EDUCATION IN A COMPETITIVE AND GLOBALIZING WORLD

DEVELOPING CROSS-CULTURAL EXCHANGE PROJECTS

A STEP-BY-STEP GUIDE

EDUCATION IN A COMPETITIVE AND GLOBALIZING WORLD

Additional books and e-books in this series can be found on Nova's website under the Series tab.

EDUCATION IN A COMPETITIVE AND GLOBALIZING WORLD

DEVELOPING CROSS-CULTURAL EXCHANGE PROJECTS

A STEP-BY-STEP GUIDE

AI-LING WANG

Copyright © 2019 by Nova Science Publishers, Inc.

All rights reserved. No part of this book may be reproduced, stored in a retrieval system or transmitted in any form or by any means: electronic, electrostatic, magnetic, tape, mechanical photocopying, recording or otherwise without the written permission of the Publisher.

We have partnered with Copyright Clearance Center to make it easy for you to obtain permissions to reuse content from this publication. Simply navigate to this publication's page on Nova's website and locate the "Get Permission" button below the title description. This button is linked directly to the title's permission page on copyright.com. Alternatively, you can visit copyright.com and search by title, ISBN, or ISSN.

For further questions about using the service on copyright.com, please contact:
Copyright Clearance Center
Phone: +1-(978) 750-8400   Fax: +1-(978) 750-4470   E-mail: info@copyright.com.

NOTICE TO THE READER

The Publisher has taken reasonable care in the preparation of this book, but makes no expressed or implied warranty of any kind and assumes no responsibility for any errors or omissions. No liability is assumed for incidental or consequential damages in connection with or arising out of information contained in this book. The Publisher shall not be liable for any special, consequential, or exemplary damages resulting, in whole or in part, from the readers' use of, or reliance upon, this material. Any parts of this book based on government reports are so indicated and copyright is claimed for those parts to the extent applicable to compilations of such works.

Independent verification should be sought for any data, advice or recommendations contained in this book. In addition, no responsibility is assumed by the Publisher for any injury and/or damage to persons or property arising from any methods, products, instructions, ideas or otherwise contained in this publication.

This publication is designed to provide accurate and authoritative information with regard to the subject matter covered herein. It is sold with the clear understanding that the Publisher is not engaged in rendering legal or any other professional services. If legal or any other expert assistance is required, the services of a competent person should be sought. FROM A DECLARATION OF PARTICIPANTS JOINTLY ADOPTED BY A COMMITTEE OF THE AMERICAN BAR ASSOCIATION AND A COMMITTEE OF PUBLISHERS.

Additional color graphics may be available in the e-book version of this book.

Library of Congress Cataloging-in-Publication Data

ISBN: 978-1-53616-160-1

Published by Nova Science Publishers, Inc. † New York

Contents

Preface		vii
Chapter 1	Cross-Cultural Exchanges: An Essential Part of Globalization and Internationalization	1
Chapter 2	Methodologies for Cross-Cultural Research Design	41
Chapter 3	Recruiting and Training Your Participant Students	65
Chapter 4	Choosing Cross-Cultural Exchange Partners	91
Chapter 5	Studying, Teaching or Working Abroad	109
Chapter 6	Developing the Tasks or Activities	169
Chapter 7	Types of Collaboration and Objectives of Cross-Border Partnership	223
Chapter 8	Assessing the Students and Evaluating the Project	269
Chapter 9	The Future of Cross-Cultural Exchanges	289
References		311
About the Author		333
Index		335
Related Nova Publications		347

PREFACE

Although I have been interested in cross-cultural exchanges and communications since I was working on my graduate degrees in the United States, I never thought of putting all my experiences and readings together to provide those who are interested in cross-cultural exchanges a systematic presentation of how a cross-cultural exchange project can be organized and implemented, especially in the field of higher education. Not until one of my doctoral students asked, after the presentation of my personal cross-cultural exchange experiences, how I got all the overseas exchange partners, did I decide to put all the best of my knowledge relevant to cross-cultural exchanges together to provide those novice cross-cultural exchange practitioners with a source of information and those experienced ones with more ideas as to what they can do in their practice of cross-cultural exchanges. Practically, this book can be a useful resource book for educators, administrators, and teachers who practice cross-cultural exchanges, international or exchange students who are heading for or are now in a host country. Superficially, this book is seen as a personal endeavor that presents my own experiences and readings. In reality, it is more appropriate to say that it is a collection of precious experiences of various devoted practitioners of cross-cultural exchanges.

As modern technologies and transportations develop and as the world is moving towards globalization, there is a tendency for international collaboration, and cross-cultural exchanges to be practiced in the commercial, diplomatic, military, religious, and educational fields. One of the benefits of cross-cultural exchanges is the added-value they bring to the participants and the creation of the effect that the sum of one plus one is greater than two. Participants from different cultures in a cross-cultural exchange can complement each other with some knowledge, information or skills that they might lack or supplement their shared knowledge with information from different perspectives. Another benefit of cross-cultural exchanges may be that cooperation or collaboration between or among participants from different cultures and the development of cultural awareness and a global view may help eliminate prejudice and conflicts and promote world peace.

In education, one of the important practices of cross-cultural exchanges is peer learning. As DeLong, Geum, Gage, McKinney, Medvedev, and Park (2011) have pointed out, peer learning "is a strategy of teaching and learning worth considering in today's diverse student populations, scare resource allocation, and rapid evolution of technology" (p. 47). They further explained that peer learning features its learning among participants of approximate equality who learn from each other in authentic situations and a mutually supportive climate. Through "social discourse, dialogue, and negotiation, they construct knowledge and make new meaning" (p. 47). Participants of cross-cultural exchanges not only learn from each other but also realize how people from different cultures perceive them and, as a result, have a better understanding of themselves.

In this book, I specifically focus on the investigation of cross-cultural exchanges of the educational field, especially higher education. However, in modern society, different fields or professions may be inter-related and inter-dependent. Educational practices may be connected to commerce, politics, religion, technology, and other fields. I do not arbitrarily and narrowly confine the discussion of cross-cultural exchanges to the educational domain. When applicable, discussions of cross-cultural exchanges in this book involve other related domains. And the term *cross-cultural exchanges* is defined in a broader sense to include student and teacher mobility, any type of cross-border cooperation, collaboration, interaction, or teamwork, partnership between or among groups of people from different cultures, a class attended by students from different cultures or is taught by a foreign teacher, short-distance and short-term cross-cultural exchanges, distance education, international volunteering, and other related cross-cultural projects. Furthermore, in this book, ways to communicate range from face-to-face to computer-mediated communications, including field trip, videoconferencing, online discussion, and many other different ways of communication. With the aims of this book in mind, I organized the book in the following manner.

This book is organized based on the ADDIE model, which stands for the five stages in the instructional design process: analysis, design, development, implementation, and evaluation (Instructional Design, n.d., Training Industry, n.d. & Kurt, 2017), that prevailed decades ago together with the common patterns revealed in most research reports on cross-cultural exchanges. After carefully analyzing and comparing the two paradigms, I found that they are actually following similar principles of developing a cross-cultural exchange project. In the 1970s, an instructional design model called ADDIE was getting more and more attention. Initially, the design model was developed for the design of training programs and instructional materials for the U.S. Army. Gradually, this instructional design model was adopted by designers of instructional materials across different disciplines. I followed the model and the patterns found in research reports to organize the procedure to develop cross-cultural exchange projects. In the first chapter, I first discuss globalization and internationalization, which are the essential causes of cross-cultural exchanges. I later divide the historical development of cross-cultural exchanges into three stages based on the development of communication technologies.

In the second chapter, I briefly describe how all the cases of cross-cultural exchange were collected, including theories applied and methods used to collect, analyze, and present all the information. On the other hand, this chapter serves to provide practitioners of cross-cultural exchanges with suggestions as to how they can start formulating a cross-cultural exchange project from a researcher's viewpoint. Researchers always need to carefully design the entire research and be prepared to report on their findings. The same is true for practitioners of cross-cultural exchanges. Sharing experiences and providing recommendations for future practices of cross-cultural exchanges can be important and valuable in an era moving towards globalization.

After these introductory and background discussions, I move to a step-by-step guide to discuss the development of a cross-cultural exchange project. In Chapter 3, the discussion focuses on the first step of cross-cultural exchange, *recruiting and training cross-cultural participants,* which corresponds to the *analysis* stage in the ADDIE model. In this stage, the teacher is required to analyze his or her students' needs and wants, their educational and personal backgrounds, level of language proficiency, interests and experiences, computer skills, and the availability of time and preferences of learning. Most importantly, the teacher has to decide on what learning goal or goals he or she wants students to achieve at the end of the program. The teacher also needs to decide on the objective of the project, which corresponds to the *design* stage in the ADDIE model. In this stage, having chosen the participant students, the teacher has to start planning the project. Based on the goals set in the first stage for the students to achieve, the teacher may have to choose ways of cross-cultural communication based on the availability of facilities, types of tasks (e.g., cooperation vs. collaboration), instructional materials needed, the schedule for the project, and any underlying theories he or she may follow in the design process.

After the *analysis* stage, in Chapter 4, the teacher *looks for exchange partners* from different cultures, which is the *development* stage of the ADDIE model. In this stage, the teacher needs to look for exchange partners who share similar educational goals and philosophy from a different culture. Having reached a consensus, the teacher has to collaborate with the partner teacher to develop the entire process of the exchange program, including schedules for different activities, tasks posed for students to achieve, facilities or equipment to be used, instructional materials to accompany the activities, and ways of assessing students' accomplishment. These are guidelines to follow in the next stage when the teacher puts the project into practice.

In the following chapters to come, namely Chapter 5, Chapter 6, and Chapter 7, the entire stage is similar to the *implementation* stage in the ADDIE model. Key to this stage is that the teacher has to monitor the entire process of the project, observe the students, and gain sufficient feedback and make instantaneous modifications if necessary. In this stage, the teacher surely has to discuss with the partner teacher and record down whatever might be helpful for further improvement and the final evaluation to come. In Chapter 5, I divide cross-cultural experiences and discuss them based on the nature of cross-cultural encounters, including studying, teaching, and working involving people from different cultures, either at home or abroad. Some guidelines, background information, suggestions, and challenges are provided for different types of cross-cultural encounters. In Chapter 6, tasks or activities that can be practiced in a cross-cultural setting and examples reported by cross-cultural practitioners are presented. Chapter 7 focuses on larger scales of cross-border collaborations or partnerships between institutions and/or organizations, either public or private and governmental or non-governmental organizations. Again, some valuable examples of either positive or negative cases are provided in this chapter.

The final stage of an exchange program *evaluation*, in Chapter 8, is broadly defined to include evaluation of students' achievement and of the entire project. In the part of evaluating students' achievement, the teacher has to design a more creative way of assessing students' performance based on the tasks given to the students in the exchange process. In the part of evaluating the entire project, the teacher has to decide who will participate in the evaluation process, for example, the teacher, the partner teacher, the students, the administrators, the sponsoring organizations, the material developers, and the technical personnel; relevant components to be evaluated include, for example, teacher's observations, students' feedback, students' performance and administrative and technical support.

Finally, after the assessment stage, possible improvements or recommendations for future cross-cultural exchange projects should be made in the final stage based on all the information gained from the experiences of the participants. The last chapter, Chapter 9, of this book is devoted to the discussion of future directions of cross-cultural exchanges based on the discussions of the entire book and an envisioning of future trends in cross-cultural exchanges.

Although the choice of research reports, personal experiences or interviews to be reported in this book tends to follow convenience and uniqueness, I paid special attention to the representativeness of each case in terms of geographical location, level of economic, educational, and technical development and religious orientation. It is particularly important in a globalizing era, not to ignore a part of the world that may in the future contribute to world peace and to the diversified yet harmonious global community.

In sum, this book aims at providing educators, including teachers, material developers, administrative personnel, and school leaders, who are interested in practicing cross-cultural exchanges in their pedagogical agenda with a guide or a source to develop a cross-cultural project, and this book is also aimed at providing students who are interested in having overseas experiences a guide as to where to look for opportunities to study or work and how to prepare themselves in a foreign country. I sincerely hope this book can be helpful for educators, administrators, teachers, and students who are involved in or who are interested in cross-cultural exchanges and for organizations seeking for collaboration with academics. It is hoped that they may frame their cross-cultural exchange plans in the light of what has happened in the field. As we can understand and predict that the nature, principles, and procedures of cross-cultural exchanges may change in different aspects and to a certain degree in the future as technology, education, politics, society, and economy change, I will keep paying attention to whatever occurs in the global community that might affect the practice of cross-cultural exchanges, and you, the most valuable readers of this book, are quite welcome to provide me with your feedback and comments for future revision of this book.

Chapter 1

CROSS-CULTURAL EXCHANGES: AN ESSENTIAL PART OF GLOBALIZATION AND INTERNATIONALIZATION

It is logical and understandable to argue that cross-cultural exchanges are the result of the practices of globalization and, in a smaller scale, internationalization in different domains, such as education, science, business, economy, religion, and politics. Lucas and Blair (2017) consider global education and international education carry two different concepts. For them, global education "emphasizes values, attitudes, and concepts that transcend the nation-state and political-institutional structures, [and] incorporates intercultural perspectives and focuses on connections between local and global contexts" (p. 208), while "international education emphasizes issues related to the relationship between nations, which is often thought about in terms of politics, economics, geography, and law" (p. 207-208). In this introductory chapter, I will first discuss the big topic of globalization as the starting point towards exploring issues relevant to cross-cultural exchanges, giving an overview of the background and development of the concept of globalization. Then I narrow the discussion down to the internationalization of the campus. Different views of internationalization of the campus are presented. Finally, I focus on cross-cultural exchanges in the educational arena, which is part of campus internationalization and which is the main topic of this book. In this book, the term *cross-cultural exchanges* is broadly defined to include cross-border collaborations and collaborations or exchanges between or among different domains or fields.

From Globalization to Glocalization

Globalization in the Globe

Globalization is a topic hotly discussed and debated in the recent decades. People around the world have different interpretations and perceptions of globalization, and they have different degrees of appreciation or apprehension of *globalization* (Kirk, 2009; Taylar, 2010). As Taylar (2010) states "there is no universally accepted definition of the term" (p. 83). For some people, globalization means establishing relationships and having more contacts or interactions and better understandings among nations and among people from different cultures, and it is "a social and economic process that is identifiable by growing levels of financial and technological integrations and interconnections in the world system" (Wiggan & Hutchison, 2009, p. 2). For example, Wiggan and Hutchison point to some globally known multinational corporations, such as Microsoft, Sony, Citigroup, Xerox, and Coca-Cola. In education, countries such as the U.S. and the U.K., Germany, France, and Australia have been hosting international students from China, India, Greece, Turkey, and other countries. On the other hand, students from these host countries also choose these same countries as their destination of study abroad. In an interview with a European Union reporter, Dr. Koen Leurs (Research eu Results Magazine, 2015) points to an existing phenomenon that European cities such as London is already a multicultural community, and the popularity of social media greatly facilitates the creation of multiculturalism. School youths may have their classmates, friends, neighbors, and digital friends from various cultures or ethnic groups. According to Dr. Leurs, "young Londoners already use social media as platforms for cultural exchange" (p. 15). For these people, as Maringe (2010) puts it, there "seems to be an increasing political, socio-economic, cultural, ideological homogeneity across countries of the world" (p. 17).

For others, globalization means a lot more than that. People who claim to be global citizens should work together against some global issues, such as inequality, discrimination, hegemony, monopoly, oppression, colonialism, religious extremism, pollution, famine, disaster, homelessness, and poverty (e.g., Winer & Ray, 1994). Shiveley and VanFossen (2001) also list some contemporary world issues between countries, such as China and Taiwan, Cuba and the United States, North Korea and South Korea, India and Pakistan, and Isreal and Palestine. There are also country-specific issues, such as HIV in Africa, human rights in China, drugs in Colombia, and debt in the third world. On the other hand, people should work together to contribute to the development of technologies and well-being for all people in the world and for the eventual goal of world peace. The historical background of the formation of globalization was the political and economic events that occurred in the twentieth century, such as the Great Depression, WWII, and the Cold War (Wiggan & Hutchison, 2009). We cannot ignore these global issues and still talk about globalization. More precisely, these scholars consider "globalization as concerned with interdependent and interconnected world systems that exist distinct from local and national life" (Shivnan & Hill, 2011, p. 155).

Still others regard globalization as a threat to their well-being, and it is a topic only for privileged people in rich and well-developed countries. They are afraid that their language and culture will eventually die out under the operation of those dominant countries and the spread of English and English-speaking cultures. As Kirk (2009) states, the term *globalization* is interpreted and understood by some people as modernity, and modernity is actually referred to as being Westernized. In periphery countries, English is not actually promoted. It is accessed by privileged and selected people only, and those people are said to possess social and political advantages. Thus, the English language actually creates a social divide in those countries. Even in some well-developed countries, traditionalists show their resistance to globalization. They are afraid "that new, unfamiliar, and untested systems are displacing their time-tested, ancestral-instituted systems" (Wiggan & Hutchison, 2009, p. 6). The term *globalization* can hardly be defined precisely without involvement of ideological thinking. In sum, there are indeed tensions and controversies existing among these different perspectives.

The two factors that facilitate the process of globalization are the development in technology and the advancement of transportation (Wiggan & Hutchisom, 2009). Modern technologies allow people around the world to get connected and to communicate either synchronously or asynchronously. Although there are inequalities in access, use, and benefits existing in the digital age (Natriello, 2006; Wang, 2015; Wang, 2018), these issues are seen as gradually being solved to a certain degree. On the other hand, due to the advancement in transportation, meeting with people from different cultures face to face is no longer a big issue for many people in the world. As a result of the advancement in transportation, greater mobility of human beings can be seen in modern world. People can travel around the world to meet different people for different purposes; for example, there is a considerable amount of literature reporting on migrations in Asia, especially Southeast Asia. Asian people move to another country for different purposes, such as marriage, education, employment, and business (Iredale, Hawksley, & Castles, 2003; Lorente, Piper, Shen, & Yeoh, 2005; Ananta & Arifin, 2004 ; Rahman & Ullah, 2012).

Although there are many countries working towards globalization, there are still a considerable number of countries regarding globalization as being potentially harmful to their survival in the world. The two big issues of globalization causing dispute are hegemony and linguistic imperialism. For those people or countries working against globalization, globalization may expedite the divide between the economically, politically, and linguistically dominant countries and the disadvantaged and oppressed countries and may work against world peace. On the other hand, linguistic imperialism, which "refers to attitudes which discriminate against people of language-related issues" (Seargeant, 2012, p. 156) may force those who speak minority languages to abandon their own language in favor of the dominant language and to accept the cultural elements of the language. Under this circumstance, it is NOT impossible that minority languages and their relevant cultures will die out eventually. It happens all the time that leaders of more powerful countries are having their summit meeting on globalization in a gorgeous meeting room; while people of less privileged countries are protesting outside the conference room. The contrasting pictures remind us that globalization is not a privilege granted for those more powerful countries; less privileged countries are the real issue of globalization. Globalization can be interpreted in a variety of ways as illustrated above and can cover a variety of domains, such as economics, culture, politics, religion, and education. Globalization can be seen as an on-going process in general. There is no real "destination" in the journey moving toward globalization, just like there is no end to technological development. We may eventually solve a global issue; however, new global issues may emerge. Today, we may interpret *globalization* in a way; tomorrow, we may perceive *globalization* in a different way. The process of globalization is slow but sure. Not until the day we reach a consensus on globalization can we really enjoy a "globalized" world. For these reasons stated above, throughout the book, I will not use terms such as "a globalized world." Instead, I will describe the world as "a globalizing world" and the time as "an era moving towards globalization." Now, I will narrow the topic of globalization down to focus on the field of education in the next section.

Globalization in Education

Globalization in education can be seen practiced in different modes of mobility and in different types of collaboration between or among institutions, organizations, or governments. Knight (2011) illustrates at least four categories of cross-border mobility, namely people (students, professionals, and researchers), programs (course, program, and degree), providers (institutions, organizations, and companies), and projects (academic projects and services). Viewed from this perspective, globalization in education is no longer limited to mobility of people and to collaborations between institutions. In this section, I will only focus on people (i.e., student mobility and teacher mobility). More detailed discussions on various types of cross-border collaboration will be presented in Chapter 6.

Cases of Globalization in Education

In this section, I will choose some issues and strategies practiced in different areas of the globe, namely the United States, Trinidad & Tobago, the United Arab Emirates (U.A.E), Germany, and China, to cover nations in different continents of the world, including North America, Africa, Middle East, Europe, and Asia. As mentioned earlier, this book focuses on cross-cultural exchanges in the field of education.

The Case of the United States

As noted by Wiggan (2009), the concept of globalization has emerged mainly in response to some issues of global economy. But how about globalization in education? Wiggan has detailed accounts on the impact of globalization on education in the U.S. He states that the nature of globalization and global competition have transformed education in the U.S. into neoliberal market practices. Like global economy, the result of globalization has created inequality in education and has favored children of high socio-economic status parents and left poor and minority students in an inferior position. On the other hand, the test-oriented practices in U.S. education has deprived American students of their critical thinking and creative skills and their ability to compete with students of other countries.

Wiggan (2009) has pointed to the fact that cross-national "studies generally indicate that U.S. students underperform relative to their counterparts in other major developed countries" (p. 29). He also points out that those countries with high levels of students' achievement are eager to recruit top graduates to join the teacher workforce. While there is teacher shortage and a large number of unqualified teachers in the United States, to solve the problems mentioned above and to respond to an era moving towards globalization, researchers, such as Wiggan, suggest that, as the trends are moving towards a 'knowledge economy,' the United States should focus on technological research and development and encourage the study of science and engineering. Another issue always discussed by researchers is that higher education in the United States is not well-prepared for and completed. Wiggan summarizes relevant research reports and states that education in the United States does not include every student. Minority and nontraditional students are always ignored in the educational arena. Compared with the United States, Cuba is seen quite different in this regard. Research reports show that the educational system in Cuba does not exclude any students, irrespective of their socio-economic status, ethnicity, and gender. That is the reason that "students in Cuba's lowest-income schools outperformed most upper-middle-class students in the rest of the region" (p. 30). Wiggan concludes that the United States failing to educate its poor students and applying a market approach to education may be its major problems in the course of globalization in education. Wiggan's accounts have pointed to a fact and a potential issue in globalization of the world. That is, minorities, including people, society, nations, and regions, are always ignored in terms of their languages, cultures, and identities and are assumed to accept the languages and cultures of those more powerful and dominant countries.

The Case of Trinidad & Tobago

Now let us turn our discussion to a developing and historically colonized country: Trinidad & Tobago (T&T). As described by Trotman and Wiggan (2009), T&T has a long history of colonialism. "During colonial times, only students of privilege were allowed to attend school" (p. 299). Poor and disadvantaged students and students with special needs were almost excluded from school education. After the colonial time, although a board was formed to administer the school system, the situation did not get any better. Discrimination, segregation and inequality in distribution of educational resources were featured in T&T's educational school system. To respond to the trends of globalization, T&T's Ministry of Education (MOE) seemed to be serious to reform the education in T&T. Their proposal, *Education for all*, sounded promising. However, on the other hand, according to Trotman and Wiggan, there were considerable problems in the language of the official papers on the one hand. On the other hand, most importantly, the documents were prepared and determined by the authority. Those immediately relevant to the plan, such as teachers, parents, communities, and even students, were all excluded from providing their opinions. In interviews with teachers, Trotman and Wiggan found a big gap between the government's perceptions of the reformed educational system and those of the teachers.

From Trotman and Wiggan's (2009) accounts mentioned above, it is quite clear that the problems with T&T's educational system and with its way of moving towards globalization lie in the gap between the government and educational practitioners. In an era moving towards globalization and given the historical background of T&T, *Education for All* may be an important initiative for T&T in their process of moving towards a modernized society. However, as mentioned earlier, Trotman and Wiggan point to the problem underlying the ineffectiveness of the policy is that policy makers did not really take educational practitioners' concerns into consideration. They argue that *Education for All* should be shifted to *Education for All by All* to include teachers, administrators, parents, community leaders, and even student representatives in the process of educational reform. Unlike the case of the United States, the case of T & T poses yet another problem of globalization in education: there is always a gap in perception of globalization between policy makers and practitioners of the policy. It implies that globalization is not a matter of only these dominant and privileged groups of people. Respecting and empowering those minority and disadvantaged groups of people are key to a globalized and harmonious world.

The Case of United Arab of Emirates (UAE)

Kirk (2009) describes the case of the United Arab Emirates (UAE) in the Arabian Gulf. The UAE has its unique and interesting historical background. It was a poor country before the discovery of oil. This country had been influenced by the British government in economic interest and education. The discovery of oil has brought to the

UAE a considerable amount of wealth. Before that, the UAE was reluctant to develop a higher education system. That is because "the ruling family sent their sons abroad for university so there seemed at first no real need to provide higher education to the population" (p. 61), and the UAE applied Western school systems mainly because it has long relied on foreign workers to do both professional and labor work.

The oil industry and the ambitions of the UAE have required the country to seek for a more competitive position on the world stage and for an education system. Because of its tradition and historical background, the UAE actually designed and imported its educational structure based on the United States or the United Kingdom educational system. Not until the UAE had developed as a nation and the government sensed the importance of being competitive on a world stage, did the UAE "government [realize] that an education system was needed in the country" (p. 61), and the education system should be able to bring the UAE to the global stage and "to compete globally in all areas of business, commerce, tourism, health care, and education" (p. 61).

In order to investigate what the preservice teachers' perceptions of teacher education in a global context were, Kirk (2009) interviewed students in teacher education in three universities from different countries, namely University of the Southeast in the United States, Middle English University in United Kingdom, and Northern Gulf University in the United Arab Emirates. Although preservice teachers in the three countries were investigated, Kirk mainly focuses on and discusses the part of the UAE. The cases of the USA and UK mainly serve as critical parts to compare and to validate the study. After all, only by comparing with others, can people understand themselves better.

One important issue raised and shared by preservice teachers in the three countries is the disconnection between courses offered in teacher training programs and actual practices and realties in the classroom and a gap between what school administrators feel student teachers should know and what student teachers really want to know before they teach in the classroom. Participants in UAE responded in interviews that they developed themselves as educators mostly by reflective practices in the classroom rather than by the theoretical training courses they took in the teacher education program.

Another issue that shows differences between participants in UAE and in the US and UK is the linkage between family history and the pursuit of teaching professions. Participants in the US and UK felt more likely to be influenced by their family members to become a teacher. Kirk's (2009) interviews with preservice teachers in the UAE shows that familial links are rarely important factors to affect their decision to be in the teaching profession. The reasons may be attributed to some factors, such as "reliance on expatriate teachers, status of the profession, incentivized alternative government position, gender inequality, small teacher education programs, [and] minimal recruitment strategies" (Kirk, 2009, p. 71). As pointed out by preservice teachers in the UAE, teaching positions are often viewed as a female job, and the positions are not actually valued and respected. Kirk poises questions as to whether the UAE wants to develop an indigenous higher-education system that will not only act as a way to educate the youth of the country...but also have elements of transferring of culture and values through the curricula? Or does the country head in the direction ...as an aspiring actor on the global stage. (p. 78)

After the comprehensive investigation and comparison, Kirk (2009) suggests that, in an era moving towards globalization, the UAE needs to seek global ties with other countries and international collaboration in student-teacher exchanges and to share ideas and research. Especially, minority issues, which should be taken into account seriously, can be viewed from different perspectives by collaborating with institutions in different countries.

The Case of Germany

In the case of Germany, Ortloff and McCarty (2009) describe how Germany moved from a monoculture German identity to a multicultural nation. Historically, institutionalized discrimination against non-Germans prevailed. White, European, German-speaking, and Christian people were considered real German citizens and Germany's "ethnocultural standard excluded all non-Germans from democratic participation" (p. 83). However, in the 1990s, the enforced monoculturalism has been challenged and Germany first granted Russian Germans access to German citizenship. Altogether, global economics, social pressures, and Europeanization have forced Germany to make some macrolevel changes in terms of citizenship laws and policies. But how about education in Germany?

Ortloff and McCarty (2009) describe the educational system and the citizen education in Germany. They state that "the most pervasive gesture of the German school structure is the tripartite division into different school forms after primary school" (p. 85). These three school forms are: Hauptschule, Realschule, and Gymnasium. Hauptschule and Realschule are aimed at vocational training, while Gymnasium is preparation for the university. Stastistically, most Germans attend Gymnasium, while most non-Germans attend Hauptschule or Realschule. This educational system has been criticized as favoring elitism and creating inequality.

Germany's citizenship education basically follows the nature of its educational system. Ortloff and McCarty (2009) analyze textbooks relevant to citizenship education and interviewed teachers to explore perceptions of teaching multiculturalism. They intended to investigate how the textbooks relevant to citizenship education may reflect multiculturalism and globalization in Germany. First of all, in 1993, topics on Islam and migration were included in citizenship education chapters and, hence, were discussed in the classroom. This inclusion of Islam religion recognized "that students in German schools will be working and living with citizens who are Muslims" (p. 89). However, according to Ortloff and McCarty, the inclusion of Muslims and migration appear far behind social realities, and Muslims are particularly referred to as Turkish-Muslims. In reality, "textbooks remain to the most part *Eurocentric*" (p. 89).

In interviewing teachers at schools with high non-German enrollment, Ortloff and McCarty (2009) point to some important issues perceived by those teachers. First, having students from diverse cultural backgrounds allows them to engage students in classroom discussions to share their culture and to talk about cultural diversity. It is important to tolerate and recognize diverse voices, especially those of minorities. Another issue the teachers interviewed pointed out is that diversity and multiculturalism education are ineffective. There are some reasons that may contribute to the ineffectiveness of multiculturalism education. For example, the home life in Islamic families, including relations "between men and women, the position of women in Islamic society, and the lower overall educational level of parents" (p. 93) can make it hard for non-German students to hold "values needed to become a citizen in a multicultural society" (p. 93). Furthermore, teachers are also frustrated because of the school's administrative system and the state's education policies. Ortloff and McCarty conclude "that the prevailing philosophy underscoring teacher practices regarding citizen education is ultimately anti-multicultralism" (p. 94). The discussions of global issues are only superficial, not historical, and the topics focus on food and fruit and restaurant, and the like. "Human rights and cosmopolitan ethics as a commitment to a shared humanity are discussed as a global topic but they get interpreted as founded in a Christian ethic" (p. 95).

Viewing the case of Germany, one can sense that moving towards globalization in education requires commitment and collaboration among administrators, teachers, students, parents and communities. Globalization in education can never be achieved if there are conflicts or biases existing among the people concerned.

The Case of China

When we turn the discussion to the case of China, we may find that the case of China is much more complicated than that of other countries in terms of globalization. Bahry, Darkhor, and Luo (2009) point to three important aspects unique to China that may contribute to the complexity of globalization in education in China: linguistic, cultural, and environmental aspects. In the linguistic domain, China is well-known for its varieties of languages or dialects spoken by Chinese people. More surprisingly yet, so many different groups of Chinese speakers share one writing system (Fromkin, Rodman, & Hyans, 2014). Bahry et al. point out that there are two different types of attitudes towards language or languages used as the instructional medium. Some people advocate that Mandarin Chinese should be the main instructional medium in the classroom. Under the circumstance of Mandarin Chinese being the dominant language spoken in Mainland China, some people advocate the use of Mandarin Chinese in the classroom. That is, teachers should lecture in Mandarin Chinese and instructional materials should be written in Mandarin Chinese. Minority groups of students who have problems with Mandarin Chinese may be provided with the so-called transitional bilingual education that offers students instruction in their mother tongue first and then gradually move to instruction in

Mandarin Chinese and move minority students to the mainstream of education so that they may be more competitive in their future career.

However, for others, especially the minority groups of people, their languages and cultures should be valued. Depriving them of their rights to use their own language and maintain their own culture and forcing them to accept the dominant language and value system is against the trend of human rights. They favor the so-called Maintance Bilingual Education. In the educational system, minority students learn the mainstream language that may facilitate their access to the mainstream society in the future. On the other hand, students may appreciate and value their own language and culture and contribute to a multicultural society and a globalized world. They insist that to learn and maintain their mother tongue will not impede their learning of the dominant language.

Viewed from the cultural aspect, global issues in education faced by China are also complicated because of its being a multicultural society. As described by Bahry et al. (2009), different ethnic groups scattered in the huge land of China are just like a flower garden and Chinese people enjoy the sense that each single flower has its unique characteristic and contributes to the beauty of the whole garden. Based on many research studies, the researchers argue for the importance of multicultural education in China. A significant gap in economy, ecology, society, culture, and education exists in different parts of China. That is, there is a great urban-rural divide that may prevent the reduction of poverty in those poor minority areas, and there is the sense that minority students feel that the cultural elements presented in the instructional materials are strange and irrelevant to their own culture at least for the time being.

In China, environmental issues and environmental education deserve special attention in the process of globalization. According to Bahry et al. (2009), China's environmental issues are actually multifold, including air pollution from factories and vehicles in "industrial and urban areas in the central and eastern regions" (p. 117) and environmental degradation such as "water shortages, erosion, and desertification of agricultural and pasture lands" (p. 117) in western China. These can be seen as local issues in an era moving toward globalization. The Chinese government hence has dealt with these issues at the local or school level. For example, the Green School movement was promoted in response to the immediate school environment. Based on the specific problems found in their school environment, students learned to plant trees in the schoolyard.

In some rural minority areas of China, where most of the people are pastoralist herders, another environmental issue relevant to their life is the desertification of grasslands. For residents in these areas, environment education means not only indigenous knowledge about the local landforms, flora, fauna, and weather, but also relevant knowledge of modern biology, meteorology, geology, economics, business, and management, all of which must be synthesized to allow effective creative problem solving to be applied to the challenges at hand. (Bahry et al., 2009, p.119)

In the case of China, only a global or national curriculum is insufficient to meet students' needs and solve the local problems.

It can be seen then from the cases illustrated above that globalization in education is actually country-specific. Each country has its own historical background, social system, economic status, political stand, and geographical advantages and disadvantages. For example, the problems faced by the United States and Germany are inequality and discrimination; while in T & T and UAE, there are always gaps between theories and practices between policy makers and practitioners in globalization. Yet, in the case of China, it seems that globalization has to address specific local issues to be practical and meaningful to specific groups of people. It may not be wise to use a one-size-to-fit-all approach to global issues in education. It has led to the creation of the term *Glocalization*. In the following section, I switch my discussion to the meaning and the phenomena of glocalization.

Glocalization

Having had numerous debates, however, some scholars celebrated yet another idea of globalization and termed it *glocalization*, which integrates global elements into local practices. Robertson (1995) deliberately describes the term *glocalization*, which is a blend word formed by *global* and *local*. He states that the idea of the term was originated from Japanese agricultural principle and business. In agricultural principle, the idea can mean "adopting one's farming techniques to local conditions" (p. 28); while in Japanese business, it refers to "a global outlook adopted to the local conditions" (p. 28). Robertson argues that the "global is not in and of itself counterposed to the local. Rather, what is often referred to as the local is essentially included within the global" (p. 35). That is, if we treat the global as a compressed world as a whole, then the world links to localities. Citing Japanese cases, Robertson argues that "modern nations have tended to promote discourse concerning their own unique difference" (p. 41). For advocates of this view, it is a hybrid type of cultural practice that maintains local traditions on the one hand and enjoys the impacts of global trends on the other. The hybridity created under this circumstance may be seen as moving between localization and globalization, and it helps the development of a multicultural society. As accounted by Wiggan and Hutchison (2009), younger generations hope for a better future. They are actually educated in hybridized institutions. On the one hand, old traditions are not easy to be ignored in a short period, and we all treasure our own cultural heritage. On the other hand, the abundant material sources and advanced technologies are indeed tempting. Why not pursue a better life that we hope for? This has led people to embrace the idea of glocalization.

Roudometof (2016) views *glocalization* from a yet different angle. He argues that the "local and global should not be seen as binary opposites, for local…has always been…the product of outside influences" (p. 38) and that *glocal* should be viewed from the concept of geographical space to that of social space. For Roudometof, local and global do not exist in scalar hierarchy like the hierarchy we traditionally view: local-national-regional-glocal-global. Rather, they interact in a social context. Applied to the educational setting, glocalization can mean institutions need to negotiate both upward with the government and even global organizations and downward with the local and individual. In cross-cultural communications, geographical locations may not be the only concern. Participants of each group need to take all the social factors into consideration, including the background and partners' purposes for participation, the contexts and ways of communication, what incidents or events just happened globally and locally, the power relations between or among groups, and how do members in different groups perceive the world differently. These may be the real meaning of globalization in cross-cultural exchanges.

Tsou (2015) discusses the case of Taiwan in terms of moving from globalization to glocalization, especially focusing on English education. Like other countries, Taiwan is following the trend of globalization. For example, in the private sector, there are increasingly a growing number of multinational companies and stores that have emerged in Taiwan. In education, a great number of international students can be seen on the campus. In response to a growing diversified society, Taiwan has had to "glocalize" its English instruction. Tsou points out some English vocabulary words or expressions specific to the Taiwanese environment and a writing format in the medical science field different from that of the traditional writing system found in international journals. She concludes that there is a need in the English education in Taiwan to transform "the English language from a global language into a glocal language" (p. 60).

In addition to Taiwan, many countries in Asia are also globalizing their social practices on their way moving towards globalization. For example, Roudometof (2016) notes that it is in India "where new ICTs audience feedback, and professional training of journalism students have become globalized, whereas news content remains highly localized" (p. 69). The same is true for the field of fashion magazines in South Asia. On the one hand, they follow the trends of globalization; on the other hand, they are designed to meet local tastes.

Another important example of glocalization described by Roudometof (2016) is ICT-based interactive technologies, which can be termed *digital glocalization*. He provides examples, such as Google Maps. The system is actually a combination of human actions and technological systems. The use of Web 2.0 or the Internet is actually glocal in nature. For example, the Internet is seen quite global; however, the digital divides, which will be discussed in detail in a later part of this book, and languages used on the Internet are quite local. Another feature of ICT-based technologies is that users of these technologies can, on the one hand, communicate with people far away from them around the world. On the other hand, they can also communicate with their neighbors, friends, and relatives close to them to maintain ties and friendships. That is, whoever they communicate with, they still live their local lives. Viewed from this perspective, ICT-based technologies are actually local.

In cross-cultural exchanges, you communicate with people from different cultures and probably speaking different languages. These cross-cultural encounters require you to think and communicate at a *global* level and expand your ways of thinking to justify and accept different views. On the other hand, under this circumstance, you are responsible and are expected to provide your *local* messages to your foreign partners. You need to be knowledgeable and confident to present your local culture. Viewed from this perspective, cross-cultural exchanges are in deed glocal activities. We can conclude from the discussions above that the concept of globalization and localization cannot stand alone and they need to work hand in hand.

INTERNATIONALIZATION

Maringe and Foskett (2011) describe the concept of globalization and internationalization as "two sides of the same coin yet are not synonymous with each other, although they perhaps share many common characteristics" (p. 1). For these researchers, globalization refers to the coming together and homogenization between nations in business, economy, politics, society, and ideology, while internationalization is relevant to how higher education applies different strategies to respond to globalization. To respond to an era of globalization, there is a call for internationalizing the campus, especially in higher education. "Internationalism may be viewed as part of globalization by its focus on relations between nations, people, and culture" (Olcott, 2009, p. 73). The rationale underlying this trend is that only an internationalized campus can prepare its students for being global citizens and can educate its students to behave properly in a globalized world. Some scholars (e.g., de Wit, Said, Sehoole, & Sirozi, 2008) view internationalization as more relevant to international cooperation and faculty and student mobility, while globalization can mean treating higher education as a tradable commodity in a competitive international market.

In terms of internationalization, different countries may have different historical backgrounds that affect the measures they apply in the process of internationalization, for example, the legacy of colonialism. De Wit et al. (2008) present two examples of this case: Indonesia and South Africa. In the case of Indonesia, the country had a colonial history under Dutch and Japanese sovereignty. After becoming an independent nation, Indonesia has been struggling to reconstruct its higher education system and make "higher education more relevant and responsive to the needs of Indonesia" (p. 243). For example, they use "Bahasa Indonesia as a medium of instruction to replace Dutch" (p. 243). As a result, many Duch professors left Indonesia and caused a brain drain. Under this circumstance, Indonesia "had to develop its own human resources by sending young graduates to train overseas, then take positions in higher education institutions upon completing their degrees" (p. 243).

In the case of South Africa, South Africa "gained its independence in the Post-Cold War era [and] inherited a good infrastructure and system of higher education" (de Wit et al., 2008, p. 243). However, the system was seen as very unequal and inefficient. For South Africa, its "immediate challenges were to redress these inequalities by increasing participation rates, redistributing funds to previously disadvantaged institutions, and striving to make the system relevant and responsive to the challenges of an increasingly globalizing world" (p. 243). The country reconstructed the system through merger to retain some of the strongest institutions and "some positive elements of the apartheid higher education system" (p. 243). The achievement seems encouraging. However, the question as to what forms it may use to decide on the degree of internationalization of a campus arises. In this section, I first discuss internationalization of the campus. Then I narrow the topic down to discuss internationalization of the classroom and the curriculum. Finally, I focus on internationalization of English instruction, which is a particularly important issue in an era moving towards globalization.

Internationalization of the Campus

Defining Internationalization of the Campus

Like the term *globalization*, *internationalization* also receives different views and interpretations, which will be elaborated in this section. First, Olcott (2009) summarizes *internationalization* and divides campus activities of higher education into internal and external dimensions. The internal dimensions include activities done at home, such as internationalizing the curriculum and research, recruiting international faculty and students, offering study abroad programs for students and exchange programs for faculty, comprehensive English language instruction, and services and extra-curricular activities for international students, while the external dimensions expand campus activities beyond the local campus to the international arena. For example, they may include recruitment of international students, establishment of branch campuses or regional offices abroad, establishment of cross-border partnerships, providing distance learning programs, and joint research and publication.

According to Olcott (2009), there are at least three factors that inevitably force the transformation of higher education around the globe into a more internationalized campus. First, the less funding offered by the government can be an important reason. It is a worldwide phenomenon that colleges or universities receive less and less financial support from the institute or the government. Under this circumstance, campus leaders have to seek financial resources on their own, and international students play a quite significant role in this regard. It can be seen that universities around the world are competing with each other for recruiting international students. Second, although there is an increasingly growing number of students seeking overseas studies, students may have different factors and reasons to take into account in the process of choosing the destination for their overseas study. This may make recruiting international students even more competitive. Universities or colleges around the world are offering more and more favorable conditions to attract international students. Third, the "growing interconnectedness of a global society and economy is creating a more diversified and mobile workforce" (p. 75) and learning English as a lingua franca to be able to communicate globally has become a fashion. Students may seek a higher degree of employability by preparing themselves for a diversified multicultural society and a globalized world. In order to attract more international students, colleges or universities need to internationalize their campuses to accommodate those foreign students.

Mertova (2013) proposes a guideline to perform the task of internationalizing the campus. Dimensions to be taken into consideration include student mobility, teaching staff mobility, internationalization of curricula, branch campuses, and institutional cooperation agreements and networks. Among these forms of internationalizing the campus, student mobility includes both outgoing and incoming students and teaching staff mobility refers to both teaching abroad and recruitment of international scholars. As Mertova states, internationalization is being associated with quality in higher education. She conducted studies, focusing on academic leaders' perceptions of internationalization in higher education. She interviewed academics in English, Australian, and Czech higher education. One of the merits of these investigations is that the interviewees represented two quite different worlds: Anglophone countries (England and Australia) and post-communism (the Czech Republic). Findings of the study revealed different perceptions in the two groups of academics. The English and Australian academics did not see connections between internationalization and quality of higher education. They addressed negative effects of internationalization such as "feelings of isolation among overseas students, difficulties with academic writing and different cultural perspectives on plagiarism" (p. 75). However, "Czech academics viewed internationalization as an emerging positive, quality enhancement trend in the Czech higher education context" (p. 75). Their experiences of difference between a post-communist and liberal education system help them enhance their teaching practice.

Unlike Olcott's (2009) and Merttova's (2013) accounts, Reid and Spencer-Oatey (2013) consider those mechanical counts of faculty and student mobility, programs and activities, curricula, and overseas campuses superficial and grass-roots. They insist that a global citizen needs to develop intercultural competencies and skills, and they apply a competency-based approach to develop a Global People Competency framework. The

Global People Competency framework lists some behavioral practices in critical situations that might need intercultural competencies. It aims at linking competencies to behaviors. According to Reid and Spencer-Oatey, this framework not only helps personal development and support study abroad schemes, but also contributes to the international curriculum, such as international business.

De Wit and Beelen (2013) echo Reid and Spencer-Oatey's (2013) ideas and argue that internationalization has moved from reactive to proactive strategic issues and from added value to mainstream. They do not think some activities such as faculty and student mobility should be the sole focus of of internationalization, and intercultural competences should be the focus of internationalization. That is, we should ask what the objectives of the activities are, not what activities we should do to internationalize the campus. De Wit and Beelen propose an idea of *Interationalization at Home*. They argue that internationalization should start from home, which is the campus, and it should be focused "on tools that generate learning outcomes and competences" (p. 157). They claim that Amsterdam is an international city with residents of different cultural backgrounds. "An increasing number of the students have a non-Dutch background…In addition, Amsterdam houses a considerable number of international companies that form an important part of the world of work in the city" (159). Amsterdam University of Applied Sciences thus initiates their policy of internationalization of the curriculum, which will be described later in the section of Internationalization of the Curriculum. Aside from recruiting international students and encouraging study abroad, internationalizing the curriculum and teaching methods to meet the trends of internationalization is also important. For those students who do not get a chance to have overseas experiences, they can have chances to develop their intercultural competences 'at home'. De Wit and Beelen use the example of the Amsterdam University of Applied Sciences to demonstrate how the campus can be internationalized.

On the other hand, Turner and Robson (2009) claim that there is a wide gap of conceptions of *internationalization* between the institutional managers and leaders and teachers and students, and administrative staff in higher education. It can be seen that the discussions of internationalization focus more on the theoretical and economic side of consideration than on experiences of teachers, students, and administrative staff in a context of internationalization. They found that "the majority of accounts to date have confined discussions to theoretical, policy or market areas rather than exploring the more varied concerns of academics, teachers and students" (p. 17).

Turner and Robson (2009) conducted a research study to explore how members of the university community perceive the ideas and practices of internationalization on the campus. They interviewed academic and administrative representatives and, then, staff and student representatives from departments with a larger population of international students at University of Newcastle in the U.K. Participants were identified as being most closely working with international students and being most directly involved in the university's internationalization agenda. Findings of the study show that there is a big gap between how practitioners of internationalization perceive and what the institution or the government expects of internationalization. The key discrepancy lies in the fact that interviewees expressed their sense of frustration in following the principles of internationalization. They perceived internationalization as being only numbers-driven and financially-oriented. The institution did care about recruitment of international students and raising its revenue. It did not really practice internationalization in an intellectually reciprocal manner. What has been practiced is conceptually colonizing. That is, the institution takes the lead in the knowledge-transfer game, and international students at the university are forced to receive academic knowledge and cultural messages in a British-dominant environment. On the part of academics and administrators, they were concerned about their job security. These phenomena may go against the core value and the real meaning of internationalization. It may be necessary that we understand the practices and phenomena of student and faculty mobility around the globe before we can discuss the role internationalization can play in a globalizing world and the real meaning of internationalization.

Student Mobility

Student Mobility in higher education plays an important role in an era moving towards globalization and internationalization of the campus. The history of student mobility can be traced to the medieval time. About "a tenth of the student population in medieval universities came from outside countries" (Brooks & Waters, 2011, p. 136). In modern society, student mobility has been seen increasingly growing in two directions, both inward and outward. Brooks and Waters (2011) provide some concrete examples of student mobility. Take the United States as an example. The United States used to be the "destination" of many students from different countries who wished to obtain a foreign degree. Nowadays, some prestigious universities in the United States, such as Harvard University and University of Minnesota, are encouraging students to study abroad.

The same seems to be true for the situation in Australia. Aside from the United States, Australia may be counted as one of the most popular "targets" for studying abroad. Now the Australian government and universities "have provided scholarships for home students to study in Asia" (Brooks & Waters, 2011, p. 136). According to Brooks and Waters, Those targeted countries as destinations for overseas study are now enthusiastically encouraging their students to study abroad especially in East and South-East Asia. For example, the number of international students at Chinese and Taiwanese universities has been increasingly growing.

In Asia, student mobility is also seen moving in two directions. On the one hand, universities are working hard to enroll international students; on the other hand, they also encourage students to study abroad and have overseas experiences. In Taiwan, take Tamkang University (TKU) as an example. TKU aggressively participates in the college expos held abroad, especially South East Asia countries such as Singapore, Indonesia, Japan, and Thailand. On the other hand, TKU has had its Junior Abroad project for many years. Students from different departments compete in a screening process to be chosen to study abroad. In its Lanyang campus, all college juniors are required to have a one-year overseas experience as partial fulfillment required for earning their degree. The destination of their study abroad has been the U.S. Canada, France, Germany, Japan, Russia, Spain, and Czech.

Olcott (2009) summarizes and explains the main factors that lead to the increasingly growing popularity of student mobility around the globe.

> First, the reductions in government funding for higher education in many countries have driven colleges and universities to become more entrepreneurial....Leaders typically offer politically correct rhetoric that focuses on educational goals such as internationalizing the curriculum, preparing students for a global society, collaborative research, and the value of diverse multicultural, global society....However, attracting more international students who pay significant higher tuition and fees is, in fact, a major motivation for many institutions. (p. 74)

Despite the fact that student mobility has contributed a lot to institutional and national economy and to the development of a multicultural campus, it did create some issues that deserve our attention. First and foremost, it has created inequality at the individual and national level. At the individual level, those who have an opportunity to earn a foreign degree are considered to be rich and privileged. Having a foreign degree with them, they may be more favored by employers and more competitive in their job hunting and financial rewards. At the national and regional level, it is an obvious phenomenon that mobile students tend to choose English-speaking countries or well-developed countries as their destination of study abroad. As a result, economically benefitted from student mobility are those nations that are rich and technologically advanced countries. The fact is that "very few national economies benefit substantially from student mobility....[T]he majority of international students are found in a very small number countries, and these countries are located in the West" (Brooks & Waters, 2011, p. 168).

Given the fact mentioned above and the increasing competitiveness of the international student marketplace, policy makers need to act in response to the issue of inequalities caused by student mobility. To open up more opportunities to less privileged students, young people should be informed earlier about their forthcoming higher education and opportunities to study abroad. Providing low-income students with financial aid or scholarships may help them fulfil their dreams of having overseas experiences and obtaining a foreign degree. Subsidiary financial support for a short-term stay overseas can provide valuable experiences for those less privileged students in their academic career. A good example of such financial support is the Erasmus Program

Scholarships. The Erasmus Programs provide UK Erasmus students, irrespective of their nationality, with subsidies for a short-term study or work overseas (Brooks & Waters, 2011; Tournès, 2018).

Inequality at the national/regional level may be lessened by encouraging students to choose less advanced and non-English-speaking countries as their destination of overseas study. Students may be educated to appreciate the strengths of different cultures and to be aware of their own needs and objectives to pursue a foreign degree. There is no need to go with the flow at the expanse of personal interests. On the other hand, to attract international students, educational institutions need to exert pedagogical reform to meet the needs of international students. In this section, I only briefly introduce some background information about student mobility as one of the phenomena of globalization in education. More details and examples relevant to student mobility will be presented in the section of study abroad in Chapter 4.

Faculty Mobility

In addition to student mobility, faculty mobility is also one of the indicators of globalization or internationalization of a university or college (Mertova, 2013). According to Vincent-Lancrin (2011), there was a considerable growth in the number of teachers or researchers who taught or did research in a foreign country, and the numbers can be seen either doubled or tripled in different areas of the world, including North America, Europe, and South-Eastern Asia.

Vigilance (2011) argues that faculty mobility is correlated with teacher shortages in the educational domain, especially in some particular fields. She points out some positive and negative sides of increasingly growing faculty mobility. Based on research reports, Vigilance states that, on the one hand, faculty mobility helps the development of the host country and migrant teachers' personal growth. On the other hand, as reported by Vigilance based on interviews with school principals, migrant teachers have caused some issues, such as "teaching outside their subject expertise, larger class sizes and the difficulty experienced by some children who had developed strong emotional bonds with their teachers" (p. 6). Another issue is that, when experienced migrant teachers leave the host country, they are always replaced with newly-hired inexperienced teachers and thus cause experience loss. More detailed discussion on faculty mobility will be presented in Chapter 4.

Intercultural Education

Intercultural education is a crucial part of internationalizing the campus. Intercultural education is developed on campus not only by targeting international students, but also by focusing on local students. Allmen (2011) states that the prefix *inter-* implies *interdependencies* and *interactions* and that the end of intercultural education is that people of different cultures co-exist peacefully and interdependently. Portera (2011) roughly describes four models of integration of immigrants: assimilation, which the dominant group does not allow any diversity and forces minority groups to accept its own system; dualistic or pluralistic integration, which people of different cultures live side by side peacefully, but they do not communicate with each other; fusion of differences, which different cultures "melted" into one and unique cultural characteristics are lost; and interactive integration, which "people of different ethnic groups and cultures try to live together and interact with each other…, with a constant exchange of ideas, rules, values and meanings" (p. 17). For Portera, among all the models of integration, only interactive integration can best serve the goal of globalization and only "intercultural education can be placed alongside the notion of interaction and interactive integration" (p. 17). For example, Allmen describes how the Council of Europe "have explored, conceptualized, promoted and implemented the intercultural perspective" (p. 42). For example, the Council first looked at "the social situation of immigrants in the industrialized countries of Western Europe" (p. 42), and they especially developed programs of experimental classes for the children of migrant workers and "launched a program for training the teachers of migrant workers' children" (p. 42). Aside from these programs, Council of Europe also worked on "human rights development, international understanding and the European Cultural Convention" (p. 43). They called for democratic stability and the need to take into account all aspects of diversity, especially diversity of religion and philosophy of life, as components of intercultural education.

Although "intercultural education" intends to teach students to accept and consider "all kinds of diversity, from social status, to cultural, to gender issues" (p. 25) and to respect each individual's rights, Portera (2011) also stresses the importance of duties. He stated that "Intercultural Education will only work in conjunction with education to lawfulness and respect of norms and limits. No form of education will work without precise, clear and accepted rules and regulations" (p. 25). Viewed from this perspective, teachers of intercultural education need to be very careful to remind their students that "the right of one's own cultural identity does not imply, and cannot lead to, educational spontaneity, normative relativism or educational permissiveness, where anything is allowed and everything has the same value" (p. 25). It is obvious from Portera' accounts that in a globalizing world, protection one's own rights and fulfill one's own duties as a global citizen are equally important. In the following sub-sections to come, I introduce intercultural education as practiced in some countries.

The Case of Australia

Clifford (2011), on the other hand, describes the differences between multicultural education and intercultural education. For her, multiculturalism simply means peaceful co-existence of culturally different groups of people. Unlike multiculturalism, interculturalism encourages interactive integration of different cultural groups. Advocates of interculturalism see "culture as dynamic and in constant evolution" (p. 316). Clifford investigates Australian higher education and argues that Australian higher education needs to rethink its colonialist practice and move from multicultural education to intercultural education. Clifford states that Australian higher education today is truly multicultural. Students enrolled in higher education include domestic diversified population, including the aborigine indigenous population and immigrants from different English-speaking and non-English-speaking countries all over the world, not to mention those international students studying off-shore. Clifford draws educators' attention to the social, political, and economic changes in Australia and in the world. She states that Australian higher education is developing momentum to consider some issues underlying multicultural education and moving toward intercultural education.

Clifford (2011) describes some attributes of intercultural education, such as quality assurance, graduate attributes, curriculum content, learning environments and teaching strategies, and attributes of staff. For her, the quality assurance agency has to make sure that overseas campuses meet both Australian standards requirements and the regulations and standards of the receiving countries. In this regard, not only "is one curriculum unsuitable in all locations for all cohorts, but the pedagogy and modes of assessment may be alien, incomprehensible or unacceptable to students from different backgrounds" (p. 317). The point of intercultural education is to balance tension between the needs of quality assurance and the needs of the students. For future graduates, Clifford points out that curricula have to meet the needs of both local and international students. She insists that international education should aim at fostering "the personal and professional growth of a diversely geographic student body, while paying attention to the development of values and attitudes toward justice, equality, democracy, sustainability of the global environment and issues of development" (p. 317).

The Case of Taiwan

In the case of Taiwan, compared with most of the countries in the world, although Taiwan is seen as a tiny island, the sociohistorical context and changes in its political and economical practices has made the island culturally diversified and has developed its multiculturalism and multicultural education (Liu & Lin, 2011). Liu and Lin claim that one of the problems with multiculturalism and multicultural education in Taiwan is that there was no local discourse at the very beginning stage of the development of multiculturalism and multicultural education. Mostly the concepts of multiculturalism and multicultural education in Taiwan were borrowed from those of the U.S., such as human rights, equality and social justice. However, as mentioned earlier in the section, Taiwan has its unique cultural, social, political, and economical contexts, and it needs to address these local issues in local discourse and develop local practices. Historically, in Taiwan around ten different indigenous peoples had resided before the majority Han people moved into the island. It is evident that Taiwan is a multicultural society, and it enforced the teaching and learning of mother tongues spoken by different ethnic groups in its multicultural education policy approximately a decade ago.

Socially, there is a phenomenon featuring female married migrants from Southeast Asian countries and new migrant children in Taiwan in recent decades. How the phenomenon actually developed is not quite clear. However, these migrants have added yet more ethnic groups to the existing ones. Their survival in Taiwan requires more efforts from the government and people in Taiwan in terms of developing a multicultural Taiwan in an era moving towards globalization. Politically, Taiwan has had an unprecedented shift of political power in the recent decades. It used to be ruled by the Kuomintang (KMT) Party for several decades until the year of 2004 when the oppositional party, the Democratic Progress Party (DPP) took the power. Since then, it seems that the two parties have had almost equal chances to hold political power. They have different political ideologies and different interests and foci in terms of multiculturalism and multicultural education. More seriously, this has created a binary opposition phenomenon. "The dominant group in a society may adopt the notion of difference to maintain control over other groups and maintain its own interests" (p. 171).

Economically, in addition to more and more international companies being established in Taiwan, there are a considerable number of people from Southeast Asia coming to Taiwan to do labor work or to work as caretakers of senior citizens (Fielding, 2016). These groups of people not only brought with them their unique cultures to Taiwan, but also made Taiwan a yet more multicultural society.

Given the discussions above, Liu and Lin (2011) conclude that, to successfully practice multicultural education in Taiwan, Taiwan needs to develop its own multicultural discourse, and the task requires collaboration among teachers, researchers, and the government. Specifically, it may be important for Taiwanese people to disregard all the biases or prejudices towards different ethnic groups and conflicts among different political parties. After all, Taiwan is a small island and cannot afford too many forms of divide.

The Case of Greece

Still another case of intercultural or cross-cultural education is the one practiced in Greece as described by Mitakidou (2011). Unfortunately, according to Mitakidou, the experience of cross-cultural education in Greece is far from being successful. Greece has its unique historical background that has created the nature of its multicultural population. In Greek history, following the collapse of the Eastern communist system and

USSR, Greece accepted a considerable number of immigrants and refugees from these areas and other countries to compensate for its potential population loss. To accommodate the influx of populations, Greece has been developing its cross-cultural education and so-called cross-cultural schools that aim at admitting minority students.

However, according to Mitakidou (2011), cross-cultural education in Greece developed by authorities and policy makers was actually "based on neo-liberal ideologies that take structural inequalities for granted" (p. 84), aiming at teaching disadvantaged or minority groups of students Greek language and culture. The eventual aim of these relevant policies may be the creation of a homogeneous society. As a result, these measures not only deteriorated the segregation and disconnection of the dominant and non-dominant people, but also created very different levels of educational quality between mainstream and non-mainstream students, with "lower expectations and watered-down syllabi" (p. 89) for non-mainstream students.

The Case of Post-Communist Countries

It is a particular concern when it comes to intercultural education in post-communist countries because these countries have undergone similar social and political changes. How they respond to an era moving toward globalization can be equally important for these countries. As described by Bleszynska (2011)

> The unstable status of the discipline, paucity of scholars and centers dealing with the problematic of IE, lack of consensus, competency controversies and the hostile attitudes of populist politicians and activists often are accompanied by a weak legal status and insufficient public relations by Intercultural Education in countries of the region. (p. 80)

Universities or educators in post-communist countries have quite divided attitudes towards intercultural education. Some modernists want "to retain the nation-state and the existing drive to maintain cultural homogeneity" (p. 79), while post modernists favor an open and a multicultural society that welcome and respect people of different cultures. Some educators consider "the phenomenon of migration as an immanent feature of global processes and progress in the understanding of human rights….Others propose to focus only on indigenous minorities and postpone programs addressed to immigrants" (p. 79-80). In sum, because of the political and historical background, intercultural education in post-communist countries is quite limited. People dislike cultural diversity and they perceive intercultural education "as a threat to national identity and interests" (p. 80).

From the discussions above, we may find that intercultural education cannot be treated and interpreted in the same way in different countries. It is because different countries have different historical backgrounds, political agendas, attitudes, priorities and interests. The contents of intercultural education cannot be fixed and should be varied based on the country's situation and priorities. Intercultural education will not be meaningful until it can benefit the entire country and its people.

Internationalization of the Classroom

Now I narrow the topic of internationalization down to the classroom setting. In the classroom, some factors that may affect students' learning are learning environments and attributes of teachers. Clifford (2011) points out that students expect a friendly learning environment that serves as a place for productive dialogue, not an inclusive approach based on Western assumptions, which may not be welcomed by international students. As for attributes of teachers, Clifford argues that teachers need to possess international perspectives that include issues related to using a non-native language of instruction, cultural differences, learning and teaching styles, the academic discipline and personal qualities.

Having an increasingly growing mobile student population, the so-called international classrooms that integrate students from different countries can be found everywhere in educational institutions. This phenomenon may be beneficial for students in the classroom. For example, Sato and Hodge (2016), reporting on Asian international graduate students' experiences of attending American universities, recount that, in the learning environment, students learn about diversity. International students establish social and peer relationships with people from different cultures. They also feel "understanding different social, cultural, and political contexts of students from different backgrounds helped them to benefit even more from their own cultural solidarity throughout their graduate programs at these American universities" (p. 10-11). Zhow and Ng (2016) also acknowledge that the enrollment of international students in the classroom does bring global perspectives and cultural diversity to the education setting because these students have better knowledge and understanding of the language and culture of the country where they grew up.

To investigate domestic and international students' perception of internationalization at the University of South Australia (UniSA), Leask (2010) surveyed and interviewed domestic and international students attending UniSA in Australia and international students in Hong Kong. Despite some issues raised by participants, she roughly summarizes three important advantages of internationalizing the classroom; they are: students being able to understand the world out there, being open and respectful for cultural difference, and being able to work effectively across cultures. First, students are conscious that the world is getting smaller because of the convenience of communication and transportation and that they need to be informed about global issues and to possess global perspectives. Most importantly, students felt that internationalization is not just about understanding and appreciating other cultures, but also one's own culture. Second, because of the intercultural training on campus, students felt that they are more open to culture difference, and this may contribute to their continuous personal growth and changes in attitudes and ways of thinking. Finally, students interviewed felt they are able to communicate across cultures and know better "how to respond appropriately in different situations" (p. 7).

Theoretically speaking, international classrooms may promote international friendships and facilitate intercultural learning. However, the reality may turn out to be the opposite. Some studies investigating interactions between local students and international students in the classroom revealed that there are several issues existing in international classrooms. Harrison and Peacock (2012) argue that an investigation of international classrooms needs to hear from three different perspectives: the international student, the practitioner, and the home student. However, the perspective from home students is always missing in research studies. Surprisingly, or unsurprisingly, their semi-structured interviews with focus groups of U.K. local students who participated in international classrooms showed that local students had overwhelmingly negative perceptions of international students who worked and learned with them in the same classroom. Generally speaking, a large group of international students tended to get together and take seats in the front rows in the classroom. There were seldom interactions between home students and international students. In groupworks, international students tended not to participate in the discussion and contributed little to the groupwork. However, they might be awarded the same credit as the home students might. Those work-oriented home students were afraid their learning and academic performance would be affected by those low-achieving international students. According to some U.K. students, working with international students has caused their intercultural anxiety. They were afraid of saying words or doing something inappropriate or offensive, and international students' level of English proficiency not only caused problems in cross-cultural communication but also slowed down their learning. Although, viewed from an outsider's perspective, one might think all the claims may involve the U.K. students' ideological thinking; the outcome is definitely not what we expected. As well-said by Harrison and Peacock, academic staff "become key agents of transformation within the internationalization agenda, transforming 'international classrooms' (a place where different cultures meet) into 'internationalised classrooms' (a place where different cultures meet *and learn from each other*" (p. 139-140).

Brooks and Waters's (2011) report also echoes Harrison and Peacock' (2010) research findings. Many researchers regard intercultural experiences as ways to help students develop their intercultural skills and construct a global view, and this intercultural competency further facilitates future professional career performance. However, Brooks and Waters also reported on the negative side of intercultural experiences. Unlike Harrison and Peacock, Brooks and Waters reviewed reports on U.K.

students who had a short-term stay abroad sponsored by the Erasmus program. That is, what they investigated was not international classrooms in the U.K. but international classrooms attended by U.K. Erasmus students outside the U.K. How did U.K. students perceive the international classrooms they attended as international students studying abroad? Unfortunately negative. First of all, the U.K. students did not think they can have intercultural learning in non-Western countries, for Western knowledge dominates the professional domain and non-Western people can hardly share their specific cultural or professional knowledge with Westerners. Second, like what was mentioned by Harrison and Peacock, Brooks and Waters also point to the fact that international students and home students tend to form their own groups and tend not to be involved in the communication of the other group because of language barriers and cultural differences. Third, one of the most sensitive issues in cross-cultural encounters might be racism or racial discrimination. Some international students did feel discriminated against by host students, especially since a certain colonial ideology may still exist in the mind of some people. Finally, Brooks and Waters recount that the degree of cultural difference may count for how cross-cultural learning can be achieved. If one goes to a neighboring country, which shares similar cultural heritage, then cross-cultural learning may be easier than for those who go to a country whose culture greatly differ from that of their own and who experience cultural shock.

It is interesting to note that issues recounted by Harrison and Peackck (2010) and Brooks and Waters (2011) are quite similar, and both of the two reports draw perspectives of U.K. students, focusing on cross-cultural classrooms. However, they are different in that the former reports on U.K. students as home students and the latter on U.K. students as international students. What does it tell us as cross-cultural practitioners or participants, administrators, educators or simply as readers of the reports? And if the students in question are not U.K. students, either as home students or as international students in other countries, will the situations change? It needs further investigation and, more importantly, requires a global perspective to view these issues. Global conflicts will never be solved and globalization will never be achieved without elimination of ideological thinking and an attitude to embrace and appreciate different cultures.

Internationalization of the Curriculum

Now I further narrow down the discussion of internationalization to an even smaller scale of topic, focusing on internationalizing the curriculum in higher education. In the area of curriculum content, Clifford (2011) has much to say about the current practice of curriculum content in Australian higher education both at home and overseas. The main issue was that the Australian government or institutions take major control of the development of curriculum content, and there is a tendency that they develop a homogeneous global curriculum that reveals pedagogical imperialism and deprivation of teachers' development of teaching skills. Clifford argues that curriculum content should be diversified to meet students' needs and show relevance to their future lives. She suggests that teachers and students can sit down and talk about what they really need of curriculum content in intercultural education.

Clifford, Henderson, and Montgomery (2013) argue that we have to internationalize ourselves before we can internationalize the curriculum. Although overseas education experience is a good source for internationalizing the curriculum, it is not always possible for all faculty members, administrators, and students to have overseas experience, and educational workshops held on the campus may be attended by only a limited number of faculty members. They further argue that internationalization does not merely mean attracting international students and celebrating diversity. It should aim at preparing students for being a global citizen, and "engagement with real-world issues such as sustainability, equality and justice" (p. 252).

Clifford et al. (2013) demonstrate an online discussion forum to explore the issues of internationalization of the curriculum. The online forum was participated in mostly by faculty members and administrators; some were in a leading or decision-making position, in higher education from different disciplines and different countries. Although the researchers did not deliberatively report participants' postings, their analysis of the postings did show that participants moved from a somewhat ethnocentric point of view to a broader way of thinking in the issues of internationalizing the curriculum. One of the merits of the online forum is that it was participated in by people from different cultures and different disciplines with different roles in the educational arena. This may enrich the discussion and encourage participants to think about internationalization of the curriculum from different perspectives.

While Clifford et al.'s (2013) example is more an approach or a guide to internationalization of the curriculum than concrete rules or approaches as to how international curriculum can be actually practiced on campus, Brooks and Waters (2011) do provide some examples of how the theories of internationalizing the curriculum are put into practice. For example, in Hong Kong, from 2012 on, students have been required to "study or work overseas for a period of time…and take a number of common core modules in addition to the specialist ones required for their degree specialism" (p. 147). In the U.K., Southampton University encourages students to attend intercultural workshops, international events or conferences, take language courses, and study, work or volunteer abroad to "earn points to add to their 'Global Graduate Passport'" (p. 148). These curriculum reforms may not only attract international students to study in the U.K. but also provide those U.K. students who do not get a chance to have overseas experiences with an opportunity to develop a global view. Still another example of internationalizing curriculum is the 'Melbourne Model' initiated by the University of Melbourne, Australia, featuring interdisciplinary approaches to curricula. According to

Montgomery (2013) the curriculum aims at exposing students to "alternative knowledge domains, methods of investigation and enquiry and different ways of knowing" (p. 178).

Montgomery (2013) describes a future curriculum for future graduates envisioned by the New London Group, a group of academics getting together in New London, New Hampshire, USA, and proposed three approaches to designing a future curriculum. First, the boundaries between university and community should be broken down. That is, the place, time, and learning materials should not be confined to the school setting. The traditional learning mode should be changed. Universities should collaborate with communities or organizations to provide students with learning relevant to the real world and their future professional career. The place for learning should go beyond the classroom, and learning should occur anytime and anywhere. Second, the interconnected world requires a curriculum design to connect different disciplines so that students may be able "to explore interdisciplinary solutions to complex and interconnected global issues" (p. 177). Finally, a future curriculum should be able to develop multiliterate graduates. That is, knowledge or information should not be transmitted by the teacher to the student unidirectionally. Students should be able to analyze, discuss, associate, and question all the information they acquire from different sources and in different modes.

On the other hand, de Wit and Beelen (2013) describe how internationalization of the curriculum at Amsterdam University of Applied Sciences was organized into three layers: the basic layer is to provide all students with a minimum of 30 European credits, the second layer is a plus option, in which 25 per cent of the curriculum is interculturally and internationally oriented, and the third layer is a complete international variety. It is an international classroom with international students and staff, and all the courses are delivered in English. In the process of internationalization of curriculum, Amsterdam University of Applied Sciences employed coaches to monitor the performance and to provide advice. "Coaches need to have a working knowledge of pedagogy and teaching methodology, including the methodology of teaching and learning in second language" (p. 166). They tend to use Socratic ways of guidance; they ask questions first and do not provide advice at the beginning.

From the discussion above in this section, we realize that internationalization of the curriculum requires educators' and practitioners' courage, wisdom, and commitment. Only by having a forward-looking perspective in designing an internationalized curriculum can students be benefitted in their future career.

Internationalization of English Instruction

Let's keep narrowing down on the topic of internationalization to the instruction of English since English has been considered an international language and is most widely used for international communications. As mentioned above and will be mentioned throughout the book, language and culture are no longer simple issues in terms of users of a language and owners of a culture due to social, political, economical, technological, and even religious changes. Multiple language proficiency refers to not only being able to speak different foreign languages but also being familiar with different linguistic accents spoken by different people in the world. English has long been seen as a lingua franca in international communications. The hegemonic control of English over other languages in computer-mediated communications mentioned earlier in the book can be traced to some historical, political, economic, technological, or educational reasons. As pointed out by Crystal (2003), in a post-colonial era, people in some countries started rejecting English as an official language or as a foreign language. The arguments underlying the change were that they wanted to promote their indigenous languages as a symbol of their identities and that they may see immediate benefits and a more promising future if they devoted more resources to foster a local lingua franca. A slightly moderate example illustrated by Kachru and Nelson (2006) was the case of Canada to challenge the dominance of English. The Canadian government practiced a bilingual policy to mandate English and French as official languages and developed its multilingual society. These practices were supported by the United Nations, who claims that human rights in language use should be protected and that promotion of a single language actually terminates minority languages and cultures.

In the colonial time, the colonized was controlled by the colonizer in almost every respect, including language use. According to Kachru and Nelson's (2006) accounts, English in colonized nations can only be accessed by elite people, and English was a symbol of power and prestige. Thus, this situation has created a serious social divide. In the post-colonial era, the social divide caused by different levels of access to English should no longer exist. Students at any level of school education should be provided with an equal opportunity to learn and use English. On the other hand, non-English speaking students should also be encouraged to maintain their mother tongue and culture so that the instruction can be said to be internationalized in terms of language use and to internationalize the classroom instruction.

From the discussions of the spread and the development of the status of English above, we may ascribe the phenomenon to "earlier colonial process and later hegemonic imposition (Kachru and Nelson, 2006, p. 311). However, the colonial era has long become history and the current status of English is not what it used to be. Citing from Canagarajah, Kachru and Nelson illustrate some strategies applied by the so-called marginalized countries, such as integrating pro-colonial discourses with personal ideologies, teaching English in the terms of native discourse, infusing local meaning in the grammar of the English language, and projecting English as a medium of scientific and technological knowledge so that everybody can learn and use it.

Both Teo and Jindapitak (2013) and Harris (2012) addressed Kachru's concentric circle model of world Englishes. In this model, Kachrou divides English-speaking countries into three circles: inner circle, outer circle and expending circle. People in the inner circle are native speakers of English and the most important countries in this circle are the US and UK. People in the outer circle are those who speak English as a second language and probably, in their history, they had been colonized by English-speaking countries. Representative countries to the circle are Singapore, India, and Philippines. People in the expending circle are those who speaking English as a foreign language, such as Chinese, Japanese, Russians, Thais, and Taiwanese.

Teo and Jindapitak (2013) and Harris (2012) argue that English instruction in Thailand and Japan are still following the inner-circle-oriented US-UK paradigm. Most English textbooks are, especially, American contents accompanied by listening materials spoken by American people. Harris especially proposes improvement of English materials in Japan to accommodate the trend of world Englishes and globalization. It is also true that the improvement is actually required for those countries in the outer and expending circles.

From the discussions above, I would like to envision a linguistically rich future of cross-cultural exchanges. In future cross-cultural exchanges, each language and its different accents will be equally valued, and language proficiency will be seen more important than a native-speaker status. Most importantly, language will be viewed as a cultural and geographical product, rather than being historically owned by a particular group of people. In the following sub-sections to come, I present some examples of English instruction practiced in different educational settings.

The Case of Bilingualism in Hong Kong

McNautht and Curtis (2009) describe the Chinese University of Hong Kong (CUHK) and its Ten-Year Vision Statement:

> CUHK's philosophy and mission is to produce well-rounded graduates well trained in their major studies and, in addition, possessing a range of skills and values appropriate to the 21st century, including a capacity for lifelong learning. Bilingual proficiency, an understanding of Chinese culture and an appreciation of other cultures are core components of the curriculum and designed to prepare our students globally as citizens and leaders. (p. 86)

CUHK developed a quality assurance framework for teaching and learning. Members of the teaching and learning committee viewed quality assurance as quality enhancement, not quality control. In the case of language policy, CUHK has its quality enhancement perspective. In 2005, it appointed the Committee on Bilingualism "to review CUHK's language policy of bilingualism. The Bilingualism Policy at CUHK should uphold its long-cherished policy of bilingualism" (p. 93). The Bilingualism Policy at CUHK features its "two writing languages and three spoken codes" (p. 97). The two writing languages are standard Mandarin Chinese and English, and the three spoken codes are spoken Mandarin Chinese, spoken English, and Cantonese. The political, societal, and linguistic contexts in Hong Kong are quite unique and complicated. Politically, Hong Kong has been under the domination of British regime for several decades until 1997 when it was returned to China. Societally, Hong Kong was seen as a hub of international trade and free market. Linguistically, people in Hong Kong speak Cantonese as their mother tongue, and, after its return to China, they were encouraged, and even required, to learning Mandarin Chinese. Cantonese and Mandarin Chinese share a common writing system; however, they are quite different in their spoken forms.

English teachers or educators in Hong Kong were in an embarrassing position to teach the language, which on the one hand has its unfavorable colonial past and on the other hand has its global future. McNaught and Curtis (2009) state that the historical situation of Hong Kong is quite similar to that of South Africa. In order to maintain a balance "between 'the two written languages and three spoken codes'" (p. 97-98), the committee on Bilingualism at CUHK states:

'For academic subjects of a universal nature, such as the natural sciences, life sciences, engineering, English will in principle, be used at lectures' (7.1), whereas 'For subjects related to Chinese culture, society and history, Chinese will in principle, be used at lectures' (7.2) and for the third linguistic possibility, 'For subjects related to local culture, society and politics and those related to philosophy of life, Contonese will, in principle, be used at lectures.' (p. 97-98)

Even though CUHK clearly states its bilingual education policy as mentioned above, it does provide teachers considerable flexibility to adjust ratios within the two languages and three spoken codes. To teach English without guilt, McNaught and Curtis (2009) echo the case in South Africa and suggest that English should be taught as a subject equally valuable and treasurous.

The Case of South Africa

Like the case in Hong Kong, South Africa also has a history of a colonial past. As pointed out by Granville, Janks, Mphahlele, Reed, Watson, Joseph, and Ramani (1998), what dominant colonizers used to do was to impose their tongues on their colonized races and downgrade or distain these local people's vernacular tongues. In the case of South Africa, prior to its independence, only English and Afrikaans enjoyed an official status. Only until very late in the history of South Africa, did the new South African constitution give official status to 11 African languages in an attempt to develop South Africa as a real multilingual country. In 1995, the government of South Africa organized a Language

Task Action Group (LANGTAG) to review the entire language-in-education policy in the country. Basically LANGTAG intended to address a multilingual policy and language equity for South Africa. However, Granville et al. (English language teaching professionals themselves) provide critical comments on LANGTAG's language-in-education policy report and recommendations for both schools and universities.

While LANGTAG recognizes the dominance and hegemony of English, Granville et al. point to some important facts or principles that it fails to address. First of all, the dominance of English was not built in one day and cannot be elimated in a short time. Parents have a preference to English. Granville et al. state that English has "both the symbolic power (attitudes) and the material power (economic capital) attached to the language in South Africa" (p. 258). Parents feel that if their children want to succeed, they need to have access to English. Granville et al. state the dilemma faced by South Africa. "If you provide more people with access to the dominant language, you perpetuate a situation of increasing returns and you may thereby contribute to maintaining the language's dominance. If, on the other hand, you deny students access to the dominant language, you perpetuate their marginalization in a society that continues to recognize the value and importance of this language" (p. 259). Granville et al. suggest that, on the one hand, providing widespread access to English may increase its hegemony; on the other hand, if English can be popularly accessed by people, then it would not be an elitist language any more. They suggest that English should be able to be equally accessed by people in South Africa and should be seen as a resource, not a problem of English hegemony.

Secondly, Granville et al. (1998) argue that language should be taught as a subject. Under this circumstance, not only students have equal rights to have access to English, but also students will make use of English as a library language "to access a wide range of internationally published resources" (p. 264) and teachers would not teach "English with guilt." This will also help "students understand that all languages are valuable and are a national treasure" (p. 268).

Finally, Granville et al. (1998) strongly suggest that "an African language be a compulsory subject in the curriculum" (p. 264). That is, all South African students should possess bilingual competence, including at least one African language spoken by White South Africans. They believe that this language-in-education policy will surely help South Africa develop as a unified multilingual country. They also admit that that some might wonder why impose a marginalized language on a dominant community. Granville et al. justify their suggestion by arguing that in "all parts of the world, but more so in multilingual countries, learners are compulsorily required to learn an additional language" (p. 265). Granville et al.'s recommendations on South Africa's language policy in educational settings echo what I mentioned earlier: on the one hand, teach English to provide students with global access and prepare them to be a global citizen. On the other hand, require students to maintain their mother tongue or learn a minority language to enjoy and take advantage of a multilingual society.

DEVELOPMENT OF CROSS-CULTURAL EXCHANGES

Having discussed globalization and internationalization, we now turn to the discussion of cross-cultural exchanges, which is an essential element of globalization and internationalization and is the main focus of this book. From a glance at the development of cross-cultural exchanges, one can find that communication technologies seem to play an important role in the ways cross-cultural exchanges are conducted. From the data collected for this book, I found that there were significant differences before and after the invention of communication technologies in terms of how exchanges programs were conducted and what can be included in a cross-cultural exchange program. I thus divide the history of cross-cultural exchanges into three stages: the stage before the invention of communication technologies, the stage when communication technologies just emerged, and the stage of modern technologies. It seems logical and advantageous to discuss cross-cultural exchanges based on the three stages.

The Stage before the Invention of Communication Technologies

Cross-cultural exchanges can be seen in various domains, such as commerce, religion, politics, diplomacy and education, and they started very early in human history. For example, in the fifteenth century, a banking family, the Medicis, in Florence, Italy, funded creators from a wide range of disciplines and cultures to get together in Florence, and together, despite the differences in discipline and culture, they came up with wonderful new ideas, and the phenomenon was later termed "the Medici Effect," a phenomenon that refers to people of different domains and from different cultures getting together and, through exchanges of ideas they came up with innovative ideas (Johansson, 2006). Another well-known example is in the field of religion about the late missionary George Leslie Mackay from Canada. MacKay traveled to Taiwan to preach Christianity in 1871, and he stayed in Taiwan for 29 years. During his stay in Taiwan, he made contributions to Taiwanese people in terms of religious belief, medical development, social service, and education. In the ancient time, without advanced transportations, he mainly travelled by boat or even on foot (Kellenberge, 2016). In education, the history of cross-cultural exchanges can be traced back to as early as the Hellenistic era in Greece. When Socrates and Plato lectured and taught in very roughly developed so-called "schools." In the ancient Greek world, they attracted a considerable number of foreigners from far-away, "leading an unmistakable 'international' flavor to an otherwise 'local' learning community" (Bevis & Lucas, 2007, p. 14). According to Bevis and Lucas, in Roman times, there were also aspiring scholars who attracted wealthy and ambitious young children from outlying regions to practice "study abroad."

In the case of Europe, the so-called "university" was developed around the tenth and eleventh centuries. As Bevis and Lucas (2007) describe, "the first great universities of medieval Europe owed their existence to the growing number of foreign students who flocked to city cathedral schools for instruction" (p. 21). These schools generally gained their reputation in particular fields, such as translations of scientific treatise, medicine, civil law, and liberal arts. In these ancient periods, "European culture was affected by an influx of new knowledge" (p. 21).

As early as the sixteenth century, scientists in the Eastern Mediterranean and those in Europe had started cross-cultural scientific exchanges. Ben-Zakan (2010), in his research study, recounts interesting stories that occurred roughly in the sixteenth century in the scientific arena. He especially focuses on the movement of Copernican Cosmology from the West to the East. According to him, for centuries, scientists and students had the ingrained belief that European and Near Eastern cultures were developed along separate, linear paths. Not until the rise of Copernican Cosmology did modern scientific knowledge flow from the West to the East. That is, the scholarly focus shifted from a single cultural site to networks of connections between cultures.

Ben-Zakan (2010) continues to explain that even an exchange of scientific ideas and practices could go across cultural boundaries and travel among different cultures. Generally speaking, scientists exchanged astronomical knowledge, books, instruments, and practices, and these changes managed to move between different cultures and accounted for the extension of European astronomical projects eastward. Ben-Zakan describes the creation of such kinds of cross-cultural exchanges. It happened that the margins of European culture and those of the Near Eastern culture overlapped so as to create a "zone of mutual embrace" Social networks were thus developed, and they allowed travelers, incidental buyers and traders, diplomats and bureaucrats, and pirates and captives to cross cultural boundaries and exchange knowledge and objects. Communications between or among people from different cultures were facilitated by translation or interpretation.

Having carefully reviewed all the literature relevant to cross-cultural scientific exchanges between the East and the West in the sixteenth and seventeenth centuries, Ben-Zakan (2010) argues that independent scientific development cannot really happen and no scientific culture is an island. "Science, like any other cultural production, consists of exchanging, altering, and borrowing from adjacent cultures and earlier time periods and is a product of socially driven networks that connect intellectual centers" (p. 7).

From Ben-Zakan's (2010) accounts, we can roughly draw a picture of early cross-cultural exchanges, featuring social networks and physical contacts. Early cross-cultural exchanges of scientific knowledge did help the creation of mutual trust, and the mutual trust, in turn, helped the expansion of scientific knowledge and the development of more mature facts derived by being looked at from culturally different perspectives.

Speaking of cross-cultural exchanges, in fact, they occurred long before and were more complicated than what we thought. Field (2016), in his accounts of Asian migrations, states that Asia has its unique economic, geographical, and societal structure that led its people to immigrate to and emigrate from other Asian countries and European and North American countries as well in its early history. He summarizes some types of East Asian migrations, including working-class migrations, migrations of the highly educated and highly skilled, trafficking, displacements because of violent conflict or natural disaster, place preference migrations, migrations of students who expect to pursue a better life and better education in Western nations, migrations because of marriage and state-sponsored migrations due to population policies or other reasons.

On the other hand, in the field of education, Stowe (1990) provides a very detailed account of the history of Chinese people learning English as a foreign language in Taiwan. In the early history of China, around the early eighteenth century, Chinese people learned the so-called Pidgin English taught by merchants and missionaries. This kind of cross-cultural exchange was basically for business and religious purposes. Later, more formal English was taught to Chinese people. Robert Morrison was the first missionary sent by the London Missionary Society to teach Chinese people English. Morrison then established the Morrison Education Society in 1835. From that time on, the U.S. started engaging in the education of Chinese people. For example, Samuel Robin Brown arrived in China in 1839 and opened his school in Macao. Again, from the example of the early stage of cross-cultural exchanges, we can imagine that contacts in person might be the only way to make cross-cultural exchanges to occur before the invention of communication technologies.

From the accounts above, we may conclude that, before the invention of communication technologies, cross-cultural exchanges were mainly achieved by human-human physical contacts. Viewed from modern perspectives, these contacts may be seen as slow and ineffective. However, it is possible that the increasing need to communicate cross-culturally and the need to communicate more effectively have urged the invention of modern technologies and transportations. Even at the present time and even from the same culture, emigration and immigration are still at work. It is evident in the case of China plus (The term is borrowed from Fielding to include People's Republic of China, Hong Kong, Macao, Taiwan, and Mongolia). Roughly speaking, people from these regions share Chinese culture. However, regional divides and political conflicts have created gaps among these regional cultures. Even though migrations take place within these regions, cultural issues are still apparent. Cultural elements, such as language ideology, religion, education and politics, still need to be adjusted for migrants. It is similar to the cases of South Korea and North Korea, and former East Germany and West Germany. On the other hand, people from these regions did emigrate to the Western world, such as North America, Western Europe, Australia and New Zealand, and visa versa (Field, 2016). It is obvious that this type of migration needs more time and energy for the migrants to adjust to the host country.

The Stage When Communication Technologies Were Emergeing

In the early stage of digital technologies, e-learning featured its electronic delivery of knowledge or information or training programs. Tabot, Oyibo, and Hamada (2013) term it *Computer-based Training*. CD-ROM's and PowerPoint were products of this stage. Basically, ranging roughly between 1984 and 1993, digital technologies were seldom used for human-human interactions. Even though later on digital devices were used to include human-human communications, as will be described in the following paragraphs, the communications were quite simple and not-well-developed in terms of the machines used for communication and the designs of the e-learning activities.

Before the development of modern technologies and the popularity of personal computers, cultural exchanges were generally limited to regular mail and simple e-mail or teleconference. Sayers (1991) describes an international multilingual computer network *De Orilla a Orilla* (From Shore to Shore) he and teachers from different countries organized in the 1980s. This network aimed at language and cultural learning and at developing relationships between and among sister schools. As Sayers mentioned, this network was a class-to-class and a team-teaching collaboration.

One of the characteristics that had made *De Orilla a Orilla* unique was that it tied minority language immigrant students in the U.S. and students from schools located in the mother culture of these minority language students. As we can imagine, meeting one's own nationals residing in another country via computer-mediated teleconferencing is quite different from meeting them face-to-face on the campus. For example, in his research report, Sayers (1991) describes how Puerto Rican minority students in the U.S. had cross-cultural exchanges and had an emerging relationship mediated by technologies with Puerto Rican students in Puerto Rico. The two groups of students had joint projects, such as the publication of classroom journals, comparative investigations and surveys, and oral histories and folklore compendia. The project featured young minority students learning their native language and culture from peer students in their homeland and students in the homeland learning a novel language and culture presented by students from their own country.

De Orilla a Orilla international learning network indicated that a variety of advantageous cross-cultural exchange activities were practiced in the early stage of the invention of communication technologies. The application of technologies in that stage was quite simple. According to Sayers (1991), this project was mediated by computerized electronic mail and real-time teleconferences. For real-time teleconferences, students had to get together in the only computer lab in the school at some designated times. Yet, students' curiosity aroused students' interests in the cross-cultural conversation. Before the teleconference, Sayers encouraged students to think about what kinds of things they would like to learn from their distant partners. For example, they may ask questions such as: "How are your schools, "What are your teachers like," "Where do you live and is it cold there?" On the other hand, a crucial element of the project, the cultural package, had to rely on snail mail service, and it took time to reach the partner's school as Sayers describes:

> I was concerned that cultural package from Puerto Rico with letters and photos and tapes had not been responded to more than a week after their arrival, since Mr. Solis had been busy pushing students through the detailed lessons in his plan book. (p. 687)

Sayers's (1991) study illustrates a rough picture of how cross-cultural exchanges were practiced in the early stage of communication technologies.

Another example of a cross-cultural exchange project that occurred in this stage was the one that I conducted in 1997. This project involved three groups of students from Taiwan, Japan, and the U.S. Basically, the three groups of students communicated via e-mailing to their exchange partners through a communication platform developed especially for this project. Compared with modern social or instructional websites, this communication platform was very simple. There were no emoticons, file attachments or pictures posted, and there were only few functions available for teachers to manage students' postings (Wang, 1997). However, students showed heightened cultural and audience awareness in the cross-cultural encounter. On the other hand, the simple encounter dud not really satisfy the students because they were not able to see each other's face and have a sense of real communication. As one of the Taiwanese students stated, "I don't even know whether my foreign partners are males or females and how they express themselves, how can I really understand what they mean by the words they posted."

The second stage in the history of cross-cultural exchanges featured its simple facilities to allow human-human cross-cultural communications. For participants, it was exciting enough to have direct communications with people far away from them. However, as mentioned above, students' reactions to and reflections on the second stage of cross-cultural exchanges further stimulated the improvement of communication technologies, which will be discussed in the next section.

The Stage of Modern Technologies

Sayers's *De Orilla a Orilla* learning network and the cross-cultural exchange project I conducted were organized in an era when computer technologies were just emerging. As technologies have been increasingly growing in their popularity and complexity and as the world has been moving towards globalization, cross-cultural exchanges have become more and more diversified in terms of the technologies used and the objectives of cross-cultural exchanges. Tabot, Oyibo, and Hanada (2013) describe the invention of Web 2.0 around the beginning of the 21st century. Web 2.0 features its more powerful capability for human-human interactions, information sharing, collaborative learning, and learner generated content, not to mention a multi-media learning environment. Tabot et al. roughly divide the evolution of e-learning into four phases: Instruction-led Training (ILT), Computer-based Training (CBT), Learning Management System (LMS), and Web-based Training (WBT). In the ILT phase, there is no use of electronic learning technologies at all. This phase featured its teacher-centered instruction, and students were consumers of knowledge and were passively learning. The second phase, CBT, emerged roughly in the 1980's. In this phase, teachers were able to make use of multimedia, such as Windows, Macintosh, CD-ROMs and PowerPoint to "cheaply mass-produce instructional and training materials on compact discs (CD-ROMs) for individuals and organizations to learn outside the classroom" (p. 9). In the third phase, LMS, the advancement of learning technologies allowed teachers and students to make use of learning management systems to manage their teaching and learning, traditionally called Virtual Learning Environment. In the Learning Management Systems, teachers and students are free to choose whatever functions they need in the management of their teaching or learning. From roughly 1994 on, the fourth phase, the development of World Wide Web "allows people to collaborate, interact, create contents, and share knowledge and information on the Internet by leveraging Web 2.0 technologies" (p. 12). Examples of such technologies are wikis, blogs, discussion forums, emails, content-generating, and management and grading tools. According to Tabot et al., there are still more to come, such as Intelligent Tutoring Systems, Virtual Simulators, and Mobile Learning facilities.

Beauchamp (2012) describes an international program *Face to Faith* that connects young students from all over the world via videoconferencing and an online learning community. This program aims at helping students learn about religion and global issues. One of the unique characteristics of *Face to Faith* program was that students dealt with issues concerning religion and belief, which were not commonly discussed in their classrooms. By not avoiding controversial religious issues, students learnt to practice empathy, build trust, and communicate respectfully with people of all faiths and beliefs. These are essential ingredients to become a global citizen. In addition to religious issues, students expanded their discussions to global issues of mutual concern, such as poverty and the environment and extended their discussions to websites, using discussion forums, blogs, and e-mail (Beauchamp, 2012). From the case of *Face to Faith*, we can see that, in the stage of modern technologies, cross-cultural exchanges can involve a considerable number of participants and can have different types of online interactions with different purposes in mind. This can be a good example to demonstrate how modern technologies work.

From the overview of the historical background of cross-cultural exchanges stated above, a rough picture of the progress of cross-cultural exchange may emerge. Cross-cultural exchanges between the East and the West have been practiced from an early time. At the early stage, the communication between or among people from different cultures started from the translations of scientific works. The objective of the exchanges was to explore scientific issues and to look for consensus among scientists of different cultures. Gradually, objectives for cross-cultural exchanges expanded to include language learning, cultural learning, and, in an era moving towards globalization, development of a global view and intercultural competence.

Ways of communication in cross-cultural exchanges went from snail mail to e-mail and from post service to digital communications. As technologies develop, computer-mediated communications have moved from written communications to include oral communications, using technologies, such as Skype, MSN, and other types of videoconferencing. In modern society, it is always the case that a cross-cultural exchange project integrates different modes of communication in cross-cultural exchanges. Professional learning also expanded from scientific exchanges to include other fields of professional knowledge, such as business management, music, journalism and fine arts (Yogman & Kaylani, 1996; Ho, 2012; Wilkinson & Wang, 2007). As we witness the development of communication technologies, we realize that modern technologies are ever-changing, and more and more functions are being developed to facilitate communications among people. We can expect more and more cross-cultural exchanges in the future, and these exchanges may have great influences on teaching and learning in the educational arena.

Haraway (2000) coins the term *cyborg* from a posthumanist perspective to describe the phenomenon in an era when modern technologies dominate human societies. A cyborg, as defined by Haraway, is "a hybrid of machine and organism, a creature of social reality as well as a creature of fiction" (p. 69). Although the changes of the human societies may be slow, we are sure that modern technologies did bring and will keep bringing great impacts on human lives. In the following chapters to come, we will see how modern technologies may facilitate and have great impacts on cross-cultural exchanges.

Chapter 2

METHODOLOGIES FOR CROSS-CULTURAL RESEARCH DESIGN

As mentioned in the introductory chapter, this book intends to provide readers with a guide to how cross-cultural exchanges can be conducted. In this case, comprehensive examples of exchange projects or activities are needed for different groups of readers to decide on their choices from various alternatives. These examples are reported from different research or exchange settings by different researchers with different objectives in mind, using different research approaches to present their results. This chapter aims to summarize some commonly used research methods in the field of cross-cultural exchanges so that practitioners of exchange programs may have an idea as to how the program can be best designed, practiced, and researched. In addition, this book itself is organized by following some of the research methods commonly used by researchers of cross-cultural exchanges. In this chapter, I also roughly explain how the data of the book are collected and how the book is organized.

Basically, a glance at the studies, the entire process of data collection and data analysis for studies on cross-cultural exchanges involves the use of grounded theory, literature survey content analysis, online methods, and statistical research paradigms. In the following sections, I illustrate how these research paradigms can be applied to studies on cross-cultural exchanges, including this book. Because this book and many studies cited in the book use grounded theory method as their theoretical framework, this chapter will devote more pages to the introduction of grounded theory.

GROUNDED THEORY METHOD (GTM)

Bernard and Ryan (2010) well-stated that grounded theory and content analysis methods "reflect the two epistemological approaches for all research: induction and deduction" (p. 265). Generally speaking, researchers start from an inductive approach to explore what we do not quite know. "As we learn more and more about a research problem, the more important it becomes to take a deductive approach" (p. 266). In this stage, as we get more and more ideas about the research problems; we need to be guided by our observation to take a deductive approach.

As Bernard and Ryan (2010) describe social processes, people who experienced similar events or activities may have their unique stories. However, by looking at all the stories, researchers may discover patterns that reveal a common process people share. That is the uniqueness of individual experiences may undergo similar social processes. Researchers then explore the hidden patterns to develop adequate theories. The theories, in turn, are sources for researchers to do deductive reasoning or to predict what the future will look like in the future. The essential steps and the future of cross-cultural exchanges generated from analysis are also patterns that emerged from the coding process of the grounded theory method. In this section, I first introduce the grounded theory method, the theoretical framework on which this book and some of the cross-cultural researchers' studies are based. Then I describe how specifically data were collected and analyzed and how the essential steps of developing a cross-cultural project were derived.

As pointed out by Corbin and Strauss (2008), the purposes and advantages of developing theoretical frameworks are that a previously developed theoretical framework can be used to complement, extend, and verify the findings and that it can guide the researcher to focus on particular points for investigation and help determine the methodology to be used in the study. In this book, I used the concepts of *essential elements* and *future trends* to guide my exploration of cross-cultural exchanges in education because I intended to explore what might be the essential steps to develop a cross-cultural exchange program and, based on the existing literature, what might be the future trends of cross-cultural exchanges. That is, from the mass of data collected for exploration, I especially look for clues of the essential elements to the development of a cross-cultural exchange program and for clues that might signal the future trends of cross-cultural exchanges. For example, by looking over a huge amount of data relevant to cross-cultural exchanges, I found a pattern of developing a cross-cultural exchange project or activity. First, researchers recruit and train their participant students and look for overseas partners. It is sometimes the case that some researchers go the opposite direction. They have contracts with their overseas partners first and agree upon some kinds of collaboration, then they recruit the most appropriate participants available. Then together with their partners, they develop and decide on cross-cultural activities and establish their partnerships. Finally, researchers need to assess students' outcomes and evaluate the entire project for future improvements.

Research done for this book mainly followed the qualitative research paradigm, applying the grounded theory method as its theoretical framework in the process of data collection and data analysis for the following reasons. First, this book aims to provide practitioners of cross-cultural exchanges with a picture of how a cross-cultural exchange program can be developed. However different cross-cultural exchange programs may have different modes of exchange and may involve different groups of students with different academic and cultural backgrounds. The data obtained from the databases stored in computer networks and my own empirical studies may be complex, non-linear, and interactive. The grounded theory method, with its inductive and theory-generating nature, can best generate the patterns to interpret the general steps to organizing a cross-cultural exchange program (Chye, Gervais, & Kiu, 2007). Second, in this book, I intend to 'explore' or 'discover' important and useful information relevant to cross-cultural exchanges, and the grounded theory method is most useful in an exploratory analysis scenario in which there are not any predetermined notions about what will constitute an 'interesting' outcome. Third, the grounded theory method developed by Glaser and Strauss is a specific research methodology aimed at building theory from data, and it denotes theoretical constructs derived from qualitative analysis of data (Corbin & Strauss, 2008). The methodology particularly fits in the nature of this book because of the various data to be collected and my own philosophical orientation. I firmly believe that the world is created and recreated through interaction. Fourth, as Stern (2007) argues, one of the vital elements of the grounded theory method is making sense, and only the audience can decide whether the research findings do make sense for them. Stern provides some examples to illustrate that some existing theories might not really make sense for participants. One of the examples was his study on discipline in stepfather families. He concludes that the stepfather should not engage in discipline until the mother and child feel that it is OK. This seems to make sense to most people, but not family therapists. Family therapists remained unconvinced until twenty-eight years later when a popular psychologist openly pointed out "that stepparents can never act as the primary disciplinarian of stepchildren because they have no history with the child, and the biological parent is a child's first love" (p. 116). The study reveals the importance of how findings of a study have to be relevant to the participants. In the process of collecting and analyzing data, I was committed to provide practitioners and participants of cross-cultural exchanges with research findings that make sense for them, and, it seems, the grounded theory method is the way to go. Finally, as Corbin and Strauss argue, something that is beyond the ability of a person to articulate or explain may occur when doing analysis and interpretation is an art that cannot be formalized. Most importantly, I strongly believe what Corbin and Strauss have stated: an event itself is not really the concern of a researcher; rather, a researcher should be aware that a person gives meaning to an event based on his or her own biography or experiences, such as gender, time and place, cultural, political, religious, and professional backgrounds. The grounded theory method features its constant comparison and its constructivist view, and researchers construct theories out of the data provided by the research participants. It particularly fits the nature of the research of this book.

In the following sections to come, before relating the organization of the book to constructive grounded theory, I first illustrate the grounded theory method from which constructive grounded theory is derived. First, I will briefly introduce the nature and principles of the grounded theory method, and then I will present the coding process generally applied by grounded theorists. Finally, I will present some criticisms that came from researchers and move to the discussion of constructivist grounded theory. In the course of presenting the grounded theory method, I demonstrate how the main topic of this book, cross-cultural exchanges, are specifically applied in the grounded theory method.

Introduction to the Grounded Theory Method

The Grounded Theory Method (GTM) emerged and was termed in the 1960s by Glaser and Strauss. As the term may imply, the two founders of GTM suggest that research studies are grounded in the data. The key spirit of GTM is theory-generating. The founders of GTM argue that theories should be grounded by logical deduction from a priori assumptions, and they encourage researchers "to go into the field to gather data without a ready-prepared theoretical framework to guide them" (Bryant & Charmaz, 2007, p. 43).

Generally speaking, the GTM is a widely used qualitative method. It does not acknowledge researchers' own standpoints and relative privileges. It encourages gathering data while you can. Glaser and Strauss claim that GTM was inductive, aiming at generating new theories rather than testing hypothesis (Byrant & Charmaz, 2007). Although most of the grounded theorists agree upon the fundamental principles of the grounded theory method, researchers actually hold varying perspectives on how grounded theory should be applied in research. For example, Holton (2007) does not regard grounded theory methodology as one of the qualitative research methods. She argues that grounded theory method "is simply a different methodology, a distinct paradigm with its own principles and procedures for what constitutes valid research within this paradigm" (p. 267). It is because, according to Holton, classic grounded theorists did their research within the traditional qualitative research paradigm and labeled it as grounded theory; however, the research frequently falls short of the criteria of the grounded theory method.

Holton (2007) describes conducting the grounded theory method as a journey to go from description to conceptualization. She argues that grounded theory is not about the accuracy of descriptive units; rather it is a conceptually abstract explanation for a latent pattern of behavior in the social setting. That is, the essential part of the grounded theory method is to *explain,* not merely *describe,* what is happening in a social setting.

Data Collection

Corbin and Strauss (2008) point out that, in qualitative studies, there are many alternative sources of data, such as interviews, observations, videos, documents, drawings, diaries, memoirs, newspapers, magazines, biographies, historical documents, autobiographies, and other sources. Stern (2007) also points out that one of the most important characteristics of GTM is everything is data, including everything the researcher sees, hears, smells, and studies and life experiences. If this is the case, then the researcher might ask: when can I terminate data collection? A rule of thumb is that when the researcher feels the data collected has reached the saturation point. That is, when consistent patterns emerge and it seems no new patterns will occur, the researcher may cease data collection (Morse, 2007).

There are, however, problems especially existing in data collection for cross-cultural investigations, for example, negligence of cultural information, inadequate translation, culture-sensitive context effects. As Schwarz (2003) reports, "minor variations in question wording, format or order can profoundly influence respondents' reports" (p. 93). He illustrates how differences in question wording format or order may affect responses from different cultures (e.g., Chinese culture) to respond to survey questions in a different way. Respondents' responses to survey questions may reflect their general thought patterns and cognitive judgements. Under this circumstance, survey results may not be readily to be compared.

The Coding Process in the Grounded Theory Method

There are various methodological guides available to illustrate the coding process required for a grounded theorist. In this book, I followed the coding process proposed by Holton (2007). Holton clearly states that the "coding process is not a discrete stage...but rather a continuous aspect of analytic nature of classic grounded theory" (p. 274). She outlines how the coding process can be executed.

According to Holton (2007), there are two types of coding: substantive coding and theoretical coding. The substantive coding includes basically two major procedures: open coding and selective coding. In the open coding process, the researcher does line-by-line coding and compares incidents to each other in the data. Researchers may ask themselves questions, such as "What do you want to study from the data?" "What category does this incident indicate?" etc. In the research process for this book, I intended to explore generally how a cross-cultural exchange project can be developed and practiced. Based on the research focus, I came up with categories, such as participants, objectives, procedures, findings, evaluations, etc. One of the purposes of open coding for the researcher is to verify and saturate categories. That is, when you, in the process of open coding, find that there is no new data emerging and no new properties and dimensions found in each category, then probably it is time for you to stop coding. This may provide the researcher with an idea as to which direction to take in the following procedures.

As open coding proceeds, patterns begin to emerge. Holton (2007) warns inexperienced grounded theorists that grounded theory is not linear in nature; rather, the overall process requires the researcher to constantly compare different incidents and the theoretical sampling to allow a core category to emerge. As pointed out by Corbin and Strauss (2008), theoretical sampling "is responsive to the data rather than established before the research begins" (p. 144). It is done based on the *concepts* derived from the existing data, and the data to be further collected will be in accord with these concepts and discovery of relevant concepts and their properties and dimensions. The term *concept* in the grounded theory method deserves special attention and explanation because one of the important tasks of grounded theorists is to abstract concepts from the data and to leave all the details behind temporarily. For example, in the process of formulating this book, I read all the data collected and labeled *concepts* relevant to the research focus, such as *objectives, participants, modes of communication, activities, findings*, etc. Then, I coded each *concept*. For example, under the concept of *objective*, there were different codes, such as *language learning, cultural awareness, enhanced global view*, and *tolerance in language, and cultural difference*. All of these codes can be seen as different kinds of learning objectives. As pointed out by Holton (2007), the "result of a grounded theory study is not the reporting of facts but generation of probability statements about the relationships between concepts" (p. 273). Corbin and Strauss (2008) illustrate the circular process and stress that grounded theorists begin data analysis immediately after the first day of data collection. That is, data collection and analysis actually occur simultaneously. "Data collection leads to analysis. Analysis leads to concepts. Concepts generate questions. Questions lead to more data collection so that the researcher might learn more about those concepts" (p. 144-145).

In the grounded theory method, constant comparison may include three different types, and it may continue through open coding to selective coding. First, incidents are compared to other incidents. Second, emerging concepts are compared to more incidents. Finally, emerging concepts are compared to each other. For example, in the case of this book, I compared different cross-cultural exchange programs and found that the objectives, the designs of the programs, the findings of the research, assessment of the project, etc. were essential elements of a cross-cultural exchange program. When the concept *objectives* emerged, I then looked for more similar objectives in different cross-cultural exchange cases for their similar and/or different characteristics. Finally, I compared the various emerging concepts, such as *designs* and *findings* to look for emerging patterns. For example, I compared the two concepts *objectives* and *designs* to see if there is a relationship between the objectives of a cross-cultural exchange program and how the program can be developed. That is, I intended to investigate whether an objective intended to be achieved in a cross-cultural exchange program required specific activities to reach the goal.

While doing constant comparison, researchers may do theoretical sampling at the same time. One of the purposes of theoretical sampling is to decide what data to collect next and where to find them, which may be controlled by the emerging theory. In the case of cross-cultural exchanges, following the example illustrated above, I would collect more data relevant to objectives set for a cross-cultural exchange to ensure the emerging pattern. The criteria of theoretical sampling are continually tailored to fit the data and the analysis. I categorized the entire concept *objectives* into different categories, such as language and cultural learning, enhancement of a global view, professional learning, etc.

A core category begins to emerge while the researcher is doing constant comparison. The core category allows the researcher to focus on a particular concern or issue in the following selective data collection. While some grounded theorists may advocate that a main concern may be asserted explicitly by the research participants, others identify or discover it as it emerges through the coding process and conceptual memoing that records the researcher's "theoretical notes about the data and the conceptual connections between categories" (Holton, 2007, p. 281), and theoretical sampling for further data. According to Holton, the process of memoing, coding, and analysis may happen at the same time to allow substantive and theoretical codes and categories to emerge. The core category accounts for most of the concerns or issues of a study and emerges as the focus of the study and can be used to explain latent patterns of social behavior.

After the process of open coding, the researcher moves to the next stage: selective coding. In this stage, the researcher identifies and selects a potential core variable, which can range from a process, a dimension, a condition to a consequence, and will collect subsequent data based on whether the data are relevant to the conceptual framework. The researcher can saturate the selected categories with little effort by focusing only on the core and other related categories. For example, in the research on cross-cultural exchanges, I focused only on *objectives*, *participants*, *activities*, etc.

Having done the two stages in the substantive coding process, the researcher may move to the other type of coding: theoretical coding. Theoretical coding is to generate hypotheses to be integrated into the theory by conceptualizing how the substantive codes may relate to each other. Holton (2007) insists that sorting of memos is an essential step to generate rich and multivariate theory. One of the purposes of memo sorting is to facilitate the researcher to look for similarities and connections between and among codes. Holton (2007) urges grounded theorists to read widely from different disciplines so that they may be open to discovery of new theoretical codes from other disciplines. She argues that patterns found in a particular discipline may well conceptually fit in another discipline. Holton considers those researchers who do not reach outside extant theory for theoretical coding possibilities may produce adequate but mundane conceptual theory, and the theory may make only a limited contribution to knowledge and may "lack the impact that the creative emergence of a novel or non-traditional theoretical code may offer" (p. 283). In the present research for this book, I compared cross-cultural exchange projects from different fields of study and different perspectives, such as science, business management, and intercultural competence.

In the process of coding, I realized that there were different kinds of computer software available for grounded theorists to use in their coding or sorting process. However, I insisted on hand coding or sorting the data. My rationale was, first, cross-cultural exchanges are complicated social activities and they involve complicated human behaviors. We can hardly quantify or clearly classify a specific human behavior by using some kind of computer software. Second some linguistic expressions have to be interpreted based on who the speaker (or the writer) and the listener (the reader) are, what the context is, and what the topic in the interaction is. A machine might not be adequate to analyze the complex human social behaviors. In speaking of computer technologies, Holton (2007) argues that while traditional qualitative research may "embrace technology's rapid and expansive processing capabilities to significantly reduce both the time and effort required to run multiple tests on vast data banks" (p. 287), application of computer-assisted coding software programs may be "counter-creative to the conceptual ideation imperative for generating good grounded theory" (p. 287). Corbin and Strauss (2008) also warn qualitative researchers that, even with computers, researchers still need to reflect on data and write memos. In other words, in the entire process of analyzing the data, I did not use a computer program to sort the data. Instead, I physically labeled different concepts, categories, and codes. I applied a cut-and-sort procedure. First, I made a xerox-copy of each piece of the qualitative data. Then I looked over all the data and looked for important messages relevant to the research and cut down the message and labeled the message with a code. Pieces of messages with the same code were then put together.

Criticisms of the Grounded Theory Method and Emergence of Constructivist Grounded Theory

The GTM did not go without criticism (Bryant & Charmaz, 2007). Critiques of GTM point to the following deficiencies. First, Gloser and Strauss, in their earlier work, stress the importance of data gathering and comparison among data. They did not really examine how researchers define, produce, and record data. It seems that the researcher does not need to be concerned with quality, range, amount, accuracy of and access to data. Second, some critiques points out that the inductive nature of GTM might fail to see the exception and that it might be impossible for any arguments from experience to be able to prove resemblance of the past to the future. A more deductive approach should be used in research based on grounded theory. Third, for some ground theorists, the traditional grounded theory method is too objective. Reading the literature on a topic should be part of the grounded theory method (Bernard & Ryan, 2010).

In response to the criticism of overplaying the inductive aspects of GTM, Strauss proposes an abductive reasoning approach, whose logic is linking "empirical observation with imaginative interpretation, but does so by seeking theoretical accountability through returning to the empirical world" (Byrant & Charmaz, 2007, p. 46). The abductive reasoning approach can be illustrated as: The researcher first analyzes inductive data, then he or she conceptualizes the data. Finally, the researcher checks these conceptions through further data gathering which brings in deductive elements. In this book, I first analyzed the existing data inductively. Then, based on the inductive data and further data collected, I envisioned the future of cross-cultural exchanges out of the deductive elements of the research reports. That is, I followed the abductive reasoning approach to conduct the research.

As GTM developed and responded to the criticism received, researchers proposed approaches for furthering the grounded theory perspective. For example, Charmaz calls her approach a "constructivist approach." Clarke refers to her method as "situational analysis," and Goulding mainly addresses her approach to management, business, and market researchers (Corbin & Strauss, 2008). Constructivist grounded theory (CGT) and objectivist grounded theory (OGT) are two of the apparent examples. Hildenbrand (2007) compares CGT and OGT and points out that the two approaches are different mainly in that data collected for OGT are real and are objective facts and both data and analyses in CGT are social constructions reflecting the process of production. The role of the researcher in OGT is played as an impartial observer who maintains distance from the subjects researched; while, in CGT, the researcher sees the world being obdurate, yet ever-changing and recognizes diverse local worlds and multiple realities.

Mills, Bonner, and Francis (2006), in addressing constructivist grounded theory, argue that the theory actively repositions the researcher as the author of a reconstruction of experience and meaning. They cite Lincoln and Cuba's words as saying that constructivism "is a research paradigm that denies the existence of an objective reality, asserting instead that realities are social constructions of the mind and that there exist as many such constructions as there are individuals although clearly many constructions will be shared" (p. 2). In this sense, constructivism emphasizes the subjective interrelationship between the researcher and participant, and the co-construction of meaning. Researchers are seen as "part of the research endeavor rather than objective observers, and their values must be acknowledged by themselves and by their readers as an inevitable part of the outcome" (p. 2).

In this book, I favor the use of constructivist grounded theory. I firmly believe that the meaning of a cultural exchange activity can only be interpreted by different individuals and that only by getting involved in the activity can a researcher construct meaning with participants of the activity, especially when the activity involves people from different cultures. On the other hand, I also believe that there is no total objectivity in a research task. The question is to what extent a researcher can report from a participant's perspective. Maintaining distance from the student and only playing the role of an observer in a cultural exchange activity, one may not be able to fully capture the real meaning of the student experiences. In this book, I, when conducting a cross-cultural exchange project, tried to get involved in the cross-cultural exchange project and reported from the participants' perspectives when it came to reporting my personal experiences in cross-cultural exchanges.

Data Analysis

As Corbin and Strauss (2008) state, many researchers have proposed various ways of managing the data collected for a study, and each analyst has his or her own repertoire of strategies for analyzing qualitative data, and they illustrate different tools as analytic strategies. Among the analytic strategies, according to Corbin and Strauss, the use of questioning and making comparisons can be said to be the most fundamental and standout ones. In this book, I thus employed these two analytic tools in the process of data analysis. Different types of questions were first formulated to allow me to better understand the data collected and the way to organize the data.

Questioning

As Corbin and Strauss (2008) point out, one of the purposes or advantages of asking questions is to familiarize the researcher with the data and to start the analyst thinking about the data. There are several types of questions that can stimulate thinking about the issues relevant to the study and lead to a more focused idea as to what to look for in the data, such as sensitizing questions, theoretical questions, practical questions, and guiding questions. In this book, I formulated the following sensitizing questions and theoretical questions to facilitate analysis of the data.

Sensitizing Questions

Facing the huge amount of unstructured data collected for this book, at the beginning of data analysis, I first formulated the following sensitizing questions to familiarize myself with the data and to decide on how to get started with the data. In this type of question, I tuned in to the data and tried to get a sense of what the data might indicate and how the data might be organized.

How can cross-cultural exchanges be categorized into different types? Do different types of cultural exchanges mean different things to the instructors and the students?

How is a cross-cultural exchange program generally developed? That is, what steps should be taken into consideration in the process of developing a cross-cultural exchange program?

- What kinds of activities can be practiced in different types of cross-cultural exchanges?
- What are the various objectives of cross-cultural exchanges?
- Who are the groups of participants selected in cross-cultural exchanges?
- Do different designs of cross-cultural exchange programs lead to different consequences?
- How is a cross-cultural exchange program generally evaluated?

In answering all the questions, I got a sense of how cross-cultural exchange programs can be generally practiced, not just based on personal experiences and imagination. Having formulated and answered the above-mentioned questions, I could roughly organize the data based on the types, objectives, procedures, activities, purposes, participants, consequences of the cultural exchange, etc. I then moved to the next step to formulate theoretical questions.

Theoretical Questions

In order to look into the details of and get an insight into each activity and the procedure of the activity, and thus to look for similarities and differences between or among different cultural exchange projects and eventually and hopefully to generate relevant theories and to predict future trends of cross-cultural exchanges, I raised the following theoretical questions in the process of data analysis.

- What are some of the general components that have to be taken into consideration when organizing a cultural exchange project?
- Among the many cases of cross-cultural exchange projects collected, what steps should be taken in organizing a cross-cultural exchange project? Are there any similarities or differences between or among different projects in terms of the steps taken in organizing the project?
- Specifically, how can each step be done, considering the objectives of the project, the participants, the facilities available, language used, and so on? What alternatives can each step have for practitioners of a cross-cultural exchange project to choose from.
- Based on findings of the research, are there any clues that reveal the future trends of cultural exchange projects that we can expect?

These theoretical questions helped me focus on some specific issues and prepare for interpreting some phenomena found in cultural exchange projects.

Making Comparison

The other analytic tool used in the book was making comparisons. Both constant comparisons and theoretical comparisons were used in an attempt to discover general patterns as well as variations of cultural exchanges from the data.

Constant Comparisons

Constant comparisons are within-code comparisons. Incidents that are coded the same are compared for similarities and differences. As suggested by Corbin and Strauss (2008), the "purpose of this within-code comparison is to uncover the different properties and dimensions of the code" (p. 74). For example, in the case of this book, I constantly compared a cultural exchange activity with another cultural exchange activity within the same group of students and also compared similar activities done in different projects. In the case of Taiwanese TESOL majors vs. American TESOL majors, I compared different activities done in the project, such as oral presentations and discussions through videoconferencing, online postings on the Moodle discussion forum on different issues, and online peer evaluation. I was trying to see if students had different attitudes towards different activities, and if different activities benefitted students differently.

On the other hand, I looked at and compared cross-cultural exchange projects that integrated different modes of activities and aimed at promoting professional growth. In making the comparison, I looked for answers to questions, such as

- What are the features or properties of the cultural exchanges?
- What kind of professional growth were they seeking?
- What were the purposes for the organizers to employ different modes of cultural exchange?

In the cases of cross-cultural exchange projects collected for this book, there were cases aiming at professional growth in mural painting (Ho, 2012), agriculture (Wals & Sriskandarajah, 2010), business management (Magnier-Watanabe, Benton, Herring, & Aba, 2011), and language and cultural learning (Ruecker, 2011). These were good sources for this type of comparison.

Another example of constant comparison was that I compared the Magaconference VI I participated in and the Face-to-Faith program because both of the programs involved participants from all over the world. Magaconference VI was organized by Ohio State University, USA and featured participation by people around the world. The videoconference lasted for 24 hours to allow people from different time zones of the world to choose a time period appropriate for them to participate and to discuss issues of common concerns. This is similar to the Face-to-Faith program reported by Beauchamp (2011). Beauchamp describes that Face-to-Faith as an educational program created by the Tony Blair Faith Foundation and is aimed at enabling students to learn directly from, with, and about each other's culture, religion, and beliefs through videoconferencing and online community. The target population of the program was students aged 12-18. While comparing the two projects, I asked myself questions, such as "What are the features specific to this kind of videoconferencing?" "What may be the differences, if any, between this kind of videoconferencing and traditional class-to-class videoconferencing?" "What are the challenges, if any, organizers of this type of videoconferencing might face?" These questions might shed light on how these larger scale videoconferencing projects might be organized and might raise my awareness of the fact that one size does not always fit all. A cross-cultural project needs to be organized based on a lot of different factors.

In sum, by doing constant comparison, I intended to look for emerging patterns. For example, there might be specific procedures to organize different kinds of cultural exchange programs, and achieving different objectives may require different program arrangements. Without comparing with others, people might not see things and see themselves clearly.

Theoretical Comparisons

To further constant comparison, theoretical comparisons will move comparison to a property and dimensional level. Corbin and Strauss (2008) analogize theoretical comparisons to frequent comparisons we make in our daily life, such as comparison of the price, size, color, shape, and juiciness of two oranges. In the case of cross-cultural exchange projects, I compared different cases and activities and looked into detailed components to compare, such things as objectives, participants, facilities, and modes of the cultural exchange projects. Some of the questions I had in mind to guide myself in the process of theoretical comparisons were: "Do different objectives set for the cultural exchange require different modes of exchange to achieve? That is, is there a particular mode or combination of different modes best suited for a particular type of cultural exchanges?" "Are there different ways of organizing the project that may lead to different consequences?" "What can be the factors that contribute to the success of a cultural exchange project, and what clues obtained from the research may shed light on the trends of future cross-cultural exchanges?"

As Corbin and Strauss (2008) have pointed out, objectivity in qualitative research is almost a myth. It is because researchers always bring with them their background, training, knowledge, perspectives, experiences, and even biases to the research context, and these ideological factors may affect how a researcher collects, analyzes, and interprets data. They argue that being sensitive to what our participants are telling us is what a researcher should care about. By "sensitivity" Corbin and Strauss mean the ability to "present the view of participants and taking the role of the other through immersion in data" (p. 33). They especially point out that what matters is not how the researcher perceives an event, but what participants are saying and doing. What the researcher sees of an object may by different from that viewed by the participants. I was aware of the importance of sensitivity and tried to maximize research sensitivity by extensively communicating with participants and reading research reports of different domains.

One specific example of theoretical comparisons in this book was that I compared the case of Taiwanese English majors vs. American journalism majors with the case of Spanish majors in Japan vs. native speakers of Spanish in Spain conducted by a professor who was teaching Spanish in Japan (Wang, 2013). I consider the former case is successful based on my observations, students' feedback, and surveys conducted for the project. The latter is considered unsuccessful as described by the Japanese professor who organized the project. He reported that communication between Japanese students and Spanish students could hardly take place at the first videoconference. I compared the two cases and looked for factors that may contribute to the success of the former case and that may account for consequences of the latter. I roughly attributed the different consequences to different levels of language proficiency and unequal benefits different groups of students received. I explain the case in detail in a later chapter.

Simply speaking, in the stage of theoretical comparison, the researcher may compare two different things or events, even though they are quite different in nature, and look for some common ground existing between them. This stage may contribute to findings of some important rules or theories.

Abduction Type of Data Analysis

Reichertz (2007) describes three types of data analysis in a research study based on the grounded theory method. They are subsumption, generalizing, and abduction. The logic underlying the operation of subsumption is that "the single case in question is subordinated to an already known rule" (p. 218). The process is that of deduction, and in this case we do not intend to invent new rules or explore new facts. The second type of analysis is to generalize the features found in the data material into an order or a rule. This is an induction type of data analysis, which, according to Reichertz, can only find new versions of what is already known. The third type of data analysis is termed *abduction*, whose process features its discovering of new things for which "there is no appropriate explanation or rule in the store of knowledge that already exists" (p. 219). The meaning underlying this metaphor is that by using the abductive process, the researcher intends to create favorable conditions for the discovery of new things. It is an attitude towards data and one's own knowledge. I followed this type of data analysis, for the goal of the research is to discover new things, rather than merely present what is already known. For example, I first analyzed the existing data relevant to cross-cultural exchanges and looked for some patterns. Then, based on the analysis, I pictured the future trends of cross-cultural exchanges.

Based on how the data were collected and analyzed as described above, a pattern of developing a cross-cultural exchange project emerged. As a rule of thumb, practitioners of a cross-cultural exchange project start with choosing participant students, and then they have to define the objectives of the project. Having decided on who will participate and the purposes for the exchange, practitioners look for exchange partners and collaborate with partner teachers to develop a cross-cultural exchange project. Having completed the project, it is necessary for the teachers to look the entire project over and to assess students' accomplishment and the project itself. Finally, I would say that it does not quite make sense if I just present what other teachers have done and outline from what has happened. I am obliged to present the future of cross-cultural exchanges based on the emerging theory of the search and the current trends of cross-cultural exchanges. In the following chapters to come, I explain each step in detail.

However, depending on your project, you may switch some steps in the course of developing the project. For example, you may be approached by a partner teacher first and asked for cross-cultural collaboration. In this case, you may need to establish consensus with your partner teacher and define the objectives of the project before you can consider which group of students may be the best choice for the project. In the following chapters, I will explain each step in detail and suggest alternatives for each step.

In addressing characteristics of the young generations, the grounded theory method may be a good research method to explore those characteristics and to discover what may evidence their multi-faceted learning style. Holton (2007), in discussing the grounded theory, urged researchers to extensively study the methodology in tandem with experiencing the method in order to truly understand classic grounded theory. She also encourages researchers to read and get involved in knowledge discovery of different disciplines. The point underlying Holton's claim was that there is no clear-cut line between two different academic disciplines. The future of cross-cultural exchanges may show that students learn from each other and learn across disciplines. A linear learning style can no longer satisfy learners in an era full of information. Participants of cross-cultural exchanges expect to learn in a hyperlink mode, just like the way Web texts are organized. As from Grounded Theory Methods, there are also different types of research methods available to be used in research on cross-cultural projects, including literature survey, content analysis, and statistical analysis, which are briefly discussed in the following sections.

LITERATURE SURVEY

The process of literature survey, according to Sekaran (2003), "is the documentation of a comprehensive review of the published and unpublished work from secondary sources of data in the area of specific interest to the researcher" (p. 63). The main reason for literature survey is to look for important variables that can be brought out in the survey. Another advantage of doing literature survey is to avoid wasting of time by repeatedly focusing on things that have been well-researched. On the other hand, a thorough literature survey can provide researchers with a clear picture of what has happened so as to predict the future trends of development of a specific issue or phenomenon. Viewed from this perspective, part of this book is actually a literature survey in nature. It is not an empirical study; rather, it is a collection of a variety of theories and empirical studies on cross-cultural exchanges. The real meaning of literature survey, as pointed out by Sekaran (2003), is to identify problems in an interested field for further investigation. However, he reminds researchers of the pitfall of identifying the "real" problem. It is quite possible that researchers regard "symptoms" as "problems" and do not really get into the problem and hence solve the problem. Sekaran suggests that

> A 'problem' does not necessarily mean that something is seriously wrong with a current situation that needs to be rectified immediately. A "problem" could simply indicate an interest in an issue where finding the right answers might help to improve an existing situation. (p. 69)

In a sense, a problem may mean the ways the researcher can find to reach the ideal situation.

In the case of cross-cultural exchanges, doing a comprehensive literature survey has enabled me to explore the real "problem" that may contribute to further improvement of cross-cultural exchanges. As I read reports on cross-cultural exchanges written from different perspectives, conducted for different purposes and in different situations, and showing various advantages and challenges, I am able to present to my readers a wider range of pictures so that they can have a better grasp of the entire project. One size can never fit all in the case of cross-cultural exchanges. For practitioners or participants of cross-cultural exchanges, there are no guidelines that can be applied to all cases. Depending on the cultural, social, political, economic, religious, and technological situations of the home country and the host country, cross-cultural exchanges may vary from case to case. One of the merits of providing readers with comprehensive sources of cross-cultural exchanges is that readers can take different situations into consideration and make the best choice.

As mentioned earlier in this book, I intend to provide the reader with a substantial guide as to how a cross-cultural exchange project can be developed. It is thus inevitable for me to resort to many existing documents and data in order to show the progress or changes of cross-cultural exchange projects. In discussing cross-cultural survey methods, van Deth (2003) argues that "using existing data is the rule rather than the exception in social research" (p. 291). She lists several reasons why using existing data in social research is appropriate and essential; they are comparability, verification or secondary analysis, and skepticism. As I have already stated earlier, the construct and data collection and analyses of the entire work mainly followed the grounded theory method, and one of the most important features of grounded theory is its constant comparison. In this book, comparing cross-cultural exchange projects practiced in different time periods is actually the main concern. As we can see, cross-cultural exchanges are complicated social activities and are dynamically processed. They change their modes, purposes, and media of communication over time because of social changes, advancement of communication technologies, and, probably, political issues. Comparison of cross-cultural exchange projects at different points of time may reveal the process of social, educational, technical, and political changes and may explain how people change their value judgments over time.

Another reason that supports the use of existing data, as stated by van Deth (2003), is that researchers do not have to collect fresh data if previous studies have similar research questions and data are appropriately collected. Researchers who attempt to use existing data may, then, analyze the data and interpret the results in a more efficient way to verify the previous studies. In cross-cultural exchanges, I realize that having investigations across countries to get a larger picture of how cross-cultural exchanges have been practiced is costly and time-consuming. It is therefore feasible for me to resort to existing documents and research reports so that I can look for patterns and dynamics from a longer history and a larger picture of cross-cultural exchanges.

According to van Deth (2003), "each and every scientific proposition should be the object of public discussion and should undergo rigorous critical appraisal" (p. 293). In the course of discussion, "the same data are scrutinized from different perspectives, analyzed with different techniques, and (re-)interpreted on the basis of additional information" (p. 294). In this book, I try to look over the existing data and see how I may have a fresh or different perspective from an outsider's view and after a course of value and social change.

In this book, I collected data from observations and video recordings of cross-cultural videoconferencing, oral and written communications with partner teachers, my own teaching logs and field notes, interviews with the teachers and students who were involved, students' learning logs and their postings on Facebook developed exclusively for the projects, assignments students turned in for a project, campus newspapers reporting on the cross-cultural videoconferencing I have conducted, and, most importantly, the Educational Resources Information Center (ERIC) online database.

I did literature survey from sources available and accessible in the library and online, including books, professional journals, doctoral dissertations or master's theses, conference proceedings, and online databases, such as ERIC. ERIC is the most important source which the book relies on because the database collects a considerable number of publications in the educational arena and keeps it updated. I searched the most recent ERIC database. Keywords such as *cross-cultural exchanges* and *cross-cultural exchange projects* were typed in to elicit relevant cultural exchange programs or activities. Data obtained from the database were considered very important because ERIC is seen as one of the largest databases in the educational arena, and reports on cross-cultural exchanges collected from the database may cover a wide range of cross-cultural exchanges organized and participated in by people from different cultures and different backgrounds for different purposes. There were more than a thousand entries relevant to cross-cultural exchanges collected for analysis. Among the entries, there were direct contact between/among teachers and/or students from different cultures, such as Chileans vs. Americans (Ruecker, 2011), Americans vs. Mexicans, and Hong Kongers vs. Germans (Chik & Breidbach, 2011); exchange teachers teaching in a foreign country, such as an American teacher teaching collective mural painting in Bulgaria (Ho, 2012) and an American teacher teaching management in the Slovak Republic; teaching in a culturally diverse classroom, such as teaching African American children (Tolbert-Hill, 2003), teaching in Australia (MacNaughton & Hughes, 2007), and teaching in Japan (Qi, 2011); evaluation of exchange programs, such as a survey of exchange students in Turkey (Icbay & Kocayoruk, 2011) and investigation of study abroad programs (Ellwood, 2011); and even programs open to students from all over the world, such as the Face to Faith program (Beauchamp, 2011). I intended to analyze all the massive qualitative and quantitative data and looked for patterns emerging from the data in my writing process.

There are, however, problems especially existing in the data collection for cross-cultural investigations, for example, neglecting of cultural information, inadequate translation, and culture-sensitive context effects. As pointed out by Mohler and Ulher (2003), "contextual and collateral information is often neglected in comparative survey documentation. In national documentation, it is of relatively minor significance, since researchers 'know' their own cultural context" (p. 315). It is not uncommon that researchers tend to focus on their own cultural context when reporting cross-cultural exchange projects. As a result, there may be an information gap or bias existing in cross-cultural research reports. To solve the problem, Mohler and Ulher suggest that "documentation could be established on a cumulative basis" (p. 315). That is, whenever researchers need any culture-specific information, they are encouraged to access relevant databases and get the information they need. In the case of this book, a comprehensive literature survey of reports on cross-cultural exchanges may enable the reader to take different social and cultural perspectives into consideration and, hence, make a better decision and broaden the scope of comprehension.

CONTENT ANALYSIS

After having discussed the grounded theory method and illustrated how the data of this book were collected, I then turn to the discussion of content analysis. As pointed out by Bernard and Ryan (2010), "content analysis is usually quantitative analysis. This is one thing that distinguishes content analysis from grounded theory" (p. 287), although content analysis is generally used to code and analyze qualitative data. Doing content analysis may help organize a huge amount of unstructured data.

Historical Background of Content Analysis

The history of content analysis can be traced to Wilcox, who "studied the content for June and September 1898, and September 1899, of 147 newspapers in the 21 most populous cities of the United States" (Bernard & Ryan, 2010, p. 288). Bernard and Ryan list seven steps to do content analysis:

1) Formulate a research question or hypothesis, based on existing theory or on prior research.
2) Select a set of texts to test the question or hypothesis.
3) Create a set of codes (variables, themes) in the research question or hypothesis.
4) Pretest the variables on a few of the selected texts. Fix any problems that turn up with regard to the codes and the coding so that the coders become consistent in their coding.
5) Apply the codes to the rest of the texts.
6) Create a case-by-variable matrix from the texts and codes.
7) Analyze the matrix using whatever level of analysis is appropriate. (p. 289-290)

In sum, content analysis is part of a research technique that applies the quantitative research paradigm to analyze qualitative data.

There are, of course, both advantages and disadvantages in applying content analysis to research studies. One of the advantages is that it saves a considerable amount of time in coding the data, compared with that done manually. However, there are also disadvantages in doing content analysis. "The obvious disadvantage is that such coding cannot readily take into account the unusual expressions or latent meanings in the text (Bazeley, 2003). Garrison and Anderson (2003) point out that there are both manifest and latent content in texts for research study. Manifest contents are much more observable and easier to code and count. Unlike manifest contents, latent contents are more complicated and problematic in terms of finding the evidence and quantifying the data.

Content Analysis as Related to This Book

In this book, as mentioned earlier, it may be unlikely for me as an independent researcher to travel around the world and interview people from different cultures to record a considerable amount of cross-cultural exchange data. I thus resorted to the use of digital data archives. The main source of the digital archive the author turned to was the ERIC database. It is because ERIC, having a history of more than 50 years, has been considered by researchers in the educational field as one of the largest collections of educational materials and research reports. It documents relevant articles or even books from different professional journals, conference proceedings, governmental bulletins, and publishers. Retrieving articles of interest from the data is quite easy. You simply key in the keywords, and you can get a list of articles that you might need. Read the abstracts to make sure you really want the articles. Then you get the articles based on the sources the database provides. This database is especially good for cross-cultural investigations, since it contains research reports written by researchers from different cultural backgrounds and from different cultural perspectives, and the organization keeps updating the database.

Having the data collected, I then moved to the next step, coding. In the coding process, I sought to answer the following research question I set to guide the coding task: What are the steps required to start a cross-cultural exchange project, and, in each step, what alternatives did practitioners of cross-cultural exchanges have to ensure the most rewarding cross-cultural experiences? In order to ensure the accuracy and appropriateness of the code, I sought to the help of an expert, who was then just conferred a doctoral degree in the TESOL field. The intercoder reliability calculated by using Cohne's Kappa (Bernard & Ryan, 2010) is $k = 0.78$, which is considered adequate intercoder reliability (Bernard & Ryan, 2010).

In addition to the ERIC database, content analysis techniques were also applied in the part of videoconferencing which I personally directed and participated in. In this part, the coders were trained to look at the videotapes of the conferences for latent content not manifested in verbal expressions themselves, such as facial expressions, body language, tone and speed of utterance, appearance, and emotions. Yet, another issue in latent content raised by Garrison and Anderson (2003) is *latent projective variables,* referring to 'the coder's' interpretations of the meaning of the content" (p. 141). According to Garrison and Anderson, some latent content variables are actually subject to the interpretations of the coder, which are relevant to the coder's cultural background, age, and personality. For example, 'use of humor', 'creativity', and 'critical thinking', may be interpreted differently by different coders. To solve the problem, I resorted to the alternative suggest by Garrison and Anderson. That is, I waited until the last stage of content analysis to look for a meaningful unit whose attributes can be reasonably assigned to an abstract code. I believe that being entirely objective may not be possible in this regard. However, by having the task jointly done by me and the coder and eventually reaching a consensus, we believe that by doing so, we are able to minimize the degree of subjectivity.

To analyze texts, Garrison and Anderson (2003) illustrate different types of units of analysis, such as sentence unit, paragraph unit, message unit, thematic unit, and illocutionary unit. Each type of unit for analysis has its advantages and disadvantages. In this book, I chose illocutionary unit as the unit for analysis. This type of unit of analysis is drawn on the theory of Speech Act. In the theory of Speech Act, illocutionary force refers to the speaker's intent or purpose to utter something. The intention to utter can be identified as to request, inform, apologize, warn, promise, etc. (Fromkin, Rodman, & Hyams, 2014). That is to say, we consider a change in purpose a unit of analysis. For us, the coders and I, this is the most meaningful and appropriate type to analyze the discourse of videoconference. However, in analyzing the ERIC database, we considered thematic unit type most suitable for our analysis. That is because, by dividing the texts into meaningful units, it may be easier for us to look for patterns existing in cross-cultural exchanges, which is one of the main purposes of this book. In sum, to borrow Boeije's (2010) words, "it is expected that the findings will have relevance for the field and can be easily transformed into interventions for practitioners" (p. 33).

Given the nature of this book, face-to-face interviews may be limited to local people or international visitors. This may not be sufficient in scope to address the big topic of cross-cultural exchanges. Searching online databases may at least partially solve the problem. Personally I favor unstructured in-depth interviews to allow participants to freely narrate their personal experiences and express their subjective views. However, as Mann and Stewart (2000) have pointed out, the "key challenge in the design of a qualitative study is to find a balance between interview methods which give participants 'the floor' and those which allow the interviewer to pursue their own research enquiries" (p. 76). Fortunately, this was less a problem for me in the process of collecting data. As mentioned earlier, I followed the grounded theory method in organizing the book. One of the key features of the grounded theory is that grounded theorists do not usually have predetermined thoughts or ideas in mind. They let the research go and the data to be collected. Beyond the required data being collected, there are also serendipitous findings that can help interpret a particular phenomenon.

ONLINE METHODS

In addition to collecting data in conventional ways, researchers can also collect data online. In introducing online methods, Mann and Stewart (2000) compare some tools of data collection with those used in traditional research methods, such as surveys, interviews, observations, and document analyses. Apparently, we may see some benefits of researching online, for example, expanding access to participants and geographically distant areas, access to closed, dangerous, or politically sensitive sites, access to interest groups, and it is cost effective and time saving. However, there are also some challenges of doing research online. Mann and Stewart also point to some challenges online researchers may face, for example, requirement of computer literacy and interactive skills online, finding e-mail addresses and making contacts with individuals, and getting participants' cooperation. Aside from problems inherently existing in cross-cultural survey questions mentioned above that will be elaborated in later paragraphs of this section, there are also problems occurring in the course of the research design. As mentioned by Mann and Stewart (2000), online methods are popularly used by qualitative researchers to collect data. It may be more practical and useful for researchers of cross-cultural exchange projects because cross-cultural exchanges inevitably involve participants who are physically apart and who are culturally different. It is thus appropriate that the researcher uses online methods to collect data if applicable, such as CMC and students' reflections or discussions online. However, Mann and Stewart also pointed out that there are both advantages and disadvantages of online survey. Although online surveys may save time and cost less and may reach more participants and secure anonymity of participants, the researcher cannot be sure of the reliability of the survey results because the same person may repeatedly submit the survey and respondents may not necessarily be members of the focused groups. Another problem is that, in case it is necessary for the researcher to follow-up some points, he or she may lose access to the participants. Furthermore, the digital world is changing rapidly, including the participants and their postings and the technologies themselves. "Statements made now may appear ridiculous in just a couple of years time" (p. 31).

To ensure multi-dimensional coverage of cross-cultural exchange projects, I used a multi-method approach suggested by Mann and Stewart (2000) in order to examine how researchers design a cross-cultural exchange project for different purposes and how they look at a phenomenon from a different perspective. I combined a comprehensive review of literature with surveys and interviews to provide the reader with a larger picture of cross-cultural exchanges.

Another problem with cross-cultural survey lies in the fact that translating a questionnaire from one language to another may lead to different interpretations, value judgments, and even different meanings for the respondents who use the translated version of the questionnaire. As pointed out by Harkness (2003), "translation is one of the most frequently mentioned problems in comparative research" (p. 44). In cross-cultural survey research, it is not uncommon that survey questions have to be translated from one language to another. This will cause fewer problems in a mono-cultural research context. However, in a cross-cultural research context, the quality of translations of survey questions may significantly affect the validity and reliability of the research.

Given the fact that "neither words, concepts, nor structures match up neatly across languages" (Harkness, 2003, p. 47), a questionnaire translator needs to be proficient in the two languages and cultures and needs to take pragmatic meaning into account in the process of translating. Harkness points out some apparently erroneous translations that occurred in empirical studies and proposes five basic procedures to produce a final version of a questionnaire: translation, review, adjudication, pretesting, and documentation. From these basic procedures, one can be easily aware of the complicated task of translating survey questions.

Another issue with online survey is about digital divides. Scholars keep mentioning issues of digital divides in the virtual world (Mann & Stewart, 2000; Wang, 2015; Hockly & Dudeney, 2017; Ragnedda & Ruiu, 2018). In addition that these inequalities may affect people's gains from making use of digital devices, it also causes problems in online survey. As pointed out by Mann and Steward (2000), the Internet is mostly accessible to wealthy and knowledgeable elites. There are differences and inequalities in access to the Internet in terms of gender, ethnicity, age, and socio-economic status. The most dominant digital group is young, white, Western males. Viewed from this regard, online survey researchers may tend to collect data from those privileged groups and ignore those disadvantaged and less representative minority groups. From the discussions above, we may realize that there are some limitations in applying online methods to research on cross-cultural exchanges. Those researchers and practitioners of cross-cultural exchanges who embrace the advantages of online methods may need to be aware of the challenges faced by online methods users.

As we can see from the above discussions, there are both strengths and weaknesses in traditional face-to-face interviews as well as in online interviews. To collect sufficient and appropriate interview data, I chose to apply both methods in the interviewing part. On the one hand, I interviewed local participants of cross-cultural exchange projects face-to-face in an in depth manner. On the other hand, I conducted online interviews to use emails to elicit responses from international researchers who have experiences of cross-cultural exchanges.

STATISTICAL ANALYSIS

Quantitative research, using statistics is best used to investigate the changes in students' intercultural competences, perceived language and communication skills, attitudes towards different cultures, and levels of satisfaction towards the cross-cultural exchange project. These statistical data are generally collected before and after the exchange activities and are used to compare and find out if the changes or improvements are significant. You may use questionnaires, tests, and different forms of recording to get the statistical data you need. It is important for the researcher to secure the validity and reliability of the data. As we can understand, cross-cultural exchanges are complicated social activities. It may not be easy to quantify every mental or physical involvement in the activity. Statistical analysis can be a good way to explore the aptitudes or preferences of the students, trends of cross-cultural exchanges, and what students really gain from the activities. It is better to be combined with different types of qualitative exploration so that the statistical data derived from the research can be meaningful to the researcher and the reader.

As is common to all research methods, each research method has both benefits and challenges. I would say striking a balance between different methods can be a wise decision in terms of ensuring the validity, reliability, or trustworthiness of a research report. This book collected research reports on cross-cultural exchange programs from different perspectives and with different research methods. By doing so, I intend to provide readers with a broadened view of issues related to cross-cultural exchanges.

Although different approaches can be used for research on different cross-cultural activities, it is suggested that a mix or integration of research methods can better demonstrate your research efforts and more precisely present your research findings. For example, you may use statistical methods to get a significant level of your students' improvements in their intercultural competences first, and then you may interview your students or search their reflection assignments for clues contributing to the improvements.

For this book, in addition to the traditional research methods used in collecting and analyzing the data, I deliberately employed the globalized research perspective as proposed by Roudometof (2016) in formulating and presenting the entire book. To be precise, because of the limitation of individual efforts, I tried to extend the scope of investigation by studying literature relevant to cross-cultural exchanges reported by researchers from different cultures and different perspectives in different areas of the globe on different issues, concerns, and interests. That is, I tried to put research reports from an individual or a local perspective in a global lens and to compare different voices. As stated by Roudometof (2016), there must be local elements situated in a global setting and vice versa.

Chapter 3

RECRUITING AND TRAINING YOUR PARTICIPANT STUDENTS

Although there are various forms of cross-cultural exchanges, especially I expand the idea of cross-cultural exchanges to include teachers as participants and practitioners from different domains, such as exchange partners, personal decisions, such as teaching and studying abroad, distance education and international volunteering. In this chapter, I will mainly focus on student-to-student, or class-to-class cross-cultural exchanges in the educational arena in which recruiting and training students are relevant. I will divide participant students into two different forms of participation: online communications and onsite experiences. Online distant communications refer to those communications other than face-to-face ones, but are mediated by communication technologies. This may include synchronous communications, such as videoconferencing and chat room, and asynchronous communications, such as e-mailing and computer mediated communications. Onsite experiences, on the other hand, are those activities when partner groups of students meet with each other face-to-face, either one group of students visits the other group of students or the two groups of students visit each other physically. Recruiting participant students to participate in the two forms of cross-cultural exchanges are totally different in terms of the procedure, the criteria, and things to be taken into account.

ONLINE COMMUNICATIONS

If you decide that a project using online communications is best for your students, then there are two modes of communications you can choose from: oral communications, such as videoconferencing, and synchronous or asynchronous written communications, such as computer-mediated communications. At the very beginning stage of developing a cross-cultural exchange project, you, as the project practitioner, need to choose your participant students. You might teach classes that are quite different in their curricular nature, students' fields of study and levels of language proficiency, and their willingness to participate in a cross-cultural exchange project. The following particulars of your class must be taken into consideration to ensure success of your exchange project.

Nature of the Class

If your language class is a reading or writing class, then it may be appropriate for you to organize a computer-mediated written communication project and have your students communicate online with partners from different cultures. If your class is an oral class, then you might want to initiate cross-cultural videoconferencing for your students so that they may improve their listening and speaking skills by communicating with students from native speakers or a different culture. If your students' professional studies require knowledge or experiences by communicating with students from another culture, such as teacher education, business management, marketing, journalism, psychology, arts, fashion design, and international relations, then you might want to look for international partners with the same field of study and organize cross-cultural exchanges for students to enrich their professional knowledge with different cultural perspectives. For example, TESOL majors may learn differences between teaching English in an English speaking environment and in a non-English speaking environment, and marketing majors can learn different strategies to promote a product in Japan and in the United States. However, in the case of aiming at enriching your students' professional knowledge, different professions can also benefit your students' learning. For example, teaching professions can be viewed from a managerial perspective in the areas of classroom management, language management, and knowledge management, and fashion design majors may learn from psychology or marketing majors as to how their designs may meet customers' needs and interests and win their appreciation. One of the benefits of this type of arrangement is that students' learning about their profession knowledge will no longer be limited to the textbook and classroom instruction. Input from different cultural perspectives can enrich their professional knowledge and develop their creativity and critical thinking skills.

Time

Another issue that deserves your attention in the case of online communications is your class time and availability of your students' time. Depending on the physical distance between your school and your partner school, there might be a time difference that you need to take into account if you will be using synchronous communication tools, such as videoconferencing. For example, in the case of American journalism majors vs. Taiwanese English majors, I had to choose a night oral English class to participate. It was because facilities for synchronous oral communication were available in the evening and because the class time for the two groups of students overlap each other.

Aside from time differences, the school calendar can also affect your decision on choosing your participant students. Your school may have a school calendar different from that of the partner school you are going to collaborate cross-culturally. A consensus must be reached before you can finalize your dates and time for videoconferencing. Even if you and your partner teacher decide to have asynchronous written communications, and you assign particular topics for students to discuss. You and your partner teacher have to check both of your school calendars to make sure that different school calendars and different national holidays will not cause any problems. What you can do is that you list the dates your students are available for collaboration, be it a week, a month, or a semester, then you ask your partner teacher to check the availability of his or her students. Dates for two groups of students to meet, say in the case of videoconferencing, may further be cut down to meet the students' schedule. The schedule for collaboration then can be finalized.

Class Size, Technical Support, and Students' Technical Skills

Other factors, such as your class size and facilities available in your school, are also important in the process of choosing your participant students. If you have a big class, then it might not be feasible for you to choose videoconferencing as a way of communication if you do not have workable facilities and rooms and trained technicians to accommodate your students and to assist you in the process of videoconferences. In this case, you can organize a small-scale online chat, such as Chat Room or Skype. However, it does not quite matter if you will conduct asynchronous written exchanges with a big class. If this is the case, you need to make sure that all of your student participants have the computer skills required for cross-cultural exchanges. You may need to organize a workshop to familiarize your students with the computer skills to communicate with their overseas partners, especially if you and your partner teacher decide to develop a website particularly for the project. In this case, you still need technical support to monitor and maintain the website in case of any communication failure.

Another issue relevant to technical support that need to be taken into account is students' preference of using, participating, and interacting in online learning environments. As also will be mentioned in Chapter 5, students prefer to be engaged in a social network learning environment, not the virtual learning environment managed by the institution. Casquero, Benito, Romo, and Ovelar (2016) suggest an integration of virtual learning environments (i.e., institution-managed learning environments) with personal learning environment (i.e., socially-oriented websites such as iGoogle, Google Groups, FriendFeed, Flicker, YouTube, and SlideShare). Findings of their study show that higher student participation and interaction were found in the groups where integration of virtual learning environments and personal learning environment were provided. That is to say, aside from technical issues, students' preferences, priorities, and other motivational factors need to be taken into consideration in the course of designing. More detailed discussions on social presence are presented in Chapter 5 of this book.

Language Skills

Another important issue you need to take into consideration is the language or languages to be used in the course of cross-cultural exchanges. Although it may not be necessary and may not be practical to assess your students' language proficiency to choose your student participants, basic language skills are required for smooth cross-cultural communications. In the case of oral communications, different levels of language proficiency may cause imbalanced participation online. More aggressive and proficient students may dominate most of their peers and leave their peers with no chances to share their ideas because of time limit. Encouraging all of the participants to learn the communication language and a different culture and to express themselves and share their ideas may be required from the onset of the project. Some strategies may be used to encourage more reticent students to speak are turn taking, awarding extra points to those who speak, and having students being prepared and practice before the videoconference, and having adequate assessments. This situation is less an issue in the case of written communications. Students can have more time to refine their wording before they post a message and one's posting will not affect other's chances to post. Theoretically, quieter students may be better motivated to participate in written communications because expressing oneself in writing appears to be less threatening.

Ethical Issues

In addition to issues mentioned above, ethical issues are also important and should be drawn to the practitioners' attention in online cross-cultural communications. Students have to be well-informed of ethical issues before they launch into online cross-cultural communications. Kurt and Simsek (2016), cited from Khan, raise different issues relevant to ethics in e-learning, including social and cultural diversity, bias and political issues, geographical diversity, learner diversity, digital divide, etiquette, and legal issues such as privacy, plagiarism, and copyright issues. Although these issues are mainly focused on design and development of distance e-learning courses and materials, they can be perfectly applied to and are equally important in cross-cultural online communications. However, they can be interpreted in slightly different ways in either oral communications or written communications. For example, in addition to respecting your partners' political stands and religious beliefs, it may not be appropriate to discuss any political and religious issues in cross-cultural communications. It is because there may not be either right or wrong solutions to issues in these fields. They are matters of ideology and cognition, and they can easily cause conflicts between people of different cultural or ethnic backgrounds. Another issue is *etiquette*, which is sometimes termed *netiquette* in the digital world to stand for Net etiquette, it can include equal treatments of and fair responses to different postings or different presenters. Ignoring these ethical issues in cross-cultural communications can cause frustrations and loss of enthusiasm in participation.

In sum, although online cross-cultural exchanges may not be so serious and tedious as are onsite ones that may need a training program before the cross-cultural activities, an orientation is still required. Teachers may provide students with guidelines to cover some of the issues mentioned above and explain to the student. A technical proficiency survey can also be done to make sure each participant student can freely operate the machine without any difficulties. On the one hand, each issue needs to be considered in the course of designing cross-cultural online communications. On the other hand, cross-cultural communications are themselves one type of learning. Students may learn different languages, cultures, technical skills, and ethical issues while communicating with their overseas peers. Teachers' encouragement and facilitation may motivate students to learn from each other and make cross-cultural learning more meaningful and beneficial.

ONSITE EXPERIENCES

Onsite experiences refer to students' experiencing a different culture in an environment of that culture. It may be much more complicated than online communications in terms of recruiting participant students, and a training workshop is essential before students head for the host country. The most apparent cases are study groups visiting the partner school, study abroad and international volunteering. In the case of study groups with a short-term visit to the partner school, it is especially important in the process of recruiting your participant students. In addition to publicizing the overseas study activities to most of the students on campus by making flyers or posters or making announcement on websites or other media, explicit regulations and criteria have to be well-stated, taking students' academic performance, language proficiency, cultural awareness, personal traits, and financial status into consideration. As mentioned earlier, many countries, especially English-speaking countries, are always welcoming international students to attend schools in their countries. On the one hand, international students may help enrich the campus culture and internationalize the campus to prepare students for being a global citizen. On the other hand, international students who pay tuition to attend the school may be of great help to the school in terms of financial contributions. Generally speaking, different countries and different institutions have different regulations and criteria to recruit international students. For example, they may require applicants with a certain degree of academic performance, language proficiency, financial support, work experiences, proofs of leadership, and/or records of social service. It depends on what they require from their prospective students and how they intend to prepare their students in their future career. In case students support themselves for the overseas study and the school is not involved in any recruiting process, then students must evaluate themselves for whether they meet the fundamental requirements needed for overseas study.

However, things have changed in the recent years. According to Bevis and Lucas (2007), for example, the United States enjoyed being the preferred choice for foreign students who are seeking it as the destination of their study abroad. This is no longer the case as an increasingly growing international competition for students among many countries. English-speaking countries, such as Australia, New Zealand, Canada, and Great Britain and member nations of the European Union are striving to attract international students. For example, European countries, including France, Italy, the United Kingdom, and Germany met in Paris in 1998 to discuss reform and harmonization in higher education. They intended "to enhance the 'attractiveness' and 'competitiveness' of European postsecondary education to other parts of the world" (p. 222). This might threaten the dominance of the United States in the international student market. Many countries may use different strategies to attract international students, such as reducing tuition, offering scholarships, and providing better facilities and accommodations for international students. As mentioned earlier, recruiting international students is the individual university's decision and is not the main focus of this chapter, I now turn to the discussion of recruiting your students for overseas trips.

Aside from recruiting students from abroad, some schools may have to assign exchange students or lead a study group to a foreign country to learn or to have cross-cultural exchanges. Generally speaking, there are only a limited number of students who can be chosen as exchange students to experience a period of study abroad. The requirements of an exchange student and the procedures to recruit exchange students vary, depending on the goal and the nature of the exchange project. Another issue that needs to be taken into consideration in the recruiting process is the issues of equality and balance. Brown and Tignor (2016) show that in the case of the United States, non-white students, males, "STEM majors, students with disabilities, and those traveling to non-

European destinations" (p. 69) are less considered in a recruiting process. It is ironical that in an era moving towards globalization, some groups of people are excluded and are prevented from joining the activities taking place in the global community. Punteney (2017) also states that while we may have rough criteria in mind as to what characteristics a student should possess in order to be eligible for overseas studies, we should not be narrow and rigid in the recruiting process. Focusing too much on some particular merits may prevent some disadvantaged and minority students from participation. Furthermore, guiding principles for recruiting overseas participants should not be "replicated year after year, rather than expanded and enhanced" (p. 72). That is, recruiting processes are actually dynamic. They may change as the process of globalization moves towards more diversified directions, then the recruiting process needs to be adjusted to meet the need for students to be global citizens.

In the following sections, I roughly present what you have to take into consideration in the recruiting process. You may not be able to get a clear picture of the students and make a perfect decision by just looking at their academic performance and by asking them some questions in the interview process. A holistic assessment of the students and an overall picture of the students may be gathered from a well-rounded recruiting team. Even though you have deliberately chosen the most appropriate students to participate in the cross-cultural exchange program, it does not necessarily mean that they are well-prepared for the forthcoming cross-cultural exchange activities. A clearly specified criterion for participation and a well-developed workshop before students head for their overseas destination is required and helpful to ensure the success of the cross-cultural exchange program. In later accounts of the chapter, I briefly introduce how a training workshop can be developed and some important issues that need to be taken into account in the course of developing a training workshop.

Language Proficiency

Among the required components to be covered in the criteria to assess students' eligibility to attend a cross-cultural exchange program, language proficiency can be said to be the most important one. It is because, without the required language skills to communicate, nothing seems meaningful and possible and it may not be easy to achieve the goal set for the program. Cross-cultural exchanges involve students from different cultures, and quite often they speak different languages. Under this circumstance, language management may be required in the process of recruiting your students no matter what objectives your exchange project might have. Depending on the language used by your overseas partner or the language upon which you and your overseas partner agree to use to communicate with each other (i.e., a lingua franca), your participant students need a certain degree of proficiency in that language. That does not necessarily mean that your students need a very high proficiency level in that language in order to participate. It is always the case that they may be interested in learning the language by immersing themselves in that language speaking environment. Your participant students may be quick learners of that language, and it is impractical to discourage them from communicating in the target language. However, it is also true that language barriers may impede the smooth process of cross-cultural communications.

To make the best decision in terms of your students' language proficiency, it is necessary for you to develop a set of rules or guidelines to manage the language issues, including criteria to assess language proficiency, threshold to participate, training programs developed for those who do not quite meet the language requirements, and particular language skills that need to be improved, e.g., speaking skills in the case of oral communications and writing skills in the case of written communications. Certainly, the contents of rules and criteria vary, depending on the nature and objectives of the cross-cultural exchange program, students' familiarity with the language to be used for cross-cultural communications, and how language proficiency may affect the cross-cultural communications.

Pre-Project Surveys

Even before the training workshops, you need to conduct a survey or an interview to explore your participants' needs and their perceptions and expectations of the forthcoming cross-cultural exchange activities. Based on the survey results, you can better organize your training workshops and develop a successful cross-cultural project. After all, a cross-cultural exchange project should be student-centered and should meet students' needs and be to their satisfaction. A good example of pre-project survey can be seen from Brown and Aktas's (2002) report on Turkish University students' hopes and fears about travel to a western country. As we can imagine, differences in religion and perceived discrimination over economic status might cause a lot of challenges for those Muslim students who were about to go on a European exchange trip. Brown and Aktas conducted unstructured interviews even before the orientation planned for all exchange students. Results of the qualitative study showed that, on the one hand, students expected to expand their horizons and to learn new cultures. On the other hand, students were anticipating attacks on their developing world status and were afraid that their Muslim religion might not be acceptable to the Western world. Having understood their students' fear of national and religious identity, the researchers then provided the students with appropriate psychological support. Exposing students to the target culture may be insufficient. Instead, participant students must be trained to develop confidence in their own culture and the wisdom to cope with things such as discrimination, inequality, and verbal abuse.

Training Workshops before Launching into the Project

For participants of cross-cultural exchanges, including teachers and students, being well-prepared is essential to ensure the experience will be fruitful and enjoyable. Hepple (2018) argues that some "study abroad researchers have found that mere *exposure* to other cultures, without adequate intercultural preparation beforehand, often leads to the deepening of existing prejudices rather than a more open mindset" (p. 19). Depending on the nature of the project, required "homework" to do before launching into the cross-cultural project may vary. However, some basic points cannot be overlooked: language proficiency, cultural awareness, and specific talent.

Language Training

It is obvious that language skill is one of the most important factors that contribute to the success of cross-cultural exchanges. You can hardly communicate with your exchange partners if you and your exchange partners do not speak a common language. However, in cross-cultural exchanges, requirements of language use are more than being familiar with and being fluent in the language. Language training workshops for your students and preparation for yourself as a teacher teaching in a cross-cultural environment can be better organized from a language-for-specific-purposes perspective. You need to analyze students' needs first. Depending on the objectives of your project, you need to prepare workshops for your students, focusing on their immediate needs and what they have been lacking, such as language required for travelling and daily life, classroom communications, cultural exchanges, and expressions of professional knowledge. Based on your analysis, you might want to develop activities or simulations to familiarize your students with the forthcoming cross-cultural environment. Speaking of language training in a language training program, Hurn and Tomalin (2013) state that if "a high degree of fluency is required, a formal structured course should begin well before the departure date and the commencement of the foreign appointment" (p. 276). On the other hand, if time is limited, you have to focus on "teaching survival elements and building confidence to encourage further learning on arrival overseas" (p. 277).

In recent years, some scholars advocate applying adaptive learning technology to language learning (Kerr, 2015; Hockly & Dudeney, 2017). Kerr describes that adaptive learning is seen as "an educational technology, rather than a method" (p. 88). The technology is designed to provide learners with personalized learning based on the learner's personal learning experience online, proficiency level, learning objectives, learner's responses to online tasks, and even learners' personal information. The online programs are able to record and analyze the data of the learner's online interactions and then deliver optimal subsequent learning materials to the learner. Given the limited time in a training workshop and the fact that language skills cannot be built in a day, teacher trainers may guide trainees to do online adaptive individualized learning and leave more class time for critical and creative discussions.

Language training in a training workshop must be devoted to more useful and meaningful discussions and can aim at language for study abroad purposes. A Flipped learning style can be applied in this context. Students are required to collect information relevant to the host country, instead of teacher providing information, raising questions, and formulating issues for discussions. The teacher's role in this case is one as a facilitator and a mediator of the discussion, rather than an information provider. In the classroom setting, as Hockly and Dudeney (2017) note, teachers can have a chance to get to know their students better and "on a more 'human' level…to help when they are struggling, having a difficult time outside of class" (p. 243). Without this higher level of discussion and problem-solving, it is just like a writing teacher who does not read students' writing pieces and lets computer programs do the entire grading job. Although the grades students get may be reasonable and logical, teachers will never know what is in the students' mind, and they are indeed depriving students of their chance to develop their creativity and critical thinking skills.

As Hurn and Tomalin (2013) has pointed out, language skills cannot be developed in a short period. Language training programs actually should be organized as a long-term enterprise. Mikitani (2012) describes the experience of Englishinization at Rakuten, Japan. As the CEO of Rakuten, Mikitani encourages and "forces" his employees to learn English, use English, and communicate in English as a way to access the global market. He developed a well-organized language management system to assess, train, and monitor employees' English proficiency. In an era moving towards globalization, English might not be and should not be the only choice in terms of having global access. The only fact is that language skills cannot be built in a day. Having a variety of language skills is inevitable in a globalizing era.

Raising Cultural Awareness

Cultural differences and raising cultural awareness have been important topics in discussions of cross-cultural encounters. However, simply telling participants some do's and don'ts in a host country can never be sufficient in terms of raising cultural awareness. In a later part of this chapter, I will describe intercultural training in detail. In this section, I first list some cultural dimensions based on Nathan's (2013) classification: strong uncertainty avoidance (people address each other very formally, and processes and communications are very clearly defined) vs. weak uncertainty avoidance (Interactions are less formal, and creativity and challenging the status quo is encouraged); collectivism (people have a preference for a loosely knit social framework in society) vs. individualism (people are supposed to take care of themselves and their immediate family members only); hierarchical power-distance (people accept a hierarchical order in which everybody has a place) vs. egalitarian power distance (people strive for power equalization and demand justification for power inequalities); masculinity (people have a preference in society for achievement, heroism, assertiveness, and material success) vs. femininity (people have a preference for relationships, modest, caring for the weak, and the quality of life); low context (people assume a high degree of shared knowledge on the behalf of a transaction partner) vs. high context (people place great value on the intangible aspects of a negotiation or a business deal); inductive reasoning (people go from detailed facts to establish general principles) vs. deductive reasoning (people move from general to specific); personal relationship (personal friendships and personal chemistry are critical elements in order to conduct business) vs. task-driven relationship (business is conducted on an impersonal basis and is driven by the deal); polychronic (people use time to accomplish diverse goals simultaneously and to interact with as many individuals as possible) vs. monochronic (time is used for ordering one's life, for setting priorities and for doing tasks in a sequential order, one thing at a time). Other cultural differences may be reflected in people's attitudes towards personal space (it refers to the amount of personal space that individuals demand or expect in their interactions with other people) and elders (it refers to the degree of respect for the elders in their societies regardless of their capabilities or achievements).

It is important that you note these cultural dimensions to your trainees and take these different factors into consideration in the process of developing a training program or assessing your trainees' performance. Although these cultural dimensions were developed basically for global e-learning projects for business practitioners, it is nonetheless applicable for cross-cultural exchanges in the educational arena. Educators, however, have to be reminded that these cultural dimensions are addressed in relative terms. That is, each one of the cultural dimensions is presented in a continuum, with the two extremes at the two ends of the continuum. Just reminding your trainees of these subtle cultural differences may contribute to enhancing your trainees' cultural awareness. It is definitely not encouraged to dichotomize between different cultures. There are also other cultural differences shown in interpersonal interactions in daily life. For example Hyde (2012) describes that in some cultures, people show respects to the speakers by listening impassively, while British culture would interpret this "as boredom or disagreement or even being upset" (p. 84), and shaking one's head in some cultures means a positive sign of engagement, rather than disagreement.

Speaking of raising students' cultural awareness, Brack (1993) has a very interesting and useful proposal: making use of international students on the campus. Having students who are heading for a foreign country communicate and discuss with international students on the campus in the same classroom can be beneficial for both groups of students in terms of enhancing cultural awareness and intercultural learning. Brack describes how University of the Pacific (UOP) makes use of international students in the overseas training programs. First, in the orientation, international students may provide information on their home country and answer questions that local students might have.

On the other hand, international students may ask local students about things that puzzle them in the host country, and local students may explain to them. Second, in the reentry phase, returned participants may share their overseas experience with international students and they may still have things that puzzle them that they would like to hear about from the 'expert' of the culture. Third, the discussion between local students and international students may be beneficial in that students learn that culture shock is a norm in intercultural encounters and that, when it comes to intercultural encounters, individual personality should be taken into consideration. In doing so, students will not be surprised when they find very different characteristics or behaviors between two people from the same culture. Most importantly, both groups of students might finally realize some of their behaviors are actually misunderstood by their cultural counterparts, and the same is true that they have misunderstood people from different cultures. Finally, a group of people from different cultures getting together in the same classroom may form a mini-global community in which students may immerse themselves. Although American students who are heading for France, as Brack describes, may find discussions of Muslim attitudes initiated by Middle Eastern peer students in the classroom irrelevant to their future overseas study, they may not be sure when they will have the chance to make use of the information they gained from the "intercultural class." After all, different ethnic groups and different cultures are getting more closely united, although we are not yet ready to say that it is a globalized world.

In case of cross-cultural encounters online, Garrison and Anderson (2003) point to the importance of *social presence,* which is the ability participants possess to participate in a virtual e-learning community as 'real person', i.e., as a full personality. They point out that an individual can never learn in isolation and that community "is the fusion of the individual and the group; the psychological and sociological; the reflective and the collaborative" (p. 48-49). They also argue that although non-verbal text communication may lack verbal cues shown in real-time face-to-face communications, it is not at all impossible to develop social presence and create a sense of belonging in a virtual community learning environment. They point out that social presence can be established "through the use of greetings, encouragement, paralinguistic emphasis (e. g. capitals, punctuation, emoticons), and personal vignettes (i.e., self-disclosure)" (p. 50).

Garrison and Anderson (2003) classified social presence into three categories: affective responses, open communication, and cohesive responses. In affective responses, participants show their interest and persistence in participating in a community of inquiry. For example, participants may use punctuation, capitalization, and emoticons to show their emotion. On the other hand, they may use humor or teasing and self-disclosure to express their goodwill and friendship. The open communication category refers to participants' response to peers' questions or discussion in a reciprocal and respectful way, showing their trust and acceptance in the virtual community. Thus, the community demonstrates reflective and insightful communications. The previous two categories of social presence actually facilitate the development of the third category: cohesive responses. With the characteristics of the two categories, it may be easy to develop a cohesive community. In the community, participants share meanings and have quality learning. This kind of community features its "addressing others by name...[and] using inclusive pronouns such as 'we' and 'our'" (p. 53).

Having discussed the importance and the categories of social presence, Garrison and Anderson (2003) remind teachers teaching in an e-learning environment to optimally use the elements of social presence. In case social presence is overly stressed, then too much politeness for people may impede discussions and or challenges in a community of inquiry and may lead to superficial and unconstructive discussion. After all, the end of a community of inquiry is the learning outcomes.

Cultural Diplomacy

A part of the training program may be devoted to encouraging students to make use of their overseas stays to promote their own country and culture. It is sometimes termed *cultural diplomacy*. Hurn and Tomalin (2013) define cultural diplomacy as "one of the means by which a country increases its visibility on the global stage and gains political and economic influence" (p. 224). It is considered as "soft power" that uses non-military means to attract people and to influence their preferences. Hurn and Tomalin list some instruments of cultural diplomacy, such as cultural missions, language and education, the arts, science and technology, tourist sites and national attractions, airlines, gastronomy, sport, national heroes and heroines, and diasporas. Although cultural missions, among others, can be "specifically created for the purpose of cultural diplomacy" (p. 228), there is still a lot that those involved in cross-cultural exchanges can do to promote their countries' image. Non-governmental organizations and individuals are actually a great power to "brand" their own countries in a slow but sure way. How one's own country is viewed by others is definitely developed in this way.

However, Hurn and Tomalin (2013) do not believe that the reputation or image of one country can be marketed or advised; rather, it must be earned. That is, how its people act and behave, how they contribute to the society and the globe, and how they collaborate with other cultural communities in sharing their cultural heritage and technological advancement are really matters in earning one country's reputation and image. This is the way people promote their country. One of the merits of cross-cultural exchanges is that one can get an idea of how his or her country is perceived through other's eyes, which "can make a critical difference to the success of its business, trade and tourism efforts, as well as its diplomatic and cultural relations with other nations" (p. 234). However, cultural diplomacy, featuring promoting one's own culture and country, alone cannot account for the success of a cross-cultural exchange program. I would like to remind the reader of one of the important features of cross-cultural exchanges: cooperation or collaboration. That is, cross-cultural exchanges, in addition to cultural diplomacy, require participants to understand, respect, and learn from their partners' culture and cooperate with them in the joint project to achieve the goal that cannot be achieved otherwise. In a training workshop, cultural diplomacy can be an important topic to address. Trainees have to be reminded that they carry their country's image with them in a foreign country. How you behave and perform may affect how people perceive your country. Well-prepared cultural information or talent shows can be a plus to your country's image and can be part of the cultural diplomacy you can do. On the other hand, you need to respect and appreciate other cultures and show your willingness to cooperate or collaborate with your cross-cultural partners.

Intercultural Training Programs

For a longer period cross-cultural exchange project, an intercultural training program needs to be organized before the participants head for the host country. In this case, intercultural training programs require competent trainers to develop. Paige (1993) categorizes trainer competencies into three domains: cognitive domain, behavioral domain, and personal attributes. As Paige states, in the cognitive domain, competent trainers need to have knowledge of international phenomena, including transition to another culture and the dynamics of cultural adjustment, cultural-specific content, and issues relevant to ethics, multiculturalism, and trainer-learner relationships. Competencies in the second domain, the behavioral domain, refer to having the ability to prepare students for their forthcoming intercultural encounters, cultural adjustment, and reentry adjustment. Also the intercultural trainer needs to be able to address some relevant issues, such as relationships between trainer and learner, ethical issues, international issues, multicultural issues and the specific culture of the host country. Finally, competent and effective intercultural trainers need to possess some personal attributes. For example, they need to be patient and tolerant of ambiguity and differences, enthusiastic and empathic, aware of personal and cultural identity. In addition, having a sense of humility and a sense of humor may greatly facilitate the work of intercultural training.

McCaffery (1993), on the other hand, reminds developers and trainers of cross-cultural training programs of unintended outcomes that happen in the training program even though the developers or trainers devote their high energy and commit themselves to the program. He illustrates some examples that deserve practitioners' attention, including deemphasizing the importance of training, stereotyping, unrealistic expectations, trainee dependency, and negative expectations. First, a short period of predeparture orientation, focusing on introducing the culture of the host country, reading some literature and watching some slides or videos of the people and the country, and sharing some do's and don'ts provided by people who have visited the country. This kind of orientation tends to reveal a message to the participant that this is all and this is enough for intercultural learning and that the learning activities are not really important. They might not be aware that there are more important and critical issues ahead of their forthcoming life abroad.

Second, stereotyping is another issue commonly found in cross-cultural training programs. In order to remind participants of cultural differences, speakers, whether professional trainers or those returned from abroad, tend to stress the points that are different from that of their own culture. These differences might be true to some extent. However, the differences can be viewed as matters of relativism, especially when we take individual preferences into account. My own experience as a college student can serve as a good example. In a conversation class, we were curious about our first American teacher and kept asking him questions like "Do Americans always eat bread and salad?" and "Do Americans always take showers in the morning?" Questions like these always confused the American teacher. He corrected us by saying "most of the Americans, not all of the Americans." The implication here is that too much emphasis on cultural differences might reinforce stereotyping. Cuenat (2018) also warns trainers of interculturality of the "over-reliance on nation cultures and exaggerated presumed differences between people coming from different countries….[simple cultural examples] bear the risk of reinforcing existing stereotypes" (p. 179). It is important to note that cross-cultural encounters are not matters of two different "national cultures," but rather are matters between people, for people may "have different identities and cultural belongings" (p. 179) in terms of their gender, profession, nationality, marital status, and the context and power relation in the cross-cultural encounter. Hepple (2018), on the other hand, also urges to "avoid essentialising cultures in restrictive binary terms" (p. 20) and assign national cultures to a pre-determined cultural dimensions.

The third unintended outcome that McCaffery (1993) illustrates is *unrealistic expectations*. In the training process, trainers or speakers may occasionally reveal some messages that may unconsciously help create unrealistic expectations in participants. For example, words such as "You are going to love the country" or "Never ask questions like…" Trainees may find later the realties are not what they expected before they go to the country. Perceptions and experiences of a country and its culture may involve a considerable amount of personal and ideological factors. It is important to keep in mind that cultures cannot always be dichotomized and are not matters of right or wrong. Instead of providing students with unrealistic expectations, trainers may encourage students to experience, explore, and learn on their own and stress the importance of personal experiences and individual gains.

Another important issue that trainers may overlook is *trainee dependency*. This is the fourth unintended outcome that McCaffery (1993) illustrates. He points to some unintended outcomes that are commonly found in professional training centers such as those of Peace Corps. McCaffery describes that staff in the training centers physically take good care of trainees in their daily life abroad and intellectually provide them with answers to whatever questions trainees might have. Under this circumstance, trainees are dependent on training staff to solve problems in their training or even volunteering process. McCaffery argues that it is not right that an intercultural training center produces dependent trainees. In the case of international volunteering, volunteers are supposed to be able to help those in need. They need to learn how to learn, especially in a culturally different environment. In other cases, such as a faculty-led study abroad, students may have leading teachers around them to help solve problems. However, if students going abroad alone to study, they may need to learn how to solve problems on their own or turn to appropriate people for help.

Finally, McCaffery (1993) points to one more unintended outcome: negative expectations. He reminds trainers of the words we commonly use to convey messages, such as cultural *shock*, *survival* techniques, and *coping* skills. We can actually express the same ideas in a more positive way, such as "adjustment to a new culture" and "being effective abroad." The idea of being politically correct may be quite useful in intercultural settings. In sum, one of the messages McCaffery wants to convey in his reminder to trainers of intercultural training programs is that a trainer needs to be objective, flexible, and not to over-generalize and over-emphasize cultural differences.

From the discussion of unintended outcomes of intercultural training programs, McCaffery (1993) proposes a new model of training programs, aiming at moving "people toward developing/enhancing the skills they need to become independently effective cross-cultural sojourners" (p. 226). The new model is actually a "learning to learn" process, focusing on skill-building. The experiential approach proposed by McCaffery has four stages: experience, process, generalization, and application. In the experience stage, trainees actively participate in activities such as case studies, role plays, simulations, games, lectures, films and slide shows, skill practice, completing an educational instrument, and living with family from another country; those listed by McCaffery (p. 232), let intercultural trainees personally experience cross-cultural encounters.

In the second stage, process, trainees work together to share, compare and contrast, and reflect on the experiences in the first stage. Together, trainees put all the thoughts together and look for meanings and patterns derived from their experiences. By verbalizing their feelings and perceptions, trainees, with the assistance of the trainer, may "conceptualize their reflections on the experience so that they can move toward drawing conclusions" (p. 232).

In the "generalization" stage, which is the third stage of the experiential approach, trainees draw conclusions and identify general principles based on the first two stages. In this stage, trainees are asked to think about what they have learned from all the activities and what all the learning means to them. Trainees first work alone to think about their personal answers to the questions, and then they share with each other their experiences and thoughts. Guided by the trainer, trainees "compare and contrast different conclusions, identifying patterns, and legitimate areas of disagreement" (p. 233).

Finally, the last stage is the *application* stage. In this stage, trainees "incorporate what they have learned into their lives by developing plans for more effective behavior in the future" (p. 233). They have to develop their own application plans, based on their profession, personal life, background, and needs.

To effectively organize a training program and be a competent intercultural trainer, Mikk and Bjarnadottir (2017) suggest some important steps intercultural trainers need to take in order to keep learning. First, trainers and trainees need to establish mutual trust in order for the instruction or training to be beneficial and for the learning to actually to occur. Trainers need to trust their trainees for what they have brought to the training environment and trust they can learn and are willing to learn. The researchers suggest that a "helpful step in the trust–building process…is be transparent from the beginning and inviting participants to collaboratively set the group expectations" (p. 129). Second, trainers need to rely on professional resources and stay current in the literature. There are various source books relevant to intercultural training whose topics include values, identity, culture-specific information, descriptions of trainer competencies, definitions of culture and intercultural competence, social justice, and professional organizations. There are also various types of literature allowing trainers to keep current the concepts and developments of intercultural competencies. Third, as an intercultural trainer, you need to know the history and development of intercultural training and intercultural competencies required as a trainer. As mentioned in the introductory chapter of this book, globalization is an ongoing process, theories and practices relevant to intercultural training may change in accordance with the change of the concept of globalization. Thus, the previously practiced intercultural training activities may not be appropriate for current practice. Trainers need to take a broader context into account and integrate different approaches to develop an approach best for their trainees. Finally, intercultural trainers need to understand different learning styles and trainees' specific learning needs and preferences. By doing so, trainers can develop different activities best for their trainees. Trainers need to keep requesting feedback from trainees or other experienced trainers.

Harvey (2017) proposes what she calls *backward design* in designing intercultural training curriculum, which puts the steps of defining key learning objectives and deciding upon feedback and assessment methods before choosing teaching and learning activities. She argues that only when you have clear objectives in mind as to what you want your students to learn and how you are going to assess students' achievement based on your set goals can you choose the most appropriate activities for your students to learn.

Kartoshkina (2017) views intercultural learning from a neuroscience perspective. She views cultural and intercultural learning involving mechanisms operated in our brain. When we learn "to speak a language, recognize intricate cultural values, and behave like a cultural native" (p. 89), there are actually two-way interactions between brain and culture. On the one hand, cultural experience affects the neural mechanisms of the brain. On the other hand, "the brain gives rise to cultural experience" (p. 89). For example,

Kartoshkina describes, based on scientific studies, that there are significant differences between North American or European people and East Asian people in their modulating "neural and electrophysiological responses when primed with cultural values of individualism and collectivism" (p. 90). It is evident from relevant empirical studies that "cultural values, beliefs, and behaviors are connected to neural structures and mechanisms" (p. 90). In this regard, it is sufficient to explain to our students "to respect rather than judge cultural differences [because those in] different cultures have different wiring of their brains due to the specific cultural environments in which they grew up and to which their brain had to adapt" (p. 90). In an intercultural training program, teachers or trainers need to remind students that intercultural experiences may benefit them in developing new neural networks and prepare them for adjusting to a new cultural environment. In the training program, Kartoshkina (2017) suggests that teachers or trainers may provide readings or show educational films relevant to the host culture, invite guest speakers from a host culture and follow a discussion section, and provide students with opportunities to reflect on what they have learned from their intercultural experiences by writing reflection journals or by discussing it in the classroom. In sum, students need to be aware that intercultural learning "provides countless opportunities for our brains to get activated and start forming new neural networks" (p. 103).

Gebhard (2017) also demonstrates how he, as an EFL teacher, teaches students some relevant cultural concepts, including adapting to the host culture, solving cultural conflicts, realizing individual differences, and studying your own culture while trying to understand another culture. First, Gebhard demonstrates to the students some non-verbal behaviors in different cultures, including "body posture, gestures, stance, and movement" (p. 135) and other things such as use of touch and use of space. Second, Gebhard demonstrates different kinds of situation in which cultural conflict occur. He ask students to think and discuss their ways of solving the problems. Third, Gebhard reminds students of the inappropriateness of generalization and stereotyping. He demonstrates and let students personally experience how people from the same culture may have different ideas and opinions. Finally, Gebhard urges students to compare across cultures and try to understand their own cultures. In this case, they may better understand other cultures and their own cultures.

Examples of Intercultural Training Programs

In this section, I demonstrate some theories and examples of intercultural training programs. Teachers or trainers may refer to those examples and adapt them to be best suited to their own situations and their trainees' needs.

Hurn and Tomalin's Guidelines for Intercultural Training Programs

Hurn and Tomalin (2013), on the other hand, provide some guidelines to teach and train students' cross-cultural communication skills in training programs. They insist that teaching cross-cultural communication skills should not mainly focus on learning cognitive knowledge; rather, it should be "interactive learning with students encouraged to participate, challenge and discuss" (p. 275). In learning activities, students may be encouraged to take "part in role playing, acting out short scenarios, practicing appropriate non-verbal behavior and learning by interaction with fellow international students" (p. 275). Using multimedia facilities in the teaching process places teachers in the role of facilitators, rather than lecturers. In a training program, Hurn and Tomalin suggest some useful activities that can be applied in teaching cross-cultural communications, for example, presentations across cultural borders, country briefings, case studies, critical incident scenarios, culture capsules, the cultural assimilator, simulation and role playing, proverbs and culture values, and exercises on stereotypes. All these activities are very useful and creative in terms of raising students' cultural awareness and developing their intercultural competences. In the following paragraphs, I will briefly integrate the ideas of intercultural training and explain activities that Hurn and Tomalin have suggested. First of all, for students who will study abroad or teachers who will teach abroad, they may have considerable chances to deliver official presentations on their own countries or on some professional topics. Presenters need to be aware of cultural differences and different presentation norms in their preparation and their course of presentation. If you use English to present for non-native English speakers, be sure to speak slowly or decide on whether or not you need an interpreter. At the beginning of your presentation, you may introduce yourself and greet you audience in your audience's language to develop a close relationship between you and your audience. If you are presenting to an audience from a different culture, pay special attention to your style of presentation. For example, your audience may have a different way of thinking or a different perception of humor or metaphor. It is important that you do not force your audience to think the way you do and that you do not violate any cultural norms of your audience.

In the training program, it is also essential for trainees to get acquainted with the country they are heading for. You, the trainer, need to prepare country briefings to introduce to your trainees relevant information needed to stay in the host country. Hurn and Tomalin (2013) suggest that country briefings should be "mainly factual input and should contain up-to-date information on a country's geography, history, politics, economics, climate, foreign relationships, infrastructure, communications, working environment and living conditions,...local customs, business practices, [and] social conventions" (p. 279). For practical training activities, Hurn and Tomalin (2013) suggest some useful classroom practices that involve students in possible real-world cross-cultural encounters. For example, case studies require students to discuss on a recently observed and hotly-debated phenomenon; while the activity of critical incident scenarios focuses on the situations that trainees may encounter in a foreign country, such as on arriving at the country, socializing with people in the country, and working with people from different cultures. Trainees are required to make judgements and decide on the most appropriate response in a specific situation. Similar to critical incident scenarios, culture capsules and the cultural assimilator, however, focus more on compare and contrast "of a particular cultural difference between a situation in a foreign culture and what would occur in the home culture" (p. 282). Other activities such as simulation and role playing require students to act out and play a particular role in a simulated situation that reflects a real-life situation, such as business negotiations.

In addition to those classroom activities, Hurn and Tomalin (2013) also suggest some paper-and-pencil exercises that may heighten students' cultural awareness and enhance their intercultural competences. For example, proverbs in a culture may reveal its cultural values. Trainers may list some proverbs of a specific cultural group and ask trainees to examine cultural values implied in the proverbs. Another way to do the exercise is that trainers may use true/false statements or cultural value check lists to check students' knowledge of other cultures. In these exercises, trainees are asked to decide on whether a statement about a particular culture is true or false or to circle one from a 9-point checklist for a series of cultural values that best describe their own culture and the foreign culture. Last but definitely not the least is the exercise of stereotypes. In the exercise, trainees are asked to write down what they think they know about the culture of the people from their host country. From all these exercises mentioned above, students may have a chance to compare how they perceive people from a culture before and after they really experience the culture.

Cuenat's *PluriMobil* Intercultural Curriculum

Cuenat (2018) describes yet another intercultural training curriculum for teachers or teacher trainers to provide them with sufficient sources or materials to enhance their students' intercultural competences before, during, and after studying abroad. The curriculum, termed *PluriMobil*, created and collected different resources in a European context to provide teachers and trainers "with materials and concrete ideas about how to create pedagogically favourable conditions for their students to maximize the learning opportunities afforded by study abroad or virtual exchange" (p. 176). This curriculum essentially covers three phases: before, during, and after study abroad. Each phase include different learning activities based on learning materials collected from "texts, pictures, videos, and other traces of experience portfolios" (p. 178).

According to Cuenat (2018), among other things, *interculturality* is especially complicated and needs to be treated carefully. "*Interculturality*" entails a number of underlying cognitive, affective, and behavioural competences" (p. 178). It has to do with one's knowledge, attitudes, skills of interpreting and relating, skills of discovery, and critical cultural awareness. For initiators and practitioners of *PluriMobil*, "cultures are not a stable and uniform set of values, beliefs, practices and traditions;...culture is seen as fluid" (p. 179). That is, we constantly negotiate with people and change our "value, beliefs, practices and traditions" (p. 179). One of the most important features of *PluriMobil* is that it applies "janusian approach" to interpreting *interculturality* in which practitioners of the curriculum view cultures in two directions at the same time or even apply conflicting theoretical concepts. This may allow overseas sojourners being able to interpret cultural issues and cultural differences from wider and more critical perspectives. Importantly, *PluriMobil* conveys a new perception in which we need to deconstruct the idea that cultures are always linked to a national territory or a particular ethnic group. Instead, we need to be aware of the diverse nature of cultures. That is, a particular group of people or even individuals may possess various cultural identities and may behave differently in different contexts, depending on where they are and whom they are communicating with. Being able to view a cultural issue from even opposing concepts may "inspire creativity, open doors to new ideas" (p. 188). The *PluriMobil* curriculum reveals a very important message to all practitioners of cross-cultural exchanges: each cultural element or incident has two sides to it. Again, we cannot judge one thing as right or wrong and say we need to "tolerate" a different culture. Rather, we need to think why people from a different culture think or behave the way different from ours.

Hepple's Global Networking Intercultural Capabilities (GNIC)

Hepple (2018) describes yet another pre-sojourn intercultural workshop in an Australian context entitled Global Networking Intercultural Capabilities (GNIC). As mentioned earlier, different intercultural training programs may apply different theoretical foundations and may use different approaches to formulate their activities. In the case of GNIC, practitioners believe in the power of peer learning and make use of dialogic peer-learning pedagogy. Like the *PluriMobil* project mentioned above, GNIC also encourages students to go beyond national diversities and enjoy their own and others' multiplicity as individuals" (p. 20), recognizing "the socialized and contextualized nature of our cultural identifications" (p. 20).

Hepple's study took place at Queensland University of Technology (QUT) in Australia. Participants of the GNIC included 63 students, who were undergoing their pre-departure training, and six facilitators. The students were in six domains of study and were heading for 21 different destinations, while all of the six facilitators were tertiary educators with different expertise, namely language teaching, counselling, and social work. These facilitators were paired in a complementary manner. That is, language teachers might be paired with social workers to make the training course more effective.

Findings of the analysis from individual written reflections and meeting or interviewing with the facilitators showed that interdisciplinary team teaching was welcomed by these facilitators. On the one hand, paired facilitators may learn each other's domain knowledge which may be complement each other's teaching and learning to accept different perspectives. However, team teaching is not without drawbacks. Teachers of different teaching styles and different personalities may not work harmoniously in the same classroom. Disagreements may occur in a team-teaching context. Another area of findings and of the facilitators' common concern is the constraint of time. They claimed that time was definitely not enough for them to conduct activities and for students to have intercultural learning. They suggest that a flipped classroom approach might be used in future workshops. In this learning context, students may work on the learning materials at home before they discuss and present their ideas in the classroom with their classmates.

Another important part of the findings is derived from the students who participated in the pre-departure workshops. The researchers found that, at the beginning of the workshops, students cared about administrative processes, country-specific information, and everyday life in the host country. However, as Hepple (2018) explains, these "country-specific processes were not the intended focus of these pre-departure intercultural workshops" (p. 27). Rather, it is more significant to explore "deeper issues, such as avoiding ethnocentrism and stereotyping…and engaging with more universal issues related to mobility and interacting with people interculturally" (p. 27-28). After the pre-departure workshops, students reflected that they did learn what they had not thought about before by communicating with their facilitators or peer participants.

As mentioned earlier, the facilitators stated the power of peer learning. The students also reflected on the value of peer learning, however, in a more positive and concrete way. They feel that meeting with other outbound-study-abroad-peer students, international or exchange students and returnee study abroad students can create a sense of community, and they do not feel alone in their journey to a foreign country. They suggested that the workshops should involve more returnee students and international students in more activities.

Commonalities in Intercultural Training

In the field of intercultural training, Brislin (1993) argues that "there are extensive commonalities in the experiences of people who interact with culturally different others. These commonalities occur despite differences in the exact jobs people have or despite differences in the exact place where the intercultural interaction takes place" (p. 281-282). Brislin thus developed a so-called "culture-general assimilator" to be used in and applied to intercultural training programs despite participants having differences in their cultural background, purposes of going abroad, and destination. Developers of the Brislin team collected information and wrote more than a hundred incidents based on real happenings or their readings in intercultural encounters. They then divided all the incidents into 18 categories such as anxiety, disconfirmed expectancies, belonging, ambiguity, and confrontation with one's prejudices. In each incident, Brislin provides alternatives to explain the situation. They asked participants of the training program to think, discuss, and choose the best explanation of the alternative.

Brislin (1993) claims that this cultural-general assimilator can be used in a variety of ways for different workshop trainees and different purposes for working abroad, for example study-abroad students, international student advisors, teachers in multicultural school districts, and college professors who teach students from different countries or teach cultural courses such as international studies, just to name some in the educational arena. However, in addition to the general assimilator, culture-specific training is still needed to familiarize the trainee with the cultural information of the country he or she is heading for. Whenever culture-specific training, for some reasons, is seen impossible or insufficient, the culture-general assimilator can be very useful for training purposes.

Brack (1993) argues that orientation and reentry should be integrated as a complete cross-cultural training. He illustrates the training program practiced at University of the Pacific (UOP) as an example to demonstrate the importance of linking orientation with reentry. For Brack, reentry after a period of overseas experience is as important as orientation before heading for a foreign country. Students' cultural learning should not end at the point of returning home. Brack points to the fact that "the problems encountered in returning can be as substantial and disorienting as the cultural shock experienced in leaving. The reverse culture-shock …can be—at least for a while—as different and strange as another country" (p. 244). For students, the overseas experience should be able to be analyzed and used as a source for future academic pursuits and personal growth.

Brack (1993) provides a conceptual framework to show how linking orientation and reentry together may provide students with more opportunities to enhance their intercultural competence. In UOP's case, the entire class goes to the same destination as a group. The freshman year is devoted to preparation for the overseas study next year. Students are required to take a basic cultural anthropology course in order to gain fundamental social cultural concepts. As for intercultural training, because "everyone was going to the same destination, the orientation tended to be cultural-specific" (p. 246).

After a one-year overseas experience, the same students came back as returnees. They are required to take a reentry seminar, and the courses offered in the seminar were actually similar to the ones offered in the orientation. The difference is that, in the orientation, the contents are a bit abstract for them, and, in reentry, students can be confident to share their overseas experiences and the intercultural knowledge they gained. More importantly, they can compare before and after the experience and identify their personal changes or development in various aspects, such as understanding of themselves and others, value judgements, and ethical dilemmas, and the enlightenment that always comes after the overseas experience. Brack (1993) argues that "the overseas experience, preceded by orientation, was only the beginning of an ongoing learning process, [and the] …orientation, the overseas experience, and reentry should be developmentally linked" (p. 250-251). Brack roughly demonstrates how UOP linked orientation with reentry in their training programs. For Brack, topical areas, such as culture shock and reverse culture shock, identity, value system, and stereotyping, in the training program can be almost the same in orientation and in reentry. In orientation, these intercultural issues are introduced at a very fundamental level, mostly using lectures to explain, define, and exemplify; while, in reentry, mostly students present in the class their experiences in a more real and concrete manner.

In both of the two forms of cross-cultural exchange program discussed above, there is also a possibility that, because of different reasons, such as limited budget, you are allowed to choose only a limited number of students to participate in the cross-cultural exchange program. Then you need to recruit your participant students carefully in terms of fairness and appropriateness. If your exchange activity is a simple cross-cultural videoconferencing or computer-mediated written communication, you may ask for volunteers to participate. If your exchange project is a more serious one, and your students need to travel to the partner school's country, whether being led by college faculty or travelling to the foreign country on their own, you need to formulate a detailed guideline to recruit your participant students, including required academic performance, language proficiency, financial support, physical state, consent form from parents, etc. In addition to the guideline, you may need to organize a training session or orientation before students leave for a foreign country.

Beyond the Intercultural Training

As Toma (2011) states, the "relationship between institutions and students…has evolved into a contractual one prompting various obligations" (p. 121). This contractual relationship is said to "protect the rights of both institutions and students" (p. 123). In this scenario, "students have come to be viewed as customers, having expectations of institutions in providing programs and performing services triggered when they pay tuition and fees" (p. 122). On the other hand, students have to abide by the regulations set by the institution, such as paying agreed-upon tuitions and fulfilling required coursework.

Viewed from this perspective, it is especially true when you send or lead a group of students abroad. In addition to students' intercultural, profession, and personal development, you are responsible for students' safety, rights, discipline, liability, and any kind of emotional change. College students are legally treated as adults. Higher education institutions are not supposed to protect them like the way parents do with their little kids. However, as 'customers' paying for the overseas trips, students are entitled to be informed of potential danger, legal rights, expected behaviors, and adjustments in a foreign country or even interacting with foreigners in their own countries. Different countries may have their specific regulations or attitudes towards, say, discrimination, privacy, copyrights, and employment. These issues are well beyond the cultural or social level. They often lead to legal intervention. It may be true that a training program cannot cover all the required information for all possible situations. Students, as adults, are encouraged to develop their independent and critical thinking skills and have the ability to collect useful information in response to cross-cultural encounters.

It is evident that in a training workshop before students head for their destination countries, language and culture are important elements in the training course. However, there are other important elements that cannot be ignored. For example, Brown and Tignor (2016) remind practitioners of faculty-led study abroad program, stating that training topics should include "risk management, health and evacuation insurance, liability, health, emergency response, mental health issues, and fiscal administration" (p. 68). Other information helpful for students' overseas trips and studies include information on "enrollment, financial aid, withdrawal deadlines, study abroad itinerary, packing list, behavioral expectations, academic expectations, etc." (p. 68). The most important thing is that students have to learn how to learn and to be independent. The role of trainers, practitioners, or teachers in an intercultural training program or a cross-cultural exchange project is actually a facilitator. The help students look for useful information, provide suggestions to solve problems, and remind students of the importance of taking the opportunity to learn and of being responsible for their own learning.

Chapter 4

CHOOSING CROSS-CULTURAL EXCHANGE PARTNERS

As stated by Sakamoto and Chapman (2011), the global economic integration and new communication technologies have driven the growth of cross-border partnerships in higher education. There "are few highly regarded colleges and universities in any country that do not participate in some form of foreign study or faculty exchange" (p. 3). Aside from the exchange of students and faculty, cross-border partnerships are actually expanding to involve "the creation of branch campuses, joint research and technology initiatives, collaboration in strengthening institutional management, testing, faculty development efforts, collaboration in quality assurance, and sharing of technology" (p. 4).

As mentioned earlier, the term *cross-cultural exchanges* in this book is defined in a very broad sense. As described by Knight (2011), new developments of cross-border education can involve "[t]raditional universities, new types of commercial providers, government higher education agencies, [and they may facilitate] international researcher work, curriculum design, faculty and student exchanges, and joint/double degree programs" (p. 16). There are also "[n]ew branch campuses, franchise and twinning arrangements, and distance education programs" (p. 16) being established. According to Knight, modes of cross-border education have to take people, programs, providers, and projects/services/new knowledge into consideration. People involved in cross-border partnerships can be students, professors/scholars, researchers, or experts/consultants. They may work on their full degree or academic credits, work as an intern, do research, or work as a consultant. The forms of establishing cross-border partnership are various, such as twinning, franchise, double/joint degree, articulation, validation, and distance education. In these cases, students may or may not have to go to another country to earn academic credits or a foreign degree. Now let us turn to a larger scale of mobility, institution/provider mobility. Education providers can be institutions, organizations, or companies, and the movement of providers can be either physical or virtual. Physically, an education provider can establish branch campuses, independent institutions, merger, study centers/teaching sites, or networks in a foreign country. Virtually, an education provider delivers "credit courses and degree programs to students in different countries through distance education using predominantly the Internet technology mode" (p. 28). Projects and services mobility is yet another element to be taken into account in cross-border partnerships. However, according to Knight, project and service mobility just moves and changes too fast to be described in a rigorous framework. The increasingly growing number and type of activities have created considerable opportunities for "international and commercial partnerships between universities and private companies. The trend to move from bilateral academic collaboration to competitive knowledge networks reflects the shift toward commercialization and competitiveness in international higher education" (p. 29). On the one hand, universities are seeking new sources of funding; on the other hand, they are pursuing international prestige.

As the knowledge economy is increasingly developed, universities are eager to gain competitive advantages by collaborating with international institutions or organizations. Knight (2011) describes second-generation cross-border activities, such as "regional education hubs, economic free zones, education cities, knowledge villages, gateways, and hot spots" (p. 29). Many countries have launched into this new knowledge enterprise. As Knight states, "the development of these hubs and education cities are positive proof of education being seen as a commodity to be acquired and used to gain a competitive advantage in the knowledge economy (p. 30).

Choosing the right cross-cultural exchange partners is critical to the success of an exchange project and to the degree to which students can learn. Having your objectives for a cross-cultural exchange project defined, you may choose your exchange partners based on your objectives. You might want to choose exchange partners whose objectives are similar to yours or whose objectives can be complementary to yours. Other factors that you need to take into consideration include communication facilities available in the school, the distance between the partner school and your school, your students' language proficiency, and the nature of the class, depending on the modes of exchange you and your partner teachers agree upon. Most importantly, both you and your exchange partners need to be enthusiastic and committed to the cross-cultural collaboration. In this chapter, I first point to some of the important principles that you have to take into consideration in the course of choosing overseas partnerships and designing a cross-cultural exchange project. Later on in the chapter, I illustrate some sources from which researchers can look for exchange partners.

Do your homework before you initially contact your potential cross-cultural exchange partners. You need to know their languages, cultures, politics, fields of study, learning styles, interests, facilities available, purposes for participation, experiences of cross-cultural exchanges, and expectations from the cross-cultural exchanges. You might want to choose partners whose expertise may be complementary to yours. Under this circumstance, two groups of students may learn from each other.

PRINCIPLES OF CHOOSING EXCHANGE PARTNERS

There are several things you need to take into account in the process of choosing your exchange partners. You may have your own criteria to choose your exchange partners, depending on the nature of your students, your specific instructional needs, and your particular expectations of your partners. As pointed out by Olcott (2009), you need to do your homework before you start to choose cross-cultural partners and establish international partnerships. He suggests that practitioners of an international partnership need to research their "partner organisation, its culture, language, history, current partners, partnership record, financial stability, and how the organisation is perceived in their own country" (p. 81). A rule-of-thumb list below may be helpful for your decision-making.

Language

At the beginning of the designing process, you have to decide which language or languages to use in cross-cultural communications. Generally speaking, there are two types of language arrangement: the tandem type and the lingua franca type. The tandem type refers to two or more languages are equally used or are used alternatively if the two groups of students are familiar with or are learning these languages. For example, if a group of American students is learning Chinese, and a group of Chinese students is learning English, they may use both Chinese and English to communicate. This may benefit both groups of students in terms of their learning of their target language. On the other hand, if the two groups of students do not speak each other's language and there is a language, i.e., lingua franca, that the two groups of students share, then they may choose the language as a means for communication. For example, both a Canadian group and a Switzerlander group of students may speak French, and they may use French to communicate in the exchange encounter. In the case of one partner group being native speakers and the other partner group being learners of the communication language, to ensure mutually benefits, learners of the language can use their native-speaking partners as language models in their learning process, whereas native-speaking partners can learn and experience a different culture from their overseas partners. One thing that deserves exchange practitioners' attention in this respect is students' language proficiency level. If one of the partner groups does not have a minimum proficiency level required for cross-cultural communication, then the cross-cultural exchange can hardly be achieved.

In regard to the language used in cross-cultural exchanges, attention should be paid to language varieties. As discussed in the previous chapter and will also be discussed in later chapters, as the result of the process of globalization, language varieties are inevitable. People from different regions of the world who speak the same language may speak it differently. The emergence of World Englishes is a good example. Although there are so many people speaking English in the world, they may speak it differently. The same is true for Spanish speakers. Spanish spoken by Spanish people may be slightly different from that spoken by Mexican people in accent, pronunciation, word usage or sentence structure. Participants of cross-cultural exchanges should be aware of and tolerate language varieties. By communicating in the same language but with slightly different varieties, participants may learn and appreciate language varieties.

Furthermore, the issue of language varieties is not limited to respecting each other's languages or dialects. It is relevant to the equality of language. As pointed out by Davies and Dubinsky (2018), there are different categories of language conflict, including indigenous minorities, geopolitical minorities, migrant minorities, dialect minorities, and competition for linguistic dominance. In a globalizing era, it may sound ironic that those minority groups or less dominant linguistic groups are ignored in the global community. On the contrary, their voice should be heard and their specific cultures deserve more attention and more exploration. In cross-cultural exchanges, practitioners are encouraged to work with less privileged groups of people and get involved in the less explored territory. After all, it is the real meaning of globalization.

Time

Cross-cultural exchanges involve students from different countries, meaning exchange partners may be located in different time zones around the world. There is less a problem in the case of asynchronous communications, such as computer-mediated communications, in terms of time differences. However, time differences can be a big issue in synchronous communications, especially in some countries such as the U.S. where Daylight Saving Time is practiced regularly. Reaching a consensus on the time for cross-cultural videoconferencing requires negotiation and compromise, and it is sometimes the case that one of the partner groups needs to adjust their class schedule in order for a cross-cultural videoconference to be able to be conducted.

Aside from time for synchronous communication, dates can be another issue. Different schools in different regions of the world may have different school calendars and different national holidays. First, you may need to list all possible dates for you to meet if it is a semester or a year-long project. Your partners then check their school calendars and then cross-out those dates that are not possible for them to meet. The dates for cross-cultural meeting then can be finalized. In the case of a field trip, checking the partner school's school calendar is even more important. Provide your partner teacher with your objectives for a field trip to make sure your goals can be achieved. For example, you might want your student to meet their foreign partners, visit specific organizations, or attend a particular lecture, make careful arrangements to make sure you are able to do all the expected activities.

Communication Facilities

For some specific types of cross-cultural exchanges, such as computer-mediated communication and videoconferencing, before engaging in practice of cross-cultural exchanges, exchange practitioners need to check that all the facilities to be used for cross-cultural communications are compatible with your partners'. Generally speaking, you need to seek for technical support from well-qualified technicians on the campus. Asynchronous text communications may be simpler to handle. Some social networking services such as Facebook may be available to be used in cross-cultural exchanges. Sometimes you may prefer to have a computer program exclusively developed and used for your project. In this case, you may ask for technical support based on your instructional and technical needs. Students may be required to log in to the computer program with an assigned account and a password. One of the advantages of having a project computer program is that it is easier for the practitioners to monitor the entire process of the exchange and collect and analyze the data.

In synchronous oral communications, such as videoconferencing, it can be even more complicated in the technical aspect. Sometimes the facilities used by two partner schools are incompatible. Other times, time lags may occur or there is no image shown on the screen or no sound is heard. In addition to having the machines tested well ahead of the times of meeting, you need to have your technicians stay on the site when a synchronous oral communication is under way in case that technical difficulties occur. Any technical problem that happens in the middle of the communication process may waste you and your participants' time and may ruin the entire activity.

Nationality and the Tendency of Regionalism

Depending on your objectives for cross-cultural exchanges (e.g., language learning or professional learning), you may particularly favor exchange partners from a specific culture or country, especially from a well-developed and English-speaking country. You aim at achieving your goal of the project. Viewed from a different perspective, however, looking for partners from a totally different culture or profession may even benefit your students more. On the one hand, they learn what they did not know before and cannot learn otherwise. On the other hand, they can contribute to intercultural understanding and to lessen the possibility of stereotyping. In his book entitled *Higher Education in Southeast Asia,* Welch (2011) describes a phenomenon in higher education around the globe. He concludes that

> scholars tend to neglect the developments of higher education in Southeast Asia, and they only confine their attention to the known world of their own higher education system....Scholars from the global North still view many of the systems of Southeast Asia as peripheral, blissfully unware, and often uninterested in, impressive development in regional higher education. (p. 159)

In reality, according to Welch, Southeast Asia's higher education has been extraordinarily dynamic with a strong desire to compete in global higher education and to share and play a role in the domain of education and "knowledge economy." A very good example of cross-border partnership between the East and the West is described by Hoult (2018). Hoult intentionally arranged his students in teacher training programs in the UK to engage in intercultural learning in South India. Compared to other cross-cultural researchers, he particularly aimed at engaging his students in intercultural communication with 'the other' in a post-colonial era. He intended to ask his students to 'unlearn' what was developed in their mind from the concept of colonialism and 'learn' from their Indian partners. In a globalizing era, it is particularly important that researchers disarm their colonial weapons and engage in research on peaceful and meaningful cross-cultural partnerships.

In other regions of the world, such as the European Union, the Mediterranean region, Arab states of the Persian Gulf, Latin America, and many other regions around the globe also deserve equal attention. The point is that each region has its unique culture and customs, specific areas of development, geographical advantages, historical background, and political practices. All of these may contribute to the harmony of the global community and may widen the horizons of the teacher and students' knowledge by mutual understanding and extended learning. It is really not a wise decision that, in cross-cultural exchanges, you purposefully ignore those minority or less-developed cultural groups.

Another possible consideration to choose exchange partners can be termed *ism*, such as regionalism, Buddhism, Catholicism, and Islamism. That is, regionally or religiously close or similar to each other may have advantages in collaboration. For example, choosing exchange partners from a neighboring country or with similar religion allows students to compare similarities and contrast differences between them and their partners. Welch (2011) describes the phenomenon in Southeast Asia, stating that "Chinese students now form a significant proportion of overall international enrolment cohorts at universities in Southeast Asia...[and] students from the Southeast Asia Five were enrolled in Chinese universities" (p. 161-162). In addition to student enrolment and offers of scholarships for students, regional collaboration between China and its Southeast Asian neighbors include bi-lateral training programs and joint staff research programs. According to Welch, Asian regionalism has brought more and more Asian students to study within their own region.

In addition to regional collaboration, a similar religion may also attract higher education institutions from the same region or different regions to work together on certain projects. For example, "Islamic higher education also has a regional dimension, with some student flows evident between Malaysia, Indonesia and, to a lesser extent, Thailand....but...also attract students from outside the region, including Bangladesh, India, Nigeria and the Middle East" (p. 162). De Wit et al. (2008) describe that data on trends in international student circulation has shown that a "regionalization South-South circulation" (p. 242). In the case of Malaysia, it recruited "students from Southeast Asia and West Asia, as well as from China and Singapore" (p. 242). The same is true for South Africa, which serves as the hub of sub-Saharan Africa, and Kyrgyzstan and Kazakhstan were mainly focusing their recruitment of international students on Central Asia.

In the case of Europe, de Wit et al. (2008) describe how members of Europe cooperate in response to the competitiveness of the global market in higher education. The European Union (EU) initiated the Bologna Process and the Lisbon Strategy, aiming at reforming European higher education by "going beyond the borders of the 25 countries of European Union" (p. 251), including adoption of Diploma Supplement, European Credit Transfer System, promotion of mobility, and promotion of European cooperation in Quality assurance. Members of the EU believed that only by cooperation among the EU states can the EU succeed in the competitive globe. In cross-cultural exchanges, similarity in region and religion may bridge the gap between exchange partners and promote discussion of relevant topics.

Another good example of regional contacts is the case of Aletheia University (AU) in Taiwan. In an interview with Wilson Lin, the then director of the Department of Continuing Education, he describes the cross-cultural contacts at AU. Generally speaking, AU has cross-cultural contacts with higher education institutions in Southeast Asian countries, including Korea, Hong Kong, Macao, the Philippines, and Malaysia. On the one hand, the regional ties and relatively close language, culture, and economic development make it easier to have cross-cultural contacts. On the other hand, from a more practical perspective and in a competitive international student market, these regional contacts may attract students from nearby countries. Viewed from a long-term perspective, these contacts may lead to future collaboration in different areas and promote mutual economic development. For example, according to Lin, those students coming from the same region (i.e., Southeast Asia) always visit local organizations or enterprises relevant to their field of study, such as transportation management. It can be seen helpful in future regional development and collaboration.

Mutuality

Mutuality here in this chapter may cover three different aspects: power relation, benefit, and obligation. In terms of power relation, Mitakidou (2011) points to the unfortunate fact that "in every exchange, power relations between the different cultures are seldom symmetrical or equitable" (p. 83). Striving for an equal power relation can be an important issue in a cross-cultural partnership. In describing the partnership between Johns Hopkins School of Nursing and Peking Union Medical College School of Nursing, Shiviana and Hill (2011) keep mentioning the importance of mutuality in a collaborative partnership. For them, "successful partnerships require commitment to a shared and significant goal, mutual respect and trust, a transparent structure for managing the collaborative work, and resources to support the activities" (p. 165). On the other hand, Brooks and Waters (2011) point to "the asymmetries in knowledge transmissions" (p. 148). The structure of knowledge transmission shows a tendency to move from the Western countries to the Eastern countries. To put it more precisely, those "more advanced and more powerful "Western countries are indeed promoting their "'national brand' of higher education" (p. 149) and are forcing other countries to accept their ideologies and knowledge structures.

Turner and Robson (2009) also point to the fact that "[p]owerful nations…are at the forefront of the internationalization of higher education. They not only take the lead in international research exchange and student recruitment, but also effectively determine the rules by which the knowledge-transfer game is played" (p. 16). They term the situation *conceptual colonialism,* featuring "a one-way colonial flow of educational influence" (p. 16). In cross-cultural exchanges, the imbalanced knowledge and cultural transfer is definitely not what we expect of the result of cross-cultural encounters. As we can see from a more global perspective, different regions of the world contribute to the world community in different ways, whether in the domain of science, politics, economy, education, religion or arts. The purpose of cross-cultural exchanges is not intended to create a melting pot that the 'pot' will eventually be represented by the dominant ones. Rather, we would like to see the development of a 'salad bowl' world in which each ingredient of the 'salad' contributes its flavor to the entire bowl and, most importantly, all ingredients in the salad are equally important in terms of enriching the salad as a whole.

Mutuality, when viewed from a different angle, may refer to the cross-border partnership being beneficial to both parties. As Sakamoto and Chapman (2011) well-state, although, for sure, each party in a cross-border partnership needs to be benefitted from the partnership, "collaborators may have different motivations for participation, assess the value of activities in different ways, seek different outcomes, and value the same outcomes differently" (p. 4). Winer and Ray (1994), on the other hand, argue that each partner of a collaborative project must have a reason to be in the collaborative team. They look to gain something, such as "money, prestige, contacts, advancement, good will, and so on" (p. 58). In this sense, benefits can mean students' academic performance, enhanced institutional prestige, and even financial gains. However, these issues may not necessarily cause problems in the cross-cultural collaboration. Partners need to negotiate and discuss to reach a consensus.

Another aspect of mutuality that may be critical to the success of cross-cultural collaborations is "equal contribution of resources and an equal share of financial risks and returns" (Fong & Postiglion, 2011, 187). As Fong and Postiglion point out, sound "business and financial models are essential for sustainable instructional operations and to ensure that financial arrangements are fair to all parties" (p. 187). They suggest that, due to different accounting, legal, political, and administrative systems in cross-cultural collaborations, it is important to state clearly all the financial obligations and distribution of returns in an agreement before launching into a collaborative project. As stated throughout the book, financial sources may be a key issue to sustain a long-term cross-cultural project. Each partner may have different financial sources from his or her government or institutions. It may be also fair that each partner school is responsible for its own financial needs in the collaboration. On the other hand, in terms of contribution to the collaborative project, you as one of the partners need to think about what to contribute to the collaboration. Sometimes it is possible that differences in some aspects can be a good chance for you to contribute to the collaboration. For example, different languages, cultures, and academic domains may be a good starting point for your collaboration, and you can contribute to the collaboration by providing your partners with what they are lacking.

For Fong and Postiglione (2011), "any indication of one partner nudging toward dictating terms or another partner being relegated to a secondary role was unacceptable" (p. 186). They describe the EMBA-Global program, a collaboration involving Lodan University, Colombia University, and University of Hong Kong. Although London University and Colombia University were already ranked on the top of EMBA program list and University of Hong Kong was then new to the field, London University and Colombia University might take the lead in organizing the program. However, because the collaborative program was operated in Hong Kong, University of Hong Kong might be familiar with regional affairs and could provide more appropriate recommendations for the locals in the decision-making process. According to Fong and Postiglione, the financial analysis show that "every effort was made to ensure that decision-making for all matters was shared equally" (p. 186). As Winer and Ray (1994) put it, "power is always present and never equal" (p. 59). Here in cross-cultural exchanges, *power* refers to different expertises, connections and financial sources; that is, things you are able to contribute to the collaboration, rather than the ones we mentioned earlier, the meaning to control and to influence decision making. In this regard, what matters is how much power you have to contribute to the collaboration and to benefit both you and your partners.

Common Goal

In addition to the above-mentioned more mechanically and operationally oriented factors, one more implicit principle that may contribute to the success or failure of cross-cultural exchanges is a shared common goal. As Gulati, Wohlgezogen, and Zhelyazkow (2012) recount, there are "extremely high failure rates for collaborative endeavors" (p. 531). Although they mainly point to strategic alliances and joint ventures, which mostly judge success or failure based on financial gains and development of the enterprise, this can be true in cross-culture exchanges in the educational domain. Included in the umbrella term *common goal* are, at least, complementary and interdependence, compatibility, mutual trust and commitment, and coordination. These are the important elements to shape a common goal and to form the basis of collaboration.

Coordination between or among partners means more than cooperation. In a cooperative partnership, more attention is paid to how much each partner contributes and how much each partner is benefitted from the cross-cultural exchanges. In a coordination perspective, partners focus more on adjustment and negotiation between or among partners so that desired outcomes can be achieved (Gulati, Wohlgezogen, & Zhelyazkov, 2012). Complementarity is indeed a tricky and sophisticated term in cross-cultural exchanges. Unlike business partnership, cross-cultural exchanges in education do not seek equal gains. To be precise, participants' gains in cross-cultural exchanges are actually not easy to measure. The point of the sense of complementarities is that students can gain what they are lacking or weak in their professional field from their partners and, on the other hand, they may strengthen their professional knowledge by attempting to provide their partners with what they know better. Compatibility in cross-cultural exchanges can mean shared philosophy of education, equal degree of enthusiasm in performing the project, common interests, similar nature and level of partners' background, etc. Incompatibility in these respects may hinder the process of cross-cultural exchanges. However, as described above, incompatibility does not mean differences in different aspects between two partners. Rather, it may mean not having a consensus to collaborate and to reach a common goal.

Common goal, in a sense, does not necessarily mean that cross-cultural partners need to be very similar in many aspects, such as historical background, managerial philosophy, and the nature or focus of the school. Sometimes contrasts between two partner schools may be advantageous for the development of cross-cultural partnerships. For example, Austin and Foxcroft (2011) describe the cross-border collaboration between Nelson Mandela Metropolitan University (NMMU) in South Africa and Michigan State University (MSU) in the United States. Although the two universities are very different in their school history, school size, and pedagogical approaches, they consider the "contrasts that exist between the collaborating institutions enhance the opportunities for learning and collaboration" (p. 122). For one thing, partners can learn from each other by providing their counterparts with what they may be good at. For another, viewed from a research perspective, an outsider's view can be even more valuable than that of the insider, and sometimes it turns out to be a critical idea that insiders have never thought of.

Financial Sources and Support

It goes without saying that a cross-cultural project needs sufficient dollars to operate. As Chapman and Sakamoto (2011) put it, "unless there is a financial advantage to all parties in the cross-border collaboration, shared commitment and the sustainability of the program will be at risk" (p. 268). Cross-cultural collaborations require considerable investment, including physical facilities, infrastructure, staffing, and sometimes long-distance transportation to operate. As a common practice, partners seek external funding. That is, they submit proposal for the project to the government or relevant organizations and request financial support. It sounds super wonderful that you are funded with sufficient money by the government or organization to run your project. However, Chapman and Sakamoto (2011) remind practitioners of cross-border collaboration of the pitfall of external funding. The government may shift their focus or support to a different domain because of economical declines or political shifts. In the case of organizational support, as we can imagine, organizational support always entails required commitment from recipients of the financial support, and the 'attachment' to the support is always initiated based on the agendas or interests of the organization. However, it may not be an obstacle that prevents the collaboration from being materialized. Rather, it can serve as a driving force that pushes the partnership to move towards its goal.

Another issue concerning financial requirements in cross-border collaboration is the commercialized higher education. Although financial return is always expected by practitioners of cross-border collaboration in order to secure the sustainability of the project, it is so unpredictable and risky. Knight (2011) and Chapman and Sakamoto (2011) are worried that the need for financial sources has pushed higher education to be treated as a commodity. Although it may be legitimate and inevitable in this regard in terms of sustainability of higher education and cross-border collaboration, the tendency may damage the quality and management of education. In this regard, practitioners of cross-cultural exchanges need to strike a balance between financial needs and educational quality. It may not be a sin to commercialize your cross-cultural project. However, it cannot be practiced at the expense of educational quality and students' learning.

SOURCES TO LOOK FOR CROSS-BORDER PARTNERSHIPS

There are several sources to look for your cross-border partners. A piece of advice to your search for cross-cultural partners is: be proactive and aggressive. Partners will not possibly come to you voluntarily. It is you who needs to approach your potential partners to express your intention to collaborate and to propose your collaborative project. Your project proposal needs to be valuable and complete enough to convince your potential partners to participate. Sometimes existing relationships between two schools may be good sources for you to look for your distance partners. These partnerships may exist in two forms: sister schools and international branch campuses. In this section, I begin with discussing these two larger-scale and more complicated cross-cultural partnerships and then go on to explore some other sources to look for cross-border partnerships.

Sister Schools or International Branch Campus

In the field of international education or in a school that stresses the importance of a global view, sisterhood between two schools is not uncommon. Many schools establish sisterhood with schools around the world. They may sign contracts or memorandums to exchange students and/or teachers, organize dual degree programs, and co-host academic conferences. As will be described in the next chapter, there are many universities around the world establishing their overseas campuses for different motives. It is also a good sources to look for your exchange partners if your school has established its overseas campuses. It may be easier for you to contact faculty members at your sister schools to find a partner teacher to work with. Among many cases of collaboration between sister schools, Fabregas Janeiro, Fabre, and Rosete (2012) describe how an international faculty-led program can be developed. They argue that one of the factors that contributed to the success of their international faculty-led program was the solid relationship between the two partner schools: Oklahoma State University in the U.S. and Universidad Popular Autonoma del Estado de Puebla in Mexico. Both of the universities have been making efforts to internationalize their campuses and to develop international relations.

Some other cases were the collaborations I conducted with sister schools of Tamkang University (TKU) in Taiwan, where I have been teaching. TKU has been devoting itself to internationalization of its campus, and it has so far established sisterhood with approximately 170 universities around the world. Several cases of cross-cultural exchanges that I conducted include collaborations with Waseda University, Japan, Nagasaki University, Japan, and University of Maryland, U.S.A. These partner schools are all sister schools of Tamkang University. Talk to the administrators in the department responsible for cross-cultural exchanges at your school, for example, in the case of TKU, the Office of International and Cross-Strait Affairs is in charge of affairs relevant to sister schools. Chances are you will realize that you are quite welcome to collaborate with them.

Academic Conferences or Professional Journals

Seize the opportunity to communicate with international scholars when you are attending an academic conference either at home or abroad. Generally speaking, educators or researchers with similar research interests would gather together at an international conference. Attend the sessions you are interested in and exchange your name card and your ideas with presenters or participants of the conference. Chances are you might find your project partners there. One of my personal experiences was that I attended a CALL conference in Scotland and one professor from France approached me, expressing his interest in cross-cultural collaboration. This contact led to the collaboration between business majors in Taiwan and in France.

It is also possible that your presentation may arouse other participants' interests and they may contact you directly. Another one of my personal experiences was at a conference held in Hong Kong, I presented a cross-cultural videoconferencing project that I conducted with an American professor, and one of the participants who was teaching in a school in Hong Kong was very much interested in cross-cultural collaboration. After several e-mail contacts, we had videoconferences between English majors in Taiwan and in Hong Kong and between international students in Taiwan and in Hong Kong. One of the advantages of looking for your exchange partners at an international conference is that you can talk to international scholars face-to-face, thus you can get details about your prospective partners and decide on the possibility of collaboration. If there are potential problems that might hinder the collaboration, you may discuss with your prospective partners and solve the problems on the spot.

Another way of getting connected with international scholars is to search professional journals or books and read the articles that you are interested in. If you find there may be a possibility that you can collaborate with the author, you can just contact him or her and propose a collaborative project. You can always find ways of contacting the author in the article. In most cases, each professional article provides the author's school name, e-mail address or other ways of contact. Politely write a letter or an e-mail to the author, expressing your intention to collaborate. There is no harm at all if you get no response.

Professional Computer Networks

There are a lot of computer networks aiming at professional discussion, such as ResearchGate, TESOL-L, and LinkedIn. You may choose the one(s) you are most interested in and register to participate. You may post your request for cross-cultural collaboration on the discussion board, or you may read the postings and look for messages calling for cross-cultural collaboration. One of the advantages of posting your request for collaboration is that your postings will reach a large number of people, and, better yet, they may be from different regions of the world. This may allow you to choose the one that can best serve your collaboration needs.

Research Grants and Scholarships

It is quite common that the university, the government, or some educational organizations provide faculty or graduate students with research grants. Teachers may propose a research project and plan an international collaboration and apply to the grants. Some grants might require grant recipients to perform some kinds of research, whereas others might evaluate your grant application based on the feasibility and expected contribution of your proposed project to the society and to the nation. Tournès and Scott-Smith (2018) devote an entire book to the discussion of the historical background and development of scholarships as they are relevant to global exchanges. Although the history of global scholarships may not be directly relevant to those who are seeking financial support and opportunities for studying abroad, new prospects may be helpful for them in their search for financial support in their forthcoming overseas study. Based on the study of the 150 years of scholarship programs, Tournès and Scott-Smith conclude with some important facts that will still be relevant to the new trends of global scholarships. First, scholarship programs are not limited to the domain of academia. It is especially true in a globalizing era. Different domains such as agriculture, medicine, sports and arts along with emerging global issues need exchanges or collaborations globally, and these collaborations, in turn, need strategic and financial supports. Second, scholarship programs are associated with power politics and are generally used "as instruments of 'soft power' and 'national branding'" (p. 323). Many more powerful nations use their scholarship programs to strengthen their political power, for example, France's promotion of the French language, China's promotion of "the Chinese language by the Confucius Institutes, the 'European idea' by the EU and technical development by India" (p. 323). Third, Tournès and Scott-Smith point to the two principles of scholarship program: unilateral and reciprocal. In the earlier history of scholarship programs, more powerful nations used scholarship programs to promote their national models, fulfill their national interests, and pursue their power politics. Gradually, scholarship programs were seen as being reciprocal, featuring *collaboration* and *exchange*. On the one hand, nations may promote their economic, political, and educational model abroad; on the other hand, they may internationalize and enrich and diversify their society, and thus promote their global status.

In the rest of this section, I can only introduce some internationally known providers of research grants or scholarships. You may search for the most appropriate ones for you to apply to.

The Case of Fulbright Program in the U.S.

The Fulbright Program is an internationally known exchange program that sponsors cross-cultural exchanges between or among the US and other countries and involves scholars, professionals, classroom teachers, teaching assistants, and students to undertake graduate study, advanced research, university teaching, etc. (Wikipedia, Institute of International Education).

To enable the reader to have a better understanding of how the Fulbright program works, I feel it obligatory to briefly introduce the historical development of the program so that prospective grant recipients will have in their mind how the money they are awarded can help them with their personal growth and devotion to the society. As accounted by Arndt and Rubin (1993), the "first Fulbright Agreement was signed with China in November 1947" (p. 13). In the 1940s, after World War II, Senator Fulbright proposed to turn the money derived from selling surplus military equipment into scholarships. At this early stage of the Fulbright program, the money was only awarded to American scholars or students for them to have overseas experiences and to learn other cultures. Not until 1950, did "the Fulbright program became a two-way flow" (p. 14). That is, international scholars or students were also invited and financially supported to come to the United States to better know American culture and their own cultures.

The 1950s witnessed the growing and flowering of the Fulbright program. In the decade, more and more countries from all over the world participated in the program for cultural and educational exchanges. Among them, there were a librarian from Belgium, a social scientist from France, a historian from Bologna, an American critic to Rome, an American couple who were a social worker and a folk artist to South Asia, and a political observer to Italy. Arndt and Rubin (1993) describe the period as "the apogee of the Fulbright program and the cradle of its myths.

However, the Fulbright program was facing a crisis in the 1960s. Budget was an issue in the first place. Political conflicts caused a budget cut by half. "The growth of new commissions and agreements overseas slowed markedly, and various agreements became inactive" (Arndt & Rubin, 1993, p. 177). In the 1970s', some changes enabled the Fulbright program to survive. First, an alumni network was established to connect Fulbrighters around the world. Second, the US Information Agency managed to reorganize to have policy made separate from cultural practices. However, there were no new agreements signed and some Fulbright Commissions in other countries were terminated because of shifts of political power in the period.

In the 1980s, "Fulbright budgets drifted upwards" (Arndt & Rubin, 1993, p. 297). People started to be aware of the lowered quality of the Fulbright program. The government was thus seeking some innovations. First, the Fulbright provided "opportunities for teachers in secondary schools and the smaller universities and colleges. Second, the experience of foreign countries tended to be shorter, such as a six-week seminar. Exchanges between countries were defined as the main purpose of the program.

In the early 1990s, as Arndt and Rubin (1993) recount, there was a tendency showing that "agreements and commissions have already begun to crop up in previously unlikely places" (p. 457), and the then President-elect Bill Clinton seemed to show his internationalist orientation. There was no wonder that Arndt and Rubin were optimistic to say that "the future for Fulbright may look brighter" (p. 458).

An example of a Fulbright-sponsored exchange program was reported by Ho (2012). Ho was then teaching in the U.S. and was awarded a Fulbright U.S. Scholarship to teach collaborative mural painting in Bulgaria for five months. The reason for her to choose Bulgaria was its rich mural painting culture. As mentioned by Ho, "the Fulbright Program has sponsored programs that endeavor to promote mutual understanding and respect between the people of America and the people of other nations" (p. 77). For this reason, Ho especially reminded herself of her obligations and opportunities of promoting "mutual understanding and respect for differences between people, cultures, and nations" (p. 77), and she insisted on integrating both American and Bulgarian cultural elements in their final mural painting product. Ho believes that art serves as an international language that blends people from different cultures together and enables people to cross "geographic boundaries, language barriers, racial differences, and cultural identities" (p. 87). To better understand and to know more experiences of Fulbright grants recipients, George's (1995) book entitled *College Teaching Abroad* has a very detailed account of the experiences of Fulbright Scholarship recipients teaching abroad.

Another example is reported by Jordan (2018). Her research is on the case of Fulbright program in Taiwan. Jordan describes that, due to political reasons, the United States and Taiwan have been maintaining an unofficial relationship, and the American Institute in Taiwan (AIT) aggressively promotes cultural and educational exchange with the support of Ministry of Education, Ministry of Foreign Affairs, and National Science Council. According to Jordan, "the program elaborated its exchanges from science and technology in the 1960s, to its social sciences and humanities in the 1970s and '80s, and to opportunities for art and cultural purposes in the 1990s" (p. 80). It is evident that cultural diplomacy as "soft power" has been getting more and more attention from the U.S. and Taiwan governments.

How may the Fulbright program or experience be related to practitioners of cross-cultural exchanges in addition to providing financial support? Most of the Fulbright recipients have changed their lives after their overseas experiences. For Americans who went abroad to other countries, they not only learned about other countries but also learned about their own country. For people who came to the United States from other countries, they had better understanding of the United States and their own countries.

Yet, some learned about themselves (Winks, 1993). This understanding may, in turn, help establish international relations. As Winks points out, the "Fulbright Experience is based … on the non-quantifiable belief that knowing about other societies increases understanding and that understanding at the very least lessens the likelihood of preemptive judgements" (p. 472).

The Case of Erasmus Program in Europe

Tournès (2018) describes Erasmus scholarship programs as being academic, economic, and political. He claims that the Erasmus program has "become the largest scholarship program in history…[and] the first truly multilateral program….in which any Member State can send scholarship holders to (or receive from) any other Member State" (p. 306). The Erasmus programs' academic, economic, and political aims are revealed in its pronounced goals: "fostering economic cooperation and development through the promotion of student mobility, with the aim of creating a single market; and promoting the global influence of European higher education through the establishment of multiple international partnerships" (p. 306). As pointed out by Tournès (2018), "from the 1990s onward, [the Erasmus program] has also been increasingly integrated into the economic strategy of the EU" (p. 308). Employability is the key. Erasmus scholarship holders did not necessarily go to universities to study; some of them stayed in a company and eventually got a position.

As the Erasmus program developed, it has expanded to serve different groups of people to cover students, teachers, and researchers and different geographic regions, not be limited to Europe. Aside from Europe, the program helped those newly independent countries after the collapse of communism reconstruct or modernize their countries. On the other hand, the program also "aimed to open up European higher education institutions to the world and to create international partnerships, both to contribute to the influence of European higher education and to attract the greatest minds from all over the world to Europe" (p. 309).

The Case of Confucius Institute to Learn Chinese

More recently in the 2000s, China started promoting learning Chinese around the world as its "soft power" to promote Chinese culture and to advance its global status. The Chinese government established Confucius Institutes around the world to inspire and engage people in learning Chinese. The government initiated "Overseas Chinese education plan" to promote "the Chinese language and above all making the Confucius Institute the 'central base' for all activities concerned" (p. 311). The plan is well-organized and the Chinese government has controlled the entire process of Chinese teaching overseas, including selection of textbooks, choice of teachers, and subjects to be taught. The language diplomacy was supported by a considerable amount of budget and well-planned scheme. The Chinese Government sent its teachers abroad to teach and train local teachers. These local teachers might then come to China to have official training and go back to their own countries to teach Chinese at Confucius Institutes or Confucius classrooms.

The entire education plan is well-supported by the government. A "policy of scholarships was put in place very early in order to allow local students and teachers to attend the institutes that had been set up in their countries, and subsequently to become teachers in the newly created classrooms" (Tournès, 2018, p. 312). Furthermore, there is also a scholarship program set up for "foreign students and researchers wanting to study Chinese in China" (p. 312).

The Case of India

As Tournès (2018) describes, one of the new actors of international scholarships after the Cold War is India. Since the 1990s, India has been rising in the international scholarship market. Unlike the case of China, India's scholarship programs are practiced "in a diverse range of fields, sponsored both by the government and by private actors" (p. 314). The governmental organizations, such as the India Council for Cultural Relations (ICCR) offered scholarships to help reconstruction of those countries such as Afghanistan after the Cold War. The case of private sectors, such as the Tata industrial dynasty, are also active in providing scholarships to collaborate with world-renowned higher education institutions, to the development of science and technology in India and its neighboring countries, and to encourage international students to study in India.

Generally speaking, India's scholarship offerings focus on Southeast Asia and Africa. The policy makers in India insist that India, located in Asia, knows the needs and issues of Asian countries better than the Western countries do. Viewed from a global perspective, India significantly contributes to the development of South-South partnerships and the phenomenon of the Global South.

In addition to the cases mentioned above, some governmental departments, colleges, or educational organizations also offer research grants for teaching and researching abroad. Sometimes the governmental institutes in your country may collaborate with the governmental institutes in other countries and offer a so-called dual collaborative project. In this case, you need to propose your research project along with your project partners. There are always serendipitous chances for you to conduct cross-cultural exchange projects.

Chapter 5

STUDYING, TEACHING OR WORKING ABROAD

As Agarwal (2008) points out, the General Agreement on Trade in Services (GATS) has categorized education service as

> one of the 12 sectors covered by the GATS and disaggregated into five sub-sectors: primary, secondary, higher, adult, and other. Like other services, trade in higher education services could occur in any of the four modes: (a) program mobility, (b) student mobility, (c) institution mobility, and (d) academic mobility. (p. 105)

It is apparent viewed from this perspective that higher education services are associated with economic development and the trends of knowledge economy. The goal of education is the well-being of human life.

In the sections to come, I focus on different modes of mobility, starting from the most common and long-standing mobility: student mobility, which is more individually driven and is a more commercially-related decision. Then, I move to discuss academic mobility, or faculty mobility, which is more relevant to demand and skills of teachers. As for program mobility and institution mobility, I leave the discussions of these two modes of mobility until Chapter 6 in which I focus on cross-border collaborations and partnerships. Just to draw readers' attention that "mobility" in this book does not necessarily only mean physically moving to a different place or country. In a globalizing era, mobility can include slower and less visible movement, such as culture, economy, politics, and education. In the case of cross-cultural exchanges, for example, teachers may teach international students in their own country and students may interact with people from different cultures in their own classrooms.

STUDENT MOBILITY

There is another type of face-to-face cross-cultural encounter. That is, students go abroad and study in a foreign country. As Barrett (2017) states, in an era moving towards globalization, having diverse educational experiences by spending a period of time studying abroad can not only enrich one's horizon in different aspects, such as culture, language, and professional knowledge, but also enhance students' employment opportunities in the knowledge economy. Student mobility can be viewed from two directions: students in a country go abroad to study or do research in another country and

a country recruits foreign students to have academic activities or careers in the country. That is, student mobility should be viewed from both inward and outward directions. De Wit et al. (2008) call the phenomenon the dynamics of international student circulation. They argue that traditionally research reports tend to view student mobility from the receiving country's perspective and focus on the direction of South to North. In an era moving towards globalization, student mobility is actually multidirectional and what motivates them to move to another country is complicated. De Wit et al. state that many push and pull factors may affect student mobility, such as "the impact of religion on flows of students, about government policies relating to foreign study, the growing impact of the European Union's internationalization initiatives, and other aspects of a high complex reality" (p. vii). De Wit et al. broadly categorize all the factors that push and pull international student circulation into four main areas: mutual understanding (political, social and cultural factors), revenue earning (economic factors), skill migration (economic factors), and capacity building (educational factors)" (p. 240). They argue against the notion of "vertical mobility," which refers to South-North and diploma or degree mobility. They view this notion as ignoring "South-South, North-South, and North-North diploma and degree mobility" (p. 238).

As mentioned in the introductory chapter, face-to-face cultural exchanges are no longer limited to a physical visit to another country for only a short period of stay. Culturally and linguistically different groups of students may sit in the same classroom and learn together. For some historical, political, economic, or technological reasons, some countries have been developed as multi-cultural nations, such as the U.S., and others are becoming more and more culturally diverse in their population, such as Australia and Canada. These and many other countries recruit international students, and local students and international students may take the same course and sit in the same classroom. This can be termed as a short-distance cross-cultural exchange. In this section, student mobility has been expanded to include different lengths of overseas experiences learning from one-week during the spring or winter break through semester or year-long exchanges to several years' degree-oriented study abroad. The term *study abroad* is seen as the "pursuit of learning beyond the boundaries of one's own community, nation, or culture and is as old as learning itself" (Bevis & Lucas, 2007, p. 1). Bevis and Lucas suggest some important factors that may motivate people to learn beyond geographical boundaries: human beings' curious and adventurous nature and ability to communicate with people of different levels and different cultural backgrounds.

Models of Study Abroad

Study abroad can be performed in a variety of ways, ranging from a home university's involvement to students' independence (Pang, 2009). Pang illustrates different models of study abroad programs and assigns them into different categories, including the island model, the direct enrollment model, the collaborative model, and the consortium model. The island model "is designed, taught, and run by the home university, and conducted at an overseas location" (p. 236); whereas the direct enrollment model is the one "in which students study in a foreign education system and take courses offered by the overseas university" (p. 236). In the collaborative model, two or more universities in different geographical or cultural settings collaborate in a study abroad project. This model features its "equal partnership and full reciprocity, where intellectual expertise, administrative support, and expenses are shared" (p. 237). Finally, the consortium model is the one in which a group of universities work together on arranging students for study abroad programs. As the types of study abroad show that in a globalizing era, students can have a variety of ways and purposes to study abroad, depending on personal conditions, preferences, and the support one gets.

Trends of International Students Mobility

As will be mentioned in the section of Challenges of Study Abroad, international student mobility is dependent on various political, societal, cultural, economic, and educational factors. Dennis (2018) roughly describes the trends of international student mobility in different regions of the globe. She predicts that "China may become the world's dominant player in international higher education in the future, both for outward mobility and inward mobility" (p. 38). In Middle East and South Asia and East Asia, there is a tendency to develop regional collaboration. In the Middle East, Middle Eastern countries collectively formed a "regional hub" to attract students from Middle East and other regions, such as Africa. In South Asia and East Asia, regionalism also works in higher education in the region. The establishment of the Association of Southeast Asian Nations (ASEAN) has harmonized "member states' education systems and increased collaboration among universities in the region" (p. 39). The community aims to "promote innovation in higher education and encourage the free flow of ideas, knowledge, expertize and skills within the region" (p. 39). Higher education institutions in Asian countries, such as Malaysia, Taiwan, Vietnam, and the Philippines have been working hard collaborating in research projects and exchanging students. In Africa, the potential of international student mobility cannot be overlooked as well. According to Dennis, African students' first choice for overseas study is France. However, more and more African students choose to "remain in Africa for their post-secondary education and South Africa is the preferred country" (p. 42). This is another piece of evidence showing regionalism at work. On the other hand, African institutions also actively collaborate with China, India, and Australia for "Joint research, Exchange and Cooperation program" (p. 43).

While Middle Eastern, Asian, and African countries are increasingly growing in international student mobility, the United States and United Kingdom are shown moving towards the opposite direction. According to Dennis (2018),

> the higher education in United States is losing its competitive advantage because of globalization and that these forces 'are helping rapidly developing Asian nations to transform their major universities into serious contenders for the world's students, faculty and resources within just a few generations.' (p. 44)

In the case of the United Kingdom, the most popular destination for international students has been shifted from the United Kingdom to Germany since "the Brexit vote in 2016" (p. 45), and the number of students enrolling from India also declined because of stricter visa regulations enforced by the United Kingdom.

As for countries such as Canada, Australia, and Germany, their gaining popularity and increased enrollment of international students can be attributed to effective recruiting campaigns and favorable policies. For example, "Canadian officials have changed application, visa and employment regulations, making it easier for international students to get a visa and work and remain in Canada after graduation" (p. 46). In the case of Australia, it attracts international students by having "a worldwide reputation for excellence" (p. 47) and providing international students with satisfactory learning experience and a safe learning environment. Germany is no exception to the recruiting campaign rules. Its strategies include "no tuition charges, courses offered in English, scholarship program for engineering students and work opportunities after graduation" (p. 48).

Tang (2018), on the other hand, investigates the reasons for Malaysian students to work on their higher education degrees in Taiwan. According to Tang, Taiwan hosts the largest number of students from Malaysia in its international student population. There are more than ten thousand Malaysian students coming to Taiwan to attend colleges or universities. He interviewed 20 Malaysian students who were working on their degrees in Taiwan. According to Tang, those Malaysian students can be categorized into two different groups identified as overseas Chinese and foreign students. For those overseas

Chinese students, because of their historical background, they feel they have a cultural tie with people in Taiwan, and some of them attended independent Chinese high schools in Malaysia before they come to Taiwan. For those who graduate from independent Chinese high schools, they are automatically eligible to attend universities in Taiwan. It is quite natural that they come to Taiwan for advanced study after their graduation from high school in Malaysia. Another reason that attracts Malaysian students to come to Taiwan is about the tuition fees. As described by Tang, colleges and universities in Taiwan offer overseas Chinese students favorable tuition fees, and it is quite easy for them to apply for admission to college or universities in Taiwan. For those Malaysian students who come to Taiwan as foreign students, tuition fees and scholarships remain an important reason for them to come to Taiwan. Other reasons may be attributed to word of mouth and the influence of the mass media. Many of the teachers who teach in Malaysia have attended Taiwanese universities before, and they would occasionally talk about their experiences in Taiwan and encourage their students to study in Taiwan. On the other hand, mass media also has a great influence on Malaysian students' choice to come to Taiwan. Some of the interviewees mentioned they are familiar with some popular Taiwanese TV programs, and the stories described in the TV program may attract them to come to Taiwan.

To ensure providing the best learning environment for international students, Olcott (2009) suggests that higher education institutions should provide a 3S global village on campus, in which international students should be able to socialize and to interact with local students, other international students, and "they need both home connections and new connections with the campus community (p. 80). In addition to *socialization*, international students need *support* from the university, including [c]ounselling, advising, employment opportunities, academic tutors, [and] health services" (p. 80). On the other hand, universities may also provide *services* to international students, such as "[d]eveloping an agenda of social activities, clubs, travel excursions, and cultural celebrations" (p. 80). Olcott briefly summarizes factors that may affect international students' destination choices for studying abroad, including the reputation of the institution and the program, social and cultural opportunities, cost, financial assistance and employment opportunities, immigration and visa requirements and procedures, opportunities to master English, the relationship between the home country and the host country, and finally research facilities and resources.

Based on her experiences of managing international enrollment, Dennis (2018) recommends essential steps to increase international student enrollment. The first step is to do research. Read important international newspapers or magazines for information relevant to geopolitical or economical changes happening in the globe, and try to think whether or not these changes will have impacts on your international student recruitment. Having the current information available, you then need to analyze the data to explore any insights that may reveal trends or potential help for your future recruitments. Aside from collecting and analyzing data, Dennis also recommends some strategies that can be taken into account to increase international student enrollment, for example, making use of technologies to offer online courses to have yearlong academic calendars, partnering with international colleges or universities, signing agreements with international colleges or universities for study abroad programs or combined degrees, and anticipating new international recruitment markets and exploring untapped market.

Before You Make a Decision to Study Abroad

Studying abroad is exciting and is full of expectations. However, to make your overseas study really exciting, rewarding, and valuable, you need to be well-prepared before you go abroad. In this section, I present very simple steps in the process of making a decision to study abroad.

Evaluating Yourself and the Host Country

Hyde (2012) provides a check list to truly understand your motivation to study in the UK. Although this check list may target students who intend to go to the UK for further studies, it can be applicable for other students who choose a different destination of overseas study. Hyde differentiates the "push" and "pull" reasons for studying abroad. Push reasons are those where you are pushed by your parents, friends, or teachers or because you are just unsatisfied with your current situation or environment and you want to get rid of them. According to Hyde, these reasons are always negative. Unlike push reasons, pull reasons come from within you. These are your intrinsic motivations. For example, you are really interested in the program, institution, and country you choose, and you like the lifestyle of the people and are willing to explore the culture of the country.

In addition to carefully analyzing your motivations to study abroad, Hyde (2012) suggests two more analyses you need to do in order to make a right choice. The first one is to analyze your personality, including your strengths and weaknesses. What you are good at and what you like to do may be advantages for your choice of study and for your future career planning. Knowing your own weaknesses may help you make improvements so as to lessen threats in your forthcoming study and increase advantages and opportunities in your future career in the workplace. The second analysis you need to do is to analyze the country you are planning to go to, especially if you have an idea to stay in the country after you graduate. The analysis includes the political, economic, social, technological, legal, and environmental situation in the prospective host country. It is important to understand if there is an imbalance between supply and demand in a particular domain.

Your Language Proficiency and Motivation to Learn a Language

Having analyzed yourself and the host country, one more important thing that you cannot ignore is your language proficiency. Whether you go to an English-speaking country or a non-English speaking country, English proficiency may be required since English is considered the lingua franca of the world for the time being. There are the largest number of English speakers, whether native English speakers or non-native English speakers, in the world. In cross-cultural encounters, if you do not know each other's language, you may use English to communicate with each other. Colleges or universities in English-speaking countries may require applicants to pass a certain level of English proficiency test such as TOEFL, TOEIC, or IELTS, or they may need to take some language courses before they can officially take professional courses. In some multi-lingual countries, such as Denmark, language use is even more complicated. Denmark is classified in the expanding circle of English usage, meaning English is not its official language. However, "Denmark...was among the first to require English of all pupils in school, and domestic and international students who come to study in college or university increasing expect a high standard of usage" (Slethaug & Vinther, 2013, p. 82). As a result, international students studying in Denmark tend to consider Denmark as in the inner circle of English usage, despite its expanding circle status. According to Slethaug and Vinther, there is a phenomenon in Europe concerning language use that "many courses and programs are not taught in English but where administrative frameworks and social discourse continue to be in a non-English local language" (p. 82). However, as Slethaug and Vinther's interviews with international students show that in daily life or outside the classroom, Danes always communicate in Danish, or even in the classroom, the teacher once in a while will switch to Danish and hands out instructional materials and give exam instructions only in Danish. Another case is group discussion, local students may occasionally switch to Danish which may cause problems for international students. In this case, international students feel a sense of loss. Otherwise, international students feel happy about having English as the instructional medium in the classroom.

If you go to a non-English speaking country, learning the local language is even more important. It may not be so difficult to learn a language in the target language speaking environment. However, it takes motivation and persistence to achieve your learning goal. You may not be wise if you do not seize the opportunity to learn the local language when you are staying in a foreign country. My assumption is that the best way to learn a foreign language is to communicate with native speakers of that language (Wang, 1997). In cross-cultural exchanges, whichever mode of exchange, language skills are essential to successful cross-cultural communications, and motivation can be key to successful language learning. According to Slethaug and Vinther (2013), there are two language learning factors that may account for the success of learning a foreign language:

motivation and structuration. Motivation refers to an individual's goal, interests, enjoyment, positive learning history, satisfaction, feeling comfortable about the local people of the target language, and some external pressures they have. These are affective factors relevant to personal personality and preference. On the other hand, structuration means using the language to interact with local people and international students. In this regard, Slethaug and Vinther formulate some open-ended questions to interview international students for their perceptions of Danish people and the social environment, for example, their perceptions of the teacher, the instruction and English proficiency of the teachers and peer students, difficulties and challenges they faced, and the level of satisfaction with the entire program.

Whether working overseas as a student or as a teacher, hosting overseas guests in one's own country or communicating with international students on the campus, language proficiency can facilitate communications. I would like to present two examples of learning a local language in a host country. The first one is Maria. Maria, who is from Panama and is Spanish-speaking, attended Tamkang University (TKU) in Taiwan as a graduate student in the time of interview. She stated her motivation to learn Chinese. Aside from the fact that she was in a Chinese-speaking environment, the real factor that motivated her to learn Chinese was the motivational factor to learn a foreign language she observed here. At TKU, there are different foreign language departments in the School of Foreign Languages and Literatures, namely English, Spanish, Japanese, German, French, and Russian. Maria observed how Spanish majors at TKU were hard-working in learning Spanish and were so proficient in Spanish. This has encouraged her to learn Chinese, especially "I am in a Chinese-speaking environment" as she noted. Her advice to language learners is: Don't just take language class. Try to communicate with native speakers of the language for real purposes.

Another example is Linda. Linda, on the other hand, has a background and situations different from those of Maria yet similar perceptions of language learning. She was a Chinese-speaking Taiwanese attending TKU as a graduate student and was unexpectedly on an assignment to teach English in a Taiwanese school in Indonesia while she was still working on her M.A. According to Linda, based on her observation, although her students in Indonesia were mostly of Chinese descent and were "forced" to learn Chinese, they prefer English to Chinese. In classroom conversations during the break, they choose to speak in Indonesian. The students' attitude towards language is apparent. Again, motivation plays an important role in language learning and use. For those Indonesian students, learning English seemed a way to develop their social status and was key to access the global community, and speaking in Indonesian they can get closer to their peers and thus establish friendships and a sense of belonging. As for Chinese language, it might be less immediate and relevant to their daily life and future career. For Linda herself, she is eager to learn Indonesian and enjoy learning the language. In an Indonesian-speaking environment, she feels that being able to communicate with local people in Indonesian can not only bridge the gap between her and local people, but also solve a lot of problems in daily life, such as calling a cab and buying stuff. As Smolcic and Martin (2018) describe it, language is an important social capital. With the social capital, you can earn a lot of benefits and can enhance your social status.

Benefits and Challenges of Study Abroad

Theoretically meeting with people from a different culture may enhance mutual understanding and hence strengthen friendship. However, students who have experiences of studying in another country may have different perceptions of the host country and different attitudes towards study abroad, either positively or negatively. On the positive side of study abroad, students may gain new knowledge, which their home country may not be able to offer. On the other hand, they may learn a new language, meet new friends, and experience and enjoy a different culture. These experiences, in turn, may widen their horizon of knowledge and prepare them for being a global citizen.

Currier, Lucas, and Arnault (2009) roughly summarize the benefits of study abroad for students in three different areas: academic knowledge and skills, personal growth, and intercultural sensitivity. They argue that, in addition to language abilities, study abroad may benefit students' domain knowledge by experiencing and gaining the knowledge in a different cultural environment. In addition to academic knowledge and skills, Currier et al. also point out that study abroad may help "increase students' confidence, maturity and self-reliance, ability to work with others, ability to clarify values, and willingness to accept new ideas" (p. 141). Finally, based on research findings, students who have experiences of study abroad show more interests in global issues and can interpret ideas from different perspectives. Because these students have opportunities to compare different cultures, they show a better understanding and appreciation of different cultures and expand their world view.

Despite the inherent advantages of study abroad, however, things do not always turn out to be that way. Bevis and Lucas (2007) describe some problems that students who are studying abroad might face: "loneliness, social isolation, lack of friends, homesickness, difficulties in adjusting to Western food [or Oriental food], unfamiliar routines and customs, hard-to-find housing - and a seeming lack of sensitivity on the part of citizens of the host country" (p. 3). Even worse, some technically advanced or economically well-developed countries tend to show their ethnocentrism and provincialism. Under these circumstances, students who are studying in another country might feel alienated and discriminated against. Janes (2010) argues that, in a class or on the campus, interactions between home students and international students probably will not happen naturally. It needs purposeful arrangement so that cross-cultural interactions become a positive activity and become a norm in a globalizing era.

Studying abroad or participating in certain kinds of exchange programs is quite common in an era moving toward globalization. Icbay and Kocayoruk (2011) list some common goals for student exchange programs: to increase the participants' understanding and tolerance of other cultures, to broaden their social horizons and increase their intercultural abilities, and to improve their language skills. Doyle, Gendall, Meyer, Hoek, Tait, McKenzie, and Loorparg (2010) also did an investigation to explore factors that may promote or inhibit New Zealand students' intention to participate in study abroad. They found that these factors may include benefits of studying abroad; ongoing support to students; social, cultural, and linguistic capabilities; and how effectively overseas study was integrated into student degree programs. In sum, we may say that students are largely instructmentally motivated to study in a foreign country, for example, to gain a foreign degree, to enhance employability, or to learn a language in the language speaking environment.

Schattle (2009), on the other hand, claim that, to become a global citizen, one needs to reveal some characteristics required for global citizenship, "such as awareness, responsibility, participation, cross-cultural empathy, international mobility, and personal achievement" (p. 3). Study abroad is definitely more than just getting a foreign diploma or certificate. The experiences you have in a foreign country can be an invaluable asset in your future career and in your development of becoming a global citizen. Many institutions in higher education recruit international students or organize exchange programs to encourage their students to study abroad and to welcome students from other countries. However, Martinez, et al. (2009), point out the issue of inequality in access to study abroad in the U.S. They argue that students from low-income families or under-represented minority groups had much less access to study abroad. They argue that equal opportunities to access to study abroad and financial support should be given to those college students. This issue can be said to be another challenge of study abroad faced by some countries.

Governmental or Organizational Support and Challenges of Student Mobility

In the following sections, I selectively describe governmental or organizational support of both recruiting international students and encouraging local students to study abroad in some countries, including New Zealand, the United States, the United Kingdom, and India. Many countries in the world cooperate to offer exchange programs for students to experience cultures other than their own and, hence, develop their global perspectives and be able to become a more qualified global citizen. In this section, I will present some cases of exchange programs that, hopefully, may be helpful for some readers who are seeking opportunities to study abroad. But before that, we need to know about the different types of exchange programs. As described earlier in this chapter, Pang (2009) categorizes study abroad models into different models. Among them are: the "island model" and the "direct enrollment model." In the "island model," the home school takes considerable control over the entire exchange program, expecting that students have their educational experiences in an overseas location; while in the "direct enrollment model," both partner schools equally share the responsibility and are equally involved in the exchange program. They collaboratively work on the program and had "equal partnership and full reciprocity" (p. 237). Whatever model an exchange program may be, the key to a successful program lies in consensus of the objectives of the partner schools. Many countries in the world welcome and offer grants or scholarships for international students to attend schools in their countries. These countries may have different goals, policies, needs, and diplomatic ties to make their decisions. However, they all provide great opportunities for students who are interested in having foreign experiences in their education.

The Case of New Zealand

In the case of New Zealand, as a member of the Colombo Plan, New Zealand has been enthusiastically involved in developing its international education and in welcoming students from developing or under-developed countries. The New Zealand government aims at helping those countries with their technological development, educational resources and life standards. They financially support students from abroad to attend schools in New Zealand, and they also assign scholars or experts to work abroad to financially, technically or educationally assist countries in need.

Tarling (2004) deliberately describes the making and changing of policies concerning supporting international students to study in New Zealand. In the 1950s, the Colombo Plan (CP) was established with four objectives : to aid underdeveloped countries in technical and practical education, to establish bilateral relationship, to create relationships that are personal and mutual, and to learn and benefit both short-term and long-term from contacting with CP countries. According to Tarling, the "'Colombo Plan' is also a phrase used in respect of a period in the history of 'international' students in New Zealand" (p. 10). There were also private students who paid tuition fees on their own.

In 1970, New Zealand established the Overseas Students Admission Committee (OSAC) to "determine the number of overseas students who could be admitted to any university or course" (Tarling, 2004, p. 45), although the universities, not OSAC, directly take applications. The main ideas of recruiting overseas students were based on a sense of obligation to developing countries and on "diversifying the student population and adding to the experience of domestic students" (p. 53). Basically, OSAC defines who had to apply through OSAC, what *ordinary resident* is, and set out "the academic requirements for entrance for overseas students in New Zealand secondary schools who sought admission" (p. 54). For example, those students whose mother tongue were not English had to pass an English proficiency test, such as Language Aptitude Test for Overseas Students (LATOS) or University Bursaries Examination (UB) in order to get admitted to a university.

In the early 1990s, a considerable number of Asian students, especially Chinese students, came to New Zealand for undergraduate study or language learning at private English language schools. As the international students market is getting more and more competitive, New Zealand was aware of the danger to rely on few or even a single country to compete in the international student market. Under this circumstance, a price penetration strategy was adopted like many institutions around the globe and like many other industries. Some problems emerged in sustaining the education in the field of international students, for example, the quality of education. As Tarling (2004) accounts:

> The fee-paying students might themselves be surprised to find so few non-Asians in the class and feel that a dimension of their international education was missing. If there were local non-Asian students in the class, they might tend to feel that students who had to struggle with the language or the mode of learning were delaying their completion of a costly course, if not down-grading its quality. (p. 227)

Under this circumstance, full-fee-paying students were seen as profitable commodities made use of by the institutions.

To respond to the Chinese-dominant situation and the need to build on research capacity, New Zealand was considering a 'niche' approach, for example, focusing on research students or attracting staff from other countries to develop relationships with other countries on the basis of research networks. However, this niche approach could not stand alone unless New Zealand was to drop its mass market. According Tarling (2004), New Zealand should combine both the niche market, which aims at high-level study or research-oriented degrees, and the mass market, which focuses on basic undergraduate and English language education. Since the Colombo Plan, New Zealand has been offering different forms of scholarships or awards, such as Aotearoa Awards and South Pacific Fees Scholarships to replace the previous ones in order to reflect equality and quality of New Zealand's international education.

The Case of the United States

In its history of recruiting international students, the United States experienced some unexpected changes. In the early age, the United States was seen as one of the most popular destinations of study abroad probably because of the prestige of American universities and the advancement of technology in the country. However, enrollments of international students were seen decreasing since the turn of the new millennium. Some predictable and unpredictable factors may contribute to the decline of international student enrollment in the United States. First of all, cited from Borjas's *National Review*, Bevis and Lucas (2007) indicate that theoretically international students can enrich both the nation's and the institutions' revenue incomes and can promote the global status and visibility of the nation and the institutions. However, there are some problems and challenges faced by the nation as a result of competition in higher education in recruiting international students. Too much emphasis on the benefits of recruiting international students has led to illegal transactions of student visas and illegal stay in the United States, and there are quite divided stands on the immigration system and admission policies. On the one hand, opponents claimed that foreign students are subsidized in their education, using taxpayers' money. Some are not here for educational purposes. They shift their status after entering the United States. They even illegally buy visas. On the other hand, advocates of recruiting foreign students claimed that every visitor to the United States received a taxpayer subsidy whether the person "landed at an airport, drove on a highway, rode a city bus, took a subway, visited a national park, went to a museum, or drank a glass of milk in a restaurant" (p. 234) and that the economic benefits the country gains from the economic activities the international students participate in are far more than the subsidy the government offers to international students. Third, opponents were afraid of the so-called "crowd-out" effect. They claimed that recruiting foreign students may force redistribution of wealth and may shift attention from native workers and taxpayers to universities and foreigners. On the other hand, highly skilled immigrants may affect "both earnings and employment opportunities" (p. 236) of local Americans.

An important issue faced by the U.S. policy makers is the decline of the international student enrollment. The September 11, 2001 incident, the increasing global competition in the international student market, and the ambiguity in the rationales for international exchange may contribute to the decline of the international student enrollment in the United States. Foreign students have been seen to shift their overseas destinations away from the United Stated to New Zealand, Japan, Australia, Canada, and other countries (Bevis & Lucas, 2007). Some policy makers see the benefits of having foreign students on the campus for reforming immigration law and the visa system and development of strategic plans to recruit foreign students to respond to the social, cultural, economic, and political change in the globalizing world.

In addition to the decrease in the number of international students attending American universities, de Wit and Rumbley (2008) point out that in speaking of international student circulation, American students who attend universities outside the United States are relatively few. Even though some students do choose to attend universities abroad, most of them choose British, Canadian, or European universities for a short period stay as part of their degree program in the U.S., rather than for degree-seeking. According to de Wit and Rumbley, participant students studying abroad were dominantly Caucasians, females, and social sciences majors. Viewing from the two directions of student mobility, de Wit and Rumbley point to some issues and challenges the United States is facing in the course of internationalization in higher education. They urge American higher education, in order to attract international students from all over the world on the one hand and on the other hand to promote study abroad programs to encourage American students to be able to equip themselves with intercultural competences to function properly in a globalizing world, to work on required strategies to balance inbound and outbound forms of student mobility and to use both push and pull factors in managing international student circulation. Given the historical background and situations of international student circulation in the United States, it might be important in a globalizing era to eliminate ethnocentric ways of thinking and to indulge in a hegemonic history.

For some scholars, (e.g., Smolcic & Martin, 2018; Brown & Tignor, 2016), it is especially important for preservice teachers to have overseas experiences. As Brown and Tignor recount, "preservice teacher population is heavily white, middle class and female" (p. 66). However, as the world is moving towards globalization, they are going to face a much more diversified student population. Overseas experiences may help them understand and deal with issues relevant to culture, ethnicity, race, and gender. It is not uncommon that preservice teachers in the United States are required to have some kinds of experiential learning abroad before their graduation. For example, Purdue University has the Honduras Study Abroad Program (Brown & Tignor, 2016) and a US-American teacher education program requires preservice teachers seeking Teaching English as a Second Language certificate to have a culture and language immersion experience in Ecuador (Smolcic & Martin, 2018). While staying abroad, preservice teachers become the minority groups and language learners. This experiential learning allows them to have a deeper thinking about the inequality in schooling in their forthcoming teaching career, rather than just show their superficial sympathy from their privileged and dominant perspectives for their disadvantaged minority students.

The Case of the United Kingdom

Unlike the case of New Zealand and of the United States, Hyde and Hyde (2014) provide detailed information for UK students on studying outside the UK. At the beginning of their book, Hyde and Hyde first present a rough picture of student mobility, institutional and professional accreditation, and an overall financial picture of tuition fees and living costs in different countries. Then they provide advice as to how to adapt to the new cultural environment, including learning a new language, different approaches to knowledge and learning, and the experience of culture shock. In the rest of the book, Hyde and Hyde briefly introduce different situations, opportunities, requirements, campus life, accommodation, application procedures, credit systems, work permit, financial aid, and particulars in different countries, ranging from the Pacific Ocean to Europe and the Caribbean, and from South Africa to Asia. This book can be very useful for UK students seeking an opportunity to study abroad. However, it can be also a useful guide for students around the world who intend to study in another country. For students from a country other than the U.K., it is also possible that they can get relevant information written from their nationals' perspectives. Local authors may better understand local students' needs, preferences, and perceptions concerning studying in a foreign country. However, you as prospective overseas students might understand that all the choice is on you. You need to take all the relevant issues into consideration before you make your decision, including your financial status, your research interests, how the host country may facilitate your career development or research studies, the relationships between your home country and the host country, how the skills or diplomas you will earn in the host country will be valued by your home country, etc.

In another book titled *The International Student's Guide to UK Education: Unlocked University Life and Culture*, Hyde (2012) provides detailed guides for students around the world who are interested in obtaining a UK diploma. He starts with making a decision to choose a university and a program of one's own interest and concludes with choices after finishing studies in the UK, either staying in UK and getting a job, moving to another country, or going back to one's home country. In between the starting point and the concluding point of studying in the UK, Hyde provides very useful information relevant to academic and social life in UK, including applying for admission to a UK university, the teaching and learning methods mostly used in a UK educational setting, the academic and administrative structure and system operated in UK higher education institutions, and, equally important, life beyond the classroom and the campus. There must be a lot of cultural elements and scenic spots worth navigating. It may beyond the scope of this book to stress all the important points. Readers of Hyde's book may pay special attention to the information that is important to them. Furthermore, governments and higher education institutions may change their policies, and political, economic, and social situations may change over time. It is always wise for readers to update the information and keep current of the status quo of the country they are visiting. For those who intend to go to a country other than the UK, it may be wise to look for books relevant to the country you are heading for and, at least, get a rough idea about how to prepare for your future overseas studies.

The Case of India

Agarwal (2008) describes how India's higher education has been impressively growing after its independence in 1947. He attributes the expansion of higher education in India to several factors: "population increase, improvements in school education, higher aspirations among the people, and the changing structure of the Indian economy that requires new and varied kind of skills" (p. 85).

In the turn of the 21st century, India started seriously taking globalization and internationalization of higher education into consideration. In outward student mobility in higher education, Indian students are the second largest pool of international students after China. Generally speaking, Indian students go to English-speaking countries or countries that provide English programs. Their destinations of overseas study are mostly the United States, and then the United Kingdom and Australia. Indian students also choose other English-speaking countries, such as Canada and New Zealand, and non-English-speaking countries such as Germany, France, and China as their overseas study destinations. In an overview of India's student circulation, Agarwal (2008) concludes that "the pattern the international student circulation in the Indian context reveals a large asymmetry" (p. 110). On the one hand, it sends the largest number of students to the United States, and it has the second largest number of students in the world that go abroad. On the other hand, this country only hosts a small number of international students who mostly come from Asia and Africa. Some significant push and pull factors may contribute to the phenomenon of the country. It may take Indian policy makers' wisdom to bridge the gap between inward and outward student mobility. After all, as described by Agarwal, India is a country full of potential and "can play an even more important role if it adopts the right approach" (p. 111).

In the case of inward mobility, India mostly attracts international students from less-developed countries in Asia and Africa, for example, Nepal, Bangladesh, Malaysia, Kenya, and Sri Lanka. An interesting phenomenon of inward mobility is that a large percentage of the international students in India are from countries with a large number of India diaspora.

Although India is seen to be promising in terms of international student circulation, as described by Agarwal (2008), host countries are competing to attract Indian students and it also hosts international students from many Asian and African countries but still faces some challenges. On the one hand, having access to higher education remains the privilege of wealthy people. The inequality in higher education is further exacerbated by the emergence of privative institutions, which get little funds from the government and need to raise their tuition fees for which only wealthy people can afford to pay. On the other hand, India has poor higher education quality "with a tiny number of high-quality institutions at the top….Weak regulatory mechanisms, inconsequential accreditation systems and financial constraints are the main bottlenecks" (p. 86).

From the discussion of student mobility in different countries above, it is apparent that in a globalizing era, there are no longer hegemonic advantages for more powerful countries in terms of student mobility. Less powerful countries are working hard both recruiting international students and encouraging their students to study abroad in order to be able to survive in the competitive global community. For policy makers, strategic plans are needed to attract international students, and well-organized study abroad programs are also needed to equip students with intercultural competences and global views. The two things may be interconnected, just like the case of India mentioned above.

The Case of Egypt

Egypt has been working enthusiastically to collaborate with foreign universities to advance their higher education and to encourage student mobility. For example, the "American University was founded in Cairo in 1919 by special agreement between the Egyptian and American governments" (Said, 2008, p. 55). Later on, in the early 21st century, the Egyptian Ministry of Higher Education granted establishment of French University, Germany University, British University, and Canadian University in Egypt respectively. According to Said, the "investment if completely Egyptian; however, the names reflect in-kind support from the respective countries to these universities" (p. 55). Being the first non-Egyptian university, the American University in Cairo aimed at creating "an English language university based on high standards of conduct and scholarship that would foster intellectual growth, discipline, and good character in future leaders of Egypt and the region" (p. 56). On the other hand, the school also believed that such a university would greatly increase America's understanding of the Middle East.

In addition to collaborating with foreign countries to found international universities in Egypt, the Egyptian government is also aggressively internationalizing the campus. Its enthusiasm can be shown in its internationalization policies. On the one hand, the government encourages "Egypt's higher education institutions to recruit and accept students from other countries….Independent efforts to improve opportunities for international student circulation…have been ongoing by both public and private higher education universities and institutions aggressively collaborate with foreign institutions in the form of "[t]winning arrangements, partnerships. Dual degree programs, student exchanges, and year-abroad programs" (p. 57).

The missions system in Egypt can demonstrate how the Ministry of Higher Education promotes and encourage cross-cultural studies and research by offering scholarships. According to Said (2008), "[t]he Egyptian missions system of scholarships…consists of five main types: external, internal, joint supervision, scientific, and study leave" (p. 61). The external type of scholarship is granted to those who intend to obtain their Ph.D. degree or receive practical training in a foreign country in basically scientific fields; the internal type is granted "to Master's degree holders who wish to obtain a Ph.D. degree" (p. 61). Recipients of the scholarship of this type are required to "spend one or two years abroad in the counterpart housing institution, attending courses, collecting materials, and pursuing practical work in fulfilling all degree requirements" (p. 61); the joint supervision type aims at providing academics with opportunities "to travel abroad and to become affiliated with counterpart institutions in collecting material relevant to their

Ph.D. dissertation" (p. 62). Both the professor at the candidate's Egyptian university and his or her counterpart host institution jointly supervise the candidate's dissertation writing; the scientific type is targeted at faculty members with the goal of conducting postdoctoral research; and the study leave type is awarded to the candidate's home institution and granted to the individual scholar.

To attract international students to study in Egypt, in addition to offering scholarships to foreign students, there are different forms of promoting inward student mobility, including "student exchange and year abroad programs, twinning arrangements, joint and double degrees, collaborative research, cross-border delivery of academic programs, partnerships, franchises, offshore satellite campuses, open universities, and such international development programs as Euro-Med Tempus III" (Said, 2008, p. 67). According to Said, Egypt's pull factors to attract foreign students are mostly positive, including language that attracts "students from Arab-speaking and Islamic countries…, cultural wealth, vibrant social life, and cost of living" (p. 77). However, Egypt also exhibits some negative pull factors, such as "strict immigration policies and restrictions on travel caused by an emphasis on national security…[and] job opportunities during and after study" (p. 77).

The push factors in terms of encouraging faculty or scholars to have advanced overseas study, training or research, according to Said (2008), are facing serious challenges. Said points to some important facts. Among them are: few Egyptian scholars are accepted by foreign universities to work on advanced degrees, because of relatively weak scientific competencies and low TOEFL scores. Other challenges include: some Egyptian scholars are not well-prepared and adjusted to the foreign culture, some remain in the host country after they complete their degree or training, and Egyptian scholars always have problems choosing appropriate foreign professors to jointly supervise their dissertation research. These issues need to be dealt with seriously so that teacher mobility can really facilitate Egypt's internationalization in higher education.

Examples of Study Abroad Programs

In this section, I present some reports on cases of study abroad programs, and these cases are discussed from different perspectives and explored for different purposes, for example, how to organize an exchange program, how we can prepare students for the forthcoming study abroad, opportunities for students to study abroad, and exchange students' perception of the host country. It is because each of the following examples has its unique point to make and has a different focused part of study abroad that deserve our attention. You as the reader of this book may read these examples and pay particular attention to those that concern you the most and may provide you with valuable information and excellent models in your course of designing a study abroad program or prepare for study abroad.

The Case of the Two Way Learning Approach

Mehra and Bishop (2007) describe a two-way learning approach in library and information science education in which international students, while studying library and information science, may help internationalizing the library in the United States. They argue that, in the new millennium, internationalizing the library to build mutual trust and cross-cultural communication may help promote world peace and international good will. In the two-way learning project, on the one hand, international students may learn the professional knowledge of library and information science. On the other hand, international students' cross-cultural experiences may be good sources for the internationalization of the library.

Mehra and Bishop (2007) chose all the 21 international students in the doctoral program of Library and Information Science (LIS) in an LIS institute in the U.S. to participate in the study. They conducted in-depth narrative interviews and had informal discussions with all the participants and applied grounded theory to analyze students' responses to questions such as: the importance of internationalization, how American LIS education can become more international, and the nature of internationalizing activities in which participants were involved.

Mehra and Bishop (2007) conclude that "two-way learning from case-participants yielded valid perspectives in terms of providing voice to an under-represented population that was directly being impacted by US-centric educational conditions" (p. 20-21). They argue that two-way learning can be applied to various other contexts of study such as academic, corporate, organizational, and public sectors and that mutual respect and recognition of diverse knowledge bases and multicultural experiences can emerge from different parts of the world. Aside from benefitting the participants, one of the advantages of the approach is that people can really understand themselves from an outsider's point of view. This is particularly important in a globalizing era that requires people to avoid their ethnocentric views and respect different viewpoints, working collaboratively with people from different cultures towards a better future.

The Case of Exchange Students

Another study on exchange students done by Icbay and Kocayoruk (2011) was a larger scale of investigation. The researchers investigated 50 exchange students in Turkey. These students were from European Union countries, Australia, Canada,

Ukraine, and the United States, and they were funded by different student exchange programs to go to Turkey. The study aimed at investigating how exchange student mainly from Western countries adapted to Turkish culture and problems they might face during their study in Turkey. The researchers mainly interviewed students and read students' personal notes, and they focused their investigation on exchange students' experiences of adapting to a new culture setting and interacting with local people.

Icbay and Kocayoruk (2011) conclude "that adaptation to a new culture was a process of transforming the existing sense-making patterns into the ones that could function properly in the new setting" (p. 36). For the exchange students, it might be easier to adjust to basic living conditions within the new environment than to acquire new values and to change the existing beliefs and attitudes. However, generally speaking, "students were open to new culture and … their prejudices were broken down….[Although] moving to a new culture and establishing new interpersonal relations and social life is a stressful experience" (p. 37).

A significant point of Icbay and Kocayoruk's (2011) study concerning exchange students in Turkey lies in the fact that the home country and the host country are quite different in their cultures, religions, and life styles. The exchange students represented the North part of the globe, and the host students the South part. Although I sporadically mention the trends of regionalism throughout the book, it may be valuable to have the North meets the South (or say the Westerners meet the Easterners). Doesn't it sound strange and contradictory in a globalizing era that we insist to differentiate Global South from Global North? The significance of Icbay and Kocayoruk's study lies in that it draws people's attention to the real meaning of *globalization*. Globalization will not make sense if people from different cultures cannot respect each other's culture and if there are still dividing lines, such as North vs. South, developed vs. underdeveloped, and majority vs. minority, existing in the globe.

The Case of Collaboration in Higher Education

Still another yet well-structured cross-cultural collaboration in higher education is the University of Pacific (UOP) program in the United States. Brack (1993) describes the historical origins of the UOP program. There are three colleges within the UOP involved in overseas programs: Raymond, Covell, and Callison. Each of these internationally oriented colleges holds a particular focus on one part of the globe. For example, Raymond College stresses Euro-American studies, Covell was a bilingual unit concentrating on Latin America, while Callison focused upon non-Western/Asian studies.

Brack (1993) himself was assigned and was located at Callison College and was responsible for the overseas program to be involved in participant observation in Asian countries. I describe the program as being well-structured because it is governed by a very systematic and well-structured school system. Freshmen in these colleges are engaged in preparation for their study abroad in the sophomore year of college. When they come back as veteran juniors after a one-year overseas experience, they are eligible to share their overseas experiences and personal growth with freshmen who are preparing for their year abroad and exchange their overseas experiences with their peers. Brack explains that college sophomores are sent abroad as a group for study. Although they are abroad, they share a sense of community and camaraderie. That is, they are going to the same nation.

One of the important points that Brack (1993) wants to make in the entire report is that integrating orientation and reentry in overseas programs can have a synergistic effect in students' entire learning process and personal and professional development. They argue that both during and after overseas experiences, students face the same issues, such as culture shock, identity, and stereotyping. Students have different types of culture shock when they are in a foreign country and when they go back to their home country (i.e., reverse culture shock), and they also perceive themselves and deal with the issues of stereotyping differently. In the discussions either in the orientation before students' departure for another country or in reentry after they come back from another country, as suggested by Brack, it may be a good practice to invite international students on the campus to join the discussion. On the one hand, they may provide useful cultural information concerning their own country and share their experiences of living in the host country. On the other hand, for those students returning from a host country, international students may explain and respond to questions concerning their countries and cultures raised by the returnees.

The Case of NUS Overseas Colleges and Its University Scholars Programme

An example of an alternative of overseas campuses is the one described by Pang (2009). Pang describes a study abroad program initiated by the National University of Singapore (NUS) called NUS Overseas Colleges. He explains that the Overseas Colleges are not really NUS's overseas campuses. Rather, it is a study abroad program in which NUS collaborates with well-known entrepreneurial hubs in the world and its partner universities close to the hubs. Students who participate in the program are required to take full-time internship with start-up companies in these entrepreneurial hubs, namely Silicon Valley, Philadelphia, Stockholm, Shanghai, and Bangalor. On the other hand, in the year abroad, students also have to take part-time courses at NUS's partner universities nearby, including "Stanford University, University of Pennsylvania, Royal Institute of Technology (Stockholm) Fudan University, and India Institute of Science" (p. 235).

Pang (2009) also describes NUS's University Scholars Programme (USP) which was founded in 2001. This program is a so-called honors program. According to Pang, participants of the program are required to attend some kinds of abroad activities, ranging "from double programs that require 2 years study abroad, to overseas field trips and summer programs that last for a week or more" (p. 235) and ranging from less formal to highly structured ones, including bicultural immersion, double degree programs, and exchange programs. Some of the programs will be discussed in other chapters for different focuses.

The Case of Science Majors Studying Abroad

Speaking of sciences, it is a common perception that sciences are less important and less logical in terms of study abroad and cross-cultural exchanges. It may be because of the universality of sciences, and place-specific knowledge and cultural differences in sciences are not as important as those in social sciences and humanities. However, as argued by Wainwright, Ram, Teodorescu, and Tottenham (2009), as studying abroad has become more and more popular and globalization of economic systems can be seen everywhere in the world, "the need and desire of undergraduates in the sciences to have international exposure and to learn about working in the global context has become more evident" (p. 381). They claim that science is seen as a global enterprise in that "international teams of scientists collaborate on traditionally defined problems and on emerging problems that have a global impact" (p. 382).

Wainwright, et al. (2009) describe the study abroad programs for science students at Emory University (EU). They roughly categorize these programs into three types: semester or year-long study abroad programs, faculty-led summer study programs, and independent research or internships overseas. EU collaborates with different countries in Africa, Australia, Asia, Europe, Latin America and the Caribbean, and Middle East. The researchers point to the potential differences in study abroad between science students and social science and humanity students. They claim that, unlike study abroad in the field of social sciences and humanities that may focus on language learning and cultural immersion, science faculty members pay much more attention to the effectiveness of the program and training of students. "Science faculty are passionate about their discipline, research, and teaching interests. They want to profile the quality of their graduate programs abroad to attract international students, and to connect researchers abroad who have complementary interests" (p. 387). On the other hand, some senior faculty members at EU are active researchers and they are responsible for operating labs. Therefore, probably short-term cross-border exchanges and lecturer track faculty are more feasible and practical.

Wainwright, et al. (2009) also point to some of the obstacles that EU faces in conducting study abroad programs in the area of sciences. First, they point out that because of the tight course schedule and sequence of science courses, science students feel unmotivated to attend study abroad programs. To turn the obstacle into opportunities, EU provides more flexible course options and develops a course equivalence database to facilitate students' choice of courses and minimize their confusion. The second obstacle came from science faculty's indifference in sending students to study abroad. It is partially because of the universality of sciences as mentioned earlier. On the other hand, science faculty members look for benefits of study abroad in the science field. For them, it is easier to measure students' improvement in language skills and cultural awareness in the field of social sciences and humanities than in the science field. In this regard, EU surveyed those science students who returned from study abroad, and luckily students' responses were quite positive. Finally, the obstacle was from some departments. Because they predominately define the objectives of study abroad as language and cultural learning, these departments give priority to some countries as destinations of study abroad. When designing study abroad programs, in addition to cross-cultural education, they found that "programs designed to join science related subject areas with research and practical experience have been very promising" (p. 393). For example, the Interdisciplinary Global Health Program in South Africa can be a good source of collaboration in the field of medical science and public health.

As mentioned earlier, the fields of sciences are quite different from those of social sciences and humanities in terms of studying abroad. Traditional perceptions are that scientific knowledge, such as chemistry, physics, math, and medical science are universal and that there is no need for science students to study abroad. However, Wainwright, et al. (2009) argue that science students need to study abroad and sciences need to go global. They use EU as their case study target to address the importance of moving science students to the global stage. In the part following this section, I do not describe how EU's study programs are developed and practiced. Instead, I describe and cite students' reflections on their study abroad experiences.

An example of science majors studying abroad is the summer chemistry studies program reflected on by Nicholas Justice on his study abroad in Siena, Italy. Justice's overseas experiences included taking courses, working on a research project with an Italian professor, and working as an intern in Italian vineyards. He describes that "the Siena experience was extremely valuable for my education and for my development both as a chemist and a person" (Wainwright, et al. 2009, p. 395). What has Justice learned in his overseas experience in Italy? He summarizes that he

> learned of inorganic chemistry in general, of instruction, of how to invent solutions quickly, of how to work in a small research group, of how the wine business is run, of how to differentiate different types of vine species, of how to behave respectfully and independently in a foreign environment, of how to meet and get along with very different people, and most of all the Italian language. (p. 395)

Justice's account clearly provides supporting evidence, showing that science majors should not be prevented from studying abroad. Students can learn a lot more beyond their professional domains in their experiences of studying abroad.

The Case of Study Abroad Program for First-Generation College Students

Martinez, Ranjeet, and Marx (2009) describe a study abroad especially organized for first-generation, low-income students. They argue that college should have equal access to study abroad. However, low-income and first generation college students are always excluded from participating in studying abroad activities. They explored the "barriers that inhibit student participation, which include: cost, lack of information about study abroad, family constraints, and individual limitations" (p. 529). They thus organized the Liverpool study abroad program, targeting at those less privileged students, at University of Connecticut. The program was tailored to meet the needs of low-income and first generation college students. By participating in the study abroad program, those students were able to go to the University of Liverpool in the United Kingdom.

Martinez et al. (2009) first describe how they created a culture that values study abroad among those students. First, they needed to promote study abroad. For students from low-incoming families, they had never thought of studying abroad because of many reasons. The team had to convince students and their parents that it is not impossible for the students to participant in a study abroad and the school will assist them to achieve the goal. They provided useful information and invited past participants of study abroad programs to help students better understand study abroad programs. Second, faculty members tried hard to intervene and help students in their process of making a decision, preparing required documents, and planning for their trip. Most importantly, they needed to establish students' confidence and empower them with required skills needed for studying abroad. Finally, it came the financial issues. The advisers of this program "openly discuss the costs of the program, the scholarship awards, and the expected student contribution" (p. 536). They believed they had to make the program financially accessible to first-generation college students if the study abroad program is valuable investments for them.

To meet the special needs of the group of students, Martinez et al. (2009) first developed programs culturally relevant to low-income, first-generation college students. Because of the financial needs and needs to support their families, it may not be practical for these students to stay abroad for one semester or even one year. A summer-long program may be appropriate for them. Second, the program content was also developed based on students' needs and interests. For example, Martinez et al. states that "many of our African American and Latino students…have developed an interest in issues of social justice and contemporary race relations" (p. 538). Therefore, their "3-week program at the University of Liverpool is titled 'Black Roots in Liverpool'" (p. 538), and students learned that the globe is actually an interconnected world. Finally, Martinez et al. suggest that faculty advisers need develop bond with the students and assist them all the way in their preparation for the trip. In the trip in a foreign country, faculty advisers' accompanying along side may let students feel a sense of security and certainty.

The Case of Student Teachers Studying Abroad

Smolcic and Martin (2018) describe another type of involving student teachers in overseas experiences. Seventeen pre-service teachers attending an American university were assigned to a period of sojourn, or immersion, in Ecuador as part of their teacher training. The activities included experiencing Ecuadorian culture and learning Spanish or Kichwa by staying with Ecuadorian families and field trips to Ecuadorian cultural sites. On the other hand, these participants visited and observed local schools and taught ESL students there. Data were collected before, during, and after the immersion, including interviews, dialogue journals, meetings with program advisors, group discussions, and teaching observations.

Findings of the study show that the overseas immersion experiences prove to be important and valuable in teachers' development. Smolcic and Martin (2018) divide the development into three domains: immersion domain, curricular domain, and teaching practice domain. In the immersion domain, homestay experiences allowed students to learn "about Ecuadorian customs routines and values" (p. 195) that may benefit their cognitive and intercultural development. On the other hand, because they were also learning Spanish or Kichwa, they experienced the way how language learners or how language minorities feel or are discriminated against and they have a better understanding of the situation of their students when they go back to the U.S. to teach ESL students at home. This can be identified as intrapersonal development. In the curricular domain, students developed their intercultural and global competencies. According to Smolcic and Martin, "the curriculum emphasized links among international and domestic diversity while highlighting the socially constructed nature of cultural identity and the role of political ideology in language learning and cultural experiences" (p. 198). In this regard, participants of the immersion program showed a change from a more ethnocentric view towards America to a more global view that values and respects different cultures. Some participant students do not see America as a 'melting pot' and do not assume the idea of US superiority; others define a bilingual as "someone who wants to be part of two cultures" (p. 199) and they do not even think that English being the dominant world language will last forever. Smolcic and Martin ascribe students' change to the application of reflective ways of curricular design in which the instructors provided guided prompts for students to respond to and to reflect upon. By doing so, students were allowed to show their interpersonal development. In the teaching practice domain, participant students were required to teach local students in Ecuador for five weeks as part of the teaching practicum. In this practice, in addition to learning how to develop a lesson plan, they learned how to teach English as a second or foreign language to non-native English speakers. Most importantly, because student teachers themselves were 'language minorities" in a Spanish-speaking environment, they learned to put themselves in other's shoes and developed empathy in terms of language and cultural learning. This reflection and awareness can be of great help in their future teaching career back in America.

The Case of International Teaching Assistants (ITAs)

It is not uncommon, especially in the United States, that international graduate students are assigned to be a teaching assistant to work with undergraduate students in their academic learning process. Under this circumstance, international teaching assistants (ITAs) need to learn the teaching norms and culture and students' expectations in the host country, on the one hand. On the other hand, they themselves might be struggling with using a new language in the classroom. Williams and Case (2016) describe some useful mentoring strategies that may help ITAs socialize into US higher education norms so that they may fully participate in the new institutional community. They claim that ITA training activities provided by the department can be more discipline-specific and pedagogically-based and more personal, and they propose that departmental mentoring can provide ITAs with mastery of the content knowledge and pedagogy. On the other hand, departmental mentoring "can help raise ITAs' awareness of the students' cultural and content background in order to facilitate instruction for their students" (p. 159).

Participants of Williams and Case's (2016) study included 20 ITAs from 15 different countries in 13 different teaching fields. They had an average of three years' teaching experience. These participants were interviewed and were observed in their teaching process. Generally speaking, these ITAs were helped through departmental mentoring by being provided with previous teaching materials and syllabi, assigned to teach courses, and they had chances to observe senior professors' teaching and were also observed by their supervisors to get feedback from them. Participants were interviewed at the end of the study.

Findings of the study showed that departmental mentoring benefitted ITAs a lot by providing them with useful materials needed in their teaching process, such as instructional materials, lesson plans, and syllabi. On the other hand, observing senior teachers' teaching and being observed by their departmental mentors also benefitted ITAs a lot. By observing their mentors' teaching, ITAs were provided "with a real-life view of what American teaching norms looked like" (p. 163). The same is true for being observed by their supervisors. ITAs, by getting feedback from experienced professors, got to know the strengths and weaknesses of their teaching, and "personalized critique with the opportunity to discuss strategies for improving their instruction is more helpful than the numerical rating of student evaluation" (p. 165).

It is without doubt that there are gaps between mentors and mentees. As described by Williams and Case (2016), it happens that professors and ITAs had different perceptions of and attitudes towards some teaching strategies or principles, especially ITAs were from countries of a culture different from that of the United States. Another issue was that ITAs were not familiar with the educational system in the United States, and did not know what college freshmen had gone through in terms of academic knowledge in their high school years. This has led to problems in their teaching of college freshmen, for example they provided students with either too easy or too difficult materials. They were not "aware of the appropriate level and typical materials used in the undergraduate classroom (p. 169).

The Case of International Volunteering

An alternative of study abroad may be international volunteering. Staying in a foreign country for a short period of learning, but not to attend school, actually has a long history in the educational field. As earlier as the sixteenth and seventeenth century, the so-called Grand Tour was quite popular among youths in England then. They financially support themselves and travel to other countries to learn. For example, according to Bevis and Lucas (2007), the frequently chosen countries were France, Switzerland, Italy, and Germany. The experiences abroad were quite helpful for their future job searching. For employers or administrators, having the ability to make one's own financial arrangement travelling abroad and having experiences of different cultures may be great traits in one's future career.

Similar to the Grand Tour, international volunteering may be a good choice for some students. For those students who may consider one or more years' study abroad is too long for them in terms of their financial arrangement and planning of academic schedule. Jones (2010) proposes that volunteering abroad for a short period of time, say three months in the summer, may be a good choice. For example, Jones describes a short-term international volunteering program offered by Leeds Metropolitan University in U.K. According to the students interviewed, the experience of international volunteering is quite different from those of study abroad. In some cases, volunteer students were arranged to stay with a host family. They may learn language, culture, and cross-cultural communication skills. On the other hand, because volunteering always works in groups, group empathy may be developed while working together abroad. Participants cooperate and collaborate and offer mutual support. Some other personal transformations that occurred in international volunteering may include "putting oneself in the shoes of others, being in the minority, sharing humanity, finding connections, reviewing one's own culture assumptions, and considering other perspectives" (p. 92). In addition to learning about self and others, volunteers were able to make use of the skills they developed in their volunteering and transfer these skills to new cross-cultural contacts. These skills may include "patience, sensitivity, meditation skills, team work and organizational skills" (p. 87).

Ngo (2014) also discusses Canadian youth volunteering abroad. She first describes that since "the 1960s, over 65,000 young Canadians have participated in volunteer abroad programs; this number continues to expand each year as young people travel to developing countries for a variety of reasons" (p. 49). There are more than 20 volunteer-sending organizations in Canada. These volunteering abroad activities aim at cross-cultural exchanges and development of global citizenship. Ngo summarizes potential benefits of international volunteering claimed by many researchers "that include language enhancement, transformative learning, building contacts between individuals and communities, developing cross-cultural understanding and working across difference" (p. 56). Aside from these benefits, international volunteering may provide volunteers with travel opportunities and has the potential to reduce conflict between former colonizing countries and colonized countries.

However, Ngo (2014) also takes a very critical view and addresses the problems of international volunteering from her standpoint. She argues with evidence that issues of power and privilege may destroy the potentially good-intended international volunteering. First of all, international volunteering should be beneficial for both the volunteer-sending country and the host country. However, most research reports focus on the gains of volunteers and what the sending-organizations have done. Little has been explored as to how the volunteer work may have impact on the host country. Second, there is always inequitable power relation between the sending country and the host country. It is always the case that volunteers and the sending organization conceive that they can offer people in the developing countries or "the third world" what they really need in spite of their lack of knowledge of the host country and familiarity with the language they need to communicate within the host community. Third, most importantly, inequity exists in the volunteer business. Sending organizations do not really provide adequate training pedagogy to enhance cross-cultural understanding. Generally speaking, they promote multiculturalism rather than reduce racism and stereotypes. Under this circumstance, volunteers may regard their volunteering work as one kind of favor done to disprivileged "others," and they may mistakenly exert their power and privilege in their volunteering work. For those who are interested in international volunteering, Ngo proposes a framework of justice oriented and anti-racist citizen. She suggests individuals should transform themselves to have a better understanding of the role they play in a volunteering context and how to interact with local people to create an outcome that both volunteers and the community they serve may benefit from.

In addition to having a positive attitude towards volunteering, one of the most important issues in the course of volunteering is safety and health. Hartman, Kiely, Boettcher, and Friedrichs (2018) point out some risks that international volunteers may encounter, such as kidnapping, natural disaster, terrorism, pickpockets, sex harassment, protests, strikes, roadblocks, road safety, and other risks relevant to individual's health condition, including malaria, yellow fever, dengue, bilharzia, polio, and altitude sickness. For all the possible risks, Hartman, et al. insist that prevention is much more important than cure. Being well-prepared before the volunteering journey can ensure your health, safety, and security in the host country. There are organizations or departments in your home country and some global support networks that provide important and up-to-date information about the country you plan to visit. As participants or leaders of a volunteering group, you need to do homework before heading for the host country to ensure a healthy, safe, and valuable experience.

In all the accounts of student mobility discussed above, we conclude that, as a student, there are a considerable number of ways to have overseas experience. In a globalizing era, colleges and universities all over the world are eager to diversify their campus and they welcome enrollment of international students. For college administrators, international students not only benefit the school's finances, but also enhance the school's reputation and diversify and enrich the community and society (Amirali & Bakken, 2005). The above cases reveal that to study abroad is both a blessing and a challenge. Being an international student in a foreign country can be a great experience to learn a new language and a new culture firsthand, and, on the other hand, international students may contribute their unique experiences and the knowledge they bring from their home country. However, adapting to a new culture can be a challenge to all international students. As a practitioner of cross-cultural exchanges, you may need to take all relevant issues into consideration and work out a win-win consequence. In the following section, I move to the discussions of some challenges participants or practitioners of study abroad may face.

Challenges of Study Abroad

In this section, I discuss challenges of study abroad at the individual, institutional, and national level. At the individual level, overseas students may face issues such as racism and stereotype and the so-called reverse cultural shock in their reentry to this home country. At the institutional level, the school may face the competition of recruiting international students and supporting its students for studying abroad. At the national level, policies concerning study abroad and recruiting international students may have impacts causing brain-drain or brain-gain. In this section, I discuss different challenges at different levels.

Issues of Racism and Stereotype

An important issue that may directly affect the quality of study abroad is *racism* and *stereotype*. Punteney (2017) indicates that people tend to label or categorize people in society and decide who are in a particular group and who are not. We tend to attribute some characteristics to a particular group and its group members. Part of the potential of this is that we are inclined to overemphasize the similarities among group members and differences between groups. For practitioners of intercultural learning or activities, this human tendency to assign identity to groups may provide them with guides to manage administrative tasks and somehow show respect to the group's culture, such as foods and religious rituals. However, in this way, we overlook the multicultural nature of individuals, including family and educational backgrounds, gender, personality, and physical appearance. On the other hand, the tendency to generalize groups may lead to stereotyping. Ritter (2016) describes some racial conflicts that occurred on campuses between local students and international students in the U.S., Australia, Japan, China, and many other countries. Aside from physical racial conflicts, racism and stereotypes are actually prevailing everywhere on college campuses. He attributes the never-ending conflicts on the campus to the historical background cultivated in people's mind and media's influence. Ritter interviewed Chinese, Japanese, and Korean graduate and undergraduate international students who were attending University of California, Los Angeles (UCLA) to investigate how these international students perceived different racial groups since UCLA is considered rich in different racial groups in its student population.

Ritter's (2016) study found that these Asian students did bring with them racial prejudices and stereotypes. The historical backgrounds these students have learned, e.g., Chinese nationalism, Sino-Barbarian dichotomy, colonialism, and the media influences, e.g., promoting and reinforcing the image of different ethnic groups such as White people, African Americans, Latinos, and Asian-Americans on TV or other mass media did contribute significantly to the construction of racial and socio-economic hierarchies in these Asian international students' mind. Interviewing with these Asian international students, Ritter found that a racial hierarchy has been created in these students' mind, with African-American and Africans in the lowest status and Latinos come slightly above them. Then come Asian-Americans and white people, including Americans and European people who are on the top of the hierarchy. The hierarchy is relevant to their decision on romantic dating, making friends, and interacting with people.

To challenge international students' stereotypes, UCLA student services applies some strategies, such as providing interracial living spaces, international center programs, and courses on race and diversity. For those students interviewed, these arrangements did change their previous stereotypes and their perceptions of a particular ethnic group, African American, for example. By rooming with people from different cultures, attending international center programs and meeting with both domestic and international peers, and taking courses on race and diversity, these international students gained more understanding of other ethnic groups, got along with people from different cultures better, and had less stereotyped image of people from a different culture. Ritter (2016) urges American scholars and administrators to "look more closely at diversity issues surrounding international student populations" (p. 148) and provide more programs or chances for interracial interactions to eliminate those negative images and stereotypes existing in our mind.

Probably racism, or racial discrimination, is a slightly different issue, although it is connected with stereotyping. In some cases, some particular groups are easily treated unfairly or unfriendly in some regions or countries. In literature relevant to study abroad, cases of racial discrimination are often reported. If you, a visitor of a foreign country, happen to be a victim of racial discrimination, you need to follow the rules or regulations of that country and seek for fair treatment. In an era moving towards globalization and increasingly growing mobile population, many countries are sensitive in protecting people from being racially discriminated. However, viewed from a different perspective, racism can be seen as two sides of a coin. How you behave or communicate with people can be reflected on how people treat you or perceive you. As a student attending an overseas school, you need to be aware of cultural differences and the rules or regulations practiced in the classroom or on the campus. In this case, chances are you will avoid misunderstandings and, hence, racial discrimination.

Issues of Reentry and Needs for Adjustment to the Home Culture

Kartoshkina (2017) views culture shock and reentry from a neuroscientific perspective. She states that people experience culture shock because they have developed their neural networks in their brain adjusted to their home culture before they encounter a new culture in a foreign country. In a new cultural environment, they need to develop new neural networks to adjust to a new environment. The same is true when they go back to their home country. They need to readapt to their home culture, and they tend to apply newly-developed neural networks abroad to their home culture environment and feel uncomfortable at home. "They may miss the people they met and the experiences they enjoyed in the host culture" (p. 101). Having overseas experiences for a period, students may need to adjust to their home environment when they reenter the place with which they were familiar before. Martin (1993) presents a communication-centered approach proposed by Kim to address returning sojourners' adaption to their home culture after returning to their home country. She demonstrates that re-entry adaption includes four dimensions : predisposition of the returning sojourner, such as the person's cultural background, personality attributes and his or her preparedness for change; home environment characteristics, such as the degree of openness and acceptance and social segregation; communication of the returning sojourner, including the person's communication competence, interpersonal communication with members of home culture and with other returning sojourners, and mass communication consumption in home culture and from former host culture; and readaption outcomes, such as the sojourner's readaption outcomes, his or her psychological health, functional fitness and intercultural identity.

Brack (1993), on the other hand, argues that orientation and reentry should be integrated as a training unit. He argues that, like those who are experiencing culture shock in a foreign country, those returnees are actually experiencing a certain degree of *reentry shock*. Brack considers a reentry program is an integral part of intercultural training and should be integrated with orientation. For those students who are preparing for their overseas study ahead, orientation is to some extend abstract and imaginative. Returning to their home country after one year's overseas experience, returnees may compare their pre- and post-experience over a long period of cross-cultural encounter. In retrospect, returnees may reflect on their personal change and growth and may share as an expert with those who are preparing for their year abroad. For the school, the long-term effect of overseas study program is worth investigating. Hartman, Kiely, Boettcher, and Friedrichs (2018) term linking pre- and post-intercultural experience in international cultural training the "sandwich model." This model "involves academic preparation and processing before and after travel experience including intercultural immersion" (p. 65). Pang (2009) also argues that we "need to track what students do after study abroad, and, much more problematically, try to tease out how their transformation (if any) is due to the study abroad experience" (p. 242). He demonstrates some outcomes of study abroad he investigated. For example, some study-abroad participants started volunteering at health care centers or hospitals after their study abroad experience; whereas others founded "the West, Asian and North African Interest Group....and has organized trips to Yemen as well as a language immersion program in Oman" (p. 242).

In line with Brack (1993) and Pang (2009), Jones (2010) and Hoult (2018) also consider post-visit reflection is as important as pre-departure preparation. Jones urges investigations of whether the transformation is enduring and has long-term effects on the participants as a result of overseas experiences. Hault, on the other hand, describes many changes that his participant students made after their overseas experience, for example, "increased confidence and an ability to critique matters, ...desire to teach overseas; ...volunteering with the homeless; changed approach to teaching about development; ...working with disadvantaged children in the UK; and...to reconnect with her family" (p. 83). He argues that post experience interventions, such as interviewing and reflective writing, are essential to provoke sustained learning.

Issues of Competition in the International Student Market

At the institutional level, as reported by many scholars, the international students in higher education are getting more and more competitive due to the development of modern technologies and the convenience of transportation and due to the changes in politics, economy, society, and education in a globalizing era (Dennis, 2018; Agarwal, 2008; Amiral & Bakken, 2015; Maringe & Foskett, 2010; Sakamoto & Chapman, 2011; Olcott, 2009). In order to survive and sustain in the global community, higher education institutions around the world are trying hard to recruit international students and, on the other hand, to encourage and support their students for studying abroad to develop a global view and to gain global access to different domains. The increasing growing competition in the international students market has led to a decrease in the market share of the United States and the United Kingdom, once the leading importers of international students (Dennis, 2018). On the other hand, the growing number of middle classes in Asia also has contributed to the increase of student mobility in Asia. Dennis states that national "visa and immigration policies, coordinated regional and national marketing campaigns, availability of scholarships and employment after graduation" (p. 10) are some of the factors that may affect students' decision for the destination of study abroad.

In addition to different recruiting strategies used to attract international students, in a globalizing era, many countries resort to the so-called "soft power," such as cultural diplomacy, to attract international students. Jordan (2018) describes "soft power" as cultural elements used to attract and affect others to get the outcomes you expect, rather than using coercion or threats. Cultural diplomacy can be viewed as one kind of soft power, which makes use of one nation's particular cultural elements to establish relationships and understandings with other nations and win the hearts and minds of their people (Jordan, 2018). In the case of the United States, Jordan describes the American experience of cultural diplomacy. As early as the era before the Cold War, the United States had been sending students and artists abroad through exchanges programs and helped terminate the Cold War. In the educational domain, the United States also developed many educational and cultural exchange programs. Among them is the Fulbright program as described earlier in this chapter. Jordan, maintains that impacts on economic growth and foreign relations may not be seen in a short-term period. However, at the individual level, Fulbrighters were reported to have considerable growth both personally and professionally.

Cross-cultural exchange programs also take place in other regions of the world, such as those between France and Germany. According to Jordan (2018), France and Germany have been maintaining a very good relationship through cultural diplomacy. They have been "twinning" their cities and have had civic, student, and sports exchanges. Students on these cross-cultural experiences contribute to attitude change. As people from different cultures get closer to each other, they gain mutual understanding and learn from each other.

Issues of Support of Study Abroad

From the discussions in earlier sections, we can find that there are considerable ways, purposes, and destinations for students to choose from, especially if we define "study abroad" in a broader sense to mean "study" as one way of informal learning. In a seemly globalized world, as Bevis and Lucas (2007) point out, there is an increasingly growing global competition in higher education in the market of international students. Several decades ago, the United States were seen to be the destination prioritized by students who were interested in studying abroad. However, many nations have been working hard to recruit international students, such as the United Kingdom, Australia, New Zealand, Japan, and Canada. They use different strategies and provide different supports, such as low tuition fee, permanent residence, and scholarships, to attract international students. For students who are seeking opportunities to study abroad, it can be good news that their choice of the host nation has been widen up (Dennis, 2018). *Supports* in this section is used in a broader sense to mean financial, academic, and other forms of support and to mean supports both from the home country and from the host country.

Currier et al.'s (2009) discussion of study abroad focuses on the nursing profession. The researchers do not really demonstrate certain types of study abroad and report on a particular case of study abroad; rather, they review a considerable number of studies on study abroad in nursing. They argue that in an era of globalization, nursing professionals especially need to possess cultural awareness. These researchers argue that nursing professionals need to move from being culturally competent to globally competent. They insist that integrating cultural elements into nursing curricula is definitely insufficient in terms of being globally competent. They argue that "nursing and health care are global issues that require an awareness of the complex cultural, social, political, and economic interrelationships within and between nations, and the moral obligations that unite us as a world community" (p. 133). The research findings on study abroad in the nursing field have shown that study abroad in a nation of a different culture is superior to international immersion programs conducted in the U.S. in terms of students' development of global competence.

Currier et al. (2009) point to some ongoing challenges practitioners of study abroad in the nursing profession might face. First, the nursing curricular arrangements tend to offer less flexible options. Students who are interested in having nursing experiences abroad probably need to think about choosing a summer or a short-term program offered on a non-credit basis. Another challenge that nursing students or faculty might face is about funding. Study abroad costs money. According to Currier et al., "grant support to find international travel to develop new programs is frequently difficult to obtain" (p. 146). For nursing students, the cost for participation in study abroad programs is considerably high, and the current American economy further prevents students from pursuing nursing experiences in a foreign country.

Currier et al.'s (2009) discussions on issues of institutional support for study abroad focuses on the nursing profession. However, these issues are also apparent in other domains, for example, the science fields mentioned earlier. It is important the higher education institutions need to consider their supports to student mobility from different aspects so that these supports can really benefit students in their decision to study abroad.

Issues of Brain-Drain, Brain-Gain, and Brain-Circulation

We now move to the national level of challenges faced by a country. At the national level, a country may face issues of brain-drain and brain gain in practicing study abroad programs. Welch (2011) describes the situation in Malaysia. In the history of Malaysia's higher education, the country first suffered brain-drain in the 1960s and early 1970s. Because Malaysia is a member of the Commonwealth and many Malaysians speak good English, they mostly chose the United Kingdom and Australia as destinations of overseas study. The popularity of gaining a foreign degree at that time and very few international students attending Malaysian universities had caused the Malaysia government problems with brain-drain. Not until the time of economic crisis, when Malaysian people had less financial resources to support their overseas study, and not until Malaysia government applied considerable strategies to attract foreign students did Malaysia strike a balance between Malaysian students studying abroad and international students attending universities in Malaysia. As well-described by Welch (2011), in "the much-touted new knowledge economy of the future, no country can afford not to cultivate and celebrate all its talent" (p. 83).

The issue of brain-drain in the Philippines is no less serious than that of Malaysia. Ironically, the "current government strategy is to export more and more of its workers to the world in order to profit from the remittances they send home" (Welch, 2011, p. 117). The issue of brain-drain was even more significant in the 1980s. Both educated and less-skilled workers are moving abroad. Those educated Filipinos are mostly nurses and doctors. As described by Welch, "only one in four doctors trained in the Philippines eventually settled permanently in the Philippines during the 1980s, while the trend was similar among the rare PhDs in the science and technology areas" (p. 118). Generally speaking, their destinations of permanent residence or citizenship are North America, Europe and Oceania. Reasons for educated Filipinos to seek for greener pastures may be, as stated by Welch, bad working conditions and some sociopolitical factors at home, such as toadying, politics and connections.

Viewing from a different perspective, whether brain drain or brain gain, Agarwal (2008) calls the phenomenon "brain circulation." For example, in the case of India, many Indian skilled professionals, e.g., IT personnel, seek to get their higher degree and settle down permanently in advanced countries such as the United States and the United Kingdom. The most apparent example was "the 'brain drain' from India to Silicon Valley" (p. 104). However, Agarwal describes the phenomenon as being

> transformed into a more complex, two way process of 'brain circulation' that links Silicon Valley to information technology hubs at Bangaluru, Hyderabad, or Kolkata....A majority of Indian immigrants in Silicon Valley seriously planned to start businesses in India in the future." (p. 104)

This reverse brain drain phenomenon in India is also apparent in that many Indianan Americans are going back to India for short-term or permanent work.

The case of India has shown that we need to redefine the concept of "brain drain." Agarwal (2008) views brain drain from a positive perspective. Traditionally, we can consider brain drain as loss of talent to other countries. However, in a globalizing world, a "country's well-being can be considered its talent pool spread globally, thus contributing to the country's interests abroad and to its home economy through the infusion of funds and cutting-edge ideas" (p. 104). In a sense, migrants in host societies can form effective networks and, if well-managed, can contribute to the development of their home country.

Bano (2018) views the issues of brain drain and brain gain from a broader and comparative perspective. She points to historically a shift of brain drain from South Asian countries to the United States, the United Kingdom, and European Countries. Based on the theory of human capital, which considers individuals' talent and knowledge important "contributor in sustaining a nation's global competitiveness' (p. 67). Historically, the United States, the United Kingdom, and some European countries are target destinations for Asian students seeking opportunities to study abroad, and those same Asian students chose to stay in the host country after their completion of study because of better job opportunities, living standard, and professional growth in the host country. The situation has gradually changed. Many Asian students chose to return to their home countries and contributed to their own countries in their countries' economical and technological development and advancement in higher education as well. Bano attributes the phenomenon to the growth of knowledge economies and competitiveness of higher education in the global market. Under this circumstance, she implies that the United States, on the one hand, needs to attract more international students to study there and, on the other hand, it needs to train their own local professionals. In Asian countries, in an age of knowledge economies, they are facing different issues, such as aging population and needs to establish education hub and recruiting foreign workers. From the discussions in this section, it is apparent that the situation of brain drain and brain gain has been changing and will keep changing in accordance with the development of globalization. It is necessary for country leaders to keep track of the changes so as to make the most essential changes for the country.

TEACHER MOBILITY: TEACHING INTERNATIONAL STUDENTS AT HOME AND TEACHING ABROAD

In addition to student mobility, teacher mobility is also an important part of international migration in the field of education. Teacher mobility may diversify the campus, create employment opportunities, provide faculty and students with intercultural experiences, and complement local and foreign educational practices. In this section, teacher mobility is defined in a broader sense to include all teachings involving students from different cultures. This may include using videoconferencing to lecture students in another country, staying in one's own country and teaching international students in the classroom, or going abroad and teaching local students in another country. In some cases, teachers might not physically move to another country. However, its significance cannot be overlooked in terms of its impacts on education in a globalizing era.

Vigilance (2012) states that there may be "a direct correlation between the migration of teachers and shortages of teachers within the educational system" (p. 6). Other impacts of teacher mobility can be seen in brain circulation and remittances. Generally speaking, teacher migration can be associated with brain drain (in the case of skilled and experienced teachers seeking to teach in other countries) or brain gain (in the case of experienced or professional teachers being recruited to teach in the host country). However, if teacher migration is viewed as a dynamic activity, then, as Vigilance states, we can term the activity *brain circulation.* On the one hand, exchange of teachers can benefit both the sending country and the receiving country in the education arena; on the other hand, teacher migration may have "the potential of remittances..., opportunities for increased international trade and investment; and the prospect of migration encouraging greater uptake of education" (p. 7). However, there are also problems with teacher migration. Vigilance also raises the issues of having migrant teachers in the schools. On the one hand, migrant teachers are always recruited to teach in the school for a short period, and they have to be replaced by newly-qualified teachers after they complete their teaching assignment and leave the host country. Experience loss can be an issue. On the other hand, students may have developed close relationships with their local teachers and may be used to the way their local teachers teach. These issues may challenge school leaders in a globalizing era. As stated by Ochs (2012), imbalance between teacher supply and teacher demand may drive either recruitment or export of teachers. It can cause serious problems if local teachers choose to leave their home country and teach overseas while their home country has problems with teacher shortage.

The Case of Lecturing via Videoconferencing

There are several ways that teachers from different cultures can work collaboratively to benefit different groups of students. For example, teachers from different cultures may lecture to each other's class via videoconferencing or they may physically visit a foreign country and teach there for a short period. George (1995) points out that traditional lecturing in the classroom, although may be warned against by some learning theorists, remains the most common form of teaching. However, she also points out that there are some problems with classroom lecturing if this is your primary teaching method, for student attention, comprehension and memory decrease as the lecture proceeds, lecturing reinforces passive listing and discourages the practice of critical thinking, and non-native English speaking students often have difficulties with comprehension of lecture material delivered in English. As mentioned earlier in this chapter, international teachers also require sufficient cultural awareness. Wiggan and Hutchison (2009) have pointed out some issues international teachers might face, "including differences in communication styles, teaching styles, teacher-student relationships, school organization, and assessment" (p.11). Teachers cannot assume a one-size-fits-all pedagogy. They need to adjust their teaching method based on the nature of their student population.

In case lecturing is part of your program agenda, then partner teachers may serve as exchange teachers to lecture via videoconferencing. This can minimize the problems of lecturing mentioned above. First, with a sense of novelty, students may pay more attention to the partner teacher. Second, lecture materials developed by partner teachers may address one issue from different perspectives. It is helpful for the development of students' critical thinking and global view. Finally, for non-native speakers of the instructional language, students may have a better understanding of the contents of the instruction if they can play and re-play the video-tape of the lecture.

Another issue of teachers' lecturing online is the transition from classroom teaching skills to online teaching skills. Exchange teachers, who only lecture students in a different country based on limited collaborative project, may not be familiar with some online teaching skills as those distance education or online teachers are. Peachy (2017) argues that teachers who will teach online need to be prepared for the transition. He suggests that online teachers first need to learn some basics of operating the facilities and how to make the best appearance and most appropriate behaviors online. To achieve the goal, Peachey recommends that observation and teacher training are required. By observing other online teachers' presentation or watching instructional videos of others or one's own may benefit online teachers for further improvement. Peachey suggests that communities for online teachers can be organized so that they can learn from each other and can eliminate a sense of isolation.

An example of lecturing via videoconferencing is the study done by Wu and Marek (2010). Their study involved Taiwanese college students enrolled in an English conversation class. This conversation class featured its live videoconference interactions between Taiwanese EFL students and a native English speaker as the teacher. Wu and Marek found that, in addition to improving their oral skills, EFL students also showed greater confidence and heightened motivation in their learning of English as a foreign language. In the case of learning English in a non-English speaking environment, it may be a good arrangement to schedule a native English speaker to address the class via videoconferencing. In this case, heightened motivation is the key, rather than the improvement of language proficiency. Language proficiency cannot be improved in a short period, say listening to or communicating with native speakers of the target language. Rather, being highly motivated to learn the target language can be enduring and have a long-term effect on language learning.

The Case of Teaching International Students at Home

As study mobility is increasingly growing in a globalizing era, it is not uncommon that you as a classroom teacher have students who come from other countries. If this is the case, you cannot just follow the way you teach your local students. You need to be particularly aware of differences between teaching local students and teaching a culturally diverse class. In a culturally diverse class, at least, you need to be aware of international student identity, understand cultural differences, and apply different teaching strategies.

International Student Identity

Chang and Gomes's (2017) accounts of international student identity in a digital environment focus on international students working on academic degrees in a foreign country. Generally speaking, these students often stay longer in a foreign country, or even move to another country, than other transient migrants whose purposes for going abroad may be volunteering, working on holidays, or short-term stay or research visits. Teachers who are teaching students from diverse cultural backgrounds cannot ignore the identity or identities they carry with them to the classroom. Identity, according to Chang and Gomes (2017), actually is not so simple. It may include "multiple factors such as ethnicity, culture, nationality, gender, sexuality, socioeconomic conditions, personality, personal interests, and more" (p. 39). For international student identity, it is even more complex "because students have more than one identity" (p. 39).

International student identity can be best described in the term *translocality*, which refers to different phenomena that not limited to national boundaries such as mobility, migration, and circulation. Chang and Gomes (2017) argue that traditional models of identity formation did not take the current issues of mobility in a globalizing era into account and only "have limited value in the digital age" (p. 41). For example, in the digital age, "international students have the means, time, and resources to maintain daily contact with people back home and those they meet along the way in the home country" (p. 40). In the digital world, international students from a digital community and feel a sense of belonging, especially if they move from non-West to West or the Global South to the Global North. They rely on social media to get information, to participate as members of a specific digital community, and to entertain. However, Chang and Gomes also point out that social media communities developed by international students may have potential barriers to the integration of international students with local students.

Given the complexity of international student identity, teachers with international students in their classroom need to be aware that international students form multiple identities in the host country. On the one hand, they need to interact with local people and explore local cultural in the host country. On the other hand, they need to be closely connected with their family and friends back home with whom they have strong linguistic and cultural bonds. Furthermore, like any other people, international students also possess various identities simultaneously, which is termed intersectionality of identity, including gender, religion, sexuality, field of study, socio-economic status, occupation, and a lot more (Punteney, 2017). Educators need to be aware of international students' special needs, and digital communities can be good resources to meet international students' different needs. One international student who attended a university in Denmark quoted by Rogers and Steinfatt recounts

> After 12 years in Denmark, I can understand/relate to Danish in environment more than my own culture. But I don't feel 100% Danish. In Denmark, I feel like I'm a stranger and in my own country I feel the same. I am somehow caught in between." (Slethoug & Vinther, p. 82)

This phenomenon is actually found in many cases. For example, in the United States, Chinese Americans always consider themselves "banana," meaning they are yellow in their skin, i.e., being Asians in their appearance, and white in their mind, they behave like Americans.

To effectively work with international students in their intercultural learning, Punteney (2017) suggests some important traits that teachers or administrators who deal with international students on local campuses need to develop and some activities they may do. First and foremost, we as cross-cultural practitioners need to increase our self-awareness, including our values, perceptions, biases, and the norms of the groups we belong to. Most importantly, we need to continue to learn and to be self-critical. Second, we need to understand our students as individuals and as group members and recognize their various identities and the historical background of the countries where they are from. Third, we need to improve our engagement with students by learning their approaches to different aspects of their life. Be careful in language use when communicating with international students. Do not stereotype and use generalizations to assume that students in the same cultural group are the same. Fourth, it is our responsibility to help students develop their intercultural competence, create opportunities for students from different cultures to meet and learn from each other. By doing so, students may deconstruct their stereotypes. Finally, Punteney (2017) suggests that, in order to develop effective intercultural programs, we need to cooperate with relevant colleagues in relationships where "each person has equal status or opportunity to contribute" (p. 83). On the other hand, policies against biases and discriminations on campus are needed in order to create a safe and equal learning environment. Do not intentionally or unintentionally ignore or exclude some minority groups in any kind of activities or recruiting process.

Chang and Gomes (2017) describe that, although international students may adapt to the host culture and social norms, they tend to get together to form a community and identify themselves as international students. It seems that they feel "only other international students are able to understand what they are going through" (p. 45).

Understanding Cultural Differences

As mentioned earlier in Chapter 3, raising students' cultural awareness is important in a training program. The same is true for teachers who are teaching a culturally diverse class. Nathan (2013) dichotomizes cultural dimensions and stresses cultural differences between the Western world and the Eastern world as mentioned earlier. Although we do not want to let the cultural classification lead to racism or stereotypes and although we do believe that the comparison is relative, rather than absolute, it is true that international teachers need to be aware of cultural differences in their teaching process. Class structures, classroom interactions, teaching and learning styles, grading systems, power relations between teacher and student, and administrative supports may vary from nation to nation and from institution to institution. It may be wise for teachers to be flexible in their classroom instruction based on their student population. Raising students' cultural awareness and fair treatment of both local students and international students from different countries may be key to successful management of a culturally diverse class.

Gebhard (2017) provides some examples of cultural contrast that may be relevant to practice in the classroom. He points to different attitudes towards *time* between Americans and Arabs. Americans are generally strict to setting timeframe to start and end, say, a meeting or an activity, while Arabs may "flow" through time. They "do not always have fixed beginnings or endings" (p. 131) in social events or appointments. In this regard, Arabs may come to the class late and do not turn in assignments on time. Another example is differences in values and behaviors. Generally, "while some Americans value direct confrontation to solve conflicts, people from Asian countries generally value avoiding confrontations. They have developed subtle, indirect ways to solve conflict" (p. 131). In a culturally diverse classroom, American students may challenge the teacher's or the textbook's authority, while Asian students may remain quiet or express their ideas indirectly. Gebhard (2017) points out that the importance of understanding cultural differences is that not only we can understand other cultures, but also, by using other cultures as references, we can understand our own cultures and ourselves better.

Bücker, Bouw, and Beuckelaer (2018) investigate cross-cultural issues in culturally diverse classrooms in Dutch business schools. They insist that a culturally diverse classroom is a society in miniature, especially those future business managers may need to deal with people from different cultures in the business field. Bücker et al. interviewed business administers from different schools to explore the underlying issues in culturally diverse classrooms. They found that business schools were facing some cultural-related challenges. In an era that requires internationalizing the campus, it is inevitable that students from different cultures sit in the same classroom and learn together. Traditionally, it is perceived as a good chance for students to learning each other's language and culture and to develop their worldview. However, as Bücker et al. point out, mere "exposure to multiple cultures does not automatically result in successful intercultural interaction" (p. 120). In culturally diverse classrooms, interviewees point to a monoculture phenomenon. That is, integration of foreign students with domestic Dutch students appear to be problematic. "Dutch students prefer to work with Dutch students; Germans prefer to work with Germans. Students in large groups of international students have the tendency to stick together" (p. 125). It seems that students show prejudices towards other cultures.

As far as teaching and learning are concerned, Bücker et al. (2018) state that, generally speaking, international students have less problems with the contents to learn and the requirements for the degree. However, they have more problems with the teaching and learning style. For example, Asian students are not used to participating in classroom discussions and are lack of critical thinking skills and sometimes they copy from existing documents and paste them to their own assignments.

From the discussions above, Bücker et al. (2018) argue that, in a globalizing era and with the requirement to internationalize the campus, teachers need to process cross-cultural competences. To reach the goal, teacher training is required to keep teachers informed of specific cultural messages and the trends of globalization and internationalization. On the other hand, teachers themselves need to be aware that student population is getting more and more culturally diverse. They need to be sensitive to cultural issues, find problems, and provide solutions.

Applying Different Teaching Strategies

As mentioned above, in a culturally diverse class, you cannot just duplicate the way you teach your local students. International students carry with them different thought patterns, life and learning styles, knowledge backgrounds, levels of language proficiency, and religious beliefs, just to name some. On the other hand, teachers themselves may not experience or be familiar with all the cultural differences and may not be able to manage the international class. In this case, specific teaching strategies can be applied to make use of the rich and valuable cultural resources available in the classroom to enrich your teaching and students' learning. The following suggestions may be worthwhile taking into consideration.

If there are only a few international students in the class, you might want to schedule some class time for those international students to present their countries or cultures. The local students may be responsible for providing feedback, raising questions, and even comparing or introducing local cultures to international students. If you happen to have a large international student body in your class, then organize students into groups or pair international students and local students to work together on assigned tasks. McGrath-Champ, Zou, and Taylor (2013) provide very useful classroom activities to do so, namely team-based learning (TBL) and reflective journals. In team-based activities, to group the students, McGrath-Champ, et al. suggest to take "work and professional experience, nationality, gender, local or international student status and prior TBL experience" (p. 30) into consideration. That is, the more diversified the group, the better. In this case, students can enhance their intercultural capabilities and communication and negotiation skills and learn to solve problems collaboratively and from different perspectives. In addition to team-based learning, McGrath-Champ et al. (2013) also required students to write critical reflective journals. In this activity, a local student was paired with an international student. They first write their weekly journals individually. Then, they read each other's journal entries and discuss, question, and even challenge each other from different perspectives.

Another issue is relevant to the instructional language you use in the classroom. You, as the teacher of an international class, need to prepare yourself in terms of the language for teaching. Being proficient in one language may not be sufficient to account for the success of your classroom practice in a cross-cultural setting. Take the English language as an example, because of the wide spread use of English, if is used as a communication language in cross-cultural exchanges and classroom practices throughout the world. There are even policies that require teachers of English to teach English in English or professional teachers to teach content areas in English (Freeman, Katz, Gomez & Burns, 2015). Freeman et al. argue that teachers should develop a useable knowledge of English and that English instruction should focus on the classroom. They further argue that general language proficiency is different from teacher classroom English. They develop a construct of language-for-teaching and argue that using "English to teach English entails using the language to accomplish curricular and interactional ends within the classroom context" (p. 133). That is, a teacher's language knowledge should include the ability to prepare and present the curricular contents to be understood by the students and the ability to manage the classroom situation in the target language, such as providing directions and responding to students inquiries.

In a cross-cultural exchange context, the teaching and learning environment is much more complicated than that of a traditional classroom in that it involves participants from different cultures. Whether you teach international students at home or you teach foreign students abroad or you conduct cross-cultural videoconferences, you cannot always manage your classroom based on your recognized culture and ideology. As mentioned by Freeman et al. (2015), teachers' language knowledge, in addition to language of the content area, includes the situated use of the language in the classroom. In a cross-cultural exchange setting, being aware of cultural differences and language varieties should be reflected in your classroom management. In case of teaching abroad, you need to be aware of the classroom culture and administrative practices of the host country. It is essential that you exert specific teaching strategies and use appropriate classroom language in front of your foreign students.

Another issue is about the language used for communication between local students and international students, especially if local students are native speakers of English, which is considered the lingua franca of the world. Wicaksono (2013) describes how her UK students interact with international students in the same classroom. "For the UK students, misguided ideas about their ownership of English can mean that the responsibility for intelligibility is rested wholly on the shoulders of the international students: if I can't understand you, you need to learn more of my language" (p. 241). She reminds UK students of the fact that "English is already successfully used around the world in multifarious ways" (p. 249). The concept of English, or other languages, varieties is an inevitable phenomenon in international communications, and successful international communications are both the speaker's and the listener's responsibility, and they are dependent on the participants, the tasks or topics, and the contexts.

In another case of teaching strategies, Daniels (2013) describes how the theory of *capability* can be applied to international students in doctoral programs in Australia. She first explains that

> [C]entral to capability theory is the idea that quality of life is dependent not just on access to, or acquisition of, commodities, but also the opportunities to benefit from those commodities through the ability to make choices based on individual circumstance and need. (p. 42)

Applied to doctoral study in education, capability can mean being able to make use of resources available for them and choose what they need and what are important for them, to discuss, negotiate, and even challenge with peers or supervisor for their ideas, and to be cognitively flexible and be able to work collaboratively in groups with people. Drawing on the capability theory, Daniels (2013) and colleagues organized doctoral writing groups for international students at La Troe University in Australia. She first describes the challenges international doctoral students may face. Aside from language problems for those from non-English speaking countries and adjustment to the Australian education system, international doctoral students face challenges, including

> working in comparative isolation, with little or no opportunity to share or receive peer support in their experience of doctoral work; minimal exposure to different ways of presenting ideas or crafting an argument; few opportunities to develop skills of critique or receive critical feedback and little encouragement to engage reflectively with their work. (p. 45)

Writing groups for international students were organized to respond to these challenges. International doctoral students attended group meetings reviewing and discussing each other's writing pieces. According to Daniels, students in the writing group became more reflexive and could consider from different perspectives. Initial findings from interviews and journaling show that participants had heightened confidence as a doctoral student and a researcher. On the other hand, they also developed not only their writing skills but also skills to critique and to reflect on feedback from group members.

Devlin and Peacock (2009) present two models of programs aiming at internationalizing the campus at Bournemouth University and Sunderland University respectively to overcome linguistic and cultural barriers to integrate local students and international students. They argue that overcoming the barriers requires institutional intervention. After all, local students and international students will not work together naturally or automatically. Bournemouth University initiated the English Conversation Club (ECC) to break the barriers between local students and international students. The program aimed at providing 19 Level-One Chinese students who were working on their Sandwich degree "with an opportunity to improve fluency and confidence in English, learn more about UK work application processes and socialise with UK peers" (p. 172-173). There were four native English speakers with work experience in UK hired to have regular informal conversation with these Chinese students, talking about issues, such as job hunting and job interviews in the UK. In interviewing the attendees at the end of the program, students responded that they did learn more about UK culture and job application processes in the UK, although the program did not really locate a job position for them. On the other hand, students felt that they did improve their speaking skills and their confidence in speaking to British people in English.

The other model initiated by Sunderland University was the Sunderland Language and News Group (SLANG). SLANG aimed at providing international students with a context that promoted their cultural understanding and language skills. The nature of SLANG was defined as a social event. The group mainly focused on discussions of news stories in different domains, e.g., local, national, and international. SLANG is actually quite autonomous and democratic. Members of the group even decided to visit local sites and had a cultural trip. Research on the program shows, as Devlin and Peacock (2009) point out, reciprocity of benefits is key to attending the meetings, for example "social support, making friends, cultural exchange, development of language skills and professional development for students interested in pursuing teaching posts both in the UK and abroad" (p. 178). Devlin and Peacock conclude that there was less enthusiasm on the part of British students to attend the programs. They claim that programs like these will not succeed with only unilateral effort.

With the advancement of modern technologies, web-based learning and computer-mediated communication have become the norm, and the objectives of cross-cultural exchanges have been moving from language and cultural learning to include professional learning. Mehra and Bishop's (2007) study involved doctoral students from different cultures and different disciplines who were working on their doctoral degree in library and information science. One of the objectives of the study, as the authors pointed out, was to justify the culturally diverse society so that under-represented voices were heard. On the other hand, the authors proposed that the cross-cultural experiences of the international students would be good sources for American libraries in the process of internationalizing American libraries. Participants in the study were interviewed to provide ideas of and comments on internationalizing American libraries. Mehra and Bishop termed the approach a *two-way learning* approach. On the one hand, international doctoral students in library and information science were learning professional knowledge in their doctoral program. On the other hand, those international students were contributing their cross-cultural experiences to the internationalization of American libraries by looking at a library from a different cultural perspective.

Improving International Student Satisfaction

In order to explore and improve international students' satisfaction with the host institutions, Yu, Isensee, and Kappler (2016), by reviewing the literature, identify four key factors that may affect international students' satisfaction: student-faculty interactions, education system in the U.S. vs. home country, language proficiency, and integration with community. They point out that, first, student-faculty interaction in the classroom may differ in the U.S. and in other countries. The American students are used to a student-centered classroom where students actively participate in classroom discussions and asking questions, whereas students from some other cultures may tend to listen to the lecturer quietly and regard the lecturer as a person with great authority,

Second, Yu et al. point to the differences in education system in the U.S. and in international students' home countries. How "much is expected for class participation, types and workload for required homework, and what to expect during office hours, etc." (p. 216) may affect students' perceptions of satisfaction with the host institution. Third, international students' language proficiency can greatly affect and challenge "their confidence for participating in class, and caused difficulties understanding examples faculty used in class and expectations for group work" (p. 216). Finally, Yu, et al. also argue that "simply mixing students from different countries across the world without purposeful facilitation doesn't guarantee that they will integrate. International students tend to build friendships from their home culture or other international students over host country students" (p. 216-217). Yu et al. point out, language and cultural barriers can be key factors that prevent international students from participating in classroom discussions and make friends with local students, and, hence, feel isolated.

Yu et al. (2016) did a campus-wide survey to explore international students' satisfaction with the campus. Their investigation had different constructs, including arrival satisfaction, learning satisfaction, living satisfaction, and interactions with domestic students. What they did with the data collected at the University of Minnesota Twin Cities was, first, seeking multiple sources of data and integrated different data to get a significant picture of international student satisfaction. Then, they disseminated and shared the data with relevant units or colleges and discussed important issues. After discussions, together they did strategic planning to work out solutions or improvement to raise international student satisfaction.

In a globalizing era, when competitiveness in recruiting international students is high, Yu et al. (2016) provide a very good framework as to how institution leaders may make use of data collected from different occurrences to shed light into what international students really need and really care about, and, hence, promote international student enrollment.

The Case of Teaching Abroad

Another possibility of teacher mobility is that you may be on an assignment to teach in a foreign country. Teaching in an environment you are not familiar with requires a lot of time and patience to adjust to a new culture. George (1995), as an American teacher and a Fulbright professor, provides valuable advice for college teachers who are going to teach abroad. She argues that "methods and techniques successful for teaching American college students and doing business in the U.S. academic context are insufficient to meet the challenges of university work across culture" (p. 3). In the following paragraphs, I do not present specific cases of teaching abroad. Rather, I summarize what George suggests for teaching abroad and after returning home because George's accounts can be seen as a comprehensive and detailed collection of ideas and experiences of those who have taught abroad.

In addition to her personal experience as a Fulbright professor, George (1995) has collected her massive information from different sources, such as interviews with American professors during their academic exchange experiences, documentary video footage of U.S. Fulbright professors shot on locations in different countries, interviews with English-speaking host colleagues and students in Southeast Asia, reports from American professors participating in academic exchanges from different countries. Based on the huge amount of data, George summarizes some important points that college teachers who are teaching abroad should keep in mind. First, teachers should examine the classroom culture and observe teacher-student interactions because, in the host country, cultural norms and university support systems may be dissimilar from your own. Second, teachers are advised to plan routine classroom procedures and effective classroom instruction. Students from different cultures may have different learning styles. Students from some cultures may be used to rote memorization, while others may prefer group discussion. Third, teachers should negotiate for a manageable teaching role, such as teaching load, class size, and students' level. In the U.S., it may be a common practice that the teacher and the superior reach an agreement on all the details before the teacher starts teaching, while in other cultures, some factors such as human relationships, status, and social reciprocities may overshadow the systematic practice. Fourth, teachers need to structure the learning environment to decide whether to have team-teaching with host professors, to set up cooperative learning systems, etc. and whether there are limitations on space, materials and other resources in the new instructional setting. Fifth, teachers need to think about how to lecture effectively in a cross-cultural setting. Other important pieces of advice are fostering connections with faculty and colleagues of the host school, implementing effective instructional strategies, and enhancing learning with technologies.

On the other hand, George (1995) suggests what teachers can do after returning home. First, college teachers who have international teaching experience may build networks to exchange experiences of teaching abroad to promote international education and to provide teachers who are going to teach abroad for the first time and students who are going to study abroad with valuable information for their forthcoming journey. She lists some organizations aiming at these objectives, such as the Comparative and International Education, the National Association for Foreign Student Affairs, and Fulbright Alumni Association. Second, there are other ways that you, who have experiences of teaching abroad, can contribute your overseas experiences, for example, you may offer lectures to share your experiences with those teachers who are planning to teach abroad or you may advise your students who are going to study abroad. Fourth, to internationalize your curriculum and to make your curriculum more meaningful, you may put your host culture into your curriculum. Those students without a chance to study abroad may benefit from your curriculum and develop an international perspective.

Finally, having experiences teaching in the host country institutions, you may help establish institutional linkages through the support of the government or a foundation. These linkages may help develop strong and long-term relationships with the host faculty.

In addition to George (1995), Ochs (2012) also provides pieces of evidence on contextual factors for teachers who are interested in teaching abroad from the perspectives of Commonwealth Teacher Recruitment Protocol. She suggests that in choosing the destination of teaching abroad, some contextual factors need to be taken into consideration, for example, the organization of education system of the host country, the gap between teacher supply and teacher demand, the relationship between the sending country and the receiving country, the level of economic development of the host country because it might affect migrant teachers' working conditions and remitting money to support family at home, and the internal and external mobility of teachers in the host country, for teacher mobility might reveal some issues existing in the educational arena in the host country.

In a globalizing era there are significant chances that you teach in a foreign country. First of all, there are many higher education institutions around the world that establish their international branch campuses in other countries. Others may sign agreements with overseas institutions to establish sisterhood and develop some kind of exchange programs. In these cases, teachers may teach in another country to local students there. As cross-cultural communications are increasingly popular in an era moving towards globalization, recruiting international teachers to teach language-related courses or courses of their expertise has been encouraged in many countries. In this case, teachers and students are learning from each other and are exchanging each other's culture. For example, Cronje (2011) describes how professors from South Africa and Master's students in Sudan worked together in a teaching and learning context in Sudan for two years. In the entire course period, the professors even participated in tours and "stayed with the students in their private homes" (p. 603). Cronje points out that professors and students had to construct shared meaning together and learn to listen and to ask questions. For example, in terms of academic products, if students try to appeal to the professors, then they reduce their cultural richness and do not enrich the professors. The same is true if the students just follow a very precise rubric and clear examples of what the professors want, then it deprives the students of their creativity.

Among all the modes of teaching abroad, faculty members are particularly encouraged to teach in their overseas campuses or in the partner universities. In this chapter, I describe different modes of cross-cultural exchanges. As mentioned at the beginning of this chapter, which one to choose from depends on a lot of factors. I just present some examples of cross-cultural exchange projects from existing literature and my personal experiences of cross-cultural partnerships. Developing a cross-cultural exchange project best for your own case requires your creativity and critical thinking and, of course, your collaboration with your partner teachers.

The Case of Teaching Local Languages to International Students

It may be the norm that international students learn the local languages in order for them to be integrated into the life of the host country and to achieve academically. It is not uncommon that a university offer classes for international students to learn local languages. Local teachers or even students are available to teach international students local languages. Martinez-Alba and Cruzado-Guerrero (2016) provide some language teaching strategies. Although they focus on teaching English to English language learners in the United States, it can be useful for teaching any local languages to international students because these strategies are derived from comparison of language teaching strategies in different countries. First, the teacher needs to establish rapport with his or her students. After all, they are from different cultures. By having conversations with international students, the teacher can better know the students' interests, strengths and weaknesses and can help develop students' social language skills. Second, in an earlier stage of learning the local language, international students may have problems understanding some vocabulary words. In this case, the teacher can use visuals, such as pictures, photos or realia to help students' understanding. Third, asking students to do choral reading and read aloud may help students with their oral fluency and may alleviate their language learning anxiety. Fourth, using technologies in teaching and learning of a language is inevitable in a globalizing era. In addition to various visuals or images online that may help students' understanding of the texts, some websites are actually language-learning oriented. Martinez-Alba and Cruzado-Guerrero envision that as the number of language learners has grown, "technology continues to expand and evolve and language instruction that revolves around technology will too. Computers, iPods, notebooks, smartphones, videos, smartboards, Google glass, and the like will assist students in building their language skills" (p. 211). Finally, Martinez-Alba and Cruzado-Guerrero suggest the teaching of idioms. It is especially appropriate in culturally diverse learning environment. Idioms cannot always show the literal meaning and cannot be literally translated. Language learners can hardly understand the meaning of an idiom unless being explicitly taught. By learning idioms, students not only learn the language, but also learn the culture and the value system of the host country.

Although teaching international students local languages may be dependent on various factors, Martinez-Alba and Cruzado-Alba's language teaching strategies can serve as a rule of thumb and can be useful to teaching local languages to international students and teaching a foreign language in general.

Volunteering Abroad

Like students, it is possible for teachers to teach minority or less privileged children abroad voluntarily. As mentioned in the introductory chapter, the real meaning of globalization is that people from different cultures work together to explore, discuss, solve global issues and people in the world towards a better future. Crawford and Witko's (2018) story of volunteering in a conflict zone is a perfect and touching example showing how teachers can contribute to the education of a problematic area by devoting their time and energy to teach children there. Initially, they were teachers teaching in the United States. They met in a Brazilian favela where they both participated in the Project Favela and volunteered to teach and work with children there.

According to Crawford and Witko (2018), the favela in Rouinha is the largest favela in Brazil and is often ignored by the government. The children there were most of the time out of school. Because of insufficient classroom space and qualified teachers, children in the favela could only attend the school for half of the day. Some of them wander on the street. Unfortunately, gunfire is always heard on the street, and conflicts between the units of police pacification and drug traffickers are seen all the time.

The two volunteer teachers taught math and English to children in the favela, including after-school programs. An important issue for Crawford and Witko (2018) was "how to effectively blend [their] ideas and ways of thinking about educational methodologies with culturally relevant approaches" (p. 89). Because of the situation in the favela and students' unique experiences, they even had to take psychological and neurological factors into consideration. As Crawford and Witko state:

> The children at Project Favela live in endemic poverty, noise, pollution, and disease. Their day-to-day lives may be serious sources of stress. Stress has psychological impact on the brain. For this reason, we seek to give the children a safe and orderly environment, giving their brains time to repair the damage caused by chronic stress. (p. 89)

For this reason, in addition to language and math, they scheduled "meditation activities throughout the day to alleviate stress, practice mindfulness, and promote well-being" (p. 89).

As far as teaching methodologies are concerned, the two volunteer teachers stress the importance of integrating relevant teaching methodologies with specific cultures in an educational setting. In their case, Crawford and Witko (2018) integrated brain research and Montessori principles with cultural elements responsive to Brazilian culture as their teaching approach. As we can tell from Crawford and Witko's report, they need a lot more devoted volunteer teachers to work together in the favela, on the one hand, for the well-being and the education of the children there. On the other hand, teaching in an educational setting as described by Crawford and Witkp can be valuable experiences that enrich your teaching career and can be treasurable sources to enhance your teaching skills and broaden your world views.

Challenges of Teacher Mobility

There are many issues and challenges faced by practitioners in the domain of teacher mobility, including teacher training and preparation, recruitment, exploitation of migrant teachers, and teachers' professional development. In this section, different issues are presented and discussed in detail.

Exploitation of Migrant Teachers

Omolewa (2012) states relevant problems from the UNESCO and Commonwealth points of view. First, teacher exploitation is a significant problem in the domain of teacher migration. According to Omolewa, "teachers are constantly being exploited both at the state of origin and abroad" (p. 16). Generally speaking, teachers' pay is often inadequate and is less than those of other professions. They leave their homeland and seek a better working condition abroad, expecting better salaries, adequate respect, and, more importantly, a promising future. However, the Commonwealth, which was organized by smaller and less powerful countries after the collapse of the British Empire, was especially concerned about two important issues: "(i) the unregulated exploitation of teacher stocks of small developing countries by recruitment agencies; and (ii) lack of protection for recruited migrant teachers in more developed countries" (p. 19). There are core values shared by members of the Commonwealth, including "a demand for equity, fairness, integrity, social justice and transparency" (p. 19). For the Commonwealth, its members concern about "the poorest, smallest and perhaps most voiceless people spread across sometimes very tiny islands through the world" (p. 19). In a globalizing era, it is especially important that, in the education arena, all teachers are equally treated and protected, be they from developed, developing, or underdeveloped countries. Globalization does not make sense if we ignore voices from minority and underrepresented groups of people. Migrant teachers are actually contributing to enriching the contents of instruction and to the development of a really globalized world.

Teacher Recruitment, Preparation, Training, and Professional Development

Other issues that also drew the UNESCO's and the Commonwealth's attention was teacher training and continued training. As pointed out by Omolewa (2012) about the importance of continued retraining, today's "knowledge will be inadequate to meet the challenges of tomorrow, so it is expected that teachers should maintain a standard of training so that their skills remain relevant" (p. 17). In addition to the above-mentioned issues, issues such as "the stability of teaching jobs, appropriate remuneration, salaries and wages, and the rewards of service in the form of promotion" (p. 17) are also concerns of the domain of teacher migration.

Although Ochs (2012) points out the importance of the issues of comparability of qualifications, she reminds the reader that "teaching qualifications and teaching quality are not synonymous" (p. 32). In addition to teacher recruitment, both UNESCO and the Commonwealth Secretariat and other international organizations also have been focusing their attention on the quality of education. They stress the importance of teacher training and retraining for adequate profession development of teachers" (p. 15).

In the domain of teacher mobility, Ochs (2012) points to the issue of teacher recruitment. In the case of the Commonwealth member countries, although the Commonwealth Teacher Recruitment Protocol was initiated in 2006, Ochs's study carried out in 2008-2009 showed that "teachers remain largely unaware of the protocol" (p. 31), not to mention the implementation of the protocol. The obstacles that prevent the protocol from being implemented include the lack of cross-national comparability of teaching qualifications. They may cause what Ochs termed "brain waste," which refers to "an experienced teacher is given a position that does not make use of the teacher's skills or prior experience" (p. 30). She urges further studies to "explore which countries use qualification agencies and/or recruitment agencies, and the process of their involvement….more information is needed to understand their specific actions and how these agencies might actively participate as stakeholders in the ethical migration and recruitment of teachers" (p. 32). As we can imagine, this may greatly facilitate teacher mobility in a globalizing era.

Quality of Education

In the case of higher education in Southeast Asia, Welch (2011) points to some facts and problems that higher education in Southeast Asia are facing. First, it is about the quality of education. As described by Welch, there is a tendency of educational reform towards privatization. It is not uncommon that academics in public higher education institutions moonlight at private institutions to meet the needs of the rise in private enrolments and, for public institutions, to compensate for their already low salaries. Under this circumstance, the quality of higher education in the region deserves attention. Academics in public higher education institutions who moonlight at private institutions generally have no time and no energy for their students in their home institutions and for research. Some private institutions offer some evening or weekend programs, and actually these programs have a very low standard of entry. It is also possible in certain countries that students are allowed to pay hefty fees and get admission to a higher education institution. Financial considerations are always the priority of school leaders. In the case of Indonesia, quality "in the private sector is also threatened by low investment and per-pupil spending rated, which often denote poor facilities and equipment" (p. 36). In India, Agarwal (2008) also points to challenges faced by its higher education: quality assurance and mutual recognition. India has "the third largest system of higher education in the world" (p. 83) and "Indian students are the second largest pool of international students after China" (p. 93). However, India has difficulties attracting international students from other countries, especially from advanced countries. Agarwal points out that UNESCO and Organization of Economic Cooperation and Development (OECD) have issued guidelines on "Quality Provision in Cross-Border Higher Education." This initiative is issued "to protect students against misleading information and low-quality provisions, and to intensify international cooperation among national quality and accreditation agencies" (p. 106). Agarwal suggests that "India needs to work toward the establishment and eventual adoption of common international standards such as the UNESCO-OECD guidelines for qualifications (p. 106).

Another issue challenging the higher education in Southeast Asia is the issue of corruption. Welch (2011) describes that many countries in Southeast Asia are not "free of the taint of corruption" (p. 164). It is the case that "too many of the resources generated within these countries are, at times, siphoned into private pocket, and that decisions taken are often not transparent" (p. 164). For example, in Indonesia, higher education institutions always use devious strategies, such as bribery and false reports, to compromise the quality of their evaluation and to get passed in the evaluation process. On the other hand, according to Welch's accounts, education "has traditional been distributed very unevenly in terms of both geography and gender…higher education was already well beyond the reach of many" (p. 27). In the case of Thailand, "Thai higher education has not been free of graft, with charges of profiteering, improprieties in entrance exam procedures and favouritism for students of powerful families (p. 85).

Non-Native Teachers' Language-Related Identity

Whether you teach foreign students via videoconferencing, teach abroad, or teach international students at home, as long as you are not a native speaker of the language you use as the medium of instruction, the issue of language-related identity arises, which may be related to disciplines, contents, students, your professional knowledge and your awareness. Gray and Morton (2018) point out that a non-native speaking teacher may view themselves as a user, a learner, and a teacher of the language. They use *English* as an example to show how these identities may function and affect non-native speakers' practice as a language teacher. In the role they play as a user of English, non-native English teachers tend to feel inferior as compared with their native English speaking counterparts. Ideologically, native-speaking English teachers consider themselves superior and speak 'standard' and 'real' English. However, according to Gray and Morton, the dichotomy of nativeness and non-nativeness in a globalizing era is no longer relevant. In "methods and materials used, teachers' and students' attitudes and institutional hiring practices, [there is still discrimination] against non-native-speaking professions" (p. 72). Gray and Morton cite Holliday's words as saying that native speakerism is "a pernicious ideology which serves to privilege those within the ELT profession who are labeled as 'native speaker' and discriminates against the majority of English teacher around the world…as non-native speakers" (p. 73).

Gray and Morton (2018) mention the value of both native and non-native speaking teachers. While native-speaking teachers are able to provide authentic language, including accurate grammars and native accents, non-native speaking teachers may have chances to recontextualize the target language for their local settings and use discourses best for their local students. However, as pointed out by Gray and Morton, non-native speaking teachers always perceived themselves as having an "awareness of a lack of proficiency,…'non-native' accent, stigma attached to speaking a local variety of English, feelings of professional legitimacy" (p. 74). It is important for both native speaking and non-native speaking teachers to note that the emerging concerns of the varieties of English, and other languages. Gray and Morton stress the importance of viewing languages as communication tools manifest and meaningful in social interactions, rather than fixed products having static grammatical rules.

Viewed from another non-native teachers' language-related identity, Gray and Morton (2018) focus on non-native English teachers' experiences of learning English. They describe preferences and perceptions of learning English as a second or foreign language. In their examples, Oriental people may favor the use of grammar-translation approach to language learning. They memorize vocabulary words and grammatical rules and translate and read the texts. On the contrary, Western people may prefer to use the language to communicate with people, rather than rote memorization. Whether non-native English teachers favor rote memorization or communicative approach to language learning, it is important that they keep learning and keep developing their language skills. That is, language is a product of social interaction whether orally or in writing. It is important to keep up with the development of language varieties, in addition to the vocabulary, newly developed meaning or usage of vocabulary words or expressions, and the sociolinguistic aspect of language use.

When non-native speaking teachers are viewed from the teacher's role they play, two main areas are relevant: professional skills and language skills. Gray and Morton (2018) argue that non-native speaking teachers' professional skills, such as professional knowledge, well-prepared instructional materials, and creative teaching skills, may compensate them for their language proficiency deficiencies. They point out that studies have shown that "students do not have a negative perception of their non-native teachers, recognising the value of experience and professionalism over being a native speaker" (p. 78). In a sense, non-native local teachers are able to better understand local students, their learning style, and their problems and attitudes towards learning, and they are able to use local resources and students' first language knowledge to address some issues of language learning.

However, non-native speaking teachers are also criticized by native speaking teachers as being resistant to change and to encourage critical thinking skills and creativity in their students. Rather, they rely on memorization and follow the textbooks, focusing "on enabling the students to pass examinations" (p. 79). The positive and negative sides of non-native speaking teachers are actually reflecting the cultural differences between the East and the West. When it comes to the culture, it is not a matter of right or wrong. However, both the ways native-speaking and non-native speaking teachers teach may benefit students and may deserve attention. While some factors may not be easy to change, such as accents, non-native speaking teachers may consider making some changes so that their students can benefits more in their learning process.

Cultural Differences and Cultural Learning

The discussions above focus on non-native English teachers teaching English in a non-English speaking educational setting. Carson (2018), a native-English speaker, describes his experiences of teaching English in a non-English speaking country, Japan. In order to internationalize the campus, the Japanese university that Carson was working hired a considerable number of faculty and staff from English speaking countries, and only "less than 10% were Japanese (p. 97). Theoretically, this may facilitate internationalization of the campus. However, "[a]lthough working with mostly Western colleagues decreases dissonance in working practices…,it may have delayed cultural learning and the development of cultural competency" (p. 97). He argues that we cannot apply the one-size-fits-all model to international education and internationalization of the campus. Carson raises three issues in his experiences of teaching in Japan: Japanese students, colleagues, and grading students.

First, Carson (2018), as a Westerner and a native English speaker, describes how he perceives Japanese students. In terms of English education, Carson states that the Japanese education system and Japanese students do not focus their learning of English on communicative skills. It is because oral skills are not easy to administer and test in an exam. Generally speaking, Japanese students do not perceive English as a means to communicate. The issue is compounded by the nature of classroom practice in Japan, which features being teacher-centered. Unlike commonly seen in a Western classroom, Japanese students are shy and reluctant to communicate in the classroom, even in a language class. They listen to the teacher attentively and seldom participate in classroom discussions.

Second, Carson (2018) also mentions some problems he had working with colleagues towards internationalization. Internationalizing the campus is a trend in an era moving towards globalization. It may include recruiting international students and foreign scholars, English instruction in the classroom, having international students and local students working in the same classroom. Theoretically, assigning international students and local students in the same classroom and instructing in English may facilitate language and culture learning and may enhance the competitiveness and reputation of the university in the global market. In reality, according to Carson, the outcomes are not always what we expect. Carson points to the fact that, in order to accommodate Japanese students and other low-English-proficiency international students, the teacher has to slow down and simplify the instruction and, as a result, the English-medium content course turns out to be a language course. Those international students with a higher level of English proficiency claim the course is too easy, and they are not motivated to take those simplified courses.

Finally, the attitude towards grading students also confuses Carson (2018). Carson believes grading students should be based on their potential to function in a global community and to contribute to society. He insists on not passing failing students. This may go against what his Japanese colleagues think, who do not always judge immediate outcomes and who expect and look for long-term effects.

Based on his experiences of teaching in Japan, Carson (2018) reminds international educators of an important perspective that "international hires in academics are often expected to contribute in the manner of working and interaction of their home cultures' (p. 113). He argues that traditional ways of learning may "not fit with the fast-paced society of constant change that is the global world today" (p. 113). He urges international educators, in addition to learning and adopting the host country culture and social norms, it is important to contribute to the host country by demonstrating themselves as sources and examples. What international educators bring to the host country may be valuable and important to students as well as colleagues who work with them. Cultural learning is actually a two-way process and can be achieved only when both cultural members can enhance intercultural competencies and learn from each other.

Aside from cultural learning, learning the local language also appears to be a big challenge for expatriate teachers. Theoretically, it must be easy to learn the local language in the target language speaking environment. In reality, things do not turn out as we can imagine, especially if you are a native English speaker. Gebhard (2017) describes the situation. We

> Get too busy to study the language,…We speak English to our students, the office staff, and administers. We make friends with other EFL teachers and with fluent English-speaking acquaintances from the host culture, and we end up speaking English with them outside the workplace. When we venture out into the country, we meet people who jump at the chance to use English with a native speaker, and we oblige." (p. 146)

Gebhard then illustrates how he "force" himself to learn Japanese when he was in Japan.

> When I moved to Japan, I purposeful lived in a place where no other foreigners lived, and when approaching the study of Japanese, I used the community. I talked with

people at the public bath, the local stoves, and the laundry. Being single at that time, I went on dates with women who I know would be willing to speak Japanese with me. I also joined a yoga club where I could use Japanese, went on weekend hiking trips with a non-English speaking Japanese, and drank a few beers each week at a place where few were interested in speaking English with me. (p. 147-148)

Gebhard's main point is that learning the local language can be successfully done if you are really committed in the learning.

LIVING AND WORKING ABROAD

As stated earlier, this book does not limited cross-cultural exchanges to the domain of higher education, although it is the focus of this book. In a globalizing era when we emphasize life-long learning and to be a global citizen, learning across culture does not end in one's life in schools. Beyond one's life in formal education, professional careers may require a person to adapt to a global community and to deal with people from different cultures in accordance with changes and new issues emerging around the globe. One of the examples is the people who work for multinational corporations and who have overseas appointments to live and work abroad for a short-term or long-term period. In this section, I focus on expatriate managers as an example of working abroad.

Like the educational domain, in the globalizing era, there are more and more multinational corporates establishing overseas branch companies or establishing a certain kind of collaboration with international companies in other countries. Under this circumstance, it is not uncommon that these multinational corporations need to assign local managers to work abroad to handle overseas business. Let's first focus on expatriate managers' everyday life beyond their professional work. Like those students, teachers, or researchers who work abroad, expatriate managers need to adapt to the host culture and to socialize with people in the host country. Spiegel (2018) interviewed expatriate managers and describes that there are different types of expatriate managers in their everyday life in terms of their spatiality and sociability. She interviewed and analyzed the everyday spatiality and sociability of expatriate managers and their families and categorizes expatriate managers into different types, ranging from the cosmopolitan type to the anti-cosmopolitan elites type. Cosmopolitans are those who embrace different cultures and enjoy making friends with people from different parts of the world; while anti-cosmopolitans are those expatriate managers who reject to have contacts with local people and learn local cultures. Instead, they confine their choice of living space and social activities to the anti-cosmopolitan elites. Between the two extremes of expatriate managers, there are different types and degrees of cosmopolitanism. Spiegel terms them "selective cosmopolitanism," "unaccomplished cosmopolitanism," and "conditional cosmopolitanism." Selective cosmopolitan expatriate managers "were simultaneously open to some cultural Others and reluctant to others" (p. 87). On the one hand, they keep local people and culture at a distance. On the other hand, they reveal their openness and curiosity to cultural differences. Those unaccomplished cosmopolitans, on the contrary, show their strong "desire to be immersed in the local culture and the impossibility to realize this desire" (p. 92). They consciously try hard to be immersed to the locality and reject "social and spatial segregation from the host country" (p. 92). Unfortunately, because of some inherent reasons such as the closed character of the local communities and language barriers, their ideal to be a cosmopolitan expatriate manager and to "look for an immersion into the locality but [trying] to control this immersion as much as they can" (p. 97) is hard to achieve. They are ambivalent in their emotion to be localized. On the one hand, they are open to the local Other; on the other hand, they somehow distance themselves "from the local culture in order to be included into joint sociability, thus trying to control and reduce the amount of difference" (p. 102).

It is evident from Spiegel's (2018) account and categorization that to what extent an expatriate manager expects to be localized and socialized in the host country is actually a personal choice, and different expatriate managers may have different degrees of comfort and different attitudes towards their daily life in their expatriate career. Yet, their professional life is as important, if not more important, as their daily life. In the following paragraphs in this section, I turn the discussion of expatriate managers' everyday life to discuss their professional life in a managerial position in a foreign country.

Bredenkötter (2018) suggests that the roles of expatriates who are assigned to work in an overseas subsidiary can be roughly classified into three kinds: controller and transfer agent, coordinator and negotiator, and learner and information seeker. That is, an expatriate manager needs to transfer all the headquarters' operations and policies to the subsidiary, coordinate between headquarters and the subsidiary for any tasks, problems, or conflicts, and learn local knowledge to help the headquarters to "adapt to its organizational environment" (p. 137). In the role as a controller and transfer agent, Bredenkötter suggests that expatriates can "make" roles as a teacher or as an entrepreneur. In the case of a teacher's role, Brdenkötter describes the case of a German expatriate manager. The manager feels that his local Chinese employees need more guidance and instruction than his German nationals do. He then makes this role as a "teacher" to "construct clearly asymmetrical relationships with [his] Chinese employees" (p. 140). He patiently "teaches" his "student employees" and understands their culture, such as being afraid of losing face in public. In another case, on the other hand, another German manager of a multinational corporation was assigned to work in its US-American subsidiary. Unlike the teacher role mentioned above, he "makes" his role as a "start-up entrepreneur" "who wants to 'build' something new and innovative with his 'team'" (p. 143). Unlike the role as a teacher, the expatriate manager expected to work "with well-trained employees…who complete their tasks largely independently after only a few instructions and explanations" (p. 143).

Bredenkötter (2018) describes yet another type of expatriate manager as coordinators and negotiators. This type of manager sees themselves as being "posted to exchange knowledge, coordinate tasks, mediate conflicts, and generally resolve problems between head and subsidiary offices or to jointly develop projects and strategies with the subsidiary" (p. 147). These types of managers play their roles in at least two modes: managers as service providers and managers as chameleon. Those who see themselves as service providers try to immerge themselves in the local work environment. They would rather be the learner to learn more about the local market and other local knowledge. They do not want to be seen as authoritative personnel from the headquarters; rather, thet would like to be observers or outsiders of the local society. Another type of expatriate managers are those who play their roles as coordinator and negotiator and see themselves as chameleon. Because they need to coordinate and negotiate between the headquarters and subsidiary, they need to "balance dual membership…[and] become a dual citizen" (p. 15). On the one hand, they need to be loyal to and closely connected with the headquarters and faithfully transfer the headquarters' policies, strategic practices, and interests to the local employees. On the other hand, they need to keep relationships with local employees, speak for their interests to the headquarters, and respect and understand their cultures. It seems they have to adjust their attitudes, strategies, and practices based on the situations and the environment like a chameleon.

From Bredenkötter's (2018) classification and the accounts above, it is clear that working abroad like studying and teaching abroad, needs to deal with different issues. However, working abroad does not necessarily limit to the business domain. Some people have overseas appointments as diplomats, missionaries, or technicians. Discussions of those domains are far beyond the scope of this book. However, one thing for sure is that intercultural competences and professional knowledge are key to successful practices overseas.

Chapter 6

DEVELOPING THE TASKS OR ACTIVITIES

Having communicated with your partner teacher, you need to start thinking about the tasks or activities you want your students to learn or to achieve. You need to keep in mind that you cannot develop the tasks or activities alone. You need to involve your students and the partner teacher and students in the developing process. Whatever activities you and your partners decide to do, most importantly, you have to make sure your proposed tasks or activities are feasible to operate, to gain administrative, technical or financial support, to be scheduled as activities, and to provide your students with their learning needs and with the most chances to learn. In cross-cultural exchanges, a task or an activity developed for participants to complete must be appropriate for and agreed upon by the different groups of students. In the course of developing a cross-cultural exchange program, it is always wise that the teacher integrates students' ideas, needs, and preferences and discusses with the partner teacher to reach a consensus at the end of the planning stage. To achieve the goal set before the exchange and to engage students in the cultural exchanges, teachers should keep several things in mind in the course of developing a project. In this chapter, I first point out some key factors that may contribute to the success of a cross-cultural exchange program, including learning materials, learning environment and experience, benefits of learning, and modes of exchange. Then, I present examples of different types of tasks or activities.

IMPORTANT CONSTRUCTS OF CROSS-CULTURAL EXCHANGES

Authenticity

In cross-cultural exchanges or other educational activities, the issues of authenticity have been brought up for discussion. At the earlier stage, when educators started discussing the concept of authenticity, they mainly referred to authentic materials or texts (Lee, 1995; Shomoossi & Ketabi, 2007). However, this concept of authenticity was gradually regarded as insufficient in terms of motivating students to learn and enhancing students' learning outcome. For example, aside from text authenticity, there are relevant terms such as learner authenticity, learning authenticity, topic authenticity, classroom authenticity, and authentic assessment emerging in the educational arena (Lee, 1995; van Lier, 1996; Lam, 2005; Gerstein, 2000; Shomoossi & Ketabi, 2007; Lombardi, 2007). Having a closer look at all these concepts of authenticity may be helpful in the development of tasks or activities for cross-cultural exchanges. An era of globalization and internationalization may contribute significantly to the increasingly growing needs of the authentic nature of cross-cultural activities. Teachers are required to develop activities or tasks that are relevant to real-world situations. In this section, I discuss authenticity viewed from different aspects of a learning setting.

Authentic Materials (Text Authenticity)

Lee (1995) defines two types of authenticity in teaching and learning: *text authenticity* and *learner authenticity*. According to Lee, *text authenticity* is about the origin of the materials, and *learner authenticity* is about learners' interaction with the materials, including their positive responses and psychological reaction to the materials. Authentic materials must be those collected from daily life. That is, these materials were not initially created for a specific teaching and learning purposes like language teaching and learning, but for real-life communicative purposes and knowledge acquisition. For example, newspapers, magazines, recipes, technical instructions, commercial ads, brochures, catalogues, movies, and realias are all authentic materials. They can be used for different types of learning. In cross-cultural exchanges, students may learn better by using, creating, and exchanging authentic materials. These materials are more meaningful to students in terms of how they may use what they have learned in their daily life.

Van Lier (1996), on the other hand, argues that authentic materials written for native speakers can benefit language learners for some reasons. First, texts written for non-native speakers are always linguistically distorted or unrepresentative of the target language in order to accommodate non-native speakers. Second, language learners may benefit from and prefer to have genuine texts in order to have a deeper understanding of how the target language is actually used in the target cultural communities. Third, genuine texts are really important and necessary for immigrants or international students to survive in a foreign country. Van Lier's point is clear that language learners may benefit the most, from a language learning perspective, by being forced to be immersed in a target-language-using environment.

Ates (2012) demonstrates a good example of the use of authentic materials in business class. His students were Turkish-speaking and were taking an ESP business course. He calls the way he conducted the course a case-based method. Ates assigned his students to read, write, discuss, and present authentic English reports on globally known enterprise cases, such as MacDonald's and FedEx, aiming at developing students' global perspective and understanding business operation in different cultures. Findings of his study show that students benefitted a lot from the instructional method in terms of developing their global perspectives, improving their language skills, and heightening their cultural awareness. Although this case may not be a real cross-cultural exchange, it can be a good alternative if a real cross-cultural exchange is not at all going to happen in your situation. Familiarizing your students with actual practices in different cultures by providing authentic materials for them to read and to discuss.

Learner and Learning Authenticity

Lee (1995) also argues that textually authentic materials are not necessarily learner authentic. Viewed from the learners' viewpoint, authentic materials should be motivating, interesting, and useful to them. She points out, in order to establish learner authenticity, five factors should be taken into consideration: material selection, individual differences, task design, learning environment, and teacher's attitude and teaching approach. Students can learn better if they are engaged in an activity that is interesting and meaningful to them. For example, students may be assigned to develop their own exchange curriculum, design their own brochures or videos of introduction to their department or school and exchange their products with their partner classes, and interview their partners via videoconferencing and publish their reports in newspapers. The novelty of working on these activities and a sense of accomplishment may be good incentives for students to learn with their cross-cultural exchange partners.

Still Shomoossi and Ketabi (2007) have a more critical view of the concept of authenticity. They argue that texts not written for language teaching and learning purposes are not necessarily authentic instructional materials. They insist that texts authenticity should be viewed from different aspects such as the learners, the teacher, and the situation of teaching. Shomoossi and Ketabi further argue that "texts themselves can actually be intrinsically 'genuine', but that authenticity is a 'social construct'" (p. 150). That is, only the interaction of the language users, the texts themselves, and the contexts where the interactions occur can create a certain kind of authenticity. Any texts, either written or spoken, cannot be considered authentic without taking the learner and the context into consideration. For example, native speakers' real pieces of conversation may appear difficult for beginning learners of the target language. It does not make sense no matter how authentic the spoken piece is if the sample pieces are unintelligible for the language learner.

Shomoossi and Ketabi (2007) conclude that the key to authenticity in learning was pragmatic appropriateness. Learners need to develop pragmatic competence in order to function in global communications. As far as authenticity of instructional material, the learner, the context, and the learning activity are concerned, pragmatic appropriateness should be the major concern in the development of cross-cultural exchange projects. That is, the partners, the language or languages used, the activities, and the materials chosen should be appropriate for students to learn and to communicate.

Lam (2005) and Lombardi (2007), on the other hand, focus their discussion on authentic learning. Lam defines authentic learning as "learning which happens by actually participating and working on real-world problems, it engages learners by the opportunities of solving real-world complex problems and finding out solutions" (p. 1). She argues that authentic learning can boost students' motivation to learn, students learn better in an authentic learning environment, authentic learning prepares students for future career, authentic learning actually makes the concept easier to be assimilated, and, finally, authentic learning is actually putting theories into practice. She points out that some characteristics are critical in an authentic learning environment, such as real-world relevance, being interdisciplinary and collaborative, aiming at creating tangible and authentic products to be used in the real world. Lam also reminds teachers who intend to provide students with an authentic learning environment of their role as facilitator and that students' outcomes should be authentically assessed. She roughly presents the different stages in an authentic learning process. First, the teacher explains the entire learning context and tasks to be done. Then, students need to discuss in groups and search for relevant information to solve the problems. After that, students start working on the main task. That is, in this stage, they are transferring the knowledge they have learned into a product. Finally, they need to present their products in the class or in the community to get feedback and to learn from other groups. A wider scale of authentic learning is international volunteering, which will be described in detail in a later section in this chapter. International volunteering brings students to another country to learn serving people and experience different countries.

Lombardi (2007) further indicates the trends of authentic learning in the 21st century. She mainly points out that information technology (IT) will play a key role in authentic learning in the 21st century. Very similar to what Lam (2005) has stated, Lombardi also considers real-world relevance, collaboration, and interdisciplinary perspective important elements in the design of an authentic learning environment. These may not have seemed as big problems before. However, as the social structure changes, making links between the classroom work and the real-world is getting more and more difficult. For example, assigning a large number of students as apprentices to relevant work sites, having science students operate expensive equipment to do important experiments, having students interact face-to-face with people all over the world may seem impractical or impossible. As IT develops, however, these and more activities have become practical and feasible. According to Lombardi, IT can do a lot of things for us in terms of creating an authentic learning environment; for example, working with remote instruments, working with research data, simulation-based learning, student-created 3D virtual reconstructions of an ancient marketplace, etc. We may conclude here that, when it comes to real-world experiences, although being as close to the real-world and to daily life as possible is the top priority, some limitations may force teachers to seek for alternatives and IT may be part of the answers, especially in the case of cross-cultural exchanges.

Task Authenticity

Koh (2017) states that the "[a]uthentic tasks replicate real-world challenges and standards of performance that experts or professionals typically face in the field" (p. 1). Herrington, Reeves, and Oliver (2010) discuss the differences between academic problems and practical problems. They argue that academic problem are present in a textual form rather than in a contextual form and are mostly irrelevant to the real-world situations. They are always well-defined and can be solved with only one approach and with only one correct answer. Unlike academic problems, practical problems are relevant to real-world situations and they are ill-defined and ill-structured. That is, students need to seek substantial and relevant information to solve the problems collaboratively. Most importantly, there is always more than one way to solve the problems, and there is not only one correct answer to deal with the problems.

Lee (1995) illustrates a practical application of learner authentic tasks. Participants of the task were BA part-time Social Work students at Hong Kong Polytechnic. In the task, students chose to work on a topic on teenage suicide, and they decided to study the death of Yu Po-Shan, a teenager who committed suicide and whose case had drawn public attention. Students were guided to fulfil the task after reading the news article. First, students might play the role of the school social worker, and, in order to investigate the causes of the tragedy, students may invite the Principal, Po-Shan's class teacher, and his mother for a meeting. After the meeting, students might write a short report on Po-Shan's death. Then students might organize a seminar for teachers and parents on teenage suicide and conduct a survey and interview teenagers. Having all the data collected, students were required to give a short oral presentation in the class.

Another example presented by Lam (2005) was the case practiced in the American Museum of Natural History. The program was organized by a primary school, aiming at training primary school students to become docents in a museum. These young students were first taught research and interview skills, then they needed to orally present in a way that the public can understand. Finally, "the students get a chance to talk to the docents in the museum and eventually became one of them" (p. 5). It might be a common belief that little kids are not capable of doing things that adults do in the real world. However, the study shows that primary school students, guided and trained by teachers or professionals, can actually perform the tasks they will face in their future workplace. Those who participated in the activity can be envisioned to be better equipped to work in their future professional career.

The two examples of authentic tasks presented above show relevance to students' fields of study and probably to their future professional career. In addition to the "real life approach," Mousani (2002) identifies yet another approach to authenticity of assessment tasks "interactionalability approach." In speaking of language testing, he defines authenticity as "the extent to which the tasks required on a given test are similar to normal real-life language use" (p. 43). In cross-cultural exchanges, in addition to professional fields, students from different cultures may be assigned to work together on particular global or local issues meaningful for them. In this case, students may have brain storming and look at one issue from different perspectives. Being connected to the real world and being meaningful to the students, authentic tasks can better prepare students for their future professional career and for being a global citizen. More about authentic assessment tasks will be elaborated in detail in a later section in Chapter 7 discussing authentic assessment. In sum, "authentic tasks are often performance-based and include complex and ill-structured problems that are well aligned with the rigorous and higher-order learning objectives in a reformed vision of curriculum" (Koh, 2017, p. 6).

Classroom Authenticity

Some researchers claim that classroom is inherently unnatural and inauthentic (e.g., van Lier, 1996), especially in a language learning classroom. Textbooks used and teacher-student interactions occur in the language classroom are all artificial. According to van Lier, language use is closely tied to the setting where it occurs, and the setting includes "a speaker's intention and a hearer's interpretation of the language used" (p. 124-125). In a language learning context, "authenticity relates to who the teachers and learners are and what they do as they interact with one another for the purposes of learning" (p. 125). Van Lier points to the fact that it is easy to obtain a piece of *genuine* spoken discourse. However, it needs learners to authenticate the piece of discourse in order for it to be authentic. In a language learning classroom, authentic language-using behaviors, such as practicing the target language in a simulated situation in the classroom, can be more addictive in terms of language learning than that of authentic language use. Shomoossi and Ketabi (2007) also claim that "authentic (listening) materials can be frustrating for beginners ….[and] unmodified authentic discourse may prove to be impractical particularly for low-proficient learners" (p. 151).

Van Lier (1996) would treat *authenticity* as *a process of validation,* or *authentication*, rather than *a product* or *a property of language.* In van Lier's sense, in the process of authentication, participants of a conversation try to fix any discrepancy or misunderstanding between or among participants and to establish relevance. For example, a linguistics teacher may, in the middle of explaining one of Grice's maxims of conversation, mention something irrelevant to the topic and students get confused. However, when the students realize that the irrelevant information is used as an example to explain the maxim of relevance and students get an "authentic" example of how the irrelevant information violate the maxim of relevance in conversation, the dialogic discourse is authenticated. In this sense, "a drill, or a recitation in chorus of an invented dialogue, can be authentic language-learning tasks within the social context of the classroom" (p. 126). In sum, van Lier's point is that only when learners are aware of what they are doing and are committed to what they are learning, can learning be authentic even though learning materials and process might be inauthentic. However, in a foreign language classroom, if the teacher uses the so-called "teacherese" to facilitate students' understanding, the language could be said to be authentic in the classroom, although it might not be authentic in the real world.

On the other hand, van Lier (1996) distinguishes between *equality* and *symmetry* in the classroom. He regards being symmetric as things such as equal rights and duties to participate, while being equal is relevant to participants' status and power. For van Lier, being symmetric is not necessarily being equal, and vice versa. For example, in classroom discussions, some more articulate and aggressive students might dominate the entire class and leave other students with no chance to express their ideas, although, theoretically, each student has equal rights and obligations to participate in the classroom discussion. That is, it "is a mistake to suppose that inauthentic interaction is due to inequality in terms of status or even power" (p. 141). Rather, authentic interactions in the classroom are always the result of unsymmetrical participation of students.

Finally, van Lier (1996) further points to the authenticity of classroom, and he states that, in terms of pragmatic authenticity in the classroom, there are at least three components to be taken into consideration: context, purpose, and interaction. The context includes the setting, participants, topic, and activity. The setting refers to the physical environment "where the language use occurs" (p. 138). Participants include people involved in the activity of language use and many other contextual forces they bring to the setting, such as their family, cultural background, personality, beliefs, and attitude towards teaching and learning. Topics are the theme being discussed at the moment. Finally, *activity* does not necessarily only mean the activities currently practiced in the classroom. It may include rules, beliefs, and norms that link to the process of the activity both inside and outside the classroom.

Authentic Assessment

Finally, we need to discuss "authentic assessment." It seems logical that, in an authentic learning environment with authentic tasks, students' learning outcomes should be assessed authentically. Koh (2017) distinguishes authentic assessment from conventional assessment. He states that standardized paper-and-pen tests in conventional assessment feature their true-false, matching or multiple choice types of closed-ended formats. These types of tests are said to be objective, easy-to-administered, and summative and are subject to behaviorist learning theory. Students are encouraged to memorize pieces of facts and teachers' teaching performances are even judged based on students' test scores. "As a result, the intended curriculum was reduced to a drill-and-practice of decontextualized factual and procedural knowledge" (p. 5). In traditional ways of assessment, learners, as recipients of knowledge, are always tested for the knowledge they acquire from textbooks or the Internet. In the assessment process, learners are required to be objective, logical, structured, and follow the so-called standard answers. Expressing feelings and emotions and encouragement of creativity and critical thinking are always ignored in the process of assessment.

Unlike conventional assessment, "authentic assessment is characterized by open-ended tasks that require students to construct extended responses, to perform an act, or to produce a product in a real-world context" (Koh, 2015, p. 5). They intend to assess students' higher-level learning outcomes, such as critical and creative thinking, complex problem solving, collaborative and communicative skills, and lifelong learning, which are required as a global citizen in the 21st century. Most importantly, the tasks assigned for students to be assessed authentically must be relevant to their daily life or future professional career. Authentic assessment is rooted in the constructivists' learning theory, which views co-construction of knowledge through social interactions in the learning process as very important.

Koh (2017) summarizes criteria for authentic assessment from relevant literature. Among them, some principles are particularly important in the course of designing assessment tasks. First, the tasks must be real and relevant to the real-world context. That is, they must reflect those real situations that students might face in their daily life or in their future workplace. Second, assessment tasks must be aimed to assess students' higher level of learning performance, such as critical and creative thinking and judgement, problem-solving, collaborative and communicative skills, and construction of knowledge. Finally, assessment tasks must be perceived by students as having values beyond school. That is, students must be able to feel the tasks interesting and useful for their life beyond school.

Authentic materials can be obtained in our daily life and authentic learning environment and activities can be developed by directly relating the activities to what may occur in our daily life, too. You do not have to go too far to get your instructional materials or to think about a particular theory to apply to your activities. Just plan your cross-cultural exchange activities as naturally as you would plan your daily life, and just make sure "that there is indeed an exchange or active dialogue taking place. Otherwise, the students may as well be watching a video" (Gerstein, 2000, p. 181). More information and details relevant to authentic assessment will be addressed in Chapter 7, focusing on assessment of cross-cultural exchanges.

Learning Environment and Learning Experience

Aside from learning materials and learning activities, the teacher should also consider the entire project as a learning experience for the students. Providing students with a pleasant and meaningful learning environment is key to successful cross-cultural exchanges and to students' learning outcomes. In the field of teaching and learning, the learning condition or the learning environment of an individual can play an important role on the effect of a student's learning outcomes. For example, what instruction has the person been given and what has his or her experience in the past hour or the past year led the person to expect in a given situation? Experiences act on an individual in a variety of ways, and these experiences may determine the effects of present experience and guide their response in new situations (Malone, 1991).

Chuah (2007) points out the importance of students' experience in e-learning and argues that online experiences should be designed to attract, inform, and invoke learners. He proposes a four-realm model for designing e-learning experiences; the design should be entertaining, educational, esthetic, and escapist. Chuah suggests that if an e-learning environment is entertaining and esthetic, it is more likely that students will be attracted and be passively immersed in the e-learning environment and eventually learn. On the other hand, students may be actively engaged in their learning if the e-learning environment, being educational and escapist, can provide them with useful information and requires students to perform many tasks. Natriello (2006) also states that there are both internal and external factors that may affect students' learning online, such as how technology-mediated lessons or activities are developed, how the international structure of online groups is formed, and what the educational decisions are. Both Chuah and Natriello are actually addressing the importance of communication tools and learners' experience with the tools. In the case of text exchanges, such as CMC, quick and constructive responses and mutual understanding may encourage students' participation in the virtual community.

The same is true for a cross-cultural exchange environment that requires students' direct physical contacts with their exchange partners, such as study abroad. A friendly atmosphere and multicultural understanding should be developed to ensure that students will have a pleasant cross-cultural learning experience. This requires partner teachers to carefully plan the activities early. Some practitioners' successful cross-cultural exchange programs have suggested that, to ensure that students will have wonderful experiences travelling to another country, teachers need to do a lot of things before their departure. For example, teachers might have to recruit enthusiastic and experienced professors and staff to survey students for their expectations of the forthcoming trip and necessary cultural adjustment to organize an orientation session, and to schedule academic visits, cultural visits and social activities (Fabregas Janeiro, Fabre, & Rosete, 2012; Brown & Aktas, 2012). In this mode of cross-cultural exchanges, raising students' cultural awareness is particularly important in terms of providing students with a pleasant learning environment and an enjoyable learning experience. It is because cultural conflicts and cultural misunderstandings can always spoil the atmosphere of cross-cultural exchanges.

Samuels (2013), on the other hand, views the learning environment and learning experience from a humanistic perspective. He refers to the 20th-century humanism as a good match for the 21st-century technology in cyberspace. He argues that "if our students feel better about themselves, they will achieve greater results as learners....the more inclined students are to share their feelings, interests, values, hopes, and dreams, the stronger and more self-confident they will be" (p. 2). In cross-cultural exchanges, either in face-to-face encounter or in Cyberspace, people communicate through "aural, visual, and written discourse;…one can reveal interests, innermost feeling, core values, and straightforward opinions" (p. 2). In cross-cultural exchanges, students have to communicate with people from different cultures. They make friends, develop their ego, discover themselves, and have a greater sense of self-esteem. The philosophy of humanism can actually fit into cross-cultural exchanges, such as developing relationships, "recognizing inter-dependence, expressing one's feeling, achieving one's potential, sharing oneself, and giving and receiving support" (p. 3).

Motivation and Benefits

Motivation is fundamental to every kind of learning and can be an important factor for successful learning. Students can be either intrinsically or extrinsically motivated to participate in cross-cultural exchanges as long as they feel that the activities are beneficial to them, for example, social, cultural, and professional learning, making friends, and language learning. In the case of language learning, Vinther (2011) argues that even though two groups of students are non-native English speakers, they can still be motivated to communicate in English and express themselves. Vinther's study involved Chinese and Danish EFL students. The theoretical framework applied to the study was mainly Vygotsky's sociocultural approach and other theories relevant to the link between motivation and autonomy. The two groups of students had e-mail exchanges with each other, sharing whatever cultural accounts and narratives they were interested in. Vinther concludes that this open-ended type of task combined with a high degree of autonomy might highly motivate students to use the target language they are learning.

Mady (2011) did a research study, exploring the long-term impacts of brief bilingual exchanges. She examined Francophone and Anglophone participants of the exchange programs sponsored by The Society for Educational Visits and Exchanges in Canada (SEVEC) and concluded that participants of short-term bilingual exchanges had confidence in their language abilities, continued to use their second language and had better bilingual job opportunities. Mady's study shows that the existence of benefits may be highly associated with willingness to learn. Wang's (2013) analysis of successful cross-cultural videoconferences echoes Mady's conclusion of the importance of the benefits of the project to students and shows that by only being mutually beneficial can a cross-cultural videoconferencing project be successful. Her study involved native English speakers in the United States and Chinese speakers in Taiwan, who were learning English as a foreign language. Although Taiwanese students might learn English from American students, it seemed that there was no reason for American students to stay at the videoconference and teach Taiwanese students English if they did not feel benefitted from the cross-cultural encounter. In reality, as journalism majors, these American students got a chance to learn how to interview people from a different culture, and their interview reports contributed to their campus newspaper received extremely favorable responses.

In describing the collaboration between Nelson Mandela Metropolitan University (NMMU) in South Africa and Michigan State University (MSU) in the United States, Austin and Foxcroft (2011) also claim that one of the factors that contributed to the success of their collaboration was the opportunities it provided for mutual learning. They account that a "critical factor in the success of the partnership is that the work has brought benefits to both institutions" (p. 122). The collaboration focused on organizational change, faculty development, and innovative approaches to teaching and learning. NMMU participants learned all the knowledge, strategies, and skills required in their current situation from experts in these fields. As for MSU, they could hardly have a chance to work with a university that is so diverse in student population and so desperately in need of a change. They had a good chance to put their theoretical study into practice in a contextual setting.

You, as the practitioner of a cross-cultural exchange project, have to remind yourself all the time throughout the course of developing a cross-cultural exchange project of the importance of keeping your students motivated to participate by showing your students that they can be benefitted from attending the project.

Collaboration vs. Cooperation, Plus Teachers' Coordination

There is no doubt that collaboration or cooperation is an essential element in a cross-cultural exchange project that involves two or more groups of students from different cultures. You and your partner teachers need to decide whether you want your students to collaborate or cooperate in the project. You might want to discuss with your partner teachers which types of exchanges may benefit both of the two groups of students the most. I describe the different natures of collaboration and cooperation in the following sub-sections.

Collaboration

Collaboration and cooperation are two terms commonly misunderstood as being able to be used interchangeably. However, the two terms are different in nature. In a collaborative task, members of the work team have a shared goal and each of the members may be responsible for a part of the task, and only as each member contributes his or her part to the task can the group achieve the goal. For example, students may be assigned to design a class newsletter. All the students in the class can be divided into different groups, based on their specialties and interests, to work as authors, reviewers, editors, proof-readers, and art designers. There is a shared goal in this case: to publish a newsletter. Members in a group are said to be interdependent. It is always the case that one can hardly fulfill his or her assignment without the information provided by other group members. Lacking one role can make it impossible for the collaborative groups to achieve their goals.

However, as pointed out be Herrington et al. (2010), "simply placing students in groups will not necessarily result in collaboration....[Collaboration aims at] 'solving a problem or creating a product which could not have been completed independently' " (p. 28). As pointed out by Winer and Ray (1994), collaboration can be seen in a task of collective responsibility. In this case, the joint identity of the group is more emphasized and is given more credit than an individual member of the group. Furthermore, one of the characteristics of collaboration is that a collaborative task may lead to a hierarchical structure, namely one member's work may affect or may be affected by other group members and how a member may proceed may be subject to the decision of other members. In a cross-cultural exchange, a collaborative project may be developed to engage two or more groups of students in the joint and valuable project so that each group can contribute its part to the project from a different perspective or a different expertise, e.g., a joint investigation of a global issue, so that the collaboration can make one plus one greater than two.

It is not uncommon that teachers receive complaints from students who feel frustrated at the collaborative task they have been assigned to fulfil. Mendeloff and Shaw (2009) describe their frustrations in an American-Canadian collaboration on which they worked. They point out some issues commonly found in a collaborative project and made some suggestions to solve these problems. First, they suggest individual work can be integrated into a collaborative project. Mendeloff and Shaw found that "students had a more favorable response to those assignments with which they had greater individual control and were much more critical of those tasks that required coordination and cooperation with others to complete" (p. 41). Second, in a collaborative project, it is always the case that some participants may be more dominant than others. Most participants may just contribute the minimum to the entire project. In this case, grouping students and grading students' achievement are particularly important. Equal accountabilities to hold and equal opportunities to contribute to the collaboration have to be taken into consideration in the development of a cross-cultural project. Finally, as pointed out by Mendeloff and Shaw, the pedagogical value of a collaborative project is not always obvious to students themselves. As one can imagine, a cross-cultural collaborative project is always deliberately developed by partner teachers. Each specific step or each task has its pedagogical objectives and is aimed at particular skills for students to learn. To the teacher's disappointment, students do not always appreciate the opportunity for them to learn. They complain that there is too much work and insufficient time for them to complete the tasks and that some tasks are just wasting their time. In a cross-cultural project, two culturally different groups of students can be encouraged to participate in the design process. Under this circumstance, students can better understand how they can benefit from the cross-cultural collaboration and can be better motivated to participate in the cross-cultural learning.

Cooperation

Unlike a collaborative learning context, in a cooperative learning context, members of a group work towards their own goals. Their goals may be similar yet personal. For example, a study group may be organized for members to encourage each other in the course of dissertation writing and exchange valuable information. Each member has his or her own research topic, schedule, and approaches to the study. However, members in the group may help each other with some necessary information, words of encouragement, and suggestions from different perspectives. Another example based on my personal experience of cross-cultural exchange is the one my partner teacher and I had. Our students (Taiwanese students and American students) communicated through videoconferences for an entire semester. There was no specific project for them to work collaboratively to accomplish. They just discussed the assigned topics and learned each other's language and cultures and probably each other's professional knowledge.

Generally speaking, the relationship between members of a cooperative group is one of being connective. There is no clear power relation between members and no clearly defined structure of the team. The relationship between members is said to be less formal, and each member is working toward his or her own goal and retains his or her authority and power. In this type of cross-cultural exchange project, participants may learn each other's language, culture, or profession. The structure of cooperation may be loosely organized. Each participant may voluntarily or randomly contribute to the cooperative group.

Coordination of the Teacher

Whether to collaborate or to cooperate in a cross-cultural exchange project may require the partner teachers' consensus. In this case, teachers in cross-cultural exchange programs actually play the role of a coordinator. Different forms of cross-cultural exchange may lead to different types of learning environment and outcomes and different degrees of involvement. For example, in a collaborative learning environment, group members may have higher involvement and also greater intensity. On the other hand, in a cooperative learning environment, group members may participate and share information at ease and their involvement will not affect other members. The way to pair or group students interculturally may depend on a lot of factors; you need to discuss with your partner teachers and even to take your students' opinions into consideration. Teachers conducting a cross-cultural exchange program need to coordinate between their partner teachers and their own students before they can develop a program that meets both groups of students' needs, expectations, and benefits. DeLong et al. (2011), researchers of an exchange case mentioned earlier, describe the way they paired their culturally different students. Their students in the design profession were first required to post a photograph, introduce themselves, and describe their interests on the common website, and students were allowed to choose their own partners based on their interests and expertise.

In either a cooperative or a collaborative project, students may not be provided with equal opportunities to contribute or to learn. Some dominant members may deprive others of their opportunities to contribute, and students' interests vary. For example, A topic interesting to some members may not be interesting to others. In sum, both collaboration and cooperation have advantages and disadvantages. Coordination always occurs because of differences. Without teachers' coordination, two groups of students with different cultures and located in different geographical areas will not have any chances to collaborate or to cooperate. Winer and Ray (1994) argue that we should not envision a scenario of melting pot anymore. Rather, people should accept and respect differences between or among them. These differences or diversities can include physical traits, such as skin color, ethnicity, and sexual orientation, styles, personalities, preferences, and family. However, Denise (1999) also points to the fact that coordination can make collaboration or cooperation more effective, but it is not necessarily related to how successful the program is and how well students achieve in the program. Partner teachers may have to work together and have the project well-planned. It may be necessary to integrate cooperative elements with collaborative elements to ensure students' learning and their level of satisfaction.

Cultural Awareness

The importance of cultural awareness has been discussed a lot in reports on cross-cultural encounters. Cultural awareness refers to not only being aware of and being able to tolerate a different culture, but also well understand one's own culture and how it is perceived by different cultural groups. Although we do not need to be so extremely sensitive to cultural issues as to stereotype a particular group of people, it is possible that cultural issues may ruin your whole exchange project. For example, in the classroom, Western students may be more discussion-oriented and they even challenge the teacher's authority, while Asian students may exhibit a so-called "listening culture." They listen to the teacher's lectures attentively and consider what their teacher says as powerful wisdom (Wiggan & Hutchison, 2007). Another example of cultural differences is that Western students tend to value individual accomplishment and personal interests, while Asian students place team accomplishment in the first place and they may sacrifice personal interests for the benefits of the whole team. You need to draw particular attention to these issues in the course of designing and assessing the exchange activities, for example, group work or individual assignment and cooperation or competition in nature. Different cultures can also cause different interpretations of or different approaches to a particular issue. Kachru and Nelson (2006) provide examples of genres across cultures. They illustrate through analysis how book blurbs may be approached differently by international publishers and local publishers. This may imply different cultural groups that may have different ways of thinking or thought patterns.

Another issue, although it may not be directly related to cultural differences, deserves cross-cultural partners' attention. It is about the distribution of power between or among partner schools. Wiggan and Hutchison (2009) term it *cognitive allocation*. As they recount, the so-called *New World Order* is actually a Western standard. The hegemonic and dominant Western cultures and social rules are actually penetrating the disadvantaged minority world. Under this circumstance, in the case of international students or teachers, "members of the dominant groups do not need to spend their energy to adjust to the school curriculum, which is an extension of societal norms" (p. 13). Viewed from this perspective, cultural awareness means more than tolerance of different cultures. It can be expanded to mean discarding a sense of superiority or inferiority toward a particular culture. That is, each culture is equally unique and deserves equal respect. In an occasion, I asked one of the international students in my class about where he was from, and he felt reluctant to answer my question. (Eventually he did not tell me where he was from.) I asked him whether he was afraid that I might not know his country, and he nodded to agree. Like some people feeling their cultures are superior, it is equally unnecessary to feel inferior about one's own culture. For me, this is the real meaning of cultural awareness. As mentioned earlier, cultural awareness is more than just understanding and tolerance of other cultures. Understanding our own culture and how our own culture is perceived by others is equally important. However, little relevant literature explores what the impact of self-awareness may have on one's intercultural learning. Intercultural learning is actually a two-way and reciprocal process. On the one hand, in cross-cultural communications, we learn from other cultures. On the other hand, we contribute to the learning of our intercultural partners. Puntney (2017) maintains that only by comparing with others can one really understand his- or her-self. Cultural elements are not matters of right or wrong and superior or inferior. Rather, they can be understood in relative terms. Only through comparison can we see strengths or weaknesses of a particular cultural element. Something we take for granted in our own culture may not be accepted by other cultures. The global community we are living in is better seen as a salad bowl in which each ingredient can contribute to the entire taste of the bowl and can complement each other to make the dish more nutritious and more agreeable for our taste.

In addition to culture itself, languages also matter. Here I do not intend to discuss different languages spoken by different groups of people. Rather, I refer it to "personal languages." That is, different people may use and interpret the same piece of discourse differently in regular communications, not to mention cross-cultural communications. To understand individual differences, cross-cultural communicators need a certain degree of sensitivity and require considerable exposure to different people and different cultures.

Design of Intercultural Learning Pedagogies

Harvey (2017) descries three kinds of pedagogies for intercultural learning: constructivist pedagogies, experiential pedagogies, and learner-centered pedagogies. A well-designed cross-cultural exchange program actually needs to integrate these essential elements into one rich and rewarding intercultural learning environment. First, in intercultural learning, learners need to be provided with chances to communicate and construct knowledge with the teacher, peer learners, experienced cross-cultural participant, and international students. Second, in an intercultural learning pedagogy, learners should be able to personally experience cross-cultural encounters with people from different cultures. A short overseas trip or interactions with students on the campus will facilitate their intercultural learning and heighten their culture awareness. Finally, an intercultural learning pedagogy should be learner-centered. That is, if it is appropriate, students can be invited to participate in the process of designing the pedagogy. Needs analysis of students' preferences, interests, and requirements is also helpful for designing pedagogy for students' perspectives.

Jackson (2018), on the other hand, insists that intercultural learning requires teachers' or mentors' interventions. She argues that intercultural learning will not automatically occur by simply putting students in a different cultural environment or in a cross-cultural a cross-cultural encounter and that current intercultural training programs always "ignore cultural diversity within groups and tend to promote Otherization and stereotyping. Students can easily miss important parts of cultural learning without optimal interventions. Jackson organized an online course to monitor students' intercultural learning before, during, and after students' overseas experiences.

Jackson (2018) offered a course entitled *Intercultural Communication and Engagement Abroad* at a Hong Kong institution. This is an online course enrolled by international exchange students. All of them were taking part in a year-long or semester-long international exchange program. According to Jackson, these students taking this course studied in host countries, including Canada, the United States. Japan, Australia, and other countries such as "Belgium, Finland, Germany, Ireland, the Netherlands, Singapore, South Africa, and the UK" (p. 124). The research collected both qualitative and quantitative data from different sources, including

> Application forms for the course and international exchange program, in-depth pre- and post-course transcriptions of interviews that were conducted in either Chinese or English,…survey questionnaire responses, forum posts, fieldwork reports and related posts, digital images, reflective essays, pre- and post-IDI reports and [the researcher's] fieldnotes." (p. 123) Stored in a computer program for management and analysis of the data.

After comparing the results of her study with other similar studies without intervention involved, Jackson (2018) found that her participants gained much more points in their IDI score than other groups of participants did. She then insists that students need to be guided and intervened in their overseas experiences in order for intercultural learning to be successful. In Jackson's own case, she used a gull-group, them-based forum, fieldwork tasks with small group sharing, and reflective essay writing to encourage students to ponder, to share, and, most importantly, to learn.

MODES OF EXCHANGES

There are different modes of interaction that can be practiced in cross-cultural exchanges. One exchange project may integrate different modes of interaction into the entire project to make the exchange project more interesting and meaningful to ensure the effectiveness of students' learning. Depending on the availability of your communication facilities, budget, administrative and financial support from the school or other institutions, and your school calendar, you need to discuss with your partner teachers to decide on which mode or modes are best for your exchange project. In this section, I discuss different modes of possible arrangement for cross-cultural exchanges, namely face-to-face fieldtrip, computer-mediated communication, videoconferencing, blended communication, study abroad, teaching abroad, and distance education.

Field Trips

Field trips refer to students' physical visits to their exchange partners abroad for a short-term stay. In this section, I first review literature reporting on field trips in a cross-cultural exchange project because physically visiting the partners of a cultural exchange project may be seen as a traditional way of cross-cultural exchanges. It takes time and costs money; yet the first-hand language and cultural messages students experience cannot really be made possible otherwise. Before the development of modern technologies for communication, a field trip to visit geographically far apart partners may be the only way to develop relationships and friendships with exchange partners. A field trip can be a short-term visit to a culturally different region or nation or a long-term exchange project and can aim at different objectives, such as language and cultural learning or professional learning.

There are at least two advantages of a field trip: change of attitude and learner authenticity. First, a face-to-face encounter may lead to change of attitude. Ellenwood and Snyders (2010) report on a cultural exchange project featuring a virtual journey coupled with a face-to-face exchange. They argue in favor of contextualism by saying that "traits are determined by multiple factors and…the individual's social environment is paramount in shaping personality" (p. 549). They further apply social judgement theory to argue that involvement in something with some people may contribute to change of attitude toward people. Based on this theory, Ellenwood and Snyders believe that if "people are exposed to individuals from different cultures, they may come to realize that their negative attitudes toward people of difference have been misplaced. Over time, exposure can result in shifts of attitude, beliefs, and opinion" (p. 540). Their findings show that at the beginning of their study, participants "had a tendency to respond behaviorally to others of difference before thinking. By the end, they were more likely to think before they respond" (p. 563).

The second advantage of field trips is that field trips may provide students with first-hand experience and information. People can be familiar with a foreign culture by exposing themselves to a lot of reading materials or audio-visual media. However, they also tend to believe something by actually seeing it. The nature of a cultural exchange program is seen as more student-centered than that of a traditional classroom. Lee's (1995) conceptual framework of authenticity mentioned earlier, namely learner and learning authenticity, can provide cultural exchange practitioners with a guide in the course of designing a cultural exchange program. The following examples of fields trips will show how field trips in other countries may have different learning objectives and students may learn in different ways and in different countries.

The Case of Faculty Led Study Abroad Program

In this section, I will briefly present four field-trip cases, which are different in nature and different in their project and research design. First, in their study, Fabregas Janeiro, Fabre, and Rosete (2012) describe how a faculty led study abroad program was organized and conducted and what might contribute to the success of a study abroad program. They first define Faculty Led Program as "short academic abroad programs, ..., where college students travel within a group, directed and supervised by one or more professors from the same institution" (p. 377).

In their study, Fabregas Janeiro et al. (2012) took 43 students of Universidad Popular Autonona del Estado de Puebla (UPAEP) in Mexico on a Faculty Led Program to travel to Oklahoma City to visit Oklahoma State University in the U.S. The authors claim that the collaborative programs were successful. After the orientation in the U.S., the Mexican students generally participated in academic and social activities around 16 hours per week during four days of the week. On Wednesdays, students were scheduled to visit organizations or institutions relevant to their fields of study, such as supermarkets, news agents, factories, and radio and television stations.

Fabregas Janeiro et al. (2012) conclude that a successful study abroad program requires detailed planning, proper selection of the professor involved in the process, and a solid relationship between partner schools. They further suggest that establishing clearer guidelines for the responsibilities of students and teachers, conducting deeper orientation sessions before arriving at the host countries, direct involvement of school authorities, and conducting open dialogues among students, professors, and members of the host university are also very important.

Another faculty-led study abroad program was conducted and reported by Brown and Tignor (2016). Brown and Tignor's account focuses on faculty-led, short-term study abroad programs for students in teacher education. They argue that faculty-led, short-term study abroad programs are particularly appropriate for students who are preparing to be teachers in a multi-cultural context and in a globalizing era. First, to be prepared as culturally competent teachers to teach in a multicultural context, preservice teachers need to possess intercultural competencies, and overseas experiences are crucial to the development of intercultural skills. Second, students in teacher education are always constrained by particular course structures and certification requirements in the field, and long-term study abroad programs may not be easy for them to manage. Short-term study abroad programs held in summer or winter break can be good choices for them. Third, overseas experiences may help preservice teachers personally be exposed to different cultures and experience cultural differences. In this way, they may be more prepared to deal with cultural, ethnical, and gender issues in a diversified classroom. This may be a typical reflective experiential learning. Preservice teachers going abroad in the host countries may observe classes taught by local teachers, do student teaching in the host countries or do some kinds of service learning or research. Fourth, leading a study abroad program may have the potential for future cross-cultural collaboration or research. Finally, according to Brown and Tignor, study-abroad programs led by faculty are more effective and money-saving. Especially, diverse "faculty members have the potential to attract a more diverse student body for study abroad programs, so recruiting faculty of various backgrounds may be an effective method of recruiting a diverse group of students for faculty-led programs" (p. 69).

In the case of faculty-led short-term study abroad for preservice teachers, choosing an appropriate destination is particularly important in that the experiential learning opportunities may be relevant to preservice teachers' future teaching environment and, hence, may familiarize them with their future student population before they start teaching a particular ethnic or religious group.

The Case of ESP Program

The second case of field trip is the one conducted by Yogman and Kaylani (1996). They describe in their research report on an English for Specific Purposes (ESP) program designed for mixed level students about some barriers they experienced. This project was a four-week program, involving a small group of college business majors from a Baltic state to take business-related courses in Pittsburgh, USA. The researchers experienced some barriers in the course of the project. Before the visit by the Baltic students, the American teachers had problems doing comprehensive needs analysis, which is an essential part in the ESP field. Because of different levels of English proficiency and different reasons for the Baltic students to take courses in the U.S., teachers felt pressured to pass on frank evaluations of the students' levels of English proficiency and reluctantly allowed students with limited English proficiency to study in the U.S.

Another barrier the American teachers experienced was finding it hard to get interfaculty cooperation. In the ESP field, it is crucial for language teachers and content teachers to cooperate to achieve their mutual goal. However, in realty, the faculty always had heavy workloads, and it was not easy to convince them to plan the joint project earlier. On the other hand, content teachers and language teachers might want to protect their "territory" and secure their professional expertise.

Based on the drawbacks the teachers encountered, Yogman and Kaylani (1996) designed the second year program and added an American culture class to the program. Aside from some improvements needed to be made, the researchers suggest two ways to go in the future of developing similar programs: one is that short-term language programs supporting content-area programs can differ according to how much language support is required by the content program, and the other one is the development of mini-projects, which can motivate students to learn and which are advantageous for evaluation.

The Case of Surveying before Departure to Another Country

Another two cases of field trips were reported by Brown and Aktas (2012) and Doring, Lahmar, Bouabdallah, Bouafia, Bouzid, and Gobsch (2012). Researchers of the two cases, unlike the previous two cases, report from students' and teachers' perspectives on their hopes and fears about traveling to another country. Brown and Aktas argue that international education has become a major export industry at university level, and the "international student market…has significant growth potential" (p. 4). Analyses of the perceptions of students involved in the study aboard in another country can motivate students to participate in such programs and may urge changes to meet students' needs.

Brown and Aktas (2012) study Turkish university students' hopes and fears about traveling to the West, and they found that Turkish students, before embarking on a European exchange trip, mostly expected their trip to be self-developmental and culturally educational. On the other hand, as Muslim students, they were afraid of their adaption to a country in the developed Western world. Brown and Aktas raise the issue of differences between the origin country and the host country. They describe that "Muslim students face specific challenges owing to global tensions that affect host receptivity and intergroup relations, and …the impact and experience of the international sojourn will be different for this group than it may be for other groups" (p. 4). In the survey, Turkish Muslim students expressed their anxiety "with respect to possible discrimination over Turkey's status as a less developed economy and as a Muslim country" (p. 15).

Similar to Brown and Aktas's (2012) study, Doring et al. (2010) surveyed a group of teachers and students who participated in a German-Algerian University exchange program. They found that teachers and students had large differences in their hopes and fears towards the academic exchange program. Doring et al. surveyed teachers' and students' perspectives of and attitudes towards a German-Algerian exchange program before they headed for the partner country. They divided the questionnaire into five topical areas: knowledge about the partner country, how the partner country is depicted in your domestic media, study and researcher conditions in their own country and in the partner country, and their intercultural communication competencies. Findings of the study showed that students and teachers from both partner universities had very different hopes and fears for the upcoming reciprocal academic exchange.

In terms of knowledge about the partner country, Doring et al. (2010) point out that both German and Algerian participants had little direct experience with their partner country. However, in terms of time spent on informing themselves about the partner country, Algerians participants demonstrated a greater degree of knowledge than their German participants. When asked how they would describe the coverage of domestic media about their partner country, the Algerian participants tended to have a neutral or positive perception of Germany, while German participants tended to have a negative perception of Algeria. Both Algerian and German participants pointed out that their domestic media do not really report sufficiently on their partner country. In the category in which participants were asked to evaluate the study and research conditions at home and in the partner country, generally German participants considered that the basic conditions they held important at their own university were rather fulfilled, while Algerian participants had a very negative attitude towards the study and research conditions in their own country. Speaking of expectations of the forthcoming foreign exchange program, the Algerian participants valued the foreign exchange and contact much higher than their German counterparts did.

Based on how Algerian and German participants responded to the above-mentioned categories of questions relevant to their perceptions and background information of their partner country, one might easily expect how they would respond to the following category concerning their interest in the upcoming academic exchange with their partner country. Generally speaking, the Algerian participants had a much stronger interest in spending a period of time at a German university studying or conducting research than the German participants had at an Algerian university. The reasons might not be too surprising. The Algerian participants were interested in working academically in Germany basically because of "the quality of German facilities, the high academic quality and reputation of German universities, as well as the overall higher standard of living" (p. 251).

By contrast, the German participants did not show really a positive attitude towards their partner country, Algeria. They indicated "that Algeria was not up to par with other European or North American countries and was therefore less attractive as a destination for a foreign exchange" (p. 251). They were concerned about the academic opportunities, the language barrier, the security situation, and cultural differences they might face in Algeria. The last category of investigation was concerned with participants' intercultural competencies. As Doring et al. (2010) note, intercultural "competency is a specific type of skill that is primarily obtained through personal experience" (p. 252). In this category, students were asked about their perceptions with regard to the partner country's people and interpersonal situations and what advice they would give to exchange students coming to their respective country. The researchers found that, because of lacking sufficient knowledge about their partner country, the participants' perception of and advice to their foreign counterparts strongly reflected cultural stereotypes and their advice to their counterparts implied how they perceive them.

The above-mentioned cases of cross-cultural exchange are typical field-trip projects. Students experienced authentic communication with their exchange partners. However, different researchers focused on different issues. Fabregas Janeiro et al. (2012) describe a successful cultural exchange project, while Yogman and Kaylani (1997) point out some issues raised in a business English class with mixed level students. Brown and Aktas (2012) and Doring et al. (2012) surveyed how students and teachers perceive field trips to another country. These cases can be valuable information for both teachers and students who are planning field trips to another country. It is important to look at face-to-face cross-cultural encounters from different angles. Generally speaking, the face-to-face mode of cultural exchange takes more of the teacher's time to organize and can cost students a considerable amount of money. However, students can enjoy the above-mentioned advantages of field trips and engage themselves in different types of learning.

Computer-Mediated Communication (CMC)

In case a field trip to the partner class's country is impossible for whatever reasons, then computer-mediated communications (CMC) online may be another good way to practice cross-cultural exchanges. As well-spoken by Molenda and Boling (2008), "educational technology is the study and ethical practice of facilitating learning and improving performance by creating, using, and managing appropriate technological processes and resources" (p. 81). Traditionally CMC refers to those discussion forums available online. Participants are allowed to post text messages and to respond to any postings. In this type of text communications, people have more time to respond to each other, but non-verbal cues are lacking. In this section, I present theories and research studies relevant to this mode of communication.

Some scholars have been debating about the nature of CMC. Is CMC oral communication or written communication? For Mann and Stewart (2000) it is a hybrid mode of communication and it should be treated as a third mode and a unique kind of communication. On the one hand, CMC possesses advantages and disadvantages of both oral and written communication. On the other hand, computer technologies in CMC play an important and a unique role in communication, which is not salient in both oral and written communication. For some researchers, the oral aspects of CMC may be superficial, unfocused, and trite, and researchers might get faulty information if they intend to collect useful data. On the other hand, some point to the spontaneous and untainted nature of CMC. This characteristic of CMC may reveal a participant's real personality and thought (Mann & Stewart, 2000). Whatever is debated, one of the biggest contributions of digital technologies is that, as described by Tabot, Oyibo, and Hamada (2013), they are able to provide the triple A's learning, learning environments that are available to anyone, anywhere, and anytime because of the ubiquity and anonymity of the computer networks. In the following sections to come, I first discuss the written aspect of CMC, which is text communication. Mann and Stewart (2000) summarize some of the positive aspects of writing that can be found in CMC. First, asynchronous CMC such as e-mail and conferencing, "allows thoughtful, organized, and detailed communication" (p. 185). On the other hand, written scripts are static and permanent. They may help the conversation stay on track, and participants may easily refer to pervious messages.

In CMC, there are at least three issues apparently important and are worth discussion, namely communication tools, communication languages, and participation in the communication. In text communication, people need a tool as a platform for communication and a mutually understood language to present their views. Furthermore, issues of how, why, and when students participate in text communications are worth discussion. These issues are discussed respectively in the following sections to come.

Communication Tools

There are several tools available on the Internet to be used for text communication, such as e-mail, MSN Messenger, Bulletin Board Services (BBS), discussion forums, Learning Management System (LMS), and web-based language learning systems. I first discuss some evaluation reports on CMC tools and issues relevant to accessing to these tools available in relevant literature.

Options of Computer Communication Tools

A web-based learning management system can be seen as a course management system, and teachers use the system to manage all the courses they are offering. In a cross-cultural exchange program, teachers from two or more partner schools may develop a system to be used particularly for an exchange program. For example, in the exchange program that involved students from Taiwan, Japan, and the U.S. that I collaborated with Japanese and American teachers, a computer program called *EXCHANGE* was developed exclusively for participants of the program. Students were required to post their responses to the questions posed by the teachers and read and comment on other participants' postings (Wang, 1997). In another case of CMC that involved Taiwanese TESOL majors and American TESOL majors, students from different countries were allowed to discuss a topic or post their findings or assignments relevant to teaching English to speakers of other languages, using the computer management system *Moodle* and a *Facebook* website organized exclusively for the project. Students were required to post their lesson plans and other assignments on the Moodle system and use the Facebook social website to chat with their exchange partners, to develop friendships, and to informally acquire professional knowledge (Wang, 2013).

There are a lot more text communication tools available for educators to use. Cheung (2007) points out that web-based learning has been widely adopted in educational institutions for its flexibility of access, and, in order to examine how different learning management systems function, she notes that "a web-based learning management system offers four main areas of functions, namely curriculum design, communication and discussion, performance assessment and course administration" (p. 220). Cheung compares three well-known web-based learning management systems: WebCT, Blackboard, and Moodle and concludes that "WebCT and Blackboard are better than Moodle, and WebCT is the best. WebCT offers more sophisticated supports and allows more flexibility in designing curriculum and study schedules. These are especially suitable for continuing education courses" (p. 227). Cheung's study targets students in continuing education. As we can imagine, different web-based learning management systems may meet different teaching and learning needs and may be appropriate for different groups of students.

Koong and Liu (2007), on the other hand, did a similar yet more sophisticated research study to examine 25 popular Web-based course delivery programs available in the institutional market. Unlike Cheung (2007), Koong and Liu classified their assessments into six main categories: communication tools, productivity tools, student involvement tools, administration tools, course delivery tools, and curriculum design tools. They found that the six features have a total of 31 attributes. They then classified the 31 attributes into four major categories: primary attributes (found in more than 75% of all the software), secondary attributes (found in more than 50% of all the software), minor attributes (found in a percentage between 50 and 25 of all the software), and unique attributes (found in less than 25% of all the software). The primary attributes include Discussion Forums, File Exchange, E-Mail, Chat (communication attributes), Calendar/Program Review, Orientation/Help (productivity attributes), Self-Assessment (student involvement attribute), Authentication, Course Authorization, Registration Integration (administrative attributes), and Automated Testing and Scoring (course delivery attributes). That is to say, the above-mentioned attributes are more widely found in and are considered more critical to these course delivery programs. Based on their research findings, Koong and Liu (2007) suggest that developers "need to provide niche features and attributes or tools that can meet the needs of specific market segments because all online institutions as well as end-users are not necessarily homogeneous" (p. 264).

Still, Tabot et al. (2013) evaluate three most widely-used e-learning models and platforms: Blackboard Learning Systems, Moodle, and Sakai Project. They evaluate these three e-learning models from different perspectives such as: availability, feedback, cost, efficiency, levels of security, usability, browser compatibility, archiving, searching, tagging, staffing needs, and ability to customize and modify code. Tabot et al. find that each model has its own benefits and drawbacks. They conclude that "the choice for any organization (university, small business, government agency, etc.) chiefly depends on the needs of that particular organization. So proper needs analysis is key to achieving that process" (p. 23).

From the discussion above, we can be sure that the choice of an online communication tool is actually domain- or program-specific. Teachers or practitioners of CMC need to consider learning goals of the course, students' needs and preferences, and effectiveness of the tool before they make a decision to choose a communication tool for their programs. Yet, commercially available CMC programs are not the only options you can choose from. You might want to talk to computer programmers or technicians for your special needs and develop one specifically for your program. As we can tell, necessity leads to invention. The current appearance of CMC tools are actually the result of online communication needs.

Digital Divides in an Age of Information Technology

Aside from choosing a tool for communication, Murray (2000) draws people's attention to the issue of differential access to the technology. According to Murray, access "to and use of computers and the Internet mirror the socioeconomic divide between rich and poor individuals and nations" (p. 409). She argues that race, gender, education, income, and mother tongue are all predictors of computer access and use. Murray further points out, across nations, per capita Internet use is high among the affluent postindustrial nations. Given all the issues mentioned above, we cannot deny that more research studies in CMC are needed to ensure that it plays a proper role as a tool of cross-cultural exchanges. The issue of socio-economic status and about money was later termed the first digital divide.

Some scholars argue that the first digital divide has shown a sign of diminishing and is becoming less apparent in society (Natriello, 2006; Hargittai, 2002; Attewell, 2001). Now comes the second digital divide. The second digital divide, according to these scholars, refers to the inequality between people in online skills, domains of knowledge, speakers of different languages, gender difference, etc. For example, flaming in CMC is sometimes turned into verbal threats or even physical attacks. Some groups of people may be especially vulnerable to cyber attacks, such as celebrities, well-known and privileged people, decision makers at a governmental or organizational level, and particular gender groups such as women and girls. Jane (2018) describes the phenomenon of how women and girls are unequally treated, threatened, and abused in the cyber world. She terms it *gendered cyberhate.* She provides a considerable number of cases showing that gendered cyberhate issues are indeed serious problems that deserve our attention. She interviewed many targets of gendered cyberhate and found that those who suffered verbal abuses online not only withdraw and disappear from the online discussion world but also "suffer psychologically, socially, professionally, economically, and politically" (p. 189). Based on various reports about inequality in the cyber world, Jane claims that, among different social groups, women and girls are particularly vulnerable to cyber abuses. Jane's study reveals that the impacts of gendered cyberhate on targeted women and girls may be far more than we can imagine, and "has the potential to impact the lives of real people in real ways" (p. 195).

According to Natriello (2006), the two divides are actually issues of access and use, and the two issues need to be examined simultaneously. He analyzes the issues from a sociological perspective and suggests that sociologists of education can play a critical role in solving the problems of unequal access and use of digital resources, and not just bring them to the attention of others. He argues that, as the new digital educational sector is emerging, sociologists of education need to develop and design new forms and new arrangements and a new digital educational infrastructure for education, and this may involve entrepreneurs, policy makers, educators, and parents.

Aside from the first and the second digital divides, Ragnedda and Ruiu (2018) raise the issue of the third level of digital divide, which is referred to as *benefits*. That is, the returning benefits people can gain by participating in any type of online activities. They connect the third level of the digital divide with social capital as the amount of social capital you possess may affect the way and the changes you make use of in the digital world and how you are rewarded in different forms of benefits. According to Ragnedda and Ruiu, different benefits that digital capital can bring to digital users, for example strong ties with virtual communities, enlarged social networks, increased visibility, and knowledge, trust, and freedom gained from participating in a virtual community. Those who possess less digital capital may be deprived of those benefits to a certain degree.

Similar to Ragnedda and and Ruiu's (2018) accounts on *benefits*, Wang (2015), on the other hand, views the third level of the digital divide from an education perspective. That is, how students can be benefitted from e-learning or m-learning through the guidance of the teacher or through interacting with peer learners. It is about the inequality of *learning* in an e-learning or m-learning environment. As Wang points out, e-learning or m-learning may be popular in the educational domain. However, little research has been done to investigate the role modern technologies can play in students' overall learning. It has become apparent that how the teacher makes use of digital technologies in the student learning process may greatly affect student motivation to learn and the learning outcomes. Wible (2005) also points out that the development and dissemination of technology and creation of digital contents are not really the problem of digital learning. Rather, the real problem is how teachers with technologies and contents handed to them can make use of digital sources to engage students into real learning. According to Wible, making the most use of digital technologies in education needs to take educational, social, and administrative structure into consideration so as to enrich the student learning experience.

The communication tools for cross-cultural exchanges mentioned above reveal at least two issues that practitioners of cross-cultural exchanges need to be aware of. One is that, in designing and choosing the communication tools, students' learning experiences should be prioritized in order to motivate students to learn and to facilitate their learning. After all, having a good time working on learning technologies does not necessarily mean really gaining useful professional knowledge. As Casquero, Benito, Romo, and Ovelar (2016) state, "Learners' acceptance of Web 2.0 technologies and patterns, generally used for non-educational purposes" (p. 112), and "students know and access services like YouTube and Twitter everyday, but generally they do not use this type of sites for learning" (p. 119). The other issue is that teachers need to make sure that each student has equal access and use of the communication tools and resources. Mann and Stewart (2000) state that use of digital devices and access to computer networks "will continue to be disproportionately concentrated among the better-off sections of society and more economically developed countries" (p. 216). As far as digital capital is concerned, it does not make sense if we mean to provide those privileged groups with more advanced digital devices to access, to use, and to be benefitted from. Merely focusing on the advancement of communication technologies might ignore the real meaning of educational technologies: to provide each student with equal learning opportunities.

Communication Languages

Mann and Stewart (2000) point out that the loss of visual cues in the virtual world has increased the "importance of language use as a social category cue" (p. 162). In addition to tools for communication, Murray (2000) raises some issues relevant to language use in CMC. She points out that, first, research studies have shown the hegemony of English. Whether members of the CMC speech communities are native speakers or non-native speakers of English, English norms may dominate in CMC. Second, control of the discourse of CMC does not seem to be evenly distributed among participants. Because there is a lack of physical cues and social norms in CMC, a phenomenon of flaming, debate, freedom from rules and adversarial argumentation can be seen in the CMC speech community. Cronje (2011) urges optimal use of available technologies in the teaching and learning context because it allows students to have more time to formulate and adjust their ideas and allows professors to see students' work beyond the written word in the case of PowerPoint files and videos. The point is: if teachers and students are speaking two different languages and are referring to two different cultures, then, how can a harmonious speech community develop?

Phillipson (2009) warns against the misconception of the term *lingua franca*, which should be referred to as "a neutral instrument for 'international' communication between speakers who do not share a mother tongue" (p. 147). He argues that any language can serve either good purposes such as facilitating and promoting communication or evil purposes, such as accelerating the division of a nation or a community as shown in the case of India. Phillipson further provides two paradigms of English: global English and world Englishes. In the global English paradigm, Anglo-American linguistic norms are stressed, and it is monolingual-oriented. There is no concern for languages other than English. The world Englishes paradigm, on the other hand, celebrates and supports diversity and a multidialectal-orientation. Advocates and users of world Englishes follow regional and national norms, and local languages have high prestige. The two paradigms reveal that a language is not just a language that we see and understand. A language has some invisible elements within it, such as culture, power, ideology, and historical background.

Another issue of language use in cross-cultural communications can be found in the case of English in Europe. Phillipson (2009) recounts that the consolidation of English in countries like the Philippines, India, or Nigeria is different from that in Europe. In Europe, two centuries ago, there were many languages consolidated as key state languages. In the mid-1900s, there was a gradual shift towards English because of the massive exposure of European people to the American mass media, TV programs, and films. On the other hand, in business and academics, executives and researchers were expected to communicate or publish in English. However, Phillipson raises yet another issue: domain loss and linguistic hierarchization. Generally speaking, the European Union (EU) is essentially a French-German project. Dominance of English might lead to domain loss and linguistic hierarchization. In Scandinavian countries, there are also concerns of domain loss and an increased use of English might marginalize other languages.

Similarly, Spencer-Oatey and Franklin (2009) also point out their concern over linguistic imperialism. They summarize some linguists' concern, saying that the dominance of English can lead to cultural domination by the originating countries, and the cultural elements can include consumerist values, religions, beliefs, scientific approaches, research, and popular culture. They argue that the key issue underlying all of the arguments is the interrelationship between language and community identity. That is, participants of CMC may choose a language associated with their community. However, there are also impacts on individual identity. If one feels less competent in English as a lingua franca, he or she might challenge his or her personal identity as a less competent person.

As mentioned above, terms such as *world Englishes*, *global English*, *English languages*, *English as a global lingua franca*, and *English as the lingua franca of the whole world* have emerged as a necessary result of the wide spread of English and of the heightened cultural awareness of the nations whose people use English as their mother tongue, second language, or foreign language (Crystal, 2003; Jenkins, 2003; Jenkins, 2007; McArthur, 2003). Although these terms have their specific definitions, they point to the fact of a diversified English as a language. There is no longer a term called "standard English"; rather, there are different Englishes existing in the world, such as American English, British English, Singapore English, South African English, Chinese English and Japanese English. In the United States, with the largest English-speaking population, whether to promote the English language as the official language has been hotly debated. The issue has been discussed from political, socio-economic, and educational perspectives. Both supporters and opponents of official English legislation have their seemingly reasonable arguments. The disputes have never reached a consensus. However, one thing for sure is that American English, and other Englishes as well, will keep being diversified. Variations in English or other languages may be caused by geographical separation, cultural differences, technical developments, mythological and religious practices, and things like lifestyles, foodstuffs, plants, animals and diseases that are unique to a particular region (Crystal, 2003).

Even in the same region, English is spoken in different ways among different groups of people. There are terms such as *dialects* (Fromkin, Rodman, & Hyams, 2014) and *varieties* (McArthur, 2003) used to describe people who speak the same language, but who speak it differently. For example, in the United States, there are a variety of American Englishes spoken by different groups of people, such as African-American English, Jewish English, and Spanglish (Spanish English) (McArthur, 2003). These varieties of English may differ in their pronunciation, spelling, grammar or vocabulary. The same is true for other languages. For example, Spanish is spoken differently in different Spanish-speaking countries or regions, such as Spain, Mexico, and other Latin American countries.

The issues mentioned above indicate that although there are considerable claims against English as a lingua franca and calls for respecting linguistic and cultural diversity, English may retain its status for the time being, and thus remain the medium of communication in cross-cultural communications. However, in the long run, we may expect and imagine that more and more languages will be used in cross-cultural communications. Cross-cultural exchange practitioners or participants have to keep in mind that "technology is not culturally neutral and even English is contextual like most other languages with potential for miscommunication" (Olcott, Jr, p. 78). As noted by Mitakidou (2011), in a society, disadvantaged groups of people do not "have to sacrifice their mother tongue in the process of acquiring the dominant language" (p. 83).

Participation and Social Presence in Computer-Mediated Communications

In addition to the issues of the language used in CMC as a communication tool, Ruberg, Moore, and Taylor (1996) raise another issue worthy of discussion: student participation and interaction in a CMC environment. They claim that the pattern of discourse in CMC is different from that of classroom face-to-face dialogue. Findings of their investigation show that, in a CMC environment, there is a shift away in status from teacher dominance. They also point out that "traditional classroom interactions typically consist of two-thirds to three-quarters teacher talk and one-third student talk" (p. 245), and in CMC the interaction type is generally a many-to-many one and is a student-centered discourse. However, findings of their study also show that the teacher is still the most influential participant and influences the outcome of the discussion a great deal in the CMC environment. In a virtual environment, there are some features not normally found in a traditional classroom, such as changes of power relations, increased student initiations, and performance not being judged. In computer-mediated communications, all participants in the discussion board are said to be equal in terms of power relations and rights to access. It does not matter whether you have a superior social status or are an expert in a particular field, you have the same right to get access to the discussion board as the other participants and have the same virtual norms to follow as the other participants.

On the other hand, Ruberg et al. (1996) also point out that, unlike the traditional initiation-response-evaluation sequence apparent in classroom interactions, students in CMC do not wait for the teacher to respond. Students can respond to their peers' questions if they know the answer or if they have some ideas. This may help develop students' self-confidence and encourage "collaborative problem-solving" (p. 261). Although Ruberg et al.'s study does not show a shift in dominance and influence from the teacher to the students, it might be only a matter of how much autonomous learning the teacher provides to the students. If students are provided with autonomous learning opportunities, computer-mediated communications may reveal students' real voices. Wang's (2008) study shows that the most taciturn students in the classroom are actually the most active participants in computer-mediated communications. It may be clear from her findings, in traditional classroom communications, time and space limits may prevent less articulate students from expressing their ideas. On the contrary, the openness and equal nature of CMC encourage those students to participate in discussions.

Tu and McIsaac (2002), on the other hand, raise yet another issue, social presence, in CMC. They first define *social presence* as "a measure of the feeling of community that a learner experiences in an online environment" (p. 131), such as intimacy and immediacy. Tu and McIsaac propose three dimensions of social presence: social context, online communication, and interactivity. They argue that task orientation, privacy, topics, social relationships, and social process are associated with social context and may contribute to the degree of social presence. For example, if the task is complex, interdependent, and it requires communication across distant locations, then the degree of social presence may increase. Another important factor that may affect the degree of social presence is social relationship. Generally speaking, CMC communicators feel less intimate and close to each other at the initial stage of online encounters. As they accumulate more information about and deeper impression of their CMC partners, their messages to their partners tend to be more and more friendly and personal.

Another factor that may affect CMC users' social presence is their language and computer skills. That is, the degree of social presence decreases and their anxiety increases if participants lack these skills to operate online. Wang (2015) points to three digital divides: access, use, and learning, in the digital age. If a person does not feel comfortable using the computer, reading the messages written in an unfamiliar language, or having no idea of how to make use of the messages online to learn, he or she may less likely feel a sense of belonging to the digital community and, thus, show less social presence.

Finally, online interactivity also contributes to the degree of social presence. Different communication styles, such as synchronous and asynchronous types of communication, may show different degrees of social presence. Generally speaking, in synchronous communications, people get immediate feedback and feel intimate with their online partners and, thus, have a deeper awareness of the existence of their online partners. Immediacy also provides online partners with encouragement and affective and cognitive learning.

Tu and McIsaac's (2002) research on the impact of social presence investigated 51 graduate students. Findings of their study show, in the dimension of social context, familiarity with recipients, informal relationships, better trust relationships, personally informative relationships, positive psychological attitude towards technology, and more-private locations are positively associated with social presence. In the dimension of online communication, the researchers identify some important factors that may increase the degree of social presence: CMC is stimulating, is expressive, conveys feelings and emotions, is meaningful, and is easily understood. In the dimension of interactivity, findings show that a timely response to messages, use of stylistic communication styles, casual conversations or use of communication strategies, appropriate length of the message, planning, creativity, intellectuality, and decision-making, and appropriate communication group size have a positive influence on social presence.

In addition to Tu and McIssaac, Garrison and Anderson (2003) also point to the importance of social presence. They describe it as the ability participants possess to participate in a virtual e-learning community as a 'real person', such as full personality. They point out that an individual can never learn in isolation and that community "is the fusion of the individual and the group; the psychological and sociological; the reflective and the collaborative" (p. 48-49). They also argue that although non-verbal text communication may lack verbal cues shown in real-time face-to-face communications, it is not at all impossible to develop social presence and create a sense of belonging in a virtual community learning environment. They point out that social presence can be established "through the use of greetings, encouragement, paralinguistic emphasis (e. g. capitals, punctuation, emoticons), and personal vignettes (i.e., self-disclosure)" (p. 50).

Garrison and Anderson (2003) classify social presence into three categories: affective responses, open communication, and cohesive responses. In affective responses, participants show their interest and persistence in participating in a community of inquiry. For example, participants may use punctuations, capitalization, and emoticons to show their emotion. On the other hand, they may use humor or teasing and self-disclosure to express their goodwill and friendship. The open communication category refers to participants responding to peers' questions or discussion in a reciprocal and respectful way, showing their trust and acceptance in the virtual community. Thus, the community demonstrates reflective and insightful communications. The previous two categories of social presence actually facilitate the development of the third category: cohesive responses. With the characteristics of the two categories, it may be easy to develop a cohesive community. In the virtual community, participants share meanings and have quality learning. This kind of community features its "addressing others by name...[and] using inclusive pronouns such as 'we' and 'our'" (p. 53).

Having discussed the importance and the categories of social presence, Garrison and Anderson (2003) remind teachers of an e-learning environment to optimally use the elements of social presence. In case social presence is overly stressed, then too much politeness for people may impede discussions and/or may raise challenges in a community of inquiry and may lead to superficial and unconstructive discussion. After all, the end of a community of inquiry is the learning outcomes.

Speaking of an e-learning environment, Khan (2016), on the other hand, provides a framework of eight dimensions of an e-learning environment. He argues that an e-learning environment should be taken into consideration and evaluated from the eight dimensions, namely institutional issues, management, technological issues, pedagogical issues, ethical issues, interface design, resource support, and evaluation. Under each dimension, there are many sub-categories or details to take into consideration, for example, in the institutional dimension educator may need to consider needs assessment, financial, infrastructure, cultural and content readiness, organization and change, implementation, budgeting and return on investment, partnerships with other institutions and stakeholders, etc., depending on the nature of the cross-cultural exchange project. There is one thing for sure, that is, evaluation of a cross-cultural exchange project in a CMC setting cannot solely rely on the communication tool. There are a lot more factors interconnected with one another that may contribute to either the success or failure of the project.

From the discussions above in this section, we may find that students' participation in CMC and their degree of social presence are closely correlated. A low degree of social presence may prevent students from participating in CMC. This may inform teachers that creating a pleasant and enjoyable learning environment can be crucial to ensure students' effective learning and participation in a virtual community. Digital natives' characteristics and needs are reflected in CMC discussion. Findings of Ruberg et al. (1996) show that, in a CMC discussion forum, students' initiations of a topic increased because of the multiple-thread nature of the CMC discussion forum. Ruberg et al. quote students' words and claim that CMC provides students with increased access to the instructor, increased involvement with course content, and more opportunities to demonstrate what they have learned.

Power Issues and Netiquette

In the virtual world, power relations are significantly minimized. Anonymity and absence of non-verbal cues blur the power divide. Perceptions of status leadership and power are less evident in the digital world. Mann and Steward (2000) describe the virtual world as a democratized setting for non-coercive and safe exchange of dialogue. Those who are hesitant to express themselves in a public space can do so in a virtual world. The virtual world is seen as being egalitarian, free and respectful. In it, gender, race, and social status seem irrelevant.

However, some people see the opposite side of the virtual world such as the digital divides mentioned earlier in this chapter. They argue that mostly participants of the virtual world are more powerful, wealthy young white men. As described by Mann and Steward (2000), based on different research studies, these views have been challenged. They argue that "awareness of social cues remains active online and ... that there are new social processes of domination and marginalization" (p. 163). These same researchers argue that research has shown that removal of social cues can lead to participants' focus on the available cue: language. In reality, language used online and perceivable online behaviors can reveal a lot about the identity of the netizen, such as age, gender, social status, ethnicity, education, and religion. For example, online users may create a picture of a member by examining the person's perspectives, attitude towards an issue, language used, and other online behaviors. There are factors that may help create divides or hierarchies in the virtual world, such as typing speed and familiarity with the language used. Those who cannot "compete" with others in a real-time chat or who may need more time to read the message because the language used in the message is not their mother tongue may turn out to be outsiders or bystanders of the online discussion community.

Speaking of power and authority in the virtual world, our view of an equal and a non-threatening place is also challenged. Hierarchies do exist in the virtual world, and they are just defined in another way. Mann and Stewart (2000) describe that, in the virtual world, more powerful and authoritative participants are those who have significant experiences and expertise with the virtual community. An insider/outsider divide is thus created. Those more powerful participants can consciously or unconsciously control the discussion and, as the mediator of a discussion group, decide on the appropriateness of a specific message and even on the eligibility of a person to participate. In some cases and to some extent, those in a higher status in an online discussion group are provided with some technical advantages or are granted the right to, say, delete a message, suspend a participant's account, and make official announcements.

In addition to issues concerning power, there are also issues relevant to netiquette in the virtual world. As in the real world, in which people are required to behave themselves, follow the social norms, and abide by the law, the same is true for the virtual world. Virtual norms and netiquette have been developed in a slow but sure way without even the awareness of netizens. Each netizen has to follow the net rules; otherwise he or she will be attacked by a group of netizens. Mann and Steward (2000) describe that netiquette can be viewed in two ways. "First, it can mean a set of conventions and rules which structure online practice in all kinds of fora. Second, it is often used to refer to standards of politeness and courtesy in the online environment" (p. 59). They argue that netiquette keeps emerging, as we can imagine, as new technologies are invented and as more and more people are joining the virtual community, new rules for community members to follow are emerging because of new functions of communication technology, changing nature of online users (after all they are digital natives), and expansion and complexity of the virtual world. The researchers view netiquette as a dynamic process rather than static rules.

Mann and Stewart (2000) further state that netiquette for different settings may vary. For example, in e-mail communication, it may be more appropriate to use formal and introductory tone for the first time contact and be aware of the correspondent's culture and language use if it is a cross-cultural e-mail exchange. In the case of one-to-one online chat, because the recipient of a message is supposed to respond as soon as possible, "typos and other mistakes are more acceptable" (p. 60). On the other hand, in a many-to-many chat setting, the online facilitators may have to first outline regulations required for group members to follow, for example, inappropriate topics to discuss. The same is true for asynchronous conferencing; common rules of netiquette must be made known by participants in advance. Also included in netiquette are confidentiality and privacy. In a cross-cultural exchange setting, it is possible that people from different cultures perceive confidentiality and privacy differently. For example, asking about a person's age may be quite OK in some cultures. However, it can violate one's privacy in other cultures. Before cross-cultural encounters, students have to be told of this and to be encouraged to learn more about how people from different cultures perceive this issue and how to avoid embarrassing encounters from happening.

In the virtual world, different settings whether private, semi-private or public, disagreements or arguments may occur, for example, flaming and other types of violations of netiquette or even the law. Flaming in the digital world, just like what happens in the real world face-to-face situation, refers to those hostile and emotional expressions which are seen as personal abuse or harassment. According to Mann and Stewart (2000), one of the reasons for flaming in the virtual world may be the narrow and limited nature of online communications. Without non-verbal cues, participants may feel frustrated in expressing themselves and understanding others well in a text only world. Another reason may be the fact that some sensitive topics can never be dichotomized as either being right or wrong, for example, politics and religion. These are matters of ideology and cannot be judged based on a global standard or social norms. In a cross-cultural exchange setting, it takes teachers' or educators' wisdom to turn the negative side of flaming and conflicts into the positive side of cooperation and mutual understanding. It is especially important in an information age when the number and diversity of people getting access to the Internet is increasingly growing.

Aside from computer flaming in CMC, however, there is a more positive phenomenon developed in the digital world, which I would like to term as *digital justice.* Digital justice refers to those words or postings responding to a controversial issue or event and are more acceptable by most of the digital participants. It is quite common and logical that there are always different views on a particular issue, and views cannot always be judged as being right or wrong. There may be ideological factors involved in the decision towards a particular issue or event. However, the tendency of CMC participants' opinions may shed light on which stands may be more acceptable to the public and may conform to the social norms. Digital justice may contribute to regulating the CMC world and encouraging participants to think from different perspectives. Like digital norms or regulations, digital justice is also developed in a slow but sure way. One hotly-debated issues or even a personally-generated incident or opinion can arouse a considerable number of responses showing different perspectives. Participants may read, think, and decide on their own, and adjust themselves to a more objective and flexible view.

An Example of CMC —MOOCs

An example of CMC is the more recently developed Massive Open Online Course (MOOC). As Brunvand (2016) describes it, MOOCs feature their application of the theory of social connectivism, whose core notion is that "learning exists when individuals collaborate to share ideas, engage in problem solving, brainstorm, produce artifacts and wrestle with difficult concepts" (p. 2). In cross-cultural exchanges, it is especially advantageous that MOOCs are "able to engage in the class from any geographic location and on a schedule that suits the learner….Having students spread across the globe in different time zones doesn't present much of a problem" (p. 3).

According to Brunvand (2016), in a MOOC learning environment, students can make use of different tools to collaborate with their peers to fulfill different tasks, including writing tools, presentation tools, social networking tools, and brainstorming tools. One of the limitations of online learning is that students always feel isolated and are hard to develop a sense of belonging to a learning community. A MOOC learning environment may encourage students to collaborate with their peers and to share information with each other.

Videoconferencing

In oral communications online, on the other hand, people have chances to see each other and to respond orally to each other immediately, thus non-verbal cues can be advantageous for people to make sense of what they are communicating. Martin, Parker, and Ndoye (2011) categorize this type of communication as "synchronous virtual classroom." Compared to asynchronous communications online, synchronous virtual classrooms add synchronicity to the communication. The researchers list some commercially available tools for practitioners to practice synchronous virtual classrooms. Generally speaking, synchronous oral communication uses videoconferencing to connect two physically separate individuals or groups of people. Similar types of communication tools, such as Skype and Chat Room, are also available for teachers to choose from. Some projects may be organized for one-on-one discussion; others may require a big screen and a big conference room to accommodate the entire class to have a class-based discussion as shown in the following figure.

Articulation plays a major role in videoconferencing. According to Herrington et al. (2010), "the very process of articulating in speech enables formation, awareness, development and refinement of thought" (p. 32). At videoconferences, participants may have different views and different understandings of a particular issue, and thus it may cause cognitive conflicts, especially in a cross-cultural communication setting. Videoconferencing provides participants with opportunities to express themselves, defend their stands, and reach a consensus with others. In the process, they learn and grow cognitively.

In an educational setting, cross-cultural videoconferencing can be conducted for different purposes and may involve people from different cultures with different levels of language proficiency, and it might be proved to be successful in some ways, but, at the same time, it might face different challenges. In this section, I use some examples to illustrate how cross-cultural videoconferencing can be conducted and what issues may be involved in cross-cultural videoconferencing.

In their study, Wilkinson and Wang (2007) bridged two culturally and academically different groups of students together in a cross-cultural videoconferencing project. In this project, Taiwanese English majors were learning English as a foreign language. Their project partners were American students majoring in journalism. The two groups of students met in a total of nine videoconferences in a semester. Before each conference, both groups of students and teachers decided on a topic to discuss at the conference, such as educational system, part-time job, culture, hobby, and holiday. Findings of the study show that students had a heightened audience and cultural awareness. During the videoconference, the two groups of students talked to their partners shown on the computer screen. In this context, students were especially aware of whom they were talking to and what may be specific of their culture. In some cases, they had to respond to a particular partner's questions on some culture issues. It is evident that, during the conference, students were eager to share their own culture with their partners. On the other hand, for the two groups of students, this project was seen to be academically reciprocal although they and their partners were not in the same field of study. In this case, Taiwanese EFL students learned English from native English speakers, and American students learned news report writing and interview skills by interacting with Taiwanese students and reporting their experiences of cross-cultural videoconferencing in their campus news.

Another example I experienced was a one-time videoconference my students had with students in Hong Kong. In 2008, I collaborated with professors at Lingnan University in Hong Kong. English majors in Taiwan met with international students learning Mandarin Chinese in Hong Kong at a videoconference. Before the conference, both groups of students were given the rundown of the conference. Students were asked to introduce themselves and their countries, cultures and schools at the beginning of the conference. Then, they were asked to introduce either Chinese or English idioms to their partners. At the end of the conference, of course, students were allowed to ask questions that they would like to get answers for from their partners. Language use at the conference was also carefully structured. Because international students were learning Mandarin Chinese in Hong Kong and Taiwanese students, whose first language was Mandarin Chinese, were learning English in Taiwan, the language used for communication was equally allocated to both English and Chinese. From the standpoint of language and cultural learning, both groups of students were equally benefitted from the conference.

Theoretically, English is not necessarily always the language used to communicate between or among people from different cultures. As Kohn (lecture) has pointed out, there are two types of videoconferencing in terms of language use: the tandem type and the lingua franca type. We have discussed the lingua franca type above, that is, using the common language known to both the two groups of people to communicate, notably English. We now turn to the other type, the tandem type. As the name of the type suggests, in a tandem type of videoconference, both the dominant language of each of the two participating groups are equally used at the cross-cultural videoconferences like the case of Taiwanese students and international students in Hong Kong I mentioned above. The situation of this type could be that the two groups of participants are learning each other's language and they take turns to use the two languages at the conferences. Another situation might be that each group of participants receives the language which is foreign to them, and they respond with their dominant language.

Languages used in a tandem type communication can be also extended to mean different social languages, such as legal language, technological language, business language and political language. In case the two groups of participants in a cross-cultural exchange program share the same domain knowledge, it is a good chance for them to share professional knowledge they have learned from, probably, their own cultural perspective. It is an excellent advantage for participants to broaden their professional horizons by adding new perspectives to their existing knowledge. Whatever type of videoconferencing practitioners may choose, it is important that participant students need to have a certain degree of language proficiency in the language they will use at the videoconference.

Issues of Videoconferencing

Just like any other pedagogical approaches, cross-cultural videoconferencing also show some challenges or issues practitioners might face, including cultural differences, participants' communicative competences, and language varieties. In this section, the focus is on these issues.

Cultural Differences

Aside from language and communication skills, cultural differences also play important roles in cross-cultural videoconferencing. Turner (2013) raises the issue of silence in the classroom. She describes that different cultures may perceive silence in the classroom differently. For example, Anglophone higher education environment is dominated by suggestions that correlate noisy, talkative students with critical thinking and learning....In this context, silence may become implicitly with a lack of engagement" (p. 228) either with peer learners or with the learning objectives. However, in Eastern countries in an educational setting, silence may mean respecting the speaker or the authority and attending to what the speaker is saying. Interruption while the speaker is speaking and challenging what the speaker says is considered impolite and offensive.

Turner (2013) surveyed both local UK students and international students at a "business school of a UK higher education institution" (p. 232), and she found there are a lot of differences in perceptions of and attitudes towards class structure and in being talkative or silent in the classroom. For example, UK students tend to be noisy and talkative in the classroom, and they favor a student-centered instructional approach and value social learning from their peers. On the contrary, non-UK students prefer a teacher-centered teaching approach. They trust teachers' and instructional materials' authoritative position. They tend to be silent in the classroom and do not want to challenge the teacher and instructional material's authority. In addition to cultural differences, according to Turner, insufficient language skills to communicate and lack of confidence in their knowledge background also contribute to the silence of non-UK students in the international classroom. In a cross-cultural videoconferencing setting, given the fact of cultural differences mentioned above, providing students with equal opportunity to speak and to express themselves takes the teacher's wisdom. Depending on the culture of your students and your partner's students, you may need to balance the talk by providing extrinsic incentives, such as offering extra points, to encourage less talkative students to talk and by setting up the rules of game to prevent those more talkative students from taking the other participants' time and dominating the entire videoconferencing. Although, in a globalizing era, cultural differences may not be so apparent as they are used to be because of the wide spread of the mass media and the convenience of transportation, students are encouraged to keep learning to improve their intercultural competence in a specific cross-cultural encounter.

Communicative Competences

When it comes to oral communication via cross-cultural videoconferencing, language proficiency and communicative competence become crucial issues. In the field of language learning and teaching, people are aware that language proficiency does not equal communicative competence. That is, being able to speak one language does not necessarily mean being able to use the language to communicate well. Brown (2000) briefly outlines the historical development of the research on communicative competence and points out that different scholars may have different ways of interpreting communicative competence. Canale and Swain's model, although not the newest version, may provide language teachers with an idea of how people perceive communicative competence. Brown describes Canale and Swain' model of communicative competence and states that communicative competence consists of four components: grammatical competence, which is knowledge of lexicon, morphology, syntax, semantics, phonology, etc.; discourse competence, which is the ability to connect sentences in discourse to form a meaningful whole; sociolinguistic competence, which is the knowledge of the sociocultural rules of language and of discourse; and strategic competence, which is the ability to use appropriate strategies which may be called into action to compensate for breakdowns in communication. From this model of communicative competence, it is quite clear that language scholars did not see being able to speak a language as enough to function well in oral communication. It is especially true in cross-cultural videoconferencing. In this type of cross-cultural encounter, participants are required to switch their language use and language styles based on their cross-cultural partners. In case of communication breakdowns because of limited language proficiency or cultural differences, participants need to effectively apply communication strategies in the communication process. Among these competences, strategic competence is especially important in cross-cultural encounters. In this context, students need to be able to adjust their communicative strategies to accommodate different cultural groups. In case misunderstandings, disagreements, or even conflicts occur, students need to be able to provide some explanations, adjustments, or negotiations to enable the cross-cultural communication to progress smoothly.

Context and Language Varieties

In addition to language proficiency and communicative competence, language varieties have raised an issue of intelligibility. To what degree of intelligibility should a speaker reach in order to communicate and to be understood? To what extent should a listener tolerate a speaker's language variety and different accents? In fact, the issue of understanding an utterance is not so simple. Kachru and Nelson (2006) describe the idea of intelligibility, comprehensibility, and interpretability initiated by Smith. This is a holistic approach to an explanation of *understanding*. Understanding of an utterance can be analyzed in three levels. The lowest level *intelligibility* simply means being able to hear the sounds of an utterance clearly, and the hearer recognizes it as a particular language. The second level of understanding, *comprehensibility* is a little more complicated. It is about assigning meaning to an utterance. There may be technically or culturally specific terms in an utterance that impede the understanding of the hearer. *Interpretability* is the highest level of understanding and is the most complicated one. With an understanding at this level, the reader or hearer is able to make inferences and interpret the utterances from the information or descriptions provided by the contexts.

Wicaksono (2013) argues that linguists

> have documented how all speakers of all languages use different styles of speaking, writing and signing…,depending on the communities they belong to, [and] any one speaker can belong to multiple communities, shifting their speaking, writing or signing style to fit who s/he is talking to and what s/he is trying to achieve. (p. 242)

Viewed from this perspective, language varieties at cross-cultural videoconferences can mean more than different accents and grammars; they take a wide range of contextual and ideological factors into consideration, including power relations between the partners, perceived ownership of the communication language, topics of the discussion, and intended goals to achieve. Davies and Dubinsky (2018) argue that "attitudes toward language varieties are tied to attitude toward a dialect (and the speakers of it) affects their behavior" (p. 305). Especially, although not really identical to face-to-face communications, at videoconferences, partner groups can see and hear each. Negative attitudes towards a particular language variety and its speaker should be totally discouraged. As Wicaksono (2013) suggests, judgement in deciding a standard version of a language is actually social, not linguistic. What a standard language is may depend on the various factors of a communication context.

In addition to communication languages, Wang (2013) summarizes some factors that may contribute to successful cross-cultural videoconferencing. She collected data from different sources and looked for patterns that emerged from a considerable amount of qualitative data. Wang concludes that well-developed cross-cultural videoconferencing first requires the practitioners to choose an appropriate conference time since cross-cultural videoconferencing may involve students from different time zones. Partner teachers need to reach a consensus for choosing an appropriate time for a conference. On the other hand, cross-cultural videoconferencing activities should be organized to develop a mutually beneficial relationship. Each group of students has to be equally benefitted from the cross-cultural videoconferencing. Furthermore, all groups of students from different cultures need to be encouraged and motivated to participate and need to be sensitive to different cultures and learn to respect other cultures. Finally, Wang stresses the importance of an optimal learning environment. In order for students to learn, cross-cultural videoconferencing practitioners need to create a student-centered learning environment to ensure that students can best learn and can be benefitted the most from cross-cultural videoconferencing. In terms of language use, participants of cross-cultural videoconferences need to apply different communication strategies, make use of contextual resources and develop their social negotiation skills in order to succeed in communicating in a cross-cultural videoconferencing context.

Last but definitely not least is about technical issues. As Gerstein (2000) points out, any technical failure can ruin the entire project. She urges practitioners of cross-cultural videoconferencing to plan well ahead of the time scheduled for videoconferences. She suggests that planning and technical tests can be done via fax or email between two partner schools. Among those that need to be meticulously planned, time difference should be, in the first place, taken into consideration, especially if the geographical distance between the two partner schools is great. Geographical distance may be one of the sources of incompatibility of the videoconferencing equipment of the two partner schools.

Blended Communication

In many cases of cross-cultural exchange projects, different modes of communication may be integrated in the project, for example, face-to-face experience being integrated with virtual journey and text communications being integrated with videoconferencing. An example of blended communication was conducted by Magnier-Watanabe, Remy, Herrig, and Aba (2011). They brought together MBA students from France and from Japan through a videoconferencing system and provided their students with a blended learning experience. The case was a joint distance learning course taught in English by the University of Tsukuba and Grenoble Ecole de Management, and was designed to blend e-learning and face-to-face instruction. The researchers conclude that generally faculty and students showed high satisfaction with the course. Students found that a course blended with face-to-face instruction and communications technologies can be particularly helpful to prepare them for a career in international business. They also mentioned that synchronous tools combined with asynchronous ones used for the course could really meet the needs of those busy working students. Another advantage of cross-cultural blended learning found in this study was that students had heightened cultural awareness. Students felt that they had an increased understanding of cross-cultural issues. This may benefit their future business career.

However, there are also challenges faced by both the teachers and students in Magnier-Watanabe, et al.'s (2011) study. Differences in age, work experience, motive, and level of English proficiency might require teachers' extra efforts in conducting the course. Some technically inexperienced students mentioned their being uncomfortable with the videoconferencing tools. These are actually issues faced by many practitioners of different modes of cross-cultural exchanges. Surveys or many types of investigation and training are needed before the project is put into practice. For example, surveys of students' time availability, work experiences, levels of language proficiency and technical skills, and objectives to attend and expectation of the exchange may facilitate the practitioners to organize the program. It is sometimes necessary for the practitioner to arrange language or technical training courses in order for the exchange program to be effectively and smoothly practiced.

Another case of blended communication was the one my partner teachers in Japan and I collaborated on. In this collaboration, Taiwanese EFL college students and Japanese EFL college students at Waseda University participated in a cross-cultural distance learning project. The two groups of students had to log in and access a digital course website to discuss topics relevant to social and global issues, such as family roles, international students, and climate change. In this case, because English was the lingua franca of the two groups of students and they were both learning English as a foreign language, they were required to use English to communicate with each other. On five designated dates, the two groups of students met on the computer screen and discussed these issues via Skype roughly in a group of four, with two Taiwanese students and two Japanese students on each side. The advantages of this type of mixed communication were that students could learn writing skills by discussing with their cross-cultural partners on a Web page and, on the other hand, they learned oral skills by communicating with their partners via Skype and that, by regular meetings, they developed friendships and were motivated to learn English.

Ellenwood and Synders's (2010) study of cross-cultural partnerships that integrated virtual journey with face-to-face exchange as mentioned earlier was yet another example of blended communication. In their exchange project, American students and South African students first had a six-week online List Serv and e-mail buddy exchange and then they had a two-week face-to-face experience. One of the purposes of so doing was that, according to the researchers, the first six week's online experience could familiarize students with each other and could develop students' cultural awareness and cultural sensitivity. After that, face-to-face encounters may provide students with first-hand learning and the excitement of witnessing what they learned from their overseas partners in the virtual world or from the textbooks.

If time and budget allow and if the facilities and administrative support are available, then teachers are encouraged to apply a blended communication mode to their project. It is because different modes of communication may serve different types of learning and may benefit students in different ways. As it has been debated about the role of teachers in a digital age, many scholars (e.g., Hockly & Dudeney, 2017; Wible, 2005; Wang,

2015, White, 2003) argue that technologies can never fully replace human beings. In digital learning, Hockly and Dudeney argue that though machines may be able to fulfil many tasks for human beings, in the educational field, teachers know "their students on a more 'human' level and being able to help when they are struggling, having a difficult time outside of class" (p. 243). They suggest that, in a blended learning environment, i.e., physical and virtual learning environment, teachers should devote most of the class time to the development of higher-level cognitive skills, such as critical thinking and creativity. Students' lower-level learning skill, such as memorization and learning of facts, can be upgraded to higher-level cognitive skills by being provided with different modes or contexts of learning opportunities.

Distance Education and Online Learning

As pointed out by Olcott (2009), cross-border higher education is getting more and more competitive, and it is sometimes the case that "home country students may forgo formal study abroad programs if foreign providers are offering flexible, culturally sensitive, academic programmes in their home language and/or English via distance technologies or a hybrid of distance and face-to-face delivery modalities" (p. 73). Distance education was seen expanding in the previous decade. Because it may involve learners from different parts of the world and from quite different cultures, distance education creates a very unique context for cross-cultural exchanges. According to White (2003), as of 2003 when his book was published, "there are approximately 55,000 distance courses from 130 countries" (p. 2). Actually, the numbers are increasing. As Dennis (2018) has noted, making use of modern technologies and online learning courses, such as MOOCs, can increase international students' enrollment and competitiveness of an institution in the international student market. Like other modes of cross-cultural exchanges, distance education has gained its popularity for at least two reasons: the advancement of communication technologies and competition for a greater market share in higher education. The development of modern technologies has made online courses easily accessible and convenient to take, compared with the old-fashioned distance education that provide print, audio and video materials, online distance education allows participants to have online interaction and collaboration. On the other hand, as the world appears to be more and more globalized, higher education is seen to be more and more competitive and entrepreneurial. Universities are competing to attract as many international students as they can, and distance education may provide people who are not able to physically attend a class an alternative to learn, and, for universities, this is a great way to expand their student population (White, 2003). In this section, I first describe the development of distance education and then discuss the challenges faced by practitioners of distance education in a globalizing era.

Development and Types of Distance Education

White (2003) roughly divides and describes the development of course models offered in distance education into three generations. The first generation course models were basically in the mode of printed materials mailed to the learners, and it always took time to mail the instructional materials and to respond to any enquiries, and there were seldom interactions between the teacher and learner and between learner and learner. The second generation course models were seen to make use of TV, audiocassettes, and videocassettes to deliver instructional messages. The models had added audio and visual effects to the instructional materials. The third generation course models feature the use of information and communication technologies. The computer technology in the models is used not only for distribution of coursework but also for interactive exchanges between the teacher and students and between students and students. For example, Computer-mediated communication (CMC) in the third generation has greatly enhanced communication opportunities.

Distance education can be practiced in different modes, for different purposes, and in different learning contexts. White (2003) illustrates four examples of different types of distance education in language learning, including a technology-based course, a multimode course in thesis writing, an English for academic purposes course, and a vocational French language course delivered by satellite. In the first example, White describes a technology-based course in an intermediate Spanish language course. It was offered at Pennsylvania State University. The university developed a technology support system to accommodate their course need, including functions for e-mail, real-time chat, computer-mediated grammar practice, and cultural expansion modules to practice reading in Spanish. Some of the drawbacks of the technology-based course include technical failure and diverse capabilities of the students' own computers which prevented some from participating in some activities. However, the researchers found that students learned some technical skills that may benefit their future career. The second example of distance education is a multimodal course, focusing on thesis writing for international graduate students at the University of Dundee, Scotland. Basically, in the six-week long course, students spent half of the time working face-to-face in the classroom, and in the other half of the class time students learned via WebCT. The third example described by White is a pre-sessional English for academic purposes course. "The audience were postgraduate students enrolled in an English-medium school of engineering at the Asian Institute of Technology (AIT) in Thailand" (p. 5). The distance course was offered to meet students' needs and to prepare them for the forthcoming study at the institute, including familiarizing them with their prospective teachers' idiolects by sending them recordings of their future teachers and building up a relationship with the students. However, the researcher notes that development and dissemination of materials require a considerable amount of time and commitment. Finally, White describes a vocational French language course delivered by satellite. This "course was developed and delivered by the University of Plymouth to a number of small businesses with an interest in advanced French, focusing on current topics such as politics and innovation in French" (p. 6). Basically, the course was delivered by satellite broadcasting, and then there were videoconferencing sessions. The researcher notes that this type of distance learning takes a considerable amount of time and money. However, this is "an example of just-in-time distance learning that is developed for a particular group with specific needs at relatively short notice" (p. 7). Whatever methods are chosen, however, as White notes, the most important components of distance education are actually "the participants and the means by which effective learning experiences are established on an individual basis within the distance context" (p. 7-8).

All the types of distance education can be roughly classified into synchronous and asynchronous learning. Synchronous learning features its communication in realtime, such as audio- or video-conferencing, chat rooms, and telephoning. It provides learners with an authentic environment to interact with the teacher, peer learners or target language speakers in case of language learning, and learners get immediate feedback in these cases. However, there are limitations to this type of distance learning, including being less flexible in temporal options. Different time zones may make synchronous interaction impossible (White, 2003).

The other type of distance education is asynchronous learning, such as printed materials, e-mail, discussion forums, bulletin boards, CD-ROMs, and computer-mediated communications. This type of learning may provide learners with greater flexibility in terms of time and place. Learners can learn at any time and in any place, and they may have more time to organize their thoughts when writing a message or responding to others' messages. However, asynchronous learning may provide learners with little or no chance to interact with other learners orally. Under this circumstance, students may feel a sense of isolation in their learning process (White, 2003). Jana (1999) reminds distance learners of the importance of carefully choosing the right type of distance learning. "Synchronous classes usually require students to attend online chats and turn in homework at specific times. Asynchronous classes let students work at their own pace" (n.d.). The two types of learning have their specific advantages. For synchronous learners, they may be required "to attend online chats and turn in homework at specific times....With a live instructor, the material could change and be dynamic" (n.d.). For asynchronous learners, the class is static; however, learners can learn "at their own pace...[and] log on, isolate the skill [they] need to learn and take only the individual lessons that relate to this specific skill" (n.d.).

For these types of distance learning, White (2003) describes how distant courses have been shifted from a linear model to an enhanced model. In the earlier stage of distance education, courses were organized in a linear way. That is, the course models in this stage featured print-based materials and teacher-directed learning. Learners used pre-packaged materials with a set learning path. Under this circumstance, "learners may be less responsive to their own learning needs, preferences, and skills" (p. 204). In an enhanced model, learners are learning from multiple sources. In this model, learners may choose from different learning resources, such as printed ones (textbook, study guide, and workbook) and those delivered through computer or other electronic technologies (TV, radio, telephone, audiocassette, videocassette, CD-ROM, e-mail, computer conferencing, video conferencing, Internet, computer-based multimedia, World Wide Web, and virtual learning environment). These learning resources can be complementary to each other or can be a reinforcement of distance learning. As described by White, some of these learning resources are static contents, others are fluid contents. The static learning materials such as textbook, audiocassette, videocassette, and CD-ROM provide learners with fixed contents, and these learning materials may be easier for learners to access the learning content. For the fluid learning resources, learners may interact with the teacher or their peer learners, such as CMC discussion, videoconferencing, and audioconferencing. Through interactions, learners may construct new knowledge and produce their own learning courses. White argues that distance learning contents are better to be revised and modified based on learners' needs and feedback. Teachers should be able to interact with the content to respond to students' needs. "Certainly both teachers and learners need to give attention to balancing the emphasis they give to the static and fluid elements within a course" (p. 202).

As educational technologies have developed into an era of mobile learning, Diehl (2013) suggests that m-learning should be seen as a subfield of open and distance education. He reminds us of the developmental history of radio and educational television. The development of radio and educational television decades ago witnessed how the invention of technologies may affect the nature, dissemination, and policies of distance education in significant ways. For example, in the early age before the invention of technologies, distance education was also termed *independent learning.* That is, learners of distance education can only read educational materials delivered by mail alone at home. As modern technologies develop, distance education learners can form digital communities and interact with peer, teachers, and the machine. As Diehl describes, as "each new technology emerges, distance educators and technologies experiment and research the potential of the new tool, and thus another subfield of distance education is born" (p. 21-22).

White (2003) concludes that the issues faced by distance educators and students can roughly be summarized as follows: feeling a sense of isolation, lack of regular classroom interaction and collaboration, absence of teacher mediation, students' awareness and self-management, potential technical failure, the gap in technical knowledge between teachers and students, and unfamiliarity with new technologies. The third generation course models have been developed to work against these potential challenges. Advancement in technologies may be less a problem than some human factors. Course providers need to develop more interesting and motivating courses based on the nature of distance education, and, most importantly, learners need to develop their awareness of learner autonomy and time management in order to maximize their learning in a distant learning environment. In the following parts of this section, I turn the discussion to the challenges of distance education

Challenges of Distance Education

Despite the convenient and technological nature of distance education, some scholars have pointed to the inherent challenges faced by institutions and teachers that offer courses through distance education, for example, differences in language, culture, and technology quality, and learner autonomy. First, distance education teachers may encounter students speaking different languages or language varieties and from various cultural backgrounds. Teaching online may cause miscommunications. The pedagogical standards and social and cultural norms you hold may not be appropriate for your distance students. On the other hand, communication technologies may not always be compatible with those of other countries and may not be able to reach those developing countries (Olcott, 2009). Second, as White (2003) points out, much of the research on distance education focuses more on the discussion of communication technologies and less on the participants and pedagogy.

> Technology *per se* is not as important as other factors such as learner motivation, and understanding of the distance language learning context and of the demands it places on participants, the responsiveness of the teacher, the accessibility of the learning context, and the overall context of delivery. (p. 2)

It is true that communication technologies are only the means to deliver the instructional materials and manage the course, and learning outcomes are actually the ends. Well-developed instructional technology does not ensure satisfactory learning outcomes.

Quality of Online Education

As Dennis (2018) has pointed out, many scholars have been questioning the quality of online courses, such as MOOCs. However, she argues that, at least, online courses offer options for those who are unable to physically attend onsite courses. She also argues that material developers and practitioners of distance education, in order to attract more online learners to learn more autonomously and effectively, may be forced to provide more interactive and interesting materials and activities.

Herrington et al. (2010) raise yet another issue viewed from a knowledge perspective. They argue that knowledge should be viewed as cognitive tools, rather than products.

They criticize that traditionally learned knowledge in the classroom is static and inert. People always fail to access relevant knowledge in case that problem-solving skills are required in a daily life situation. They argue that emerging technologies and their applications should be able to be used as cognitive tools and constructive learning. They propose participatory e-learning, suggesting that an authentic e-learning environment needs to involve learners in creating and constructing knowledge. It may be less meaningful if material developers or teachers just duplicate the pedagogy and instructional materials used for traditional face-to-face instruction. Herrington et al. suggest that "Web 2.0 functions allow the creation of collaborative, shared knowledge (example include Wikipedia, YouTube) and the development of *participatory cultures*" (p. 9). They argue that these online tools and "emerging technologies of 'participatory culture' on the Web comprise powerful cognitive tools for authentic learning environments" (p. 8).

Distance education in a globalizing era may involve learners from different cultures and different disciplines. It may be a perfect context to share and exchange knowledge and create joined wisdom to solve common or individual problems. Public postings or messages are not tested and may not be valid or reliable in a sense; however, they may encourage learners to have higher level of thinking and learning and cognitive development, rather than just memorizing facts and accepting fixed knowledge.

Learner Autonomy

One issue that is unique to distance learning and that deserves distance educators and course developers' attention is *learner autonomy*. As Peachey (2017) points out "many online products encourage procrastination for those students who lack self-discipline" (p. 144). Unlike face-to-face classroom instruction, distance education may have little or even no instructors' appearance. Under this circumstance, the importance of learner autonomy is particularly apparent. White (2003) argues that the distance mode of learning does not necessarily give rise to learner autonomy. Learner autonomy needs learners to independence and control. However, both of these important factors do not stand alone. For example, learner independence needs learner proficiency and support. That is, learners, on the one hand, need to develop a certain degree of competency to be able to work independently to learn, including necessary technical skills to work online independently and sufficient learning strategies and heightened awareness of self-directed learning. This may require learner training and learner involvement. First, learners should be guided and taught about the nature of distance learning, how to develop required distance learning strategies, and how to explore learning materials and resources. Second, learners should be provided with opportunities to be involved in the decision-making of learning materials, learning syllabus, and learning pace based on their learning preference, especially if the learning involves learners from different cultures. On the other hand, distance learners cannot actually learn alone. The new generation of communication technologies and emerging paradigms of distance education feature interdependence and collaboration and control. From sociolinguistics and constructivist perspectives, learning is facilitated by interacting with the teacher and peer learners, especially in language learning. Thanks to the advancement of communication technologies, computer-mediated communications appear to be very convenient and popular in distance education. Learning is not achieved exclusively from printed materials, audio- and video-cassettes, and Web pages. Interactions with people online provide yet another very useful way of constructing knowledge and building up learning strategies.

From a cross-cultural learning perspective, distance education may be a good learning environment. In a distance education setting, learners may come from different cultures and different parts of the world. Sensitive and well-trained learners may take advantage of this learning environment to experience and learn cross-culturally. This type of learning may be slow but sure. As you communicate with people from different cultures, you may gradually gain a sense of those cultures and, consciously or unconsciously, contribute to the cultural awareness of others. As mentioned earlier in this section, the emerging paradigms of distance education feature its freedom of decision-making on the part of the learner. You may particularly focus on learning of different cultures if this is the preference of your distance learning. Under this circumstance, you may be highly motivated to learn, and your learning experiences is not only enjoyable but also rewarding.

Building Rapport and Applying Paralinguistic Communication

For distance teachers, it may be harder for them than for traditional classroom teachers to develop relationships with their students because it is much harder for them to apply paralinguistic communications online, such as facial expression, tone of voice, hand gestures and body movement, as they do in a physical classroom (Peachy, 2017). The tool set that can be used in a virtual classroom, such as "a whiteboard, colored markers, flash cards, wall posters, and perhaps even a multimedia interactive whiteboard" (p. 45) is quite limited. These limitations may prevent teachers from interacting with students and, thus, developing relationship. In this regard, distance teachers need to use different strategies, such as personal email communications or sharing of pictures of personal collections, to increase interactions between teacher and student and student and student. Another way to build rapport in a virtual educational setting is the use of webcam as suggested by Peachey. According to Peachey, being able to see the students and use paralinguistic communications and more teaching tools may facilitate development of rapport and may reduce students' sense of isolation. In addition to oral communications, text chat facilities are also good tools.

In addition to developing relation with distance learners, some scholars (e.g., Tweney, 1999) are worried that distance learning is going to replace real-world education and teachers are going to be replaced by modern technologies. However, Tweney argues that "distance learning is a powerful tool, and will play an increasingly large role in adult, post-collegiate education, [and] corporate training, where the primary objective is the rapid, efficient acquisition of specific knowledge" (n.d.). For college students, knowledge acquisition in only a small part of college life. "Face-to-face interaction with professors, living away from one's parents, and socializing with a diverse group of people count for a lot in college education" (n.d.).

The Future of Distance Education

As new technologies are being invented to accommodate learners' needs and to enrich the functions used for learning, however, as recounted by White (2003), technological advances are not equal to progress in learning. That is, advancement in learning technologies does not necessarily mean better learning results. Rather, the future of distance learning is viewed from quite different perspectives, including technological innovations, access to modern technologies (e.g., cost and electronic literacy), the development of virtual communities, and the emerging global online education and collaborations between or among universities. White (2003) urges practitioners of distance education to rethink all aspects of practice and for all participants completely, including "working with an interconnected community of learners, using a number of new media … and it means higher levels of interaction and collaboration" (p. 229).

In a globalizing era, distance education has paid significant attention to the learners themselves. We can imagine the future of the virtual learning community will feature participants from various cultures, speaking different languages and using different types of technology. Under this circumstance, there are enormous tasks or issues facing practitioners of distance education, especially in distance language learning, such as cultural differences, language varieties, and technological incompatibility. According to White (2003), in the new era of distance language learning, learners' needs and learning environment should be the top priorities of the pedagogical agenda. Distance education teachers are required to do needs analysis before launching into course design to explore what their learners expect of the course and what they really want to learn. Another important task for the teacher is to create a virtual community in which learners support each other in academic learning, solving technical problems, and even collaborating on research work. Additional benefits of the virtual community is that learners will learn each other's culture and language and that the sense of isolation generally faced by distance learners will be minimized.

CHALLENGES OF DEVELOPING CROSS-BORDER ACTIVITIES

From the discussions in the entire chapter, including student mobility, teacher mobility, and distance education, I would like to summarize as a whole the challenges of developing activities involving people from different cultures. As cross-border partnerships are getting more and more important and popular in higher education, to respond to the increasingly growing competitiveness in the international student market, some issues may emerge. Knight (2011) points to some issues that may be faced by practitioners of cross-border education, such as student access, quality assurance, accreditation, recognition of qualifications, the nature of higher education, and brain drain/gain/train. She first raises the issue of equity of access and she wonders whether only those who are financially sound and who possess required language skills can have access to cross-border education. Not many countries have conducted a survey as to the distribution of population enrolled in cross-border education. The second issue is about quality assurance. Since the increasing number of cross-border institutions, be it public, private or commercial, issues of quality assurance have emerged. There are different opinions on existing quality standards developed by agencies outside the education sector and about international standards for quality assurance as well. A third issue has to do with accreditation. Knight points to the fact that "in order to increase competitiveness and perceived international legitimacy" (p.37), institutions or providers of courses or programs are striving to gain accreditation status. This has not only led to commercialization of accreditation but also made it hard to tell a real and official accreditor from a rogue one, and accreditors may not be objective or legal to award accreditation. Forth, recognition of qualifications is also a challenge for cross-border program providers. For students, the credits or certificates awarded by the providers are critically important. They expect that the credits or certificates they earn will be recognized by prospective employers or academic institutions and will be helpful for their future job hunting or advanced study. Fifth, the General Agreement or Trade in Services (GATS) has seen higher education as "a tradeable commodity or … an internationally tradeable service" (p. 38). Academic mobility, such as students, professors, programs, or providers are seen as a profitable business. It has caused debates that international trade law is seen to regulate cross-border education.

Finally, one more issue that seriously concerns many countries in an era of knowledge economy: the brain drain, gain, and train. Mobility of human capital can affect higher education both positively and negatively. For example, sending countries may experience brain drain, while receiving countries may enjoy brain gain. Yet there is another phenomenon that is termed *brain train*. Knight (2011) describes the increasingly popular phenomenon as one in which individuals receive their education in their home country and have a more advanced degree or their internship in another country, and then they work in yet another country, and eventually they return "to their home country after

8 to 12 years of international study and work experience" (p. 38-39). As the trend goes, "higher education is now working in closer collaboration with immigration, industry, and the science and technology sectors to build an integrated strategy for attracting and retaining knowledge workers" (p. 39). In sum, professional labor mobility and the development of the knowledge economy together with an aging society and low birth rates have created new challenges in the higher education sector.

Chapter 7

TYPES OF COLLABORATION AND OBJECTIVES OF CROSS-BORDER PARTNERSHIP

As O'Brien and Richardson (2015) describe, a "partnering relationship can range from the more informal personal relationship built on mutual respect and trust to formalized contractual agreements" (p. 193). Barnett and Jacobson (2010) roughly categorize cross-border partnerships in higher education into three types: organization-sponsored partnerships, university-sponsored partnerships, and faculty-driven partnerships. Organization-sponsored partnerships refer to those cross-border collaborations sponsored by a "large-scale organization, such as UNESCO, the Organization for Economic Cooperation and Development (OECD), and the World Bank" (p. 258), including non-government agencies. The type of university-sponsored partnerships include those promoted by universities, such as faculty and student exchange programs, collaborative research projects, cross-border team teaching, and professional development. Finally, the third type of cross-border partnerships are initiated by individual university faculty. In addition to organizations and universities, it is also quite common that individual university faculty has connections with colleagues in other countries for various reasons, such as international conferences or invited lecturers to another country. By having contact with each other, they may initiate joint research programs, collaborative teaching projects, exchanges of students' works, and physical visits. The above-mentioned different types of cross-border partnerships indicate that there are always chances for educators or teachers who are interested in cross-border practices to establish their overseas partnerships.

Before illustrating empirical studies reported by practitioners of international partnerships, I would like to first discuss some issues of managing cross-border partnerships. It can be imagined that cross-border partnerships are much more complicated than in the case of just collaborating with local partners. In order to sustain the partnership, according to Olcott (2009), you need to diversify your investment. That is, probably you have only one partner, but you need "additional stakeholders who perceive value in the endeavor and may invest money, people, and time" (p. 81). On the other hand, an international partnership requires you to build contingencies and conduct extensive market research. In the global setting, economical, political, social, and technological changes may affect the partnership. For example, in the international student market and student mobility in higher education, the trend of globalization, advanced technologies, and convenient transportation, students "are becoming more mobile and more selective with more higher education choices" (p. 182).

In this chapter, as the term *cross-cultural exchange* has expanded beyond the domain of higher education in this book, I would like to organize cross-border collaborations into the following types: collaborations between academic institutions, collaborations beyond the instructional setting and for non-instructional purposes, and collaboration sponsored by organizations. For each type of collaboration, practitioners need to have clear objectives in mind in order for a cross-cultural exchange project to be successful, and your objectives may affect the way you develop the project and how you choose your cross-border partners. For example, if you identify your objective as language and cultural learning, then you might want to choose native speakers or language learners of the same target language that your students are learning, and your development of cross-cultural activities may focus on language development and should be able to motivate students to learn the target language. If your objective focuses on professional learning, then you might want to choose for your students a group of partners in the same field of study to complement each other's professional knowledge or in a different field to supplement students with the knowledge they might lack. On the other hand, in this book, cross-border partnerships are not confined to cross-cultural exchanges between two academic institutions. Partnerships across borders may refer to collaborations between academic and financial institutions, two governments, or even collaborations between institutions and individuals as demonstrated below in this chapter. In this chapter, I summarize some objectives identified by practitioners of cross-cultural exchange reported in the literature or obtained from other sources, such as personal experiences and interviews with experienced cross-cultural practitioners. I first present some cases of different objectives commonly seen in collaborations between educational institutions. Then I move on to present some collaborations between educational institutions and non-educational organizations, whose contributions to a globalizing era can hardly be ignored.

COLLABORATIONS BETWEEN ACADEMIC INSTITUTIONS

In many cases, collaborations between academic institutions aim at language and cultural learning and development of intercultural competences and a global view in a globalizing era. Other objectives of cross-border collaborations may include professional learning of different domains. This chapter focuses on illustrating different objectives, types, and examples of cross-border partnerships.

Language and Cultural Learning

Language and cultural learning may be the most common objective practitioners of cross-cultural exchanges claim to hold. It is understandable that language and culture are important elements in a cross-cultural exchange project. Language teachers might want their students to learn a language and its culture from native speakers of the target language or learners of the same target language. Direct contacts with members of the target culture can also provide students with authentic cultural messages and real cross-cultural experiences. In this section, I present typical cases of cross-cultural exchanges, aiming at language and cultural learning. There are several ways to organize language and cultural learning, focusing on either oral or writing skills.

Language and cultural learning, focusing on writing skills, can be organized in different ways. For example, among the following three cases Wang's (1997) case used a discussion forum to elicit students' responses, while Ruecker's (2011) and Schenker's (2012) cases focused on language exchanges. Wang's and Ruecker's studies focused on cross-cultural written communication. Wang's study, as mentioned earlier, involved non-native speakers of English from Taiwan and Japan and native speakers of English from the U.S. All of the three groups of students were either in the field of second language acquisition and learning (Taiwanese and Japanese students) or studying the history of language and culture (American students). They were assigned to do research on some linguistic issues, such as tag questions and the origin of some very common English words, and post their ideas, comments or findings on the assigned topics relevant to language and culture on the designated website in English. Findings of the study show that the three groups of students had heightened audience and cultural awareness and had no problem communicating in English. By responding to the same assignments differently, cultural differences among the three groups of students can be easily identified.

Ruecker's (2011) study, on the other hand, paired language learners with fluent speakers of the target language, i.e., English speaking students in the U.S. (learners of Spanish) and Spanish speaking students in Chile (learners of English). Pairs of students worked together to review each other's writing pieces, using the two languages alternatively when pairs of students were discussing their writing pieces. Ruecker found that cross-cultural peer review not only helped students develop language proficiency and writing abilities in their second language, but also enhanced greater cross-cultural understanding between the two groups of students. This advantage may not be easy to find in a traditional peer review class. In the dual-language cross-cultural peer review writing class, students felt like they were in an expert's position when reviewing and commenting on their cross-cultural partners' comments better than being limited by their local peers' comments in a traditional writing class. However, Ruecker raises another issue easily found in this type of writing partnership: native-speaker prejudice. That is, language learners quite often trust native speakers of the target language and they consider what native speakers write or suggest is always correct. Ruecker thus suggests that, when recruiting cross-cultural partners, we should focus on their language fluency, rather than their native-speaker status.

Another study done by Schenker (2012) also focused on students' writing skills in the target language. Her study involved sixteen American students enrolled in a German class at an American university and sixteen German students enrolled in an English course at a German high school. The two groups of students were paired and were required to send their partners two e-mail messages in English: one was their opinion on each week's cultural topic, and the other one was their response to their partner's message. This project was termed *telecollaboration*. The e-mail transcripts were collected as qualitative data for the study.

In the study, American students who were learning German as a foreign language communicated in writing with German students who were learning English as a foreign language over a twelve-week period. Schenker investigated the American students, focusing on their syntactic complexity in writing e-mails in German with their German exchange partners. Her research findings show that students improved significantly in their global complexity and complexity via subordination, although their improvement in subclausal complexity did not show statistical significance. The quantitative findings may not be so inspiring, compared with the qualitative findings. Schenker carefully analyzed the qualitative data collected for her study and summarized the main reasons for their impact on students' syntactic complexity in writing: a friendly context, request for feedback, and responding to a peer. These are key characteristics of cross-cultural e-mail exchanges like this one. First, the students from different cultures were totally equal in terms of their power relations and language status and thus create a friendly environment. In this learning environment, they felt comfortable and were not afraid of being judged for their language proficiency. Second, because of the friendly environment, students felt free to write and to request for feedback and to comment on their partners' writing. Generally speaking, enthusiastic language learners are eager to learn the target language from native speakers, and they trust native speakers. As the exchange proceeded, as Schenker described, students made correction based on their partners' suggestions. In this regard, we may say that native-speaking partners help the language teacher a lot. Finally, in this learning environment, students feel confident to respond to their partners' queries and may be curious about their partners' culture. On the other hand, they felt obliged to satisfy their partners' curiosity by explaining in detail and producing more meaningful and complex sentences. On the other hand, they were really interested in and curious about their partners' culture. These factors drove them to produce comprehensible sentences in order to be understood and to satisfy their own curiosity. In sum, cross-cultural e-mail exchanges like this create an authentic learning environment and students are writing to real audiences. In this learning environment, it may be more effective to learn a target language.

Little, Ushioda, Apple, Moran, O'Rourke and Schwienhorst (1999) did a research study similar to that of Ruecker (2011). They initiated and evaluated a tandem language learning by e-mail project participated in by students at Trinity College, Dublin, Ireland who were native speakers of English learning German as a foreign language and students at Ruhr University, Bochum, Germany who were native speakers of German learning English as a foreign language. The authors define the basic principles of tandem language learning: reciprocity and autonomy. That is, "both tandem partners commit themselves (i) to their own learning and (ii) to supporting their partners' learning" (p. 1). On the other hand, learners need to be responsible for "their own learning but also…for supporting their partner's learning" (p. 2). Basically, the two groups of students communicated via e-mails written bilingually. Students in each pair, one Irish student and one German student, were responsible for giving comments and correcting their partner's message written in the target language. On the other hand, as native speakers, they were required to provide linguistic input to support their partners' language learning.

Little et al.'s (1999) divided their analysis of all the data into the affective part and the linguistic part. In the affective data, they found that tandem language learning by e-mail has at least several advantages that may benefit students' language learning. First, because students communicated on a one-on-one basis, they feel at ease to write about their own interests and concerns. They feel like they are using language in an authentic situation and, unlike in the textbook, they were using the language for real purposes and learn everyday language. Second. email communications provide fast responses and immediate feedback, and students loved the feeling of immediate responses to their questions or curiosity. Third, in terms of language learning, by dealing with two languages and having chances to compare two languages, students had heightened language awareness and language learning awareness. They had better understanding of not only their own language, but also the target language and its culture.

In the linguistic part of analysis, Little et al. (1999) mainly focus on four areas of concern: Bilingualism, language register, coordination between partners, and error correction behavior. In terms of using the two languages, the authors found almost 90% of e-mail exchanges were bilingual and almost "equal amounts of L1 and L2 were used" (p. 26). In the area of language register, the authors found that students tended to use colloquial and informal forms of language. For example, they used discourse fillers and non-standard punctuations. Next, the area of coordination refers to partners' discussion and negotiation about the tandem language partnership itself to better work together on language learning, including error correction, contents of correspondence, expectations of the tandem program, frequency of correspondence, etc. For the authors, these are pieces of evidence showing that partners had heightened awareness and willingness to work together in this language learning environment and to achieve better outcomes. Finally, Little et al. analyzed tandem learners' error correction behavior. They concluded that

> [s]tudents spent considerable time on corrections and in many cases tried very hard to give as much support as they received. In may exchanges the equal position of both partners as learners of a foreign language played a major role in establishing a true partnership....Many exchanges show that students were fully aware of the fact that in order to make the partnership a continuing success, they had not only to negotiate common procedures for correcting one another, but give mutual support on a number of levels. (p. 50)

Little et al. (1999), in their report on tandem language learning, point out that students' correction of their partners' messages tended to focus on the grammatical part of the language. They suggest that similar projects need to encourage students to provide critical reflections so that can be benefitted more in the process of language and cultural learning.

From the four cases described above, we may conclude that e-mail exchanges between people from different countries can be an easy and effective way to language and cultural learning, and the activities or tasks focusing on improving writing skills can be organized in a variety of ways. Both the input and output of written language in different language learning activities can benefit learners in different ways. For example, in Wang's (1997) case, the form of discussion group can provide language learners with comprehensive input and a wide range of cultural perspectives, while in Ruecker's (2011), Schenker's (2016), and Little et al.'s (1999) cases, by working in pairs, students may develop long-term relationships and have sustained learning. Their relationships will not end as the project completes. Yet, in addition to writing skills, other language and cultural partnerships may focus on learning and development of oral skills as will be described in the following cases.

Some research studies focusing on language and cultural learning may aim at the development of oral skills such as the study done by Wilkinson and Wang (2007). Wilkinson and Wang's study involved two groups of students: learners of English in Taiwan and native speakers of English in the U.S. They communicated via videoconferencing on designated dates, discussing topics of common interest, such as education, friends and family, sports, food, travelling, holidays, and work experiences. Learners of English in Taiwan reported that communicating with native speakers of English was a very interesting way of learning English and they have learned a lot of authentic expressions in English by communicating with their American partners. On the other hand, American students reported that they learned a lot of Chinese culture from Taiwanese students. The Taiwanese students were eager to introduce Chinese culture, such as traditional Chinese holidays and what their school looks like to their American partners, and the American student listened with great interest and curiosity. As a result, American students published an article in their campus newspaper, reporting on their oral exchanges with Taiwanese students.

We may be aware that language and cultural learning in a cross-cultural setting may not be simply the learning of a language and its culture. Communication skills may be especially important when communications involve people from different cultures. In the field of business management, in addition to communication skills and business norms, emotional awareness may be an important factor that contributes to the success of business communications, especially in a cross-cultural setting. Ozcelik and Paprika (2010) report on an interesting study, focusing on emotional awareness in business communication. They argue that international business negotiations involve a great deal of uncertainty and may lead to misunderstandings. Their study involved business majors from a Hungarian university in Budapest and an American university in northern California. The two groups of students communicated via videoconferencing. The researchers claim that this videoconferencing approach can alleviate uncertainty and a potential for misunderstanding in cross-cultural interactions in which two groups of students could see each other and could really "experience, express, observe and reflect on emotions" (p. 671). Although face-to-face encounters may be essential in business negotiations, Ozcelik and Paprika's study presents an alternative in the training process and points to the importance of communication skills in the course of business negotiations.

As Wang (1997) has pointed out, one of the best ways to learn a foreign language is to communicate with native speakers of the target language. As the examples illustrate above, direct contact with native speakers of the target language can not only offer immediate feedback and learning of the language and culture from native speakers of the language, but also improve their communicative competence. In addition to the above-mentioned examples, there are many more ways to organize cross-cultural activities, aiming at language and cultural learning. It is also possible and encouraging that practitioners of cross-cultural exchanges integrate different modes of activities into a long-term project. By doing so, they may provide students with multimodal learning environments and may greatly motivate students to learn.

A final thought relevant to language and cultural learning in a cross-cultural setting is the emergence of World Englishes and Language varieties. As the development of the concept of world Englishes and language varieties and the rejection of the notion of native/nonnative dichotomy, learning a second or foreign language cannot be viewed as a simple social activity; rather, it involves ideological, societal, cultural, political, and pedagogical aspects of interrelated components that have changed the way we view language and language learning. First of all, each language has its dialects or varieties. To take English as an example, Kachru (1992) categorizes English speakers into three circles: the inner circle, the outer circle and the expanding circle. People in the inner circle are native speakers of English, such as Americans and British people. The outer circle includes people who speak English as a second language. They may have a history of being colonized by English speaking countries. Representative countries in the outer circle are India, Singapore, and the Philippines. People in the expanding circle are learning English as a foreign language, such as Japanese, Chinese, Thais, and Vietnamese.

Even though Kachru's classification is quite clear, Schmitz (2006) argues that there is no longer a clear-cut between native speakers and nonnative speakers. As far as nativeness is concerned, it may be "used in different senses by different scholars in the literature of the subject" (p. 7). Native speakers may be defined based on their race, nationality or ethnicity, age of acquisition, level of language proficiency or even their loyalty to the language. However, as Schmitz claims, "the distinction between 'native' and 'nonnative' is becoming more and more blurred" (p. 20). For example, people in the outer circle or even in the expanding circle may outperform in their English proficiency those in the inner circle. On the other hand, as a result of globalization, "inner circle nations are fast becoming more and more multilingual and multicultural" (p. 20). The native/nonnative dichotomy may suggest hegemony and dominance of the native speaking countries, on the one hand, and nonnative speakers being depowered and discriminated against. In cross-cultural exchanges, in addition to language learning, students need to have heightened awareness of language varieties and tolerance of different accents and ways of expression.

Enhancing Intercultural Competence and Global View

Another objective commonly seen in cross-cultural exchange projects is to enhance students' intercultural competence and global view. Being able to communicate interculturally is a basic skill required to function well in modern society. However, we might ask: how can we define intercultural communicative competence? and to what extent does one's intercultural communicative competence have to be developed in order to participate in a culturally diverse community? In this section, I will present existing theories relevant to inter-cultural competence before presenting examples of cross-cultural exchange projects aiming at enhancing students' intercultural competence and global view. I choose Spencer-Oatey and Franklin's (2009) Intercultural Interaction Competence (ICIC) model to illustrate how the model can be related to cross-cultural exchanges targeted in this book. It is because Spencer-Oatey and Franklin regard intercultural interaction competence (ICIC) as an umbrella term that covers issues such as cross-cultural communication competence, intercultural competence, communicative competence, etc. In this book, I use the term consistently to refer to the ability to communicate with culturally different people appropriately and effectively. Spencer-Oatey and Franklin discuss the goals, components, and conceptual frameworks of ICIC in detail from psychological, applied linguistics, and international business perspectives.

Psychological Perspective

As stated by Spencer-Oatey and Franklin (2009), psychologists drew their attention to the *appropriateness criterion* of ICIC and considered the context and people's capacity to be contextually flexible in their behavior important. However, the criterion may not be easily defined "because assessments always entail subjective judgements by the participants concerned....[Self-report data and observation data generated by an outsider]...are insufficient on their own....They need to be complemented...by competence judgements from significant others" (p. 54). Spencer-Oatey and Franklin have pointed out one of the shortcomings of the appropriateness criterion is its being often interpreted as the creation of cultural appropriateness with respect to the other interactant(s), rather than as communicative appropriateness with respect to the communication situation.

From their review of relevant literature, Spencer-Oatey and Franklin (2009) identify some of the components of ICIC, including open-mindedness, non-judgementalness, empathy, tolerance for ambiguity, flexibility in thinking and behavior, self-awareness, knowledge of one's own and other cultures, resilience to stress, and communication or message skills. Although the studies were criticized for their inconsistent use of terminology, relatively restricted range of populations, lack of methodological rigor in measurement, etc., a conceptual framework was developed by synthesizing the research findings.

Spencer-Oatey and Franklin (2009) illustrate three conceptual frameworks developed by psychologists and identified the key components and attributes of these frameworks. They highlight from these frameworks some points relevant for assessing and developing ICIC. First, communication skills and knowledge or cultural awareness are important. Second, being mindful, which entails openness and a focused attention on process, is also important to the development of ICIC. Third, psychological adaptation and personal attributes can also contribute to the development of ICIC. All elements of ICIC probably cannot be fostered equally well in all adults, and personality traits may militate against or may be susceptible to the development of ICIC.

Applied Linguistics Perspective

As pointed out by Spencer-Oatey and Franklin (2009), "the fields of applied linguistics and foreign language education have paid relatively little attention to researching and conceptualizing ICIC" (p. 63-64). Generally speaking, applied linguists have paid more attention to the study of communicative competence, which is narrowly interpreted as appropriate language use. The study of ICIC in the field of linguistics has been quite limited.

In a traditional second/foreign language context, people tend to take native speakers as the model to judge a speaker's language proficiency. However, as modern technologies and transportation develop, more and more cross-cultural activities can be seen in modern society, and the activities do not necessarily involve native speakers. In the field of applied linguistics, people tend not to judge one's language competence based on his or her ability to speak and write according to the rules of the profession and the social etiquette of a particular social group, but on his or her ability to adapt to a given social context of language use. In this respect, those with ICIC can be regarded as having the ability to see and manage their own and their interactional partners' cultural beliefs, behaviors, and so on (Spencer-Oatey and Franklin, 2009).

Spencer-Oatey and Franklin (2009) cite Byram, Nichols, and Stevens's model from the applied linguistics perceptive and conceptualize ICIC and list some components of ICIC, including linguistics competence, which is the ability to apply knowledge of the rules of the language to produce and interpret the language; sociolinguistic competence, which is the ability to give to the language produced by an interlocutor meanings; discourse competence, which is the ability to use, discover and negotiate strategies for the production and interpretation of the language; and intercultural competence, which includes one's attitudes, knowledge, skills of interpreting and relating, skills of discovering and interacting, and critical cultural awareness. Byram's "model is located firmly in the context of the teaching and learning of foreign languages in schools" (p. 67) and generally needs long-term exposure for ICIC to develop. It may not be "applicable to non-school contexts, where more immediate results are desired" (p. 69).

Wible (2005) raises yet another important issue of collocations and polysemous words. The fact that a vocabulary word always possesses multiple meanings depending on the context of use, and that certain words need to collocate with certain words to form a particular meaning confuses language learners a lot. He proposes a contextual view of word meaning, arguing that word meaning should be contextualized and language learners should be provided with opportunities to have authentic use of the target language. In a cross-cultural exchange context, the large amount of linguistic input and different communicative contexts may heighten learners' awareness of the multiple meanings of a word and appropriate use of collocations.

International Business Perspective

Scholars in the international business field started showing interest in ICIC a few decades ago. Researchers reported the reasons for the failure for expatriate managers to adjust to the new environment. Research findings showed that, among other things, inability of the manager and the manager's spouse to adjust to a different physical or cultural environment, family-related problems, the manager's personality or emotional immaturity, the manager's inability to cope with responsibilities posed by overseas work, the manager's lack of technical competence, and the manager's lack of motivation to work overseas may contribute to the failure of expatriate managers.

Not surprisingly, the dominant criterion for business people is effectiveness rather than appropriateness. In the international business field, researchers used three approaches to identify components of ICIC; they asked representatives of companies to describe the characteristics of their successful international managers, generating characteristics on the basis of a selective reading of the management literature, survey, and anecdotal and experiential evidence derived from the business press, and questioning international managers themselves. Although factors that contribute to the success of expatriate managers identified by studies of different approaches may seem inconsistently or unclearly defined, some critical indicators of ICIC in the international business field are still apparent: tolerance of ambiguity, empathy, sociability, behavioral flexibility, meta-communicative competence, non-judgementalness among others (Spencer-Oatey & Franklin, 2009).

According to Spencer-Oatey and Franklin (2009), a conceptual framework of ICIC developed by the company WorldWork Ltd. is probably the most widely used in international business and management. The company has identified 10 key competencies covering 22 different factors that may be required for people to be effective in unfamiliar cultural settings; they are: openness (new thinking, welcoming strangers, acceptance), flexibility (flexible behavior, flexible judgement, learning languages), personal autonomy (inner purpose, focus on goals), emotional strength (resilience, coping, spirit of adventure), perceptiveness (attuned, reflected awareness), listening orientation (active listening), transparency (clarity of communication, exposing intentions), cultural knowledge (information gathering, valuing differences), influencing (rapport, range of styles, sensitivity to context), synergy (creating new alternatives).

Higson and Liu (2013), on the other hand, argue that, when it comes to international students, universities always center on the issues of how they may help international students quickly adapt to the host culture. They ignore what international students can bring to the campus and can contribute to the society. The authors insist that it does not quite make sense if students are taught only country-specific cultural knowledge. It is important that students are trained in intercultural communication skills. Higson and Liu propose arts-based methods for intercultural training. They argue that arts are engaging and fun, and "practicing arts can make people communicate deeply, even without speaking their own language" (p. 114). For Higson and Liu, arts can be in any form, and through arts people are trained to be interculturally competent.

Spencer-Oatey and Franklin's conceptual frameworks of ICIC as illustrated above show that one's intercultural interaction competence depends on the contexts of interaction and how the competence is defined. In a cross-cultural exchange activity, one actually needs to adjust to different cultures, different contexts and different activity purposes. Competence of being able to interact interculturally may not be able to develop fully through only one single inter-cultural activity. This kind of competence is actually an accumulation of experiences and improvement of language skills and cultural awareness. In the following part of this section, I present some examples of empirical studies on intercultural competence.

Schenker's (2012) study as described earlier is an example of cross-cultural exchanges focusing on cultural learning and enhancing intercultural competence. Her study involved American students who were learning German at an American university and German students who were learning English at a German high school. Schenker applied Byram's model of intercultural communicative competence to her study. Analyses of the surveys and e-mail transcripts show that American students had a general understanding of German culture and a level of agreement with general German stereotypes and that students were able to exhibit their attitudes of curiosity and openness of intercultural communicative competence and their critical cultural awareness in their e-mails. Although this telecollaborative e-mail project seemed simple in terms of research design, Schenker points out that asynchronous e-mail communication can make second language learning and cultural learning go hand in hand and can make "it easier for students from different countries to communicate without interference of time difference" (p. 461). However, she also suggests that synchronous communications should also be considered and investigated because they provide students with a more direct and authentic means of communication.

Intercultural competence and sensitivity may also be viewed from a different perspective, for example, local teachers teaching international students or foreign teachers teaching local students. Nieto and Booth (2010) investigated how intercultural competence and sensitivity may have influences on the teaching and learning of international students. They used a mixed method to examine ESL instructors and non-ESL instructors in the U.S. Their study showed that instructors showed a higher level of intercultural sensitivity than college students and that there was a significant difference in interaction engagement between ESL instructors and non-ESL instructors. It revealed that instructors' linguistic background may affect the way they perceive ESL students' language learning. From the issues of intercultural communication competence discussed above, to prepare students for a more internationalized society, practitioners of cross-cultural exchanges may design a project, focusing on the development of intercultural competence and intercultural sensibility.

Spencer-Oatey and Franklin's ICIC model and Byram's ICC model, Pang's (2009) example of collaboration between institutions demonstrate how intercultural interactions can enhance students' intercultural communication competences. His first example concerns the collaboration between George Washington University in the U.S. and National University of Singapore in Singapore. In this program, the two groups of students had different modes of communication: cyberspace, videoconferencing, and exchange visits. They discussed about assigned global issues and compared each other's ideas and perspectives. For example, one of the topics they discussed was HIV/AIDS. Through discussions and traveling to each other's country, visiting hospitals and national health organizations, students learned from their partners how measures are practiced in their partners' country to prevent HIV/AIDS and they were also more open-minded and "in tune with the global practices and norms" (p. 239).

Intercultural Perspective

In addition to the perspectives and practical research designs relevant to cultural learning, Allmen (2011) views the issues from a different perspective: the intercultural perspective. For her, "intercultural" implies "interaction," "interdependence," "exchanges," "reciprocity and solidarity," and capacity to question various forms of egocentrism, such as ethnocentrism, sociocentrism, culturocentrism, and europeocentrism. The aim of intercultural activities is to develop a critical and open spirit that accepts diversity and being empathic to others. Allmen argues that every life, every relationship is dynamic, every "culture is diverse, gets adjusted to changes and gets transformed....We are all migrants, creoles, hybrid, of mixed origin (p. 34).

Allmen (2011) presents a model, revealing an intercultural perspective in Europe. Historically, Central and Eastern Europe featured their ethnical diversity and conflicts. Allmen describes that "the Council of Europe was given the task to develop information, exchanges, and cooperation between the countries of Central and Eastern Europe and the countries of Western Europe" (p. 39). The Council of Europe, according to Allmen, is an intergovernmental organization, aiming at promoting human rights and protecting individuals. It cooperates with academic, educational, social, and political networks. Allmen continues to state that the Council of Europe first was concerned about "the social situation of immigrants in the industrialized countries in Western Europe" (p. 42) and adopted a resolution on school education for the children of migrant workers. The Council then organized teacher training programs for those teachers who were teaching migrant workers' children; later the programs were extended to cover all teachers. Since its establishment in 1949, the Council of Europe has been sponsoring different programs or activities, such as "Democracy, human rights, minorities: educational and cultural aspects" (p. 44) and "Education for Democratic Citizenship and Human Rights" (p. 45), dedicating to issues of human rights, minority groups, and religious conflicts, and intercultural education. In sum, viewed from this perspective, intercultural learning is to unlearn what resides in our mind about ourselves and others and to learn about ourselves and others from different perspectives. On the other hand, intercultural learning is about learning to listen (Hoult, 2018). In cross-cultural encounters, listening carefully to our partners may imply our better understanding of different cultures and why people from different cultures think and behave in a certain way. It also provides us with chances to present our own culture and express ourselves.

Professional Learning

In addition to language and cultural learning and development of intercultural competence and a global view, cross-cultural exchanges can also be commonly seen to be targeted at different fields of professional learning. Some professional fields, as you will see in this section, require global perspectives and critical thinking skills if professionists aim to succeed. If two culturally different groups are from the same field, it is a good chance for participants to learn how to learn. Because they are in the same field, they share the same interests, concerns, and professional knowledge. It may stimulate participants to explore ways beyond their traditional learning. For example, Hoult (2018) describes how his UK students sojourned in South India, indicating that learning to learn happened in this cross-cultural encounter and "was almost certainly strengthened through the mutual endeavors of learning to be a teacher with whom the Indian and UK-based participants were engaged "(p. 84). In this section, I illustrate how practitioners of cross-cultural exchanges in different professional fields practiced enhancing their students' professional knowledge. These cases of professional knowledge include music, literature and history, political science, diplomacy, business management, design, nursing, and administration. In addition to professional knowledge, cross-cultural exchanges may facilitate the development of critical thinking skills and a world view. As Shiveley and VanFossen (2001) has pointed out, critical thinking skills are required to prepare students for participating in the civic life in their own communities, their own countries, and eventually the world. They argue that social studies, including a variety of disciplines, require students to develop skills to collect, analyze, and organize information and eventually to make decisions. Another trait that needs to be promoted is, as Shiveley and VanFossen state, understanding and appreciation of multiple perspectives. A pluralistic society can be achieved "only when its diverse groups really believe that they and those around them are an important part of the institutions and social structure in which they are immersed" (p. xvii). Viewed from this perspective, professional learning in cross-cultural exchanges is seen as a great opportunity to develop critical thinking skills and a world view. In the following sections to come, I present some examples of empirical studies on professional study to show how a cross-cultural exchange project aiming at professional learning in different domains can be organized.

Learning about Music

As we can expect, learning music requires international experiences. That is, international experiences can benefit students in the musical field a lot. Not only can they have chances to present themselves and win international recognition, but also they can learn from other performers from all over the world to experience how music is presented and interpreted differently in different cultures. However, as pointed out by Robinson (2011), budget availability or financial support can be a big issue for musical teachers and students who plan to perform on an international stage. Robinson suggests that, although we have to think globally, we can go locally. He insists that it is not always necessary that you need to go abroad and spend a lot of money in order to have cross-cultural exchanges and international experiences. There are international musical festivals or competitions held in a place not far from you, and you can have your students stay in your own country and still have international experiences. Just take itineraries, performance venues, educational value versus expense into account and you can organize an enjoyable local trip for your students. It takes the organizers' creativity and research of relevant information.

One of the cases Robinson (2011) describes is the Burton band's journey to Norfolk to attend the Norfolk NATO Festival in Norfolk, Virginia. According to Robinson, the previous Norfolk NATO Festival in Norfolk "features an adjudicated concert, a parade featuring marching bands and performers from all 28 NATO nations" (p. 48). The band director Stewart cooperate with a travel consultant and eventually they went to Norfolk by motor coach. Other cases Robinson describes include the ones organized by Labrie, Orchestra director at McLean High School in Virginia. In addition to larger trips to go to other countries, Labrie also organizes local U.S. trips to, for example, New York, Boston, Atlanta, and Myrtle Beach with her high school Orchestra groups for clinics and music competitions.

Robinson's (2011) research report demonstrates how a learning opportunity can be created through purposeful planning, and cross-cultural learning can take place anywhere. In his article, Robinson does not actually present an empirical study to point out what specific points of music the students were learning; however, he provides music teachers with a new perspective that international experiences for music students can be gained locally. As one can imagine, musicians have very different musical skills, and there seems no national boundaries in each skill. That is, music is an international language, and, thus, having international experiences is key to accomplishment in the field. However, as Robinson has pointed out, you can think globally, but go locally. You do not have to go too far to have international experiences. Speaking of winning international recognition in a globalizing era, it may not be really difficult to disseminate your performance globally, making use of modern technologies.

Learning about Literature and History

Sheley and Zitzer-Comfort's (2011) cross-cultural exchange project virtually connected students from Cyprus and students from California, USA. The project focused on the discussion of American Indian literature and history and the conflicted American dream. The two groups of students read the same materials, viewed the same videos, and followed the same course syllabus relevant to American Indian literature and history. They used Discussion Board on the Internet to discuss issues posed to them, such as what the causes of conflicts are and how protest literature is defined, and read relevant articles.

The researchers conclude that framing "a joint e-learning study around American Indian literatures and histories in order to provide a collaborative learning experience for two disparate classrooms proved to be more successful than they imagined in the planning stages" (p. 87). They describe that both teachers and students were so engaged in the exploration of the lives and stories of American Indians and that the world of the two groups of students "expanded as they read new materials, learned new histories, shared responses with peers across the globe" (p. 88). One of the advantages of the collaboration is that through cross-cultural communications, students were aware that literature and history can be viewed from different perspectives and each different perspective should be appreciated. Some historical conflicts may be caused by ideological or ethnocentric ways of thinking. Moving away from ideology and ethnocentrism to appreciate and embrace different perspectives is critical to be a global citizen.

Learning about Political Science

Mendeloff and Shaw (2009) point out that the traditional lecture or seminar-style approach to design peacebuilding courses for political science majors has serious limitations. They argue that contemporary peacebuilding is increasingly multinational and it is an ideal opportunity to expand students' exposure and appreciation of different national and cultural views. The researchers designed a collaborative peacebuilding course to involve college students from the U.S. and Canada. The two groups of students had the same required readings, assignments, and graded components. In addition to independent lecture and seminar discussions, the two groups of students had online interaction and collaboration, using Web-based and videoconferencing technologies. However, the core of the course, according to Mendeloff and Shaw, was the role-play simulation on peacebuilding in Afghanistan. "The simulation was organized around a meeting of a fictional 'Afghanistan Consultation Group' …convened to help draft a 'Plan of Action' for effective peacebuilding in Afghanistan" (p. 32). The simulation design aimed to encourage student interaction and collaboration and to allow students to experience the challenges involved in international coordination and cooperation to solve complex international problems. Mendeloff and Shaw's study reveals that only by direct contact with people from different cultures, can people learn to appreciate and respect each other.

Learning about Diplomacy

One of the good examples of internationalization of academic programs and learning about diplomacy was the one offered at Tamkang University (TKU), Taiwan. An interview with the chair of the Department of Diplomacy & International Relations at TKU, Dr. Chin-Mo Cheng, who was also the leader of a short-term study group travelling to Prague, Czech Republic, may reveal how professional learning can be realized through field trips and physical experiences in person. The Department of Diplomacy &

International Relations at TKU features its English-only instruction and a considerable number of international students as stated by Cheng (2016). The international students enrolled in the program include students from Pacific Islands, Africa, Middle East, and South America, and a smaller number of students from the U.S. and Japan. In this instructional context, students are used to communicate interculturally. Although the department was just established one year ago and the students just finished their first year of college, they were able to participate in a cross-cultural activity and professional training.

In the summer of 2016, Dr. Cheng led a group of local students enrolled in the program to Prague, Czech Republic. This trip to visit European countries was made possible by the support of both the government and private organizations. The Ministry of Education (MOE) in Taiwan offered a Pilot Overseas Internships Grant to financially support college students for a short-term study abroad, while the organization in the private sector, Institute of Central European Political and Economic Studies, acted as a think tank and played an advisory role to help organize and schedule the whole program. Better yet, the institute also offers certification for students who participate in some kinds of professional programs or training. Learning activities arranged in the study abroad program included visits to the Prague Castle, Charles University in Prague, Ministry of Industry and Trade, Czech Tourism, and simulations of international conferences, such as on the topic of anti-terrorism. Students were responsible for all of the planning of the simulated conferences. According to Cheng (2016), one of the characteristics of this study abroad program was that it not only deepened students' professional learning, but also extended the diplomatic profession to the business domain. Aside from visiting governmental organizations and educational institutes, students also visited SKODA Auto University, which is affiliated with the Volkswagen Group. In the university, students not only attended lectures by internationally known scholars but also had chances to communicate with students from all over the world. "Diplomacy and international trade are actually interrelated," says Cheng. In that sense, students are better prepared to compete in the global market. Having classes with students from different parts of the world, witnessing European styles of architecture, learning some Czech culture and language, and experiencing the facilities for physically disabled people are cultural learning that cannot be achieved otherwise. Cheng, who himself is familiar with the Central and Eastern European affairs and European Union and who got his Ph.D. from a European university, concluded in the interview that being familiar with the destination of a field trip and planning with students' needs and interests in mind may be key to successful cross-cultural exchanges. "This study abroad program is only the start and an example of an internationalized curricular program. Many more cross-cultural activities such as visits to Japan or Korean are expected to come in the nearest future" says Cheng.

Learning about Business Management

For business majors, it is important to learn cross-cultural communication skills to prepare for their future career because, in a business setting, it is not uncommon that business people have to deal with people from different countries. I conducted a cross-cultural exchange project with a French teacher who was teaching English in France, focusing on students' learning of business management. Both the Taiwanese and the French groups of students were in business management and were learning English as a foreign language. The project was named *International Collaborative Contest*. One or two of the students from Taiwan were grouped with one or two of the students from France. Each group was assigned a team name. The task for each group to do was that each student had to discuss with his or her partners via Skype and create and construct a scenario of a professional situation, presented as dialogues in English, such as interviews, business negotiations, meetings, claims, and promotion of products. The task was defined as a *contest*. After the presentation of the final product, the best three teams were chosen and awarded with a prize. One of the merits of the project was that students got a chance to simulate what might happen in their future career and what cultural differences may affect business transactions.

Another two cases of cross-border partnerships, aiming at learning about business administration, were reported by Fong and Postiglione (2011). Unlike the case described above, this project focused on college MBA learners; the researchers describe the joint collaboration by University of Hong Kong, London University's Business School, and Colombia University's Business School. The program is called EMBA-Global Asia. According to Fong and Postiglione, because of the prestigious and renown status of the three institutions, the program soon attracted many high-end participants, including "high-performing leaders, top-level global executives, and successful entrepreneurs with international exposure to Hong Kong, mainland China, the Asia-Pacific region, other parts of the world with at least 10 years of work experience" (p. 180). Classes were held once a month in Hong Kong, Shanghai, New York, and London respectively and were equally taught by experienced faculty members from the three collaborating institutions based on their expertise. Participants of the program eventually got a joint degree signed by the three institutions.

Fong and Postiglione (2011) describe yet another cross-border collaboration between University of Hong Kong and Oxford University in London, called the Oxford-HKU Senior Executive Program in Corporate Leadership. This program roughly focused on management, organizational operations, and corporate leadership and was "suitable for chief executive officers, board directors, senior managers, senior civil servants, and other senior executives with high-level strategic responsibilities" (p. 182). This program was conducted in an intensive 5-day workshop format, focusing on the Asia-Pacific region. The courses were equally designed and delivered by HKU and University of Oxford in Hong Kong. The researchers state that participants of the program were benefitted by exposing themselves to a higher level of thinking on the challenges organizations are going to face and practices for dealing with them, having chances to learn from distinguished professors and experts from two renown universities, and having a deep understanding of business in Asia and a chance to integrate East and West in management education.

Learning about Design

DeLong, Geum, Gage, McKinney, Medvedev and Park's (2011) study involved college students from Korea and from the U.S. Participants were in the design profession or related fields, such as merchandising and fine arts. Like the professional areas mentioned above, designers need international experiences and perspectives and cross-cultural competence. DeLong et al.'s study was a three-semester project and was a blended communication one, which integrated different modes of communication as will be explained in a later chapter of this book. After a cultural orientation, one-on-one conferencing, and video lecture sharing, paired students selected a common theme for their collaborative works. In the second semester, "students from South Korea traveled to the United Students for 2 weeks to meet their partners face to face …. Together they mounted an exhibition of their work in a design gallery at the university" (p. 47). In the third semester, American students and faculty travelled to South Korea to participate in a symposium to present and publish papers on their cross-cultural experience.

In their concluding remarks, DeLong et al. (2011) remind the reader of the importance of peer learning in cross-cultural exchange projects. They suggest that different tasks might lead to different learning outcomes. The tasks included in the project were "a team project, public presentations, publications, and a 2-week travel exchange" (p. 41). Although, in any cross-cultural exchange project, partner groups of students may have different school calendars, the difference in school schedule can be used for cultural orientation. DeLong et al. stress that the public exhibition and symposium part of the design projects "allowed for partners to learn of professional standards of the other culture while representing their own" (p. 41). As they describe it, the two tasks "provided accountability beyond a classroom grade or instructor review" (p. 53).

Learning about Nursing

As mobility of people around the world is increasingly growing as a result of advancement of technologies and transportation and the trend of globalization, cross-cultural exchanges and intercultural competences are seen to be more and more important in the nursing profession. As Shivnan and Hill (2011) report, the "nurse's role is critically important to promote health, relieve suffering, and improve quality of life" (p. 153). Nurses are no longer facing only their own nationals who speak the same language and share the same culture with them. Chances are they have to face people from different cultures and have different ways of thinking and different value systems. Shivnan and Hill point out universal "issues contributing to the nursing shortage include inadequate workforce planning, uneven distribution of available nurses, insufficient capacity in educational systems, and limited incentives" (p. 154) to prevent people from working as nurses.

Shivnan and Hill (2011) continue to argue for the importance of developing a global perspective and establishing multinational collaboration in nursing education. They deliberately introduce how Johns Hopkins University, School of Nursing worked with the Johns Hopkins Hospital on nursing education and on developing nurses' global perspectives. Collaboratively, they established the Office of Global Nursing aiming at "excellence in scholarship, teaching, research, and patient care, and a commitment to share best practices with external audiences" (p. 158). One of the examples of the Office's collaboration with external academics is its cross-cultural collaboration with the Peking Union Medical College School of Nursing. To be direct and precise, Johns Hopkins University, School of Nursing helped the Peking Union Medical College, School of Nursing in Beijing, China establish the first doctoral program for nurses in China in 2004. Faculty from Johns Hopkins offered courses in Beijing, and students in Beijing also had chances to go to Baltimore, U.S. to take courses at John Hopkins and to experience a different culture. By having experiences of studying abroad, nursing students may "develop a greater appreciation for the influence of culture, socioeconomic status, history, the political environment and other factors that impact on health beliefs and practices and health care systems in another country" (Currier, Lucas, & Arnault, 2009, p. 140). As stated by Shivnan and Hill, the graduates of the doctoral program "are prepared to assume leadership positions in education, research, and practice" (p. 165).

Learning about Educational Leadership and Administration

In a globalizing era, as schools around the world are getting more and more diversified in their student population, school leaders and administrators need to adjust their administrative practices to accommodate the needs of students from different cultures. Barnett and Jacobson (2010) describe a collaboration between University of Calgary (UC) in Canada and University of Waikato (UW) in New Zealand, focusing on learning about school leadership in another culture. At the very beginning, students from the two universities communicated via a shared e-mail discussion group called Change Agency listserv to discuss their reflections on articles that they were assigned to read. Later on, students requested the arrangement of face-to-face interactions. As a result, students from the two partner universities travelled to each other's country for a short study tour, engaging in summer school courses. Workshops, and seminars to learn each other's educational context and culture. Finally, the two universities signed an agreement to solidify the partnership and to include more participants by team-teaching, offering online courses, and publishing an academic journal to report studies and activities relevant to international experiences and leadership.

Like all cross-cultural projects, the collaboration between UC and UW also has its advantages and challenges. Barnett and Jacobson (2010) describe that the UC and UW collaboration benefitted students, faculty, and institutions. For students, they learned to value other perspectives and to clarify their own views on educational leadership. For faculty, they expanded their research productivity and learned new teaching strategies. As for the institutions, they enjoyed having the opportunities to include international faculty to enrich students' learning experiences. However, Barnett and Jacobson also point to some challenges found in the collaboration. For example, international partnerships require mutual trust and commitment of all participants. On the other hand, institutional support is critical to sustaining partnerships. It may mean that cross-cultural collaborations need not only cooperation from the overseas partner, but also commitment from local participants.

Learning about Public Policy

Pang (2009) describes a project, Lee Shiu Summer Programme, involving students from Singapore, Hong Kong, and China and aiming at the discussion of public policy, focusing on "public governance, economic development, education, and social services" (p. 239). The three regions share some similarities and contrasts in some aspects. In this regard, it is particularly valuable that they learn "from each other's practices as well as understanding each other's thinking" (p. 240). According to Pang, selection of participants was quite competitive and students were chosen from the most outstanding applicants. Participant students joined the four-week program and stayed together in three places, namely Hong Kong, Shanghai, and Singapore respectively. In their stay abroad, they listened to lectures delivered by "prominent intellectual, government, business, and community leaders" (p. 240) and visited relevant government departments and nongovernmental organizations. In addition to lectures and visits, participants also had transnational group discussions to work on their group project.

One of the merits of this program is that, by involving students from different cultures, students can think beyond their borders "by broadening [their] minds to larger issues and building international networks ….This network will last and [they] can learn from each other and help each other in the days to come (p. 240). They researched and discussed many practical and relevant issues, such as, in the case of China, corruption, government transparency, English instruction, economic development, and environment sustainability. Under this circumstance, they can be said to really contribute to the well-being of the country and the global community.

Learning about Religious Harmony

Religious conflicts are actually becoming a global issue. Understanding and tolerance of different religions is indeed a lesson to be learned in a globalizing era. Pang (2009) describes the Interfaith Dialogue Study Program initiated by National University of Singapore (NUS), aiming at providing students with opportunities "to observe firsthand how different societies address religious harmony" (p. 241). Students involved in the dialogue were from Istanbul, Kuala Lumpur, and Singapore. The three cities feature their "Muslim population, and yet are cosmopolitan, modern, and multireligious" (p. 241). There is a good opportunity for students to have comparative study. In this program, participant students travel in Istanbul, Singapore, and Kuala Lumpur respectively. They held seminars and "visited mosques, churches, and synagogues, and had discussions with religious leaders" (p. 241). As Pang describes, one of the valuables and interesting findings that students' observed in the program is that "dialogue doesn't necessarily mean literal discourse; rather, it can be metaphorical, carried out through art and architecture" (p. 242).

Religious conflicts are particularly important issues in a globalizing era. Being unaware of and not tolerating other religions are real sources of religious conflicts as can be seen in the world today. The world can never be globalized without religious harmony. This program sets a very good example of how we can work together cross-culturally on global issues to move towards a really globalized world.

Learning to Do Research Cross-Culturally

Wainwright, Ram, Teodorescu, and Tottenham (2009) describe a collaborative research team called International Research Experience for Science (IRES). The research team was led by a renowned research advisor at Emory University, who was well-known for both his research expertise by his colleagues and his familiarity with and experiences of international collaboration. It encourages research collaboration between students and students or faculty and faculty in different countries.

Basically, student and researchers were guided by both an Emory advisor and an international advisor in another country jointly. The Emory advisor was responsible for preparing students for upcoming research tasks overseas. Participant students had to stay in the host country for at least 10 weeks, working closely with the host advisor as well as the Emory advisor. They also had to present their research findings upon returning to their own country. According to Wainwright et al. (2009), students who came back from IRES were said to gain new research skills and new perspectives. They were able to publish research papers and continue their research endeavor in graduate schools.

Interdisciplinary Learning: East vs. West, Sciences vs. Humanities

Cross-border partnerships can actually go beyond disciplinary boundaries. Wainwright et al. (2009) describe the Emory Tibet Science Initiatives, aiming at developing a science curriculum for Tibetan monastics. In the collaboration, Emory students in the United States collaborate with Tibetan students and, more recently, Emory scientists and Tibetan scholars in religion, philosophy, and other fields work together on new curriculum. In one of the activities, Emory students and faculty had a one-semester study abroad in Dharamsala, India, focusing on Tibetan Buddhist studies. In another activity, faculty and students attended "lectures and activities in cosmology, life sciences, and neurosciences" (p. 396). In sum, according to Wainwright et al., These programs are "to build bridges of communication between practitioners of Western science and Buddhist science so as to create new knowledge in areas such as cognitive neurosciences and mental health" (p. 396),

Learning to be Engaged in Global Issues and to Develop Global Competencies

As mentioned earlier, this book is focused on, but not limited to discussions of higher education. As we may be aware that global competencies should be developed at an earlier age, especially since the young people have been born in a globalizing era and are "global natives." Smith (2018) describes how American fourth graders collaborate with Taiwanese students connected through the Internet and eventually went to Taiwan to meet with their partners and experience a foreign culture in person. According to Smith (2018), his fourth graders are from low-socioeconomic families in a small Midwestern town. They were first connected with students at a bilingual school in Taiwan and developed the *World Problems* project. American students and Taiwanese students identified, researched, discussed, and provided possible solutions through e-mailing. In the process of communicating with each other, the researchers found not only the two groups of students were enthusiastically discussing global issues, but also they heightened their interest in learning each other's language.

Having developed friendships between the two groups of students, the American teachers came up with the idea: Why don't we let American students fly to Taiwan to meet their Taiwanese friends? This idea soon raised many potential questions for the teachers to think about, such as sources of funding, support from the school, the administration, and the parents, safety abroad, cultural differences, and intercultural training and learning. After the teachers carefully and collaboratively solved the problems, including fund raising, getting support from the school and parents, recruiting participant students, and holding pre-departure training and making homestay arrangements, the seemingly impossible became possible.

The visit to Taiwan was arranged as "International Summer Camp" and was "a combination of tours and activities as well as classroom sessions for projects, art, and guest presenters" (p. 10). In addition to visiting cultural spots, enjoying local food, and experiencing traditional Chinese festivals, in the classroom sessions, both teachers from the U.S. and from Taiwan taught lessons about Chinese and American languages, foods, and traditions. That is, both Chinese students and American students learned each other's culture in the same classroom. Smith's (2018) story shows that collaborative efforts and commitments are key to providing students with a meaningful and rewarding cross-cultural experience. In a globalizing era, thanks to the advancement of technologies and transportation, different forms of cross-cultural exchange seem much easier to accomplish. Smith's case sets a good example as to how potential problems ahead of a cross-cultural exchange project can be solved by collaborative efforts.

There are a lot more cross-cultural exchange cases aiming at professional learning, for example, Ho's (2012) case of teaching mural painting and Magnier-Watanabe, Benton, Herrig, and Aba's (2011) case of teaching business management, which will be described in later chapters. There is one thing in common in all of the professional learning cases: The professional knowledge can be best learned by collaborating or interacting with people from a different culture.

INTERNATIONAL BRANCH CAMPUSES

Establishing international branch campus has become one of the important practices in higher education in response to the advent of a globalized world, and it may provide local teachers with opportunities to teach abroad. As recalled by Chapman and Sakamoto (2011), new "forms of cross-border partnership have necessitated new organizational arrangements as colleges and universities launch programs and construct campuses in foreign settings" (p. 267). It is much more complicated than just developing sisterhood between two schools. Lane (2011) defined International Branch Campuses (IBCs) as "higher education institutions operating in one nation and owned, at least in part, by a university in another nation" (p. 67) and students, while being physically present in the host country, can earn a degree from the home campus" (p. 68). IBCs may target recruiting nationals of the host country or international students from different parts of the world. Theoretically, establishment of IBCs may benefit both the source, or home, country and the host country. Partners in the host country may "help the source country institution navigate the local bureaucracy, establish facilities, identify suppliers and staff, create relationships with companies, and recruit students" (Croom, 2011, p.46). On the other hand, the partner in the source country may be credited with its contribution to the financial, educational, and cultural development by providing materials, resources, technologies or professional knowledge that the partners in the host country may be lacking.

In reality, IBCs may involve unpredictable political, financial, educational, cultural, legal, and even religious factors that may affect the practice of an international campus. They can include rights of the land, quality assurance, awarding of degrees, human subjects issues in research studies, and intellectual property rights (Chapman & Sakamoto, 2011). Due to all the factors involved in the practice of international branch campuses, practitioners of IBCs may face different degrees of success or even failure. In this section, I quote some research reports on IBCs around the world to demonstrate how IBCs were practiced and what factors that may affected their operation.

The Case of Japan

Croom (2011) describes international branch campuses and compared the cases in Japan and in the Gulf region. Interestingly and importantly, the comparison happens to demonstrate factors that may contribute to the success or failure of the establishment of international branch campuses. According to Croom, Japan developed its international branch campuses in the 1980s. Many institutions from Western countries, such as the U.S., made quick decisions and sought to develop branch campuses in Japan, hoping "to grab a piece of the perceived economic pie" (p. 50). In the case of the United States, its higher education institutions were facing falling enrollments and they were seeking new sources of revenue. Just in the period between the late 1980s and early 1990s, there were "more than 30 U.S. institutions [that] established a branch campus in Japan" (p. 50).

However, at the beginning of 2000, only a few branch campuses survived. Croom (2011) summarized some factors that might contribute to the failure of international branch campuses in Japan as saying that "naïve negotiations, unmet educational expectations, lowered standards and institutional commitment, awkward governance structures, problematic costing mechanisms, financial and legal manipulation, and power and control issues among partners" (p. 50). There were still other reasons contributing to the failure of IBCs in Japan, including recognition of US degrees, plummeting student population, cultural differences between the East and the West, and some economic factors. It is all clear from the Japanese experience that establishing overseas branch campuses needs a wide range of considerations before launching into the educational enterprise as will be described in the next case of the Gulf Region.

The Case of the Gulf Region: Dubai and Qatar

The Japan experience did not really dissuade higher education leaders and decision makers to open branch campuses abroad, and the case of the Gulf region seems to be a more successful one. Croom (2011) describes two cases of the branch campuses in the Gulf region: the Education City in Qatar and the Dubai International Academic City. The Education City in Doha, Qatar is closely tied to and financially sponsored by the Royal family. This spacious compound aims at enhancing the City's capacity and prestige and at bringing together higher education, research, and commerce to promote Doha as an international city. Currently, there are six U.S. universities operating in the Education

City. Their specialized fields include design, computer science and information systems, medical science, foreign service, and journalism and communication. As stated by Croom (2011), the Qatar Foundation financially supports the operation of the Education City, and revenue generation is not the major concern of the City. "Rather, Qatar appears to target quality, image, and prestige in order to attract top institutions and researchers to its campus" (p. 55).

The other case in the Gulf region described by Croom (2011) is the Dubai International Academic City (DIAC) in Dubai. The investor of DIAC intends to develop the City to promote knowledge economy, bringing "together a number of higher education institutions with plans for shared facilities and services among them" (p. 55). This knowledge community houses academic institutions from a wide range of countries, such as France, India, and the United States. As I note in the book sporadically, there is a tendency showing that higher education has been moving towards a more entrepreneurial orientation. This is the operational nature of DIAC. Unlike the Education City in Qatar, DIAC actively promotes their Academic City and invites institutions and students from different parts of the world to join the multi-cultural community.

Having compared the two cases of cross-border partnership in the Gulf region, Croom (2011) points to the important factors that might affect the operation of an overseas campus and the development of partnerships. Despite the very similar cultural environment, the Education City and DIAC are very different in at least five categories, namely capital investment and sources of revenue, the ability to adjust to a changing environment and educational demand, practice of institutional recognition, the impact on the partnership of long-term support for the educational endeavor, and visions and principles of investors or educators running overseas campuses. Although there is really no better or worse model in operating overseas campuses, Croom reminds those "institutions looking to establish education sites overseas [need to] understand these differences and take into account how the opportunities align with their own goals, resources, risk assessment and, most importantly, institutional mission and vision" (p. 60).

The Case of Malaysia

It is possible that different countries have different purposes to develop IBSs or to participate in IBCs abroad. In the case of Malaysia, Lane (2011) describes the purposes as: providing something superior than what is available in Malaysian higher education system, providing something different from what exists in Malaysia, to meet the increasing demand for higher education, and to generate demand to attract new foreign students to Malaysia. Lane points out that cross-border partnerships in higher education roughly fall into three types of collaboration: government relations, the academic corporation, and strategic alliance. In the first type of partnership, government relations, the home institution and the host institution are generally regulated and administered by the government and are considered public entities. There are intergovernmental relationships in this case. In the academic corporation type, the partnerships are established between academic and non-academic corporations. This can be seen as one kind of joint venture in that "two or more partners create a new legal entity to pursue a joint objective" (p. 71). Lane describing the third type of partnerships, strategic alliance, states a "strategic alliance occurs when two or more partners enter into an agreement to collaborate in the pursuit of joint objectives, but partners remain legally separate entities" (p. 72). The three types of cross-border partnerships in Malaysia show that cross-border partnerships have gone beyond the educational arena and have their educational, political, economic, and societal significance.

Like Croom (2011), Lane (2011) also presents two IBCs established in Malaysia: the Monash University Sunway Campus Malaysia (MUSCM) and the Royal Melbourne Institute of Technology's (RMIT) Adorna Institute of Technology, Malaysia. Interestingly, like Croom's examples, Lane's examples in Malaysia also show that one was successful and the other stopped partnership just after four years of operation. Contrastive analysis may provide insights into the key issues in cross-border partnerships. Lane (2011) investigated and discussed the two cases from three different aspects: "transaction costs, strategic behavior, and the acquisition of organizational knowledge" (p. 81). In the first aspect, transaction costs, it is easy to understand that academic joint ventures try to lower the operation costs and share the risks of loss. On the other hand, partners in this type of collaboration will lose a certain degree of management and control over the entire operation. In the case of MUSCM, the operation costs were low and the partners had a certain degree of familiarity with each other. Welch (2011), in another article, also describes that MUSCM was joined by Sunway Group Malaysia, and Sunway provides the infrastructure facilities under a lease arrangement, while Monash University is responsible for academic matters including providing teaching staff. They have jointly provided the capital of MUSCM. According to him, "the campus is currently exceeding its budgeted profit" (p. 75).

The second aspect, strategic behavior, aims at improving a firm's competitiveness to maximize profits. In the case of RMIT, there exists a lot of uncertainty, for example, "the location of the campus and the short-term viability of the endeavor" (Lane, 2011, p. 82). The strategic alliance in the RMIT's case means that "RMIT's potential fortunes were based on an entity of which it had almost no direct control" (p. 82). Finally, the aspect of the acquisition of organizational knowledge points to the fact that firms collaborate with academic organizations to acquire organizational knowledge and skills and knowledge about the local economy. In the case of RMIT, the two indigenous investors "have almost no role in the governance of the institution" (p. 83). In this case, the partnership might break down in case the investors are no longer willing to financially support the partnership. That may lead to, as described by Lane, "one partner is subject to the fate and fancy of the other partner" (p. 84). In the case of MUSCM, "the two partners are responsible for the areas that fall within their expertise....both share responsibility for the campus [and] each principal has say in decision making" (p. 84). Like Lane, Welch (2011) also calls the joint venture of RMIT a failure. Similarly, he ascribes the failure to a poor choice of site…, difficulties in attracting appropriate local staff, poor building standards, over capitalization, lack of experience in education on the part of the Malaysian partner, high requirement of local investment, poor prospects for private education, and the impact of the Asian currency crisis on the value of the local partner's significant property portfolio" (p. 76-77).

In sum, cross-border partnership may be full of uncertainty, such as cultural differences, decrease of student market, and change of the government and its policies. One way to deal with the uncertainty is, as suggested by Lane (2011), is "to create a joint venture, which can align organizations with different expertise and knowledge as well as protect the academic institution from some of the financial risk" (p. 86).

The Case of Taiwan

In Taiwan, establishing sisterhood with overseas universities and developing cross-cultural exchange programs are also quite common. For example, Tamkang University (TKU) in New Taipei City has develop sisterhood with more than two hundred universities throughout five continents in the globe. Exchange activities with its sister universities include exchange faculty and students, junior abroad, dual degree programs, internships, international conferences, international volunteering, etc. Among these activities, the junior year abroad program is particularly worth mentioning. The program has been practiced for 25 years. TKU offers studies of six languages in its College of Languages and Literatures, namely English, French, German, Spanish, Japanese, and Russian. Students from these departments are particularly encouraged to study in a foreign country in their junior year at TKU to experience the language and culture they are learning. In its Lanyang campus, participating in the Junior Abroad program is even mandatory. The students in the TKU Lanyang campus are well-prepared for their junior year abroad studies. Stated in its University Development Blueprint for academic year 2018-2022, TKU expects to reach a number of more than 10,000 students participating in the Junior Year Abroad program.

In fact, TKU's exchange activities are bi-directional and bi-lateral. On the one hand, TKU sends its students to study abroad; on the other hand, TKU welcomes international students to attend its academic programs. In 2018, TKU hosted more than 2000 international students from 72 countries. It is especially significant in an era when Taiwan is facing difficulty of low birth rates. There are Chinese language classes arranged for those international students to familiarize them with the host language, culture, and environment. On the other hand, they may be arranged to teach their mother tongue to local students here in Taiwan. In its Lanyang campus, TKU intentionally develops the campus as an international community. Students in the community can experience a variety of cultures, life styles, and, of course, languages.

Another case of establishing overseas campus is Ming Chuan University (MCU) in Taiwan. MCU has its overseas campus in the U.S. Students participate in a so-called "Learning away from Home" program to take courses on their U.S. campus for five weeks in the summer. Participants are recruited through a screening process, and candidates are not limited to English majors or a particular field of study. Courses offered in the program are taught by American teachers. "The courses offered each year are not the same," according to Lilie Tsai, the then chair of the Department of Applied English in an interview I had with her, "and because of the success of the U.S. campus, MCU is planning to expand the program to the graduate level and to establish its overseas campus in the U.K. and Japan.

The Case of the United States

The United States has been a popular destination for overseas studies. It has hosted a considerable number of international students in its colleges and universities. Especially, New York is considered a cosmopolitan and multicultural city. For example, New York University (NYU) not only has a diverse student and faculty population, but also establishes more than 10 overseas campuses in important cities around the world, including Acca, Abu Dhabi, Berlin, Tel Aviv, Prague, London, Sydney, Shanghai, Paris, Florence, Buenos Aires, and Madrid. The list of NYU overseas campus shows concerns of global coverage in a globalizing era. Under this circumstance, the power of alumni cannot be ignored. In the case of NYU, it has well-organized Alumni Associations around the world. These associations not only organize national or regional alumni gatherings or activities, but also arrange overseas trips for the President of NYU or deans of different colleges to visit different countries and connect with alumni. In a globalizing era, there are various meanings for these global visits. On the one hand, they may strengthen connections between NYU alumni and gain sustained support from their alma mater. On the other hand, in a competitive international student market, it is an important way to publicize and promote the university. Especially, in these occasions, NYU welcomes its alumni to invite their family or friends to participate.

It is also evident from the case of NYU that both inward and outward student mobility account for the internationalization of the university. "New York University is home to the highest number of international students in the United States with over 17,000 international students and scholars from over 140 different countries" (New York

University). NYU also offers various international exchange opportunities for current NYU students. Its global services include overseas travel payment, working and hiring, research and academic programs and regulatory issues.

From all the examples demonstrated above, we can be quick to conclude that considerations of cross-border partnership in higher education cannot overlook the importance of the financial factor. For not-for-profit educational cross-border collaboration, financial gains are definitely not the major concern of the partner institutions. However, having no financial support is critically impossible for partnership to survive. Partnerships in IBCs are comparable to those in the commercial field. Gulati, Wohlgezogen, and Zhelyazkov (2012) discuss collaboration in strategic alliances in business. They mentioned some factors that may cause collaboration failures, such as task interdependencies, environmental uncertainties, misallocation of sources, and incompatibility of activities intended to be complementary. Conversely, elaborately stated and well agreed-on contracts can ensure that partners' contributions are efficiently used and process costs or losses are reduced.

The situations mentioned above may be applicable to cross-border partnership in education. As mentioned earlier in this section, cross-border partnerships may, or even better should, involve partners from the private sector or commercial organizations. In this collaborative scenario, the relationship between partners can be said to be complimentary. A possible type of collaboration can be commercial organizations contribute to the management of physical properties and financial allocation, and the academic institutions are responsible for academic arrangements, such as recruiting faculty and students, developing school calendars, and offering courses.

In sum, Cross-cultural exchanges involve partner schools from two or more different countries; hence it involves at least two governmental entities. Chapman and Sakamoto (2011) point out that university partnerships, in general, are initiated by individuals who are interested in establishing cross-border partnerships and who have connections or friendships overseas. They then may win governmental or organizational support because of their enthusiasm and the benefits or academic prestige the government or organization can expect to gain. Lance (2011) also points out, "the government is especially important as IBCs [International Branch Campuses] must deal with at least two governments; those of the home and host countries" (p. 74). Each country has to secure its own people's interests and benefits and has to make sure that participation in IBCs will not affect their academic reputation and integrity. Lance illustrates the example of the relationships between the Malaysian and the Australian government in the areas of cross-border partnerships. The two governments signed a memorandum for the academic collaboration established between them for mutual assistance and mutual benefits of both parties. For the Malaysian government, they have "to ensure that their citizens are not unduly harmed by the services provided or the competition with other providers" (p. 74). The same is true for the Australian government. The Australian government wants to make sure that "the foreign endeavors do not negatively affect the home campus or the reputation of Australian higher education" (p. 74). In this case, each government has its rules or regulations to monitor and to operate the IBCs, depending on the consideration of educational system, political status, economic situation, and cultural differences.

Governmental support may be critical to the success or failure of IBCs. You as teachers or educators seeking for cross-cultural partnership need to do enough homework in search of exchange partners. At home, you need to check local regulations for extending campus abroad or for establishing IBCs within your own nations and if your proposals are encouraged by government. For the part of your overseas partners, it is even more important that you well study and get familiar with the situations of your prospective partners overseas before you make your commitment to the partnership. In addition to the principles mentioned above, you also have to take their governmental support into consideration. Sometimes it is not your partners' problem, but the disconnection or failure of a partnership may be because of the government. It includes policy change, change of national leaders, political instability, and economic crisis. It is an ideal situation that both governments encourage and support cross-cultural partnerships and that they have established favorable relationships and are politically and economically stable.

COLLABORATIONS BEYOND THE INSTRUCTIONAL SETTING AND FOR NON-INSTRUCTIONAL PURPOSES

As mentioned earlier, collaborations whether between educational institutions or with non-educational organizations, are meaningful only when they may improve human life, acquire knowledge, and move towards a more harmonious globe and better the well-beings of its residents. Viewed from this perspective, it is not necessary that collaborations are limited to activities collaborated between or among educational institutions. As pointed out by Walsh and Kahn (2010), "breaking through boundaries can provide creative spaces for innovative practice and for collaborative working beyond the academy (p. 103). In this section, I choose to describe some examples of collaborations beyond the instructional setting and for non-instructional purposes to show how these collaborations may really contribute to a globalizing era.

Collaboration between Educational Institutions and Farmers

It is not necessary that cross-cultural exchanges have to happen between two educational institutional institutions. The case of collaboration for instructional technology systems in agriculture described by Maharjan and Sakamoto (2011) is a good example of universities collaborating with farmers across borders. The researchers describe how a web-based, image processing diagnosis program may help overseas farmers identify plant diseases. The computer program was developed by a Japanese institution of higher education, and it helped Nepalese farmers to improve their agricultural techniques by using the computer program stored in a mobile phone to quickly identify the disease and to minimize the possible financial loss. Nepal is said to be an economically and technologically deprived country. With the development of the plant disease diagnosis program, Nepalese farmers have been greatly benefitted from the cross-border collaboration. This is a perfect example showing how modern technologies and domain knowledge can be integrated to help people in different fields to solve real-world problems. This model can be applied to different areas of concern and can show how professional knowledge can be connected with real-world practice.

Commercial Collaboration between Industry and Academia

Whaley (Walsh & Kahn, 2010) describes how University of Dundee collaborated with technological developers to develop Blackboard "Self and Peer Assessment System that engages students in reflective learning" (p. 106). Like any other collaboration, there were boundaries existing ahead of the collaboration. However, partners can finally cross the boundaries and successfully reach the goal of the project. As well-said by Walsh and Kahn, "boundaries can present barriers; or they can provide opportunities" (p. 103). The boundaries apparent in collaboration include not only "a large geographical distance between Scotland and the United States…, [but also] different internal structures and working practices…between a university and a commercial company" (p. 108). According to Whaley, the technical partner knew better of technical intellectual property and legal matters, while the higher education is better of pedagogical practices and students' needs.

Whaley (Walsh & Kahn, 2020) claims the collaboration to be successful in that "a year after the collaboration began, Blackboard released version 8.0 of its Learning Environment, which incorporate the new self- and peer-assessment system, to over 3,6000 global clients" (p. 109). The system can be used for different class sizes, subject areas, and purposed. Furthermore, they learned some important collaboration methods and strategies useful for future collaborations, such as different terminologies used, different sub-cultures in different domains, different locations, and even different languages spoken. For example, in terms of geographical distance, the partners had to use web conferences, phone conferences, and face-to-face meetings, with one partners group travelling to the other partner group's place.

Cross-Border Collaboration between Development Bank and Higher Education

As mentioned in the introductory chapter, globalization should target the synergy of working together to solve global issues. Having advanced communication technologies and convenient transportation are only a means to reach the goal. Among the global issues, poverty is a critical one because it can create various social, political, and economical problems. Collins (2011) argues that economic prosperity will not lead to poverty reduction. Rather, advancing scientific and technical knowledge and enhancing self-sufficiency will eventually lead to poverty reduction. To achieve the goal, higher education institutions play a critical role in the era of a knowledge economy. He illustrates two cases of loan collaboration between development banks and developing countries: Thailand and Uganda. In the case of Thailand, the World Bank funded and collaborated with Thai universities to strengthen and upgrade teaching, learning, and research in science and engineering in a project entitled the Universities Science and Engineering Education Project (USEEP). Assessment of the achievement of objectives stated at the beginning shows that the project met its objectives and the outcomes were satisfactory. It also shows substantial poverty reduction. Although, as Collins states, "Much of Thailand's population still exists in poverty....There was strong belief in the potential for research, knowledge creation, and distribution to make contributions to the country's human capacity for these types of roles" (p. 241).

In the case of Uganda, the Ugandan government had a Poverty Eradication Plan (PEAP), and the Millennium Science Initiative Project (MSI) was approved and funded by the World Bank with its objectives to enhance productivity, competitiveness and income of the labor market and improvement of human development through emphasis on science and technology in higher education. The MSI is still underway. However, according to Collins (2011), "the government of Uganda had made concrete links between the development of science and technology, university education, and poverty reduction" (p. 243). Thus, the government has been encouraging students to major in science and technology.

The examples of Thailand and Uganda revealed that knowledge economy may be the answer to poverty reduction, and, to promote knowledge economy, universities and colleges play a key role. There might not be an immediate effect to promote science and technology in terms of poverty reduction. However, in the long run, the knowledge economy may eventually help developing countries in their combat with poverty. In this regard, collaborations between universities and financial organizations become extremely important.

Cross-Border Collaboration between Two Institutions in Higher Education for Non-Instructional Purposes

An example of collaboration between two universities for non-instructional purposes is reported by Austin and Foxcroft (2011). They report a one-decade-long collaboration between Nelson Mandela Metropolitan University (NMMU) in South Africa and Michigan State University (MSU) in the U.S., aiming at institutional change and faculty development. The project started with the initiative of an American Fulbrighter, who was expert in "higher education, organizational change, academic staff development, and teaching and learning issues" (p. 118). They first helped NMMU with their organizational change, teaching and learning approaches, faculty development, and broadening of the student base.

The collaboration then expanded to include visits to each other's universities. For example, NMMU faculty and higher education leaders from other universities visited MSU in the U.S. and attended national conferences of an American higher education association. On the other hand, the American Fulbrighter also visited NMMU in South Africa several times after she went back to the U.S. The collaboration was later expanded to include members from MSU visiting NMMU to assist them with their merger with other universities and with required changes in post-apartheid South Africa.

Austin and Foxcroft (2011) consider the collaboration between the two universities successful due to some important factors. First, it provided opportunities for mutual learning and benefitted both universities as I describe earlier in this chapter. Another factor that might contribute to the success of the collaboration was that the project got support from both sides to lead the project and had committed participants. Still another factor that could be ascribed to the project's success was that willingness "of MSU and NMMU staff to familiarize themselves with the educational contexts in the country of the partners" (p. 125). Under this circumstance, participants were sensitive to the local context when they were offering ideas for their partner university. On the other hand, they also linked the ideas to international practices and research purposes.

Cross-Border Collaboration Aiming at Assessing Curriculum Design

Hodges, Watchravesringkan, Yurchism, Hegland, Karpova, Marcketti, and Yan (2015) report a 3-year long collaboration involving faculty at four American universities and faculty and industry professionals in Thailand, India, Russia, and South Africa. The main focus of the collaboration was on assessing curriculum design for developing students' entrepreneurial knowledge and small business skills. In responding to the globalizing market and the increasingly growing importance of small business in the United States, the project aimed at designing a curriculum for business students to develop their global competencies, entrepreneurial knowledge and small business skills in the workplace. The project started with collecting data from international entrepreneurial and small businesses, involving interviews with small business owners and entrepreneurs in Russia, Thailand, South Africa, India, and the USA (p. 317). They conducted a total of 35 interviews in the five countries through a snowball sampling technique. Interviewees were asked questions relevant to challenges and benefits of running a small business, the characteristics and skills they look for when hire new graduates, and their perceptions of the future of small business in a globalizing era.

In the second phase of their project, Hodges et al. (2015) focused on the development of curriculum for targeted students. They develop the curriculum based on their findings in the first phase and students' needs in their future career in a globalizing workplace and market. They integrated interviewees' perceptions of the characteristics required as a small business entrepreneur in a globalizing era and developed instructional and training materials, aiming at preparing students for being global entrepreneurs. These instructional materials were available in different modes, including "compilations of readings, videos, collaborative projects, and case studies based on Phase I data" (p. 317) and were organized into different modules, such as "global sourcing, consumer behavior, and product development" (p. 317).

In the third phase of the project, Hodges et al. (2015) focused on the delivery and assessment of the instructional materials developed in Phase II. Participants were asked to fill out a questionnaire both before and after the delivery of the instructional materials to investigate the effectiveness of the designed instructional materials. There were six constructs included in the questionnaire, namely "intercultural social skills, networking skills, financial skills, personality, entrepreneurial knowledge, and entrepreneurial skills" (p. 139). The quantitative research findings show that, according to Hodges et al., networking skills are important in terms of enhancing entrepreneurial knowledge.

In the qualitative part of research findings, Hodges et al. (2015) analyzed participants' responses to the open-ended questions and found three thematic areas were important: running a small business, developing a global outlook, and thinking like an entrepreneur. First, students felt that the instructional materials helped them "become more aware of what is required to start and maintain a successful business" (p. 321). Second, students responded that activities in the learning process allowed them to learn how businesses are run in different countries and how they are interconnected, and how they may be affected by the global economy. They have a heightened awareness of the role small businesses play in the global market. Finally, as reported by Hodges et al., students learned to be more creative to approach issues confronting small businesses, and they felt that "making and maintaining connections with others can also expand one's own thinking" (p. 323). Hodges et al.'s study, like other collaborations beyond educational settings, show how educational instructions can be and should be connected with real-world practices.

Cross-Border Dialogue Program Aiming at Global Issues

Pang (2009) describes a collaborative program involving students from George Washington University, National University of Singapore, and University of Chile. They discuss issues of global relevance and exchange their ideas on cyberspace or via videoconferencing, and they also had physical visits to each other's country. In reality, the dialogue program changed its theme "year to year which [was] selected for global relevance" (p. 238). For example, in a global health program, they focused on the discussion of HIV/AIDS, and visited hospitals and health institutes in their partners' country. This type of collaboration may really draw students' attention to global issues and encourage them to collaboratively contribute to the solution of these global issues. As Pang stated, this "was an important step in cultivating a society that is more open, diverse, and in tune with the global practices and norms that are needed for a global city" (p. 239).

Establishment of a Rural Library Supported by Overseas Librarians

In an era of fast-growing information technology and knowledge economy, collaborations between or among research libraries and with public and private organizations appear to be more and more important. O'Brien and Richardson (2015) and Abungu and Law (2015) describe the changing role of academic libraries and librarians in an era of globalization and rapidly growing information technology. They argue that the main causes of the change are the technological evolution in the field due to publication and the development of the knowledge economy. As O'Brien and Richardson suggest, "the Internet has enabled new models of scholarly communication.... New publishing and pricing models are being explored for journals" (p. 197-198). On the other hand, as the knowledge economy has been a new trend in a globalizing era, almost everything is commercial product, including knowledge, skills and capability, and knowledge keeps moving forward. As new knowledge emerges, old knowledge may be outdated. In this regard, academic libraries can no longer be viewed as only places that collect information and data. Rather, they need to effectively collaborate with authors, researchers, other divisions of departments, and other libraries or organizations to manage and preserve various forms of data to maximize the impacts of research findings. For librarians, they need to actively communicate with authors, researchers, and other librarians to *create* knowledge and disseminate valuable research findings to benefit the public.

Abungu and Law (2015), on the other hand, describe the efforts made by cross-cultural partners and local community members to construct a library in a rural village in Kenya. The entire story is touching, and it sets a good example of how collaboration or partnerships can make a difference. According to Abungu and Law, the project started with a two-people cross-cultural partnership. One of the partners is from the small village, Ndwara, in Kenya, and the other one is from Canada. Both of them are experienced librarians, who believe that "a public library could inspire and support both "economic and cultural development in the village [Ndwara] (p. 160-161). They met and started planning; their goal was to build a public library in Ndwara, Kenya. The partner from Kenya is familiar with the local culture of the Ndwara community.

As stated by Abungu and Law (2015), the library started without even a building. They needed to plan well the entire project, communicate with community people and products for their support, and most importantly to raise funds. In addition to writing a grant application and seeking local community support for the project, the project mainly got financial support from Canada and Korea. Because one of the two initial partners is from Canada, she was able to do some fundraising activities in Canada, and she raised "enough money to pay the legal fees to deal with the land transfer and the setting up of the library committee as a legal entity" (p. 166). In the region of Korea, fund raising activities were made possible by one of the initial partners who had a trip in Korea and who was asked to speak to a group of club members. The story of the Ndwara Library touched Korean people and was able to gain support. As Abungu and Law describe these kinds of financial support from abroad, "the first one was very small, intended to engage individuals and create a list of potential donors" (p. 167). In addition to money, people also donated books, newspapers, and laptops for the library.

The story of Ndwara Library set an example to cross-cultural collaborators as to how efforts made to support kids in less-developed countries can make a difference for them. Abungu and Law's (2015) report concludes by addressing the importance of project management skills, teamwork and collaboration, adaptability, and strategies for fund-raising. However, we do believe the story of Ndwara Library will not stop here. We can envisage a compelling picture of Ndwara kids studying diligently in the Ndwara Library and expect the follow-up report from the initial partners.

Cross-Border Collaboration Sponsored by Governments or Organizations

An example of a large-scale of cross-border collaboration sponsored by an international organization is the International Intervisitation Programme (IIP) described by Barnett and Jacobson (2010). This program was sponsored by the University Council for Education Administration (UCEA), aiming at improving administrative practice and leadership preparation in universities of higher education. At its initiative meeting in 1966, IIP brought "scholars from Australia, Canada, England, and Scotland to institutions of higher education in the United States" (p. 260). According to Barnett and Jacobson, participants claimed that this meeting has broadened their vision to break down their provincialism to perceive administration from a wider international conception.

From then on, IIP took place every four years in different countries with each time focusing on different issues of leadership and administrator preparation. More importantly, the spirit of organizational partnership has led to "the formation of both the European Forum on Educational Administration and the British Educational Administration Society" (Barnett & Jacobson, 2010, p. 261). Although, later on, IIP was transformed to a different type of partnership and was sponsored by UCEA, international partnerships and collaborations to work on developing educational leadership to respond to greater cultural diversity and to prepare students to become global citizens.

For the international collaboration, Barnett and Jacobson (2010) state some advantages and limitations. The most important benefit for participant institutions or organizations was that, by examining school administration from other cultures, they can view university administration from a different cultural perspective and would limit their use of educational ideas to their single national contexts. However, there are also some limitations that have drawn participants' attention. It seemed that, since the partnership was initiated in the United States, partners felt that they were imposed to accept American or Western viewpoints, and they claimed that local cultures and values should be respected and preserved. On the other hand, they also claimed that the entire practice of the partnership seemed to ignore the existing problems in a nation's local schools. They argue that international collaboration should take a variable-sum perspective so that international collaboration can "always inform domestic educational leadership research and practice" (p. 262).

Another case is collaboration or cooperation between or among governments. Keskin (2014) describes the dilemma faced by Turkey. On the one hand, Turkey is eager to join the European Union (EU), but EU is reluctant to grant Turkey membership particularly because of Turkey's poor record of human rights and democracy. On the other hand, Turkey thinks of an alternative to join Shanghai Cooperation Organization (SCO) mainly led by China and Russia. Generally speaking, SCO welcomed Turkey's application for membership mainly because of some economic reasons. However, there are still obstacles to Turkey's SCO membership, such as Turkey's NATO membership and its democratic future. To join EU or SCO, according to Keskin, is a difficult choice for Turkey. Turkey's case shows that ties between or among countries are always based on economic and political considerations. However, as Keskin stated "the holistic view of stability that the SCO espouses implies that significant cultural and educational links between the central Asian region and Turkey cannot be denied (p. 125).

Cross-Border Collaboration Organized by Non-Profit Networks

International Education and Resource Network (iEARN), established in 1988, is an international education network that connects teachers and young students around the world for project-based learning. In its iEARN Project Book 2016-2017, iEARN claims that it "supports over 50,000 teachers and 2 million youth in more than 140 countries to collaborate through a global online network in projects designed to make a difference in the world" (iEARN Project Book 2016-2017, p. 3). Its goal is to connect classrooms with the world and to encourage young students to learn with the world. Each year iEARN organizes different projects, aiming at learning about language arts, humanities and social sciences, science, technology, engineering and math, and others. Participant schools can access iEARN Online Collaboration Center to look for projects they are interested in and participate. Collaborations between or among participant schools can be either online or face-to-face by visiting their partners' countries.

In addition to connecting young students from all over the globe, one of the important merits of iEARN is that it encourages young students to work together on solving global issues we are facing and how to make a better globe. Viewed from this regard, what young students are doing or intend to do deserves great encouragement and support. As mentioned in Chapter One of this book, globalization should not be focused only on different types of mobility. Rather, it is more important to work together to solve global issues.

Collaboration among Participants for Sustainable Development

Nomura, Natori, and Abe (2011) describe an international network of universities for sustainable development in the Asia-Pacific region: the promotion of sustainability in Postgraduate Education and Research Network (ProSPER.Net). As noted by Nomura et al., higher education for sustainable development (HESD) networks were just emerging in the Asia-Pacific region. ProSPER.Net was launched in 2008 and was participated by higher education institutions in Asia and the Pacific, sponsored by the Japanese Ministry of the Environment. According to Nomura et al., "sharing resources through joint activities and information sharing are the two major objectives to be achieved" (p. 220). They consider face-to-face meetings and email exchanges are effective ways to share information and to generate ideas. On the other hand, the nature of networking also allows members of the network to share "resources through joint activities" (p. 222), for example, summer school and initiatives of graduate courses relevant to sustainable development. ProSPER.Net keeps encouraging its members to propose new ideas in the field of sustainable development.

Nomura et al. (2011) conclude that "ProSPER.Net has contributed to the development of a cross-border collaboration in the field of education for sustainable development in the Asia-Pacific" (p. 223). They point to some important features of ProSPER.Net: collaboration based on a network and a network led by an agency not from the education sector, and claim that collaboration among higher education institutions "can be made and utilized to cope with emerging social issues, if an institute in a given sector provides resources.

Collaboration for Quality Assurance

As Al-Barwani, Ameen, and Chapman (2011) state, the fast growth of enrollments in higher education has led to a decline of quality. As a result, some higher education institutions seek overseas collaboration to ensure the quality of their education. Al-Barwani et al. describe the situation in Oman. The Government of Oman (GoO), sensing a forthcoming post-oil economy, and the need for highly educated citizens, encouraged the establishment of private higher education institutions. As the number of private higher education institutions increased, the quality of private higher education become increasingly important. To respond to the need of assuring the quality of private higher education institutions, GoO initiated its unique policies to mandate that each private higher education institution was required to affiliate with an international counterpart institution whose responsibility is to oversee the quality of the Omani institution.

In this international affiliation system, according to Al-Barwani et al. (2011), there are minor variations in practicing the collaboration. For example, in a so-called franchise system, the courses offered in Oman should "be identical in all important respects to the program offered at the affiliate institution" (p. 135). Although the courses are taught by local teachers in Oman, tests "are graded both in Oman and again by staff at the affiliate institution as a double-check on comparability of outcomes" (p. 135). However, what attracts students in the system is that students earn diplomas from the affiliate institution. Foreign diplomas may add to the students' prestige and help them in their future employability and mobility. In another case of collaboration called 'validation system', instructors in Oman need to develop their own programs to be approved by the international affiliate. Students get a local diploma in this case.

Having practiced the international affiliation system for decades, the effectiveness and challenges of the system have been debated and discussed, and Oman is planning to move the quality assurance system in higher education to a local accreditation system. Al-Barwani et al.'s (2011) study surveyed and interviewed senior administers in colleges for their perception of the affiliation system. Basically a majority of the respondents felt positive about the affiliation system in terms of helping the institution "meet acceptable international standards" (p. 142). However, some issues were pointed out by interviewees. First, because Omani institutions have to pay for the international affiliates' services, the fee can cause financial burden for some private institutes. Second, the involvement of international affiliates varies. Some international affiliates may supervise the quality and improvement of their Omani institutions attentively, while others may just be loosely involved in the practice of the Omani institution and may be more interested in financial rewards. Finally, because the involvement of international institutions from different parts of the world, the programs may reveal different features; it causes problems for students to transfer credits they have earned across institutions.

Curriculum Development in a Developing World Context Supported by International Organizations

It is sometimes the case that international organizations' financial support can make a difference for kids in a marginalized environment. Mfum-Mensah (2009) describes the School for Life (SFL) program developed in Northern Ghana. This program did not really involve kids in cross-cultural encounters; however, the significant curriculum development program would not be able to operate without financial support from international organizations such as the World Bank, the International Monetary Fund, the US Agency for International Development, and the Danish Consortium in Denmark.

According to Mfum-Mensah (2009), SFL had great achievement in terms of providing complementary education programs to those deprived and disadvantaged kids in Northern Ghana, which is less favored then South Ghana, for literacy and numeracy skills and knowledge, and moving them into the mainstream education. This program applied two important approaches to curriculum design and development: technical approach and critical approach. The technical approach follows the traditional procedures to design a curriculum, in this case: deliberation stage to decide the aims and objectives of the curriculum, the design stage, the implementation stage, and the outcome stage. The critical approach refers to the involvement of different groups of people, in this case, including parents and community members to make sure the curriculum designed really meets students' needs and is helpful for their daily life and community practices. Mfum-Mensah concludes that the program is quite helpful, with an enrollment of more than fifty thousand in the program and 22,090 being moved to the official schools in 2006, due to the involvement of different groups of relevant personnel and the financial support they got from international organizations. It is evident from here that a well-designed and successful program, whether local or cross-cultural, requires participation of all relevant groups of personnel and financial support from international organizations if local funds are not available or sufficient for the program. Although international organizations may be not experts in the academic field, it is occasionally possible for them to offer useful strategies. For example, one of the strategies applied to the SFL program was *decentralization*. As Mfum-Mensah states, "decentralization was one of the World Bank's education sector reforms in Ghana in the 1990s" (p. 145).

Collaborations among Corporate Universities

The term *Corporate university* is relatively new, and it still confuses many people. Dealtry (2017) proposes a definition which is thought to catch the core meaning

> The corporate university is a management intervention that takes a company or organization into a new robust and sustained phase of business development that it would not achieve with its current levels of opportunity for though leadership and styles of learning behavior." (p. 5)

This is a somewhat abstract concept at the first glance. In this sense, the nature of corporate universities concerns more about corporate development than about that of academic institutions. Then, the discussions of corporate university may seem less relevant to this book, which mostly focuses on educational institutions, especially higher education. However, the concept of corporate university reveals a very important message: collaborations between educational institutions and commercial organizations can complement each other and benefit both, as I conclude in the last chapter. Practically speaking, the idea of corporate university is that a business organization apply basic educational practices in their management and development, including "quality instruction, facilitating research and advanced learning and giving recognition to the level of learning achieved" (p. 8). Dealtry (2017) proposes that a company's programs can be linked to a university, business school or college and credits can be offered for those who participate in the programs. "External alliances and learning partnerships with the intellectual supply chain should be formed on the basis of specific learning needs allied to particular strategic learning initiatives" (p. 11). The main idea of corporate university is to make use of the resources, theories and practices in learning and research, and knowledge in the management and development of businesses. European Corporate Universities and Academies Network (ECUANET), as will be described below, is a good example of this type of collaboration.

Dealtry (2017) describes ECUANET as an independent transnational networking development project. It is a transnational network joined by different European countries. One of the projects ECUANET achieved is "developing the quality of Vocational Education and Training (VET) systems and practices" (p. 66). Partners of this project did action research and provided relevant information and experiences. They even provided strategies in improving the quality of vocational education and training and in a demand-led learning. According to Dealtry, the partners of the corporate universities and their collaboration range from "large corporate companies to the higher education, charitable organisations, multi-company collaborative clusters, national policy-driven interventions, etc." (p. 71).

Conclusion: The Functional Model for the Analysis of Cross-Cultural Exchanges

From the different cases of cross-cultural activities described above, it is clear that cross-border collaborations are not necessarily limited to the collaboration between or among educational institutions and the focus has gone beyond instructional purposes. Cross-border collaboration between academic institution and government, an institution and organization, and a government and government can all significantly contribute to global development.

Sakamoto and Chapman (2011) demonstrate a functional model to analyze cross-border partnerships. They state that cross-border programs have been seen moving from instruction-oriented to non-instruction-oriented ones. At the earlier stage of cross-cultural exchanges, the exchange programs were generally developed for instructional purposes, such as student and faculty exchange, dual degree program, and establishment of branch campuses. As cross-border partnership expands its practice, non-instruction-oriented cross-border partnership expands its practice, and non-instruction-oriented cross-border programs emerged. These non-instruction-oriented cross-border programs "aim at such things as faculty development, research, joint science and technology initiatives, quality assurance, technology sharing, and delivery of non-academic services" (p. 4).

Sakamoto and Chapman (2011) roughly divide the reasons for establishment of cross-border partnerships into four factors: organizational, financial, individual, and context factors. Organizational factors are relevant to those specific to the institution, such as being aligned with the missions of each partner institution and being benefitted from participation in order to gain revenue, prestige or valued outcomes. Financial factors refer to those opportunities that institutional funding is available to support cross-border programs. Another factor, individual factors, may be more personal than organizationally driven. Faculty members may have impressive cross-border experiences, and they feel benefitted from the cross-border encounters and would like to continue their endeavor to specific shared research interests. Finally, investigations on "how different context factors faced by each participating institution shapes the nature of collaboration" (p. 9) and presentation of how different "regulations concerning academic freedom, protection for intellectual property right, ethical treatment of human subjects, financial accounting rules, and ownership of jointly developed materials and products" (p. 9) can be good topics to explore in the field of cross-cultural exchanges. According to Sakamoto and Chapman, these four domains of factors may contribute to the establishment of cross-border partnerships. However, as they also mention, there is a tendency that there are more and more non-instruction-oriented programs that will be developed. This topic will be further explored in Chapter 8 The future of cross-cultural exchanges.

The opposite term of *collaboration* is *competition*. In the course of collaboration, it is important not to turn collaboration into real competition. Punteney (2017) discusses the issue of competition between groups from a socio-psychological perspective. She argues that humans tend to compare and compete with others. In the field of cross-cultural collaboration, there is no harm at all if students from different cultures are competing for excellence or for learning gains. Theoretically, it is not real competition because one group's gains will not cause the other group's losses. The real competition is that two groups of students are competing, say, for limited resources, power relations, or political, historical, or religious debates. It takes cross-cultural practitioners' wisdom to avoid this kind of negative stereotypes or conflicts from happening.

CHALLENGES OF ESTABLISHING CROSS-BORDER PARTNERSHIPS

You, practitioners of cross-cultural exchanges, may face some challenges in the course of looking for overseas partners. First, financing may be a critical issue in cross-cultural partnerships, especially it requires both partners' commitment. As Austin and Foxcroft (2011) put it, a "partnership that involves commitment of resources by only one partner seems far less likely to succeed for any length of time" (p. 128). As a common practice, cross-cultural partners may seek for financial support from the government or organizations. However, political instability or shifts, decline in finance, or outbreaks of some social incidents may damage the sustainability of a cross-cultural collaboration. It may be wise to take all political, social, economic, and educational factors into consideration before launching into cross-cultural collaboration.

Second, any cross-cultural partnership may encounter resistance from some colleagues or even participants of the project. In addition to being resistant to change, a subtle power relation existing in a collaborative project may be critical to participants' resistance. Cross-cultural collaborations are supposed to be mutually beneficial and an equal power relation for both partners. Resistance may occur because of the seeming expertise apparent on the partner's side. As Austin and Foxcroft (2011) state, expressions of "genuine, humility, respect, and eagerness to learn as well as to share are necessary ingredients" (p. 127) in cross-cultural collaborations. Third, collaboration is "dynamic and fluid, rather than static and fixed" (p. 131). The collaborative agenda needs to be discussed and revised in the process of collaboration. Some of the timeline needs to be flexible and should be reserved for any ideas or activities that come out as a result of discussion or feedback from participants.

Another challenge of cross-border collaborations or partnerships is *regulation,* which is especially notable in the Philippines. Welch (2011) describes the situation in the Philippines. The Philippines saw a considerable growth in international enrollments in the early 2000s. However, this may be due to the incursions of transnational providers into Philippine higher education. Some well-known international institutions establish programs in the Philippines in partnership with local institutions. According to Welch, these programs are actually of low quality and are not well-regulated. Some of them "offers diplomas and bachelor degrees in about 30 branches in the Philippines most of which are in Shoemart shopping malls" (p. 126). Actually, the "academic staff from overseas institutions only visited the Philippines occasionally" (p. 126), and they just make use of local teachers' instructional materials.

The above-mentioned situation is only the case of the Philippines. However, as there are more and more cross-border partnerships in higher education in a globalizing era, regulatory issues cannot be ignored. Proliferation of cross-border partnerships cannot guarantee the quality of partnerships. Although students may be temporarily tempted by the benefits or rewards claimed by program providers, sustainability is the key. Like partnerships in business, partnerships in education cannot eventually survive if not well-regulated. Choosing your exchange partners is only the beginning of collaboration between you and your partners. As Winer and Ray (1994) put it, "the collaborative road begins by assembling people, building trust, creating a vision, and agreeing on desired results" (p. 45). From that point on, working closely with your exchange partners and making whatever changes or adjustments needed in the course of collaboration is key to successful cross-cultural exchanges.

As mentioned at the beginning of this section, it is important to carefully evaluate the feasibility of a cross-cultural collaboration before you launch into a project. The considerations should take a large number of factors into account your evaluation process. Kelly (2018), before an unsuccessful collaboration with a young educated woman in Malawi, led a group of students in the U.S. to Malawi for service learning with the support of a Fulbright Study Abroad program. According to Kelly, these experiences were quite successful in terms of working on girls' and women's issues. However, the one that take place in 2010 was a failure. In this case, Kelley worked with an educated young African woman, who was ambitious, articulate, and modern, on helping girls and women in their education and career. Unfortunately, their collaboration did not turn out to be what they expected and the money was not appropriately used to reach the goal of the project.

Kelly (2018) faithfully reflects on the unsuccessful experience in Malawi and suggests some important factors for practitioners of cross-border collaboration to think about. First, cross-border partners need to "take the time to build relationships that enable consensus building and shared purpose. It is especially true when a project involves people from different cultures. People from different cultures may perceive and approach things differently and may have different priorities and purposes. Having enough communications and building good relationships may partially be the key to successful collaborations. Second, cross-cultural collaborations need to take partners' cultural norms into consideration. Many times, we tend to view and judge things based on our cultural norms. We need to be reminded that cross-cultural collaborations are matters of two different cultures, and the outcomes or benefits are to be shared by culturally different groups. Failure to hold this perspective may make it difficult to collaborate. Third, question and do not insist on one's own assumptions. More often than not, we tend to insist on our assumptions and think based on our ideology. According to Kelly, our assumptions need to be tested before launching into a collaborative project to minimize chances of failure. Fourth, you should listen carefully to each other and engage in inclusive dialogue. Yet there are always power relations existing in dialogue. The more powerful and authoritative ones may fail to listen to their less powerful partners carefully, and thus miss messages that are critical to the success of the collaboration. Finally, Kelly points to an important perspective that cross-cultural collaborators should possess. That is, the collaborations should be built on an on-going and long-term basis. Only by holding a forward-looking perspective, can collaborations be sustainable and generate long-term effects.

Chapter 8

ASSESSING THE STUDENTS AND EVALUATING THE PROJECT

As mentioned earlier, to ensure the success of a cross-cultural exchange project, it may be helpful to do a survey or interview students before the implementation of the project to get some ideas from the students who are going to participate in the project and to take students' opinions into consideration. However, it is even more important you assess the project after you complete the entire project so that you may have a chance to improve any future projects.

Some scholars distinguish *assessment* from *evaluation* (e.g., Garrison & Anderson, 2003; Herrington, Reeves, & Oliver, 2010) in formal education. Simply put it, assessment refers to assessing students' achievement of learning and *evaluation* refers to evaluating the entire course, program or project. Lucas and Blair (2017), on the other hand, consider that "assessment is an ongoing process of collecting, using, and providing feedback to improve practice" (p. 191), while evaluation "typically happens at the end of a program, or other efforts intended to judge the work against preset criteria" (p. 191). Generally, I consider an ongoing process of assessment to assess students' cross-cultural experiences can be an effective and appropriate way and both assessing students' accomplishments and evaluating the entire project are important and are interrelated. In this chapter, I discuss the two scales of assessment you need to do during and after completion of the project: students' overall performance and an overall evaluation of the entire project.

ASSESSING THE STUDENTS

Ways to assess students' accomplishment in cross-cultural encounters may vary, depending on the types of cross-cultural exchange. In the case of teaching international students in one's home country, natural observations or participant observations may be good ways to collect data from an outsider's view. Observations may include international students' learning of a new language, adaption to a new culture, interaction with local students or other international students, and observed intercultural competences. In the case of participant observations, the teacher may, for example, participate in international students' virtual communities or online discussion groups to actually understand what in their mind, their learning experiences, and how they perceive their own country and their host country. In this case, the teacher is viewing international students' cross-cultural experiences from a more insider's view. Assessing or testing students' learning outcomes after completing a period of instruction is a common practice in education. However, testing is more than an educational practice and its impacts are far beyond the educational setting (Seargeant, 2012). As Herrington, et al. (2010) put it, "we assess what we value and we value what we assess" (p. 137). Seargeant, for example, discusses the issue of how English should be tested in an era of globalization and points out that the impacts of the testing of English are far beyond the classroom and has its influence at the societal and political level. How a specific variety of English is valued depends on its practicality in terms of employment and education opportunities. At the political level, the government of some countries requires those who are applying for immigration to their countries to be familiar with their language varieties and social and cultural norms. Whether you decide to follow the traditional assessment paradigm or the authentic assessment paradigm, which will be discussed in the following sections to come, you need to keep in mind that the way you assess your students and the test questions or assessment tasks you provide may affect the way how students perceive the cross-cultural project and may have greater impacts beyond the educational field.

On the other hand, Lucas and Blair (2017) argue that a backward design approach in which program designers "first define the desired learning outcomes, then determine the methods to assess those outcomes, and finally design the academic intervention" (p. 191) may be effective and logical. In this way, assessment tools can match desired learning outcomes, and the desired learning outcomes, in turn, can inform the instructors about what to intervene in the instructional process.

Traditional Assessment

In the case of cross-cultural exchanges, you first need to assess students' performance in the exchange program. Strictly speaking, you need to provide your students with formative feedback throughout the course of the cross-cultural exchange project and provide them with summative assessment at the end of the project. It may not be really valuable and not sufficient that you only take students' relevant statistical counts in your assessing process, such as time spent online, number of postings contributed to online forum, encounters with people from a different culture, duration of volunteering overseas, and number of email exchanges with overseas partners. These pieces of information can be used only as supporting evidence to assess students' accomplishment. Based on the objectives of the exchange project, you can develop your ways of assessing students' accomplishment in the form of paper-and-pencil test, observation of attitudinal demeanor, oral presentation, written project report, role play, simulation, poster exhibition, competition, learning log, etc., depending on the nature of the project. You have to state well ahead as to how you are going to evaluate your students' performance. Especially in a cross-cultural project, the degree of cooperation from project partners or group members may affect students' performance. In this case, you might want to apply strategies for grading group work to your cross-cultural exchange project.

As mentioned earlier, the nature of cross-cultural exchanges can be either cooperative or collaborative. Under this circumstance, assessing students' performance is more complicated than what we know about traditional ways of assessment, especially an exchange project involves students from a different culture and interdependence is important to ensure good quality of performance. In a cooperative learning project, Olsen and Kagan (1992) suggest that both individual-performance grading and team-performance grading should be taken into account to ensure that both individual accountability and group accountability are important and interdependence works in a cooperative learning project.

In the case of study abroad or international volunteering, assessing students' performance can be even more complicated. The three main areas of concern, academic knowledge and skills, personal growth, and intercultural sensitivity, mentioned earlier, should be included in the assessment of students' learning outcomes. Traditional quantitative (e.g., questionnaire, paper-and-pencil tests or statistical facts) and qualitative (e.g., interviews, group discussion, student journals, and open-ended questions) methods can be applied in the assessing process. In addition, comparisons of different study abroad programs, including home countries and host countries, training programs before study abroad, and long-term effects after study abroad are important topics that deserve further investigation. Jones (2010) argues, in this type of cross-cultural exchange, assessing students personal growth and long-term effects of the cross-cultural encounter are the most important ones. Focusing on the program alone may turn the assessment into measures of students' level of satisfaction with the program. To trace the long-term effects of students' overseas experiences, a discussion forum or a Web page can be organized, dedicated to the discussion and reflection of students' overseas experiences. This may provide researchers with good sources for longitudinal studies. However, students may feel it is irrelevant and not important to provide information on long-term effects of their cross-cultural experiences after they leave the school. This issue can be solved by encouraging students to participate in school activities as alumni, such as contributing articles to campus newspapers, delivering speeches to campus students, and participating in the overseas study recruitment committee.

When it comes to traditional assessment, the first thing that comes to people's mind is paper-and-pencil, norm-referenced, and standardized tests. Although these tests are seen to be more objective and fair, they are criticized as only testing students' lower-level of knowledge acquisition, not the higher level of creative and critical thinking skills and they view things in society into a right-wrong dichotomy. However, traditional assessments can also be organized very differently and creatively. For example, Russell and Vallade (2010) describe how the College of Agriculture at Purdue University (PU), USA assesses the outcomes of international study and volunteering programs through guided reflective journaling. According to Russell and Vallade, the College of Agriculture at PU has various well-established and popular international programs. However, it does not consider counts of international students, overseas campuses or students who have overseas experiences quite relevant to the success of internationalization. Rather, it is more important how the overseas experiences and cross-cultural encounters have impacts on the students.

Even though you follow a traditional assessment paradigm and you choose to apply paper-and-pencil tests, your test questions can be creative and your students can have chances to show their critical thinking skills. For example, rather than asking your students to provide comments and reflections on their cross-cultural experiences, you may ask your students to envision or design a cross-cultural exchange project based on their cross-cultural experiences in an essay question. Or you may ask your students to work in groups to develop their own test questions, again based on their cross-cultural experience, for their classmates in other groups to answer. Teachers just need to be reminded that the major goal of assessing students' performance is to evaluate students' intercultural learning, personal and professional development as a result of cross-cultural experiences. In your test questions or questionnaires, do not turn the assessment into assessing students' levels of satisfaction towards the project or the project itself.

Authentic Assessment

Another more practical way of assessing your students is authentic assessment (Callison, 1998; Wiggins, 1990; Mueller, 2014; Center for Innovative Teaching and Learning, 2015; Herrington, et al., 2010). At the beginning of Chapter 6, I point out some important factors that should be taken into account in the process of developing tasks or activities for cross-cultural exchanges, and the first thing mentioned in that chapter is *authenticity*. Since using authentic materials and creating authentic learning environments in cross-cultural exchange activities are encouraged, we argue that assessment of students' learning performance should also be authentic. As Herrington, et al. have pointed out, authentic assessment needs to be applied to authentic learning, and it is often neglected. Simply compared with traditional assessment, authentic assessment requires students to perform a task rather than to select a response that is considered the only right answer, connects the task to the real-world rather than contrives a situation, requires students to apply what they have learned and construct their own knowledge rather than just recall and identify what they have learned, is constructed by students rather than by the teacher, and is direct evidence of students' learning rather than indirect evidence.

Wiggins (1990) argues that authentic assessment prepares students for future career challenges because it reflects the real-world situations that students might encounter in their professional life in the future. He insists that authentic assessment may improve both teachers' instruction and students' performance. Although authentic assessment may appear time-consuming, costly, and labor-intensive, each single effort may prove to be worthwhile. The most important characteristic of cross-cultural exchanges is that they connect people from different cultures to have real interactions either orally or in writing. It may seem unrealistic to administer traditional paper-and-pencil multiple-choice exams in a cross-cultural exchange project. Different collaborative projects or joint research assignments relevant to real-world issues may be good sources for assessing students' performance.

In an e-learning or a distance education setting, authentic assessment may be interpreted in a slightly different way. Garrison and Anderson (2003) point out most of the distance educators' concern as to whether students do learn or whether the assignments turned in are really performed by the students themselves, since students are not physically present in a formal learning environment. Garrison and Anderson suggest that essay questions and task-based projects can better solve the problems mentioned here and have assessments closer to real world practices. On the other hand, they further propose to include student participation in the assessment process. They argue that, by having them comment on or negotiate the assessment system, students can control their own learning and set their objectives of learning and moving towards their learning goal. In a sense, assessment tasks themselves are one kind of learning. By engaging in the assessment tasks, which are relevant to their future professional career and to the real world, they may stimulate their creativity and critical thinking skills and, by having chances to compare with their classmates' or distance partners' performance, students can be better equipped with required skills to respond to the challenges they will face in their future workplace and around the world.

Herrington, et al. (2010) list some important characteristics of authentic assessment, including engaging the learner, encouraging student to apply what they have learned to the assessment tasks, and meaningful tasks that are relevant to the real world and to students' future career. They provide a framework for authentic assessment and include context, student, task, and indicator components in the framework. In the context of authentic assessment, the task should be relevant to the real world beyond the classroom and would normally occur. For the student, the task should be able to promote students' problem-solving and higher order thinking skills. As for the task itself, Herrington et al. suggest that it should involve "complex, ill-structured challenges that require judgement, multiple steps, and a full array of tasks" (p. 142). Finally, these authors suggest that the assessment task should be able to provide multiple indicators of learning with appropriate scoring criteria for different products. They illustrate some examples of their own practices to show how the assessment can be aligned with the task. For example, in a course related to leaders in educational technology, students were required to interview a renowned expert in this field and write an indepth report and contribute the article to a professional magazine. In another case, in an introductory course on digital technology, students were assigned to apply a range of electronic tools they have learned "to create attractive and effective documents, interfaces and graphics across a wide range of computer-based applications" (p.144). Finally, in a course on design research, students were required to choose a significant educational problem and present it at a conference. In this example, students not only learned the traditional procedure to conduct research, but also experienced the tradition of conference practices.

Authentic assessment for authentic learning sounds the right way for cross-cultural learning to go. However, Herrington et al. (2010) point to the limitations of authentic assessment: pressures from the institutional policy. In terms of assessment, teachers are required to conform to set standard enforced by the institution. Cases are that schools require the assessment to be norm-referenced and to use a standardized test to measure individual students' accomplishment. In this case, interpersonal skills in group works and other social contexts, problem-solving skills in the real world are seldom taken into consideration. In this case, interpersonal skills in group works and other social contexts and problem-solving skills are commonly ignored.

Theoretically speaking, each way of assessment has its potential advantages and disadvantages and may be appropriate for a specific project. Mueller (2014) suggests that teachers can mix the two types of assessment in the assessing process. The traditional assessment may evaluate students' acquisition of the domain knowledge the teacher has taught and may be easier to administer, while the authentic assessment may provide students with an opportunity to construct and apply all the relevant knowledge they have learned in a real-world context. In a cross-cultural exchange project, it may be even easier for teachers to practice authentic assessment. Students may be required to present their collaborative products with their overseas partners to demonstrate different cultural perspectives on a global or societal issue, or to pose questions to their peers based on the knowledge they have acquired from their direct interactions with their overseas partners.

Paper-Based Testing vs. Computer-Based Testing in Language Proficiency Tests

In cross-cultural exchanges and in a globalizing era, language learn and language proficiency play critical roles in being able to function well in communicating with people from different cultures. Hence language proficiency tests have become very important in evaluating students' ability to study abroad, participating in cross-cultural exchange programs, receive financial support, and/or even take some forms of positions, such as being teaching or research assistants and student workers. In this section, I will focus only on discussions of assessment of language proficiency. In discussing language proficiency, Saville (207) distinguishes digital assessment from traditional paper-based assessment. It is arguable that, in a digital age, digital assessment has become trends in language proficiency test. Saville discusses some advantages and disadvantages in applying digital assessment to language proficiency tests. Digital assessment may reduce logistical and administration costs, provide faster score reporting, have greater flexibility to arrange locations and timings, enhance security at test venues, and cut down storage costs and handling test materials. However, Saville also points out some drawbacks that test providers and candidate may face, including the high cost to set up computer-based system and being difficult to administer some sorts of test, such as open-ended items and speaking tests.

As we can imagine that in the field of digital assessment in language learning, relevant educators, providers, or system programmers keep making improvement to make the digital assessment system to more accurately and efficiently assess students' language proficiency. Saville (2017) demonstrates the development of the so-called computer adaptive approach to language testing. This approach features its presenting "the test items to the candidates according to the response they give while progressing through the test" (p. 201). In this case, it is possible that "no two candidate see the same set of questions or even the same number of items" (p. 202). Adaptive assessment works hand in hand with currently popular *adaptive learning*, which tailors learners' learning based on their responses to the computer questions as discussed in Chapter 3 of this book. In a screening or placement process, this approach can be a good practice.

Another issue that practitioners or providers of digital assessment is the assessment of productive skills, i.e., writing and speaking skills. According to Saville (2017), developers of relevant systems "use natural language processing (NLP) techniques to model the performance of human raters" (p. 203). They claim that the system can train itself "to recognize similar features in other essays of a similar king" (p. 203) identified and scored by human raters. As for assessment of spoken language, developers are also working on a system to "build web-based automated assessors and feedback systems" (p. 203) to assess spoken language, and written language as well. However, no matter how advanced and efficient these systems may be, they are problematic when viewed from a perspective in a globalizing era. First, in a globalizing era, writing teachers are required to help students develop a global view and to understand what in students' mind and how they perceive the globalizing world. Without personally reading students' "mind," students' writing becomes meaningless, even though there is a score assigned to it. Second, in assessment of spoken language, the system may be able to judge speakers fluency and accuracy based on native speakers' standard. Again, this may sound problematic in a globalizing era. The divide between native speakers and non-native speakers has become blurry because of the advancement of modern technologies and the convenience that transportations can provide us. On the other hand, greater population mobility has led to the development of language varieties. It is not uncommon that people speak the same language with different accents and morphological, syntactic, and semantic varieties. Even though an assessment system may cover all or most of all the varieties, language varieties keep emerging. At least in the nearest future, writing teachers and speaking teachers may need to personally get involved in the assessment of students productive skills and keep informed with the dynamics of globalization.

Assessing Learning across Cultures

In a cross-cultural setting, it is particularly difficult and complex for the teacher to choose to assess students' accomplishment, especially when teachers intend to assess students' intercultural competence. Some public or private agencies have developed rubrics for assessing students' learning across cultures or their intercultural competence. However, according to Lucas and Blair (2017), there are some challenges especially faced by practitioners of cross-cultural exchanges. First, some outcomes are not really measurable and are hard to directly observe, for example, *value* and *respect*. Lucas and Blair suggest using more creative descriptions to make themselves clear as to what they expect their students to do, for example, actively engage in cross-cultural activities. Second, social bias is another issue in the process of assessments of learning across cultures. According to Lucas and Blair, research studies show that "low-ability individuals tend to overestimate their abilities and individuals with high abilities tend to underestimate when self-rating" (p. 200). Lucas and Blair suggest that a better practice is to integrate students' self-reported statements with other assessment instruments, such as direct observations. Finally, Lucas and Blair remind teachers to avoid stating "learning outcomes that are overly parochial, political, or ideological" (p. 202). The real purpose of cross-cultural learning is to engage students in a global context and to raise students' awareness of cultural differences and global issues rather than to indoctrinate them that a certain way of living is right, which is associated with the teacher's own values. In sum, traditional ways of assessing students' learning accomplishments may not work in cross-cultural learning settings. Scholars have suggested using of refection papers and portfolios in the process of assessing learning across cultures as will be discussed below.

Reflection Papers

Many scholars in the field of studying abroad or intercultural learning advocate the use of reflective practice to evoke students to learn and to assess students' learning (e.g., McGrath-Champ, et al., 2013; Gross & Goh, 2017; Hoult, 2018; Brown & Tignor, 2016; Colwell et. al, 2016; Crozado-Guerrero & Martinez, 2016; Herrington, et al., 2010; Hartman et al., 2018; Jackson, 2018). Gross and Goh devote an entire chapter especially to the discussions of reflection in intercultural learning. They argue that "reflection is a key ingredient in active, meaningful learning" (p. 167), and the goal of intercultural learning is to develop the ability to interact in a culturally complex setting successfully. These "skills include empathy, teamwork, creativity, problem-solving, integrated reasoning, interdisciplinary thinking, conflict resolution, networking, communication, and intercultural competencies" (p. 168). However, Gross and Goh also point to some challenges practitioners of reflective approaches might face. For example, students tend to care much more about their grade or teachers' evaluation than how much they really learn. Students tend to consider instructors' instructions as authoritative and right and they cannot cope with the instructor not "providing important content that is related to the knowledge needed to succeed in the course" (p. 173), and it is not uncommon that students fake their reflections for reasons that they want to protect their ideas and thoughts and do not like to be judged.

Russell and Vallade (2010) propose a method of phenomenological analysis to measure students' learning, change, and achievement by using guided reflective journals. They argue that assessment of students' overseas experiences needs to take students' personal growth and changes, professional knowledge and skills gained, and intercultural competences and global views into consideration, and traditional quantitative studies cannot really measure the subtlety of all the changes before and after the overseas experiences. Instead, the researchers in their study required the students to write reflective journals. Before their departure for another country, students were asked to write about their expectations for the international journey and preparations for coping with linguistic and cultural differences and other challenges they might face. After staying in a foreign country for a period, they were asked to respond to some guided questions to reflect on their international experiences, such as comparison of foreign cultures with their own culture, any challenges or difficulties they have encountered, and, most importantly, what they have learned and how they perceive they have changed from the overseas experiences. For Russell and Vallade, these guided reflective journals are valuable, trustworthy, and informative sources to assess and report on students' overseas experiences.

To promote authentic reflections and to facilitate reflective practice in the process of intercultural learning, Gross and Goh (2017) argue that a working relationship between teacher and student has to be developed. They point to three basic elements in reflective proactive: being genuine or congruent with people of different cultures, unconditionally and nonjudgmentally accepting others, and having empathy that enable an individual "to truly and accurately think and feel for the other" (p. 176). To ensure quality reflections, Gross and Goh suggest some guiding principles for teachers who apply reflective practice in their instructional process, including learning by doing, engaging with real people, soliciting reflections from the other, cross-cultural simulations, intentional and designated time and space for group and individual reflections, and instructors giving feedback on students' reflections. Reflection activities can vary, for example, reflective interviews, reflective journals, and group processes and debriefing. Herrington, et al. (2010), on the other hand, consider *reflection* as a process and a product. They argue that reflection can occur only when students collaborate on tasks with others and are aware of and pay attention to others. They further suggest that teachers not only have to provide students with prompts to reflect on or questions to respond to, but also have to provide students with "an authentic task within a authentic context" (p. 31). For Hartman et al. (2018), Clayton and colleague's DEAL model can provide participants with "essential steps for systematic critical reflection…[including] Description of experiences…,Examination of those experiences…,and Articulation of Learning" (p. 64). They consider the DEAL model "helpful for structuring reflection and …is applicable before, during, and after immersive learning experiences" (p. 65). It is important that teachers provide participant students with guided questions to enable students to connect their experience with discipline-specific learning, and make use of course concepts to real life. Hartman et al. (2018) suggest four Cs for reflective writing: they should be "Connected to academic assignment…,Contextualized in the community experience and broader social issues; …Continuous by happening before, during, and after service experience; and Challenging …students reflect and question ever more deeply" (p. 70).

By the same token, Weber-Bosley (2010) also advocates the use of student reflection in long-term study abroad to assess students' overseas learning outcomes. She argues that students' study abroad needs teachers' intervention in order for real learning to occur. Intercultural learning will not automatically take place simply by putting different cultural groups together. Students need teachers' guidance in the course of their overseas study. When they are abroad, they need to take a so-called "course" to turn in their assignments, especially reflections not only on cognitive and academic learning, but also on "personalized affective learning via self-reflection and direct experience with cultural difference" (p. 57). Weber-Bosley makes use of the writing-centered course to guide students' overall learning in the overseas experience, including the stages of predeparture, during-semester, and re-entry. She argues that "without explicit and intentional intervention into the study abroad experience, students, in general, will limit themselves to surface-level observations and experiences abroad" (p. 57). It is because many times we are not aware that we are actually engaged in cultural activities and because our intercultural experiences are relevant to the context we are in.

Hartman et al. (2018) describe that participants in Weber-Bosley's study were "asked to reflect weekly on and write about their experiences by posting these on the home university's Blackboard Site. The work is accessible to the instructor at the home campus and to the other students in the course" (p. 61). In this case, students can read each other's postings written from different contexts and different perspectives and compare and comment on each other's reflections. The key here is that students, by reading each other's postings, will eventually understand that the meaning of every single cross-cultural experience is idiosyncratic and context-dependent. In the case of studying abroad individually, without the intervention of the instructor, students may not be so conscious to record down each piece of intercultural experience and be aware of the value and meaning of the experience. Without regularly recording their overseas experiences, these students may have fewer opportunities to discover their own development of intercultural competence, share their intercultural experiences with others, and most importantly develop these experiences as acquired knowledge and personal assets that may benefit their future life.

To assess students' intercultural learning from their reflection papers, it may be a good idea to apply a content analysis approach. According to Petty, Bracken, and Pask (2017), content analysis must stick to "the three basic principles of the scientific method….It must be objective, systematic, and the results must be generalizable" (p. 128). Applying content analysis to assessment of students' intercultural learning through students' reflection papers, we may look for evidence of students' intercultural competences and/or various areas of growth from an outsider's perspective and with the involvement of intercoders and the available criteria of being interculturally competent, our assessment can be objective, systematic, and generalizable. As coders, we may first decide on the unit of analysis, including sampling units, which may be each reflection essay entry and recording units, which may be each paragraph or each sentence of a reflection essay entry. In the following coding process, we create coding categories based on what we are looking for, e.g., characteristics of intercultural competences such as being able to explain to the host family members a specific home cultural element and respond to their questions. By doing so, we may objectively count and assess students' learning or improvement of their intercultural competencies.

In reflective writing, Hoult (2018) particularly emphasizes the importance of *reflexivity*. He argues that learning should not be "confined to gaining new experiences rather than challenging any pre-conceptions about Self or the Other" (p. 80). Reflexivity can be viewed as a concept more than reflection. As mentioned in the book sporadically, people tend to view others, especially people from a different culture, through their own eyes and from their own perspectives. As a result, they tend to judge other people and ignore how people perceive them. In a sense, reflexivity is a deeper awareness of Self. It is important in that people do not live alone. Intercultural learning indeed involves others. Ignoring how others learn from you and how others perceive you in cross-cultural encounters may reveal ignorance and arrogance.

Portfolio Assessment

An alternative to the use of reflective assessment is portfolio assessment. Cho (2018) considers "portfolio assessment is one kind of authentic assessment" (p. 113), and it can be used to record students' growth in different aspects over time. In assessing learning across culture, students' learning or growth is actually multifaceted, including language, cultural and professional learning, intercultural competences, and development of a global view. Not all of these sophisticated changes can be evaluated from simple, standardized tests. In cross-cultural exchanges, portfolio assessments can capture students' learning, growth, and development in different aspects as long as the teacher, as the reviewer of the portfolio, can carefully spot each single piece of evidence of students' change. It is even more effective and useful if the portfolios are combined with the use of technologies, which is termed electronic portfolio assessment. Cho states some advantages of applying electronic portfolio to assess students' learning across cultures. First, it may expand the notion of literacy to include technical skills and being able to read, write, and understand information other than words, Furthermore, since multi-media products can be viewed by a lot of people, they cannot only motivate students to present their learning outcomes, but also develop a sense of responsibility in students for their authorship.

In sum, both reflection papers and portfolios are valuable qualitative data to investigate students' growth and changes in their cross-cultural experiences. They feature their various aspects of investigation, and chances are researchers may spot some valuable information that may not be obtained otherwise. As van Lier (1996) advocates, assessments of communicative language curricula should be instantaneous and continuous. He suggests that if "public and comparative assessments are important to learners…, our teaching will have to reflect this importance" (p. 211). In the case of cross-cultural exchanges, criterion-referenced assessments, reflections, and portfolios can be good alternatives to assess students' real learning and growth in the activities.

The Role of Feedback in Assessment

Teachers may provide different forms of feedback in their process of assessment, either traditional assessment or authentic assessment. How students view and treat teachers' feedback, either in the process or at the end of students' performing the tasks cannot be overlooked since it is part of the assessment and students' views should be respected. Generally speaking, teachers' feedback is always descriptive comments, either written or spoken, along with an assigned grade. In a cross-cultural context, even in a classroom with a considerable number of international students, which is not uncommon in a globalizing era, attitudes of students from different cultures towards teachers' feedback are worth investigation. After all, teachers' feedback is not always perceived by students from different cultures as positive and helpful for their future learning. Robson, Leat, Wall, and Lofthouse (2013) did a research study on international MA students' and staff's perceptions of feedback. According to the researchers, the university where the participants studied had "almost 4,000 international students from over 110 countries" (p. 51). Mostly, they studied humanities and social sciences.

Robson et al. (2013) interviewed two focus groups of Master's students. The 29 students in the first group were in five disciplines from nine countries, and the second group were 16 students in education from five countries. All the interviewees were asked to write about what they think the most useful and the least useful types of feedback are. The researchers then analyzed the data and ranked "feedback types in order of usefulness according to several priority levels" (p. 57). On the other hand, 18 academic staff members from different disciplines were also interviewed "to elicit their views about the role that feedback played in influencing students' learning" (p. 57).

Robson et al.'s (2013) findings show that students had little experience of receiving feedback from their teachers in their home countries despite they "had clear ideas about what they would like from feedback" (p. 59). Generally speaking, they consider face-to-face, immediate feedback most helpful. Students hoped that teachers could provide assessment criteria and highlight what they did well and areas for improvement. On the other hand, those subjective, personal, authoritative, or negative comments are considered least helpful feedback for further improvement. On the part of academic staff, they mostly provide oral feedback, and they indicated that "they provided oral feedback with the intention to provide immediate clarification, to correct misunderstandings or to challenge students' assumptions" (p. 61). They expressed their problems with limited time and heavy workload. Under this circumstance, they urge students to be proactive and seeking for feedback voluntarily. Based on responses from graduate students and academic staff, the researchers summarized that, in order for feedback to have positive impacts on students' learning, teachers need to provide quality, appropriate type and timely feedback.

Olesova and Richardson (2017) also conducted a research study on feedback in online courses for "non-native speakers of English enrolled in an asynchronous online course delivered in English who remained in their own countries" (p. 81). They basically investigated how the instructor's language background, students' levels of language proficiency, and the types of feedback delivery methods, either text feedback or audio feedback, may affect the quality of students' following postings. Findings of Olesova and Richardson's study show that the instructor's language background and types of feedback delivery method did not significantly affect the quality of students' postings. However, low-level language proficiency students did show problems with understanding the instructor's feedback and, hence, made little improvement in their further postings. The researchers attribute the reasons to, in addition to limited language proficiency, not being familiar with the culture of English-speaking people and the educational practices of Western universities.

Finally, let's turn to the discussion of peer assessment as many teachers tend to assign their students to comment on each other's performance. As far as peer assessment is concerned, Robson et al.'s (2013) study shows that students did not like peer assessment in general. They are not confident with their peer's ability to provide useful and appropriate feedback. Rather, they trust the teacher's authority and professionalism. However, in cross-cultural exchanges, peer assessment can be viewed from a different perspective. In a cross-cultural setting, participants are from different cultures. They may be eager to introduce their own cultures to their cross-cultural partners and learn their partners' cultures. Under this circumstance, feedback can be seen as cultural learning, knowledge building, and development of friendship, rather than criticism and judgement of the end-product. Cross-cultural participants see their partners as experts in their culture and language, and they are willing to learn from each other. In this circumstance, they are said to develop an equal power relation.

EVALUATING THE PROJECT

In addition to assessing your students' performance, it is also very important to assess the entire project. An entire cross-cultural exchange project can be reviewed from different perspectives for future improvement and directions. Because it is a larger scale of assessment, the assessment may involve teachers, student representatives, school administrators, network technicians, sponsors of the project, partner teachers or students, developers of communication tools and materials and even external evaluators hired from outside. As Herrington et al. (2010) have pointed out, an external evaluator can be more objective and can look at things from an outsider's perspective, not being biased in favor of the project in the course of evaluating the project. Procedures to evaluate an entire cross-cultural exchange program may vary, depending on the nature of the program. A useful framework is that you might need to assess the entire program for different levels of concern, i.e., the individual level, the institutional level, and the national level and the international level. Evaluation focusing on different levels, which will be discussed in this section, are quite different in their nature; however, they are equally important.

The Individual Level

The individual level may involve different groups of individuals, such as students, teachers, administrators, and developers of instructional materials. Among them, students are the most important ones because how they perceive the programs and their levels of satisfaction may play a decisive role in the sustainability of a certain cross-cultural program. It is important that you survey your students' level of satisfaction with the project. You can hand out a questionnaire or some open-ended questions, assign students to write learning logs or reflections, interview students, browse students' postings on the discussion board, and compare and contrast the similarities and differences before and after the project. For example, Smolcic and Martin (2018) use guided reflected journals to assess students' learning abroad and their immediate feedback concerning the project. One of the purposes of this assessment is to get the students' real voice so that the project can be really student-centered, and, on the other hand, students' opinions can be valuable sources for improvement of future cross-cultural exchange projects.

For teachers as practitioners of cross-cultural exchange programs like you, you may need first to compare against the outcome criteria set before the project, such as cost and benefits and students' learning and level of satisfaction. More importantly, you need to communicate with your partner teachers for any issues you might not be aware of and for any issues you want to draw your partner teachers' attention to. Cross-cultural collaboration is the two sides of a coin after all. It is definitely impossible that you work alone on a cross-cultural exchange project and you claim the project to be successful.

For administrators, developers of materials, and sponsors of the project, communications with teachers and students are crucial. First of all, they have to make sure what they have offered, either administratively, academically, or financially, meets teachers' expectations and students' needs. Communications between or among individuals who are playing different roles in a cross-cultural exchange project should occur occasionally so that adjustments or improvements can be made in the course of a cross-cultural exchange project.

For administrators, in order for the project to be sustainable, they need to focus on the control of budget, facilitation, and adjustment to any kinds of claims. They act as coordinators between teacher and student for whatever incidents that might happen in the course of a cross-cultural project. As for developers of instructional materials, it is especially important that they need to listen to both the teacher and the student for their needs and for whatever improvements are required. Instructional materials need to reflect issues relevant to a globalizing era and benefit students to become global citizens.

The Institutional Level

At the institutional level, the head of the institution has to evaluate the significance of the entire project, considering whether the project contribute to the promotion of the school, the well-being of teachers and students, and the internationalization of the campus. Given the competitiveness of higher education in a globalizing era, recruiting students can be an important task for an institution. Collaborating with overseas partners to promote students' intercultural competences and enhance their employability can be a very important factor to attract students and to uphold the institution's status in the global market. Evaluation of a cross-cultural project should examine if the goals of the cross-cultural project, for example, increased student enrollment and heightened institutional status, were achieved.

At the institutional level, these statistical accounts may be important and practical. However, it is more important in terms of the sustainability of the cross-cultural project. As mentioned earlier, cross-cultural projects are long-term enterprises for an institution. The heart of an institution needs to be attentive to global changes and reflect on their decision-making or policy-adaptation. In the evaluation at the institutional level, participant evaluators need to possess a forward-looking perspective and take all the factors that may affect the future of cross-cultural project into consideration.

The National and International Level

At the national and international level, evaluation of a cross-cultural project should be focused on whether the project responds to the call of the government for internationalizing the campus and for diversifying the student population and curricula. On the other hand, consider whether the project is able to move towards the trends of globalization and hence prepare students for a globalizing world and being a global citizen. Evaluation of a cross-cultural project at this level requires the involvement of more people who are concerned, and the evaluation needs to be viewed from different perspectives. It may be important that you include criteria to evaluate your project in your project proposal. Herrington et al.'s (2010) suggestions, although focusing on evaluating authentic e-learning projects, can be applied to cross-cultural exchange projects especially when we view cross-cultural exchanges as authentic and real-world encounters. Herrington et al. argue that evaluating authentic e-learning projects requires careful planning, and the evaluation process needs to be participated in by relevant personnel. They propose a framework to roughly cover the required elements in evaluating a proposal submitted for conducting a project, including introduction, background, purposes, stakeholders, decisions, questions, methods, participants, limitations, logistics, and budget. For the authors, each component is essential and is key to successful evaluation. They remind practitioners of authentic e-learning projects of some important things in reporting evaluations. First, do not just report the facts. Rather, you need to explain how the data are collected, why you interpret the findings this way, and, most importantly, what recommendations you would make based on your findings to make improvements in the project. Second, do not try to impress your team members with your technical or professional expertise. Rather, focus on important facts relevant and important to the improvement of the project, Third, at the end of reporting your evaluation, be sure to recommend possible solutions or alternatives most helpful and feasible for improvement of the project. Sometimes, you need to negotiate with members of the evaluation teams because team members may have different interests, values, and goals.

Examples of Evaluating a Cross-Cultural Project

In this section, I demonstrate some examples of evaluating cross-cultural projects. These examples show that evaluations can be very meaningful and creative.

First, Yogman and Kaylani (1996) demonstrate a very good example of how a post-program evaluation may help develop the second year program. Their study involved visiting students from a new business college in one of the former Soviet Baltic republics who visited and worked in the same classroom with American business students in Pittsburgh for about four weeks. They found in their overall post-program evaluation that there are several issues that need to be taken into consideration in the development of future exchange programs, such as students at the beginner level of English proficiency had great difficulty in participating in many classroom activities, mismatch between students and teachers in expectations relating to classroom culture, mismatch of objectives with program length and students' ability levels, students' extreme concerns with accuracy, etc. Based on the lessons they learned from the first project, Yogman and Kaylani provide guidelines for designing short-term exchange programs. They suggest using miniprojects, using technology, keeping textbooks not required, using a portfolio approach to assessment, etc. Their example may exemplify how an overall assessment may lead to improvement of future exchange projects.

Another example of assessing a cross-cultural project is done by Mendeloff and Shaw (2009). Mendeloff and Shaw's study on a postconflict peacebuilding project mentioned earlier in this book was another good example of how a cross-cultural exchange project with American and Canadian students can be and should be evaluated. The researchers raise three questions as guidelines for evaluation of the course, namely how well did the various course components work, how effective was the overall course design in achieving the course goals, and how well did it advance student learning. First, Mendeloff and Shaw explain that they rely mainly on their observations throughout the course and students' evaluations of the overall course, and the individual course components to assess the impact of the course design on student learning because there were so many uncontrolled variables in this regard. Then they evaluated each course component, namely blackboard discussions, videoconferences, online simulation, and individual vs. collaborative activities. In each component, Mendeloff and Shaw truthfully recorded both positive and negative sides of evaluation, either from their observations or from students' evaluations of the overall course and each course component throughout the course. They mention that imbalanced class size, heterogeneous backgrounds of the students, and the students' sense of novelty wearing off might be some of the reasons that caused enthusiasm for the discussions to mute across the board. On the other hand, the researchers consider the videoconferences to be successful partially because the students liked having direct contact with each other and because Afghanistan's Ambassador to Canada was invited to the videoconference. The students appreciated the flexible and creative nature of the activity.

One unique example of how assessment of a cross-cultural exchange project can be done is seen in the Cross-Cultural Distance Learning Project collaborated upon by faculty members from Tamkang Uuniversity in Taiwan and Wasada University in Japan. After several years' collaboration, the two partner universities collaborated to publish a book whose articles were contributed by members of the project team (Tsai & Redmer, 2014). Teachers from the two universities wrote about their experiences involving the project, how their students were benefitted from the project, and their students' suggestions for future practice of the project. Because each author presents his or her experience from a different perspective, the entire book can be seen as an overall assessment of the project. Each project team member can easily see how the project is perceived by other members and by members of the partner team. It is not uncommon in reports of cross-cultural exchanges that researchers tend to focus on reporting their own participants because it is easier and more direct to observe and interact with their own participants. Reflections from the partner side of collaboration are always neglected. Publishing a book to gather all the participants' experiences, comments, and recommendations can faithfully evaluate the entire project from different perspectives.

In some cases, group interviews can be good sources to provide practitioners of cross-cultural exchanges with valuable or complementary information. Using group interview approaches may have similar effects in terms of evaluating a cross-cultural exchange project. Generally speaking, group interviews refer to focus groups. "In group discussions, we often see that certain perspectives are majority views and certain others are minority views" (Pettey, Bracken, and Pask, 2017, p. 90). In group interviews, participants often share the same interests or attend the same activities. A group leader can be chosen to conduct the discussions. There are some strategies in the interview process, such as providing guiding questions for discussion, recordings, and interruption for clarification. As Pettey et al. remind us, as researchers, we do not make too many assumptions in order not to view things through our own "personal/social/cultural/historical lens" (p. 92) but from the participants' lens. Be sure to provide participants with enough time, space, and freedom to discuss so that you can get real voices and useful feedback from the people involved in the cross-cultural project.

Because, as illustrated earlier, there are different kinds of cross-cultural exchange programs, involving different numbers of participants and aiming at different objectives, types of evaluation may vary. From the examples of assessing a project above, we may understand that no cross-cultural project is perfect the first time it is practiced. Different groups of students may have different needs or different degrees of preference. Only when you assess your project thoroughly can you get your students' real voice and can you really attain the goal of your project.

Finally, evaluation of a cross-cultural project may not end right after the completion of the project. Tracking the long-term effect of the project on the participants, for example, how do students reflect their cross-cultural skills on their performance in workplaces and whether participants still keep their friendship with their overseas partners several years after the project, may also be valuable information to sustain the cross-cultural exchange project on a long-term basis.

It is important to keep in mind that assessing students' performance in a cross-cultural exchange program and evaluating a cross-cultural exchange project have one thing in common: they are not the end of the project, sustainability and long-term effect are. Researchers of cross-cultural exchanges are encouraged to trace the process of students' experiences and follow up any changes, improvements, and benefits found in the students. A longitudinal research study may be time-consuming and energy-exhausting. However, with a carefully-planned project and well-developed friendship, longitudinal research in cross-cultural exchanges can be more valuable and, for researcher, more rewarding.

Chapter 9

THE FUTURE OF CROSS-CULTURAL EXCHANGES

As mentioned earlier in this book, among other things, I intend to provide "nuggets," rather than just recording what is already known and what has been done. The term "nuggets" may be too serious and too exaggerated for an ordinary researcher like me. However, in the process of practicing cross-cultural exchanges and collecting relevant data, I am sure that existing reports and records, along with ever-changing technologies and new ways of thinking and educational approaches, may allow us to envision the future trends of cross-cultural exchanges. Based on what has happened in the field of cross-cultural exchanges and the patterns emerging from the investigation, I would like to invite you, enthusiastic practitioners of cross-cultural exchanges, to pinpoint the trends and some characteristics of future cross-cultural exchanges so that we may have better practices of cross-cultural exchanges in a globalizing era. Most importantly, we need to collaborate actively with each other to *build* and *construct* the future of cross-cultural exchanges, not just follow we have learned in our previous experiences. The following characteristics of future cross-cultural exchanges may provide us with a guide to organize our future exchange projects. If you have never thought about conducting cross-cultural exchange programs, it is hoped that this book can be an incentive to motivate you to join the great enterprise of globalization.

A MULTI-FACETED LEARNING ENVIRONMENT

As mentioned earlier, Montgomery (2013) describes the New London Group in the U.S. and works on framing school curriculum to respond to an era moving towards globalization. The group claims that the future curriculum should reflect multimodal ways of learning and should be able to develop multiliterate graduates. In Internet communications alone, as described by Mann and Steward (2000), users can switch "between text, voice, video and graphics, and between synchronous and asynchronous communication" (p. 218). Given the various modes of learning in modern society, cross-cultural exchange can be a very important part of learning activity. Cross-cultural exchange programs in the future can be expected to be organized with a multiple-learning purpose in the organizer's mind. As described throughout the book, cross-cultural exchanges can be practiced or integrated in a variety of ways. The modes of exchange can be either written or spoken, physical or virtual, long-distance or face-to-face, short-term or long-term, and visible or invisible. A multi-faceted learning environment, in this book, refers to a learning environment in which learners can learn different things through different modes at the same time or in different occasions and can learn across disciplines. However, learning environments definitely are not confined to those visible and conscious contexts. Learning can occur unconsciously and invisibly. In a multi-faceted learning environment in an era moving towards globalization, learning outcomes of cross-cultural exchanges cannot actually be quantified. Personal growth, change of attitude, widened horizon, and development of creativity and critical thinking skills can be derived from invisible contexts, such as the atmosphere and norms developed in a cross-cultural setting, the enjoyments or frustrations felt while communicating with foreign partners and stories heard from others.

As a result of multi-faceted learning environments, creative use of languages and mix of cultures or creation of new cultures may be seen as a phenomenon in an era moving towards globalization. Williams (2017) describes in vivid language how young multilingual speakers in Cape Town, South Africa creatively make use of their languages, mix and remix them to create their unique Hip Hop culture and to perform their marginalized voices. Their Hip Hop is actually an integration of different languages, including Kaap, African American English, Sabela, isiXhosa, and others. They integrate their multilingual practices and their marginalized voices into Hip Hop performance. Behind the hip hop culture, there are creativity, authentic selves, and a multi-faceted presentation of language and culture. Viewed from this perspective, a multi-faceted learning environment does not simply refer to different modes of learning. It can also mean that, in the globalizing environment, there are a variety of ways to present oneself and connect oneself with others, and mobility is the key. As Williams (2017) states, South Africa's social transformation features its significant mobility. An important implication here is that cross-cultural exchanges are not only multimodal but also dynamic. An exchange may lead to another and a single partnership may lead to creation of global collaborations.

Prensky (2001) points out that digital natives, who grew up with new technologies around them, have a learning style very different from that of the older generations. They learn faster, have more random access to the information, and can learn different things at the same time. Prensky urges senior educators, aside from learning new stuff, to learn new ways to do old stuff. Given the characteristics of the new generations, organizers of a cultural exchange project have to take all the factors into consideration in the course of planning the project. As stated above, organizers and practitioners of cultural exchange programs need to prepare a multi-faceted learning environment for students and prepare students for multiple learning. This goal can be achieved by working together with teachers from different disciplines, different age levels, and even from different cultures.

Wang (2015) argues that the word *learning* in the educational setting should be redefined. In the traditional view of education, educators are regarded as "transmitters" of information and knowledge, and learners are consumers of the information and knowledge. Under this circumstance, then the role of educational technologies can simply be perceived as facilitators to make the transmission easier and faster (Wible, 2005). However, educational technologies can and should be used to do a lot more in the students' learning process. After all, getting access to educational technologies does not necessarily mean *learning*. In the digital age, students did learn a lot of things which are not easily learned in a traditional classroom. In the digital world, virtual activities are always participated in by a considerable number of people from a variety of cultural and educational backgrounds. Although students may not seriously make use of mobile devices to learn academic knowledge, by virtually communicating with people from different cultural groups, different educational backgrounds, and different fields of study, they may consciously or unconsciously learn social and interpersonal skills, learn to think critically and creatively, and with so much information available on the Internet and, with so many people participating in virtual discussions, they may learn how to respect others and to protect their own and others' privacy. As Wible states, we are expecting the day to come "when the use of learning technology spreads not because it is mandated but because it actually works" (p. 128).

A FLIPPED INSTRUCTIONAL MODEL FOR LEARNING IN A CROSS-CULTURAL SETTING

The theories of flipped classroom emerged around a decade ago. It is one kind of e-learning, and it features its being students-centered. However, all these concepts are not new. Many teachers may be quite familiar with how to apply modern technologies to their teaching practice and with the importance of making classroom instruction student-centered. The flipped classroom model features its reverse sequence of teaching and learning. Teachers prepare instructional videos for students to learn at home first, and then students discuss and ask questions in the classroom (Bergmann & Sams, 2012; Keengwe, Onchwari & Oigara, 2014; Carbaugh & Doubet, 2016; Young & Moran, 2017). This learning model can be actually applied to different modes of cross-cultural exchanges. Teachers are not able to experience a cross-cultural encounter for students.

Teachers are responsible for providing students with an optimal cross-cultural learning environment, similar to the flipped classroom model in that teachers have to provide learning materials for students to learn on their own before the teacher's instruction. After students personally experience cross-cultural encounters, teachers may ask them to present, share, compare, and discuss their experiences with their peer students. As modern technologies and transportation systems develop, cross-cultural communications in cross-cultural exchange activities can be organized into different modes. For example, participants can interact with their partners on the web, through e-mailing, or videoconferencing, or they can pay a physical visit and talk to each other face-to-face. One of the advantages of different types of communication is that cross-cultural interactions can be extended beyond the class time and the classroom, and through more frequent contacts, a learning community and a long-term friendship and life-long learning opportunities can be developed.

A short-term meeting in a cross-cultural exchange program will not benefit the students a lot. Practitioners of cross-cultural exchange programs in the future should keep a long-term objective in mind when developing a program. Online communications at a videoconference or physically meeting with each other may be insufficient for learning to occur or for friendships to develop. Written communications after a videoconference may be helpful for the development of a long-term relation and extended learning.

The emergence of student-centered learning communities can also be viewed from a student-teacher-relationship perspective. Students always feel ambivalent about their relationship with their teachers. On the one hand, students rely on their teachers in their learning process to enrich their knowledge; on the other hand, they perceive their teachers as a judge, who has an absolute power to decide for them what to learn and how to learn it. Even worse, teachers are also responsible for evaluating students' learning performance by assigning grades to students. In the real world, the relationship between teacher and student is seen, as described by John (1996), in a collaborative-vs.-confrontational negotiation situation. On the one hand, students intend to pursue their own interests; on the other hand, they have to maintain good relations with their teachers whose interests conflict with theirs. Teachers may force students to work harder and to learn more, while students expect to have a more relaxing learning environment. In a cross-cultural exchange context, students have a greater autonomy and freedom to decide on what to learn and how to learn it. In future cross-cultural exchange programs, there is a possibility that students may be asked to propose their own cross-cultural exchange programs with teachers serving as consultants or facilitators. Students, as members of a learning community, may contribute ideas to the community. One of the advantages of a flipped type of cross-cultural exchange activity is that students can decide on what they want to learn and how they are going to learn it. In this regard, students feel a sense of accomplishment and are more willing to engage in the activity.

With the help of modern technologies and given a student-centered learning environment, the future of cross-cultural exchanges can be expected to be really student-centered, and students can be granted more responsibilities in the process of developing a cultural exchange program. In a sense, cross-cultural exchange programs are actually a "flipped classroom," with teachers looking for cross-cultural partners and setting up required facilities (similar to teachers preparing video-taped instructional materials for students in the flipped classroom), students experience cross-cultural encounters and learn on their own (similar to students watching videotapes at home and learning on their own), and students discuss, and raise questions in class after the experience of cross-cultural encounters (similar to students discussing and asking questions relevant to the instructional videos they have watched at home). There is no doubt that human-human interactions will decrease and human-machine interactions will increase in a digital learning environment. However, Wible (2005) poises a question: "What is the purpose of bringing [all the students] together in the same room when they have a computer?" (p. 216). Theoretically, they can stay where they are and learn, and human-machine interactions can take the place of human-human interactions. As we can see, human-human interactions can never and should not be replaced by human-machine interactions. Human-human interactions are seen as important social activities that foster learning. The flipped instructional model stresses the equal importance of human-machine and human-human interactions.

However, applying a flipped type of learning structure to cross-cultural exchange programs is not without challenges. As mentioned sporadically in this book, students from different cultures have different perceptions of learning and different learning styles. For examples, in the West, students are seen to more actively participate in classroom discussions and even challenge teachers' professional knowledge and authority; while in the East, those who sit quietly in the classroom and listen to the teacher attentively are considered to be "good students," and they value what the teacher says and consider the teacher's judgement fair and important. Under this circumstance, practitioners of cross-cultural exchange who apply flipped-type of classroom structure to cross-cultural exchange activities must be aware of cultural differences and different attitudes towards learning. For example, Young and Moran (2017) describe various good examples of flipped classroom practices. However, most of their examples focus on students learning English as language arts in American language classrooms. In a cross-cultural exchange setting, differences in language, cultural, technology, education system, and other factors may affect the practice of a flipped classroom model. Partners of cross-cultural exchanges need to work together to bridge the gap between the two groups of students to meet their real learning needs.

REQUIREMENT OF MULTILINGUAL AND MULTICULTURAL SKILLS

The development of modern technologies has contributed to the change of international communications. English is no longer the exclusive language used for international communications. People have started learning each other's languages. The trend in international communication is evident in language planning or policy, too. The governments in many countries offer language proficiency tests for different languages, such as Japanese, French, and German, and for different purposes, such as admission to a university, application for a job, and promotion to a certain level of position. Many higher education institutions in the world offer studies of different languages. For example, in Taiwan, some universities organize different language departments to offer study of a specific foreign language, such as French, German, Russian, Italian, Spanish, and Japanese, for example Tamkang University, Fu Jen Catholic University, and Chinese Culture University. In Japan, Tokyo University of Foreign Studies even offers more than 30 different languages for students to learn.

Learning more than one foreign language has also become a trend, and bilingualism or multilingualism in a society, such as Singapore and Ottawa in Canada, are seen as successful cases of developing a bilingual or multilingual society. Promoting bilingual or multilingual policies allows people both to maintain their native languages and, on the other hand, to participate in the global community. Many colleges or institutes in the world are offering language courses for students to learn different languages. As international communication is getting more and more common, being able to speak your conversational partners' language can significantly bridge the gap between you and your partners. In the case of the U.S., where English is traditionally considered the most important language, people have sensed the importance of learning foreign languages. Kolb (2009) calls for American people's attention to a critical American priority: international studies and learning of foreign languages. He reminds the American people of the intense global competition they are going to face in the 21st century. Technological, economic, political, educational, and social factors that have contributed to the creation of a new era require students to increase their foreign language skills and cultural awareness.

Wang (2016) explores language policies of the United States. Providing English with an official status and even developing an English-only country has been hotly debated in the most-chosen destination of immigrants. Therefore, there are a great number of languages spoken in the U.S. Wang argues that a variety of languages spoken by different groups of immigrants will not segregate people in the U.S. On the contrary, different groups of people may co-exist harmoniously and help enrich each other's culture and enhance linguistic knowledge.

In the U.S. history, the debates over English only and later bilingual education have never stopped. Wang (2016) proposes the idea of *English Plus* in the language classroom.

He argues that "Americans need to expand the *English plus* policy to produce well-developed skills in many languages to enhance international competitiveness and national society" (p. 38). In a monolingual teaching approach, immigrant students learn English in an English immersion environment. However, in a multilingual teaching approach, students' mother tongues are respected, and students are encouraged to use their language resources to construct their linguistic knowledge.

Furthermore, viewed from cognitive and linguistic perspectives, being able to speak more than one language does not merely mean being able to communicate with people of different cultures. The well-known Sapir-Whorf hypothesis "holds that the language we speak determines how we perceive and think about the world" (Fromkin, Rodman, & Hyams, 2014, p. 22). This idea may imply that a person who can speak more than one language may have the ability to think about things from a wider perceptive, and this, in turn, may facilitate his or her negotiation or communication with culturally diverse people in the world.

It also has become a trend that the private sector applies the idea of language management in their enterprises as reported by Chun Shin Limited (2012). In order to be recognized in the global market, Rakuten consortium in Japan employs a language management system, Englishization, as one of their managerial strategies. Depending on their needs and frequency to use English in their positions, employees in the Rakuten consortium have to reach a certain level of English proficiency to secure their job. The same is true for cross-cultural exchanges in the educational arena. We can expect that, in the future of cross-cultural exchanges, a certain level of language proficiency will be required in order to functionally participate in an exchange program or an international learning community. Of course, the language used in future cross-cultural exchanges will no longer be limited to English. Each language can be the lingua franca of two groups of students.

Speaking of language learning, Ruecker (2011) raises yet another issue called native-speaker prejudice as mentioned in Chapter 7. Roughly speaking, it refers to an attitude towards native speakers of the learner's target language. As pointed out by Ruecker, the two groups of participants in his study (one English-speaking group who were learning Spanish and one Spanish-speaking group who were learning English) favored each other's native-speaker status and considered the language their partners used was ideal and could not be wrong. This prejudiced attitude might be lessened or even changed in the future of cross-cultural exchanges. Language learners will be more aware that language learning, either the native language or foreign languages, depends on different individual and social factors. Native-speaker status does not necessarily guarantee language fluency and accuracy. In the future of language learning communities, learners will be seen to be more aware of the importance of individual language proficiency and will not treat native speakers as equally competent in both language and professional knowledge.

EMERGENCE OF SHORT-DISTANCE CROSS-CULTURAL EXCHANGES

As we can see, there are more and more cross-cultural contacts in modern society, and a small social community, such as a school or a company, can be seen more and more internationalized. For example, a school may recruit international students or hire international scholars, and a trading company may assign managers from the headquarters abroad. The same is true for a traditional classroom. In a classroom as a learning context, learners may be culturally diverse. O'Neal, Ringler, and Rodriguez (2008) argue that the number of English language learners (ELL) is increasingly growing. An ESL classroom may have students from different cultures; a regular class may also more or less have international students. Traditional teacher preparation programs that focus on content knowledge, cognitive, psychological and linguistic development, and pedagogical theories and methodologies can no longer meet future teachers' needs. Multilingualism and multiculturalism have been added to teacher preparation programs. However, O'Neal et al. conclude based on their research findings that future teachers do not feel they are well-prepared to teach a culturally diverse class and that teacher preparation programs do not really provide them with sufficient training needed for teaching a culturally diverse class.

Another research study relevant to short-distance cultural exchanges was reported by MacNaughton and Hughes (2007). They claim that "Australia is one of the most culturally diverse societies in the world" (p. 189) and that the Australian government has a much-proclaimed commitment to multiculturalism. They surveyed 60 teachers of early childhood in Victoria, Australia. Findings of their study and other studies show that there is a mismatch between law and policy and early childhood teachers' practice. Most of the Australian early childhood teachers claimed that they did not have sufficient training and information in response to the growing number of culturally diverse groups of students. MacNaughton and Hughes finally point out that some components may be needed in a culturally diverse classroom, including the laissez faire policy, special provisions to meet students' special needs, equal opportunities for different groups of students, cultural understandings, and anti-discrimination. They argue and conclude that there is little professional learning that features in-depth exploration of issues relevant to cultural diversity in practice. However, this kind of learning "has been shown to change participants' attitudes and practices towards culturally diverse children and their families" (p. 201).

Similarly, Green and Edwards-Underwood (2015) point out that in the United States there is an increasingly growing population of culturally and linguistically diverse students attending public schools. There is a desperate need for schools to equip their teachers, students, and administrators with a multicultural insight to create a learning environment that focuses on educational equity and social justice. They urge the practice of multicultural education in classrooms. In the case of the United States, an educational setting as small as a classroom can be seen as a linguistically and culturally diverse society. It is thus the trend that cross-cultural exchanges will no longer be defined as long-distance communications.

In the case of Southeast Asia, social structures are changing and population mobility can be seen quite popular in Asian history. According to Fielding (2016), because of economic, political, educational, and other reasons, migration flows have been great in Asia. He lists several types of Asia migrations: labor migration of working class and the highly educated and highly skilled, trafficking, displacements due to a threat to one's personal security, place preference, life course migrations for a better life or better education or for marriage, and state-sponsored migration. As we can imagine, the great migration may lead to some cross-cultural concerns. Although Asian migrants may be considered more similar in culture, differences can be found in a variety of aspects. As a result of high population mobility and societies becoming more multicultural, we can no longer instinctively consider cross-cultural exchanges as always involving long-distance partners.

MORE AND MORE COLLABORATION BETWEEN/AMONG STUDENTS FROM DIFFERENT CULTURES

To develop an equal and a friendly global community and to work together on some global issues, cross-cultural collaboration can be a good way to achieve the goal. Based on analysis of the data collected for the book, I can envision a prosperous future for cross-cultural exchanges. The future is expected to see more and more team projects collaborated by culturally different groups of students, such as team teaching, joint research on a global issue of common concern, a language learning community participated in by students from different linguistic and cultural backgrounds, and publications co-authored by people from different countries. These types of collaboration can range from the small-scale one such as the Australian case mentioned above to one that involves students from all over the world, such as the international iEARN organization mentioned in Chapter 7.

Expanded collaboration features having more groups of students working on a project, and the collaboration can be more powerful in terms of reaching its goal. Chang's (2006) idea of making collective intelligence as a source of teaching and learning materials may be seen as a future trend of cultural exchanges and may involve more participants from different countries. Chang creates what she calls a *transcultural wisdom bank*, which "is the collection of the set of possible 'solutions' from many different cultures or societies to recurrent problems that are common to the human condition and that no one culture has (ever) managed to solve completely" (p. 371). Computer databases can be used to store information, surveys, research studies, cultural perspectives, etc. for analysis, problem solving, and comparison and contrast.

On the other hand, as the development of Web 2.0 and with the explosion of information, learners may unconsciously develop their critical thinking skills. In the age before the creation of digital technologies, people received instruction-led training, featuring teacher-centered learning (Tabot, Oyibo, & Hamada, 2013). In this learning context, learners were seen as consumers of knowledge. They passively received the knowledge presented in the textbook and delivered by the teacher. For them, the teacher and the textbook were authoritative, and they could hardly be challenged. As the digital technologies moving towards the Web 2.0 stage, featuring interaction and collaboration, learners are overwhelmed by a considerable amount of information. Under this circumstance, learners naturally and unconsciously learn to choose the information they really need and make use of the information in a critical way, That is, they may, on their own, judge a piece of information either favorably or unfavorably, or they may respond to a piece of information with their own ideas or comments.

In cross-cultural exchanges, this can be even more apparent to everyone due to interactions between or among different cultures. Due to the advancement of transportation, it is not uncommon that one interacts with people from different cultures face-to-face. By exposure to different cultures and witnessing how people from a different culture behave and respond, one can develop cultural patterns and make better decisions as to how and when to say what to whom. In this case of computer-mediated communications, although flaming in CMC is not encouraged and appreciated, flaming does help participants develop their critical thinking skills. In a CMC setting, when an issue is brought up, all participants are arbitrators. One needs to be aware of the CMC subculture and to be critical, logical, and persuasive in order to gain consensus on widely debated issues. As Lea, Oshea, Fung, and Spears (1992) describe it, if one does not have critical audience awareness, he or she may receive a bunch of reminders of the specific group norms.

PEDAGOGICAL IMPLICATIONS FOCUSING ON A SOCIOLINGUISTIC APPROACH AND SOCIOCULTURAL LEARNING MODEL

The latest approach to teaching a second or foreign language has been the communicative approach, which features communications between or among language users or communications with native speakers of the target language. However, many scholars have argued that having linguistic knowledge and being able to communicate with people appear not to be sufficient if we mean to have successful communications and to develop good relationships with others. Especially, these scholars claim the importance of having sociolinguistic competence (e.g., Mede & Dikilitas, 2015; van Lier, 1996; Kachru & Nelson, 2006). Having sociolinguistic competence includes the "specific ability to use L2 in various ways that may fit in various social settings in which the communication takes place" (Mede & Dikilitas, 2015, p. 16). Mede and Dikilitas argue that in an era moving towards globalization and with more and more cross-cultural contacts between or among people in the world, sociolinguistic competence is gaining more and more attention. However, teaching and learning of sociolinguistic competence is seldom integrated into language teaching. Mede and Dikilitas investigated EFL teachers in Turkey about their perceptions of sociolinguistic competence in second language learning and teaching. Findings of their study show that there are problems with teaching and learning sociolinguistic pragmatics in a second language learning context. EFL teachers who participated in the study revealed some practical problems that impede the teaching and learning of sociolinguistic competence. Most importantly, non-native English teachers mentioned that they themselves have problems with their sociolinguistic knowledge and they themselves have limited exposure to different cultures. Secondly, it seems there is no need to teach sociolinguistic knowledge. Aside from the fact that there are few sociolinguistic elements included in the curriculum, second language teaching and learning is always exam-oriented, and sociolinguistic elements are not easy to be included in the assessment process.

Kachru and Nelson (2006), on the other hand, view the issue of sociolinguistic approach from a language-variety perspective. They regard the study of English varieties around the world as a sociolinguistically inspired enterprise in that cultural and contextual factors promote the development of language varieties. For example, nativization of English in different parts of the world has led to creation of different English varieties. Kachru and Nelson continue to argue that it "is clear that correlations between cultural features and linguistic expressions lead to variety differentiation, and may cause difficulty in communicating across Englishes" (p. 320-321). That is, "cultural differences caused different uses of shared linguistics forms and processes" (p. 321).

On the other hand, Esteban, Ramos, and Seco (2011) discuss different types of learning theories. Among them, constructivism, cooperative learning, collaboration, and sociocultural learning require interactions with people or the environment in order for learning to occur. However, advocates of sociocultural learning argue "that constructivism and collaborativeism force the cultural minority into adopting the understanding derived by the majority" (p. 320). For them, nothing in the world can be treated as external reality, and any part of instruction should not be delivered as a single interpretation of reality. Rather, students need to participate in social interactions on their own terms. That is, in a cross-cultural exchange context, students not only have to understand, appreciate, and respect other cultures but also have to protect, justify, and value their own culture.

As mentioned in earlier chapters, cross-cultural encounters may cover different modes of practice and different areas of learning. That is, cross-cultural encounters may be presented in different genres that require interpretations or negotiations of language use or nonverbal behaviors from a broader perspective. For example, in business or diplomatic negotiations or writing of news reports, we need to understand, respect, and be more tolerant of different points of view or different speech acts of our overseas partners.

Van Lier (1996) thoughtfully categorizes utterances into three kinds of design: audience design, message design, and interactional design. Audience design refers to the way a speaker may design or adjust his or her speech to accommodate the listener to actually express the speaker's own intention and attitude and to save the face of the listener by showing decorum, politeness, and mutual respect. Message design, on the other hand, refers to the arrangement of the message themselves. For example, the messages are logically, sequentially, and cohesively organized in a written or an oral discourse. Finally, because a conversation or dialogue involves at least two participants, interactional design has to be taken into consideration in different forms of communication. That is, communications between or among participants need to follow some kinds of interactional rules, such as turn taking, management of the topic, and marks of relevance. In a cross-cultural exchange context, these three designs of discourse can be even more important because it is much easier to lead to misunderstandings or conflicts in the course of communication if it involves communications between or among different cultures.

Another issue in the area of cross-cultural communication that deserves discussion here is *accommodation*. Van Lier (1996) raises the issue of *accommodation*, stating that when we talk to foreigners, we naturally adjust our ways of talking to "accommodate" those foreigners in order for them to understand, just like the adjustment we make when we talk to babies or children. In a sense, if we do not accommodate to foreigners' being less proficient in our native language, then it could mean that we are not quite comfortable with the foreigner we are talking to and we purposefully show our signs of reluctance and unfriendliness.

However, chances to be exposed to different cultures are increasingly growing because of the availability and advancement of technologies and transportation. There are many alternatives and contexts from which teachers can choose to teach students sociolinguistic knowledge in a cross-cultural exchange setting, for example, tour guiding, interviewing, cultural presentation, online social networking, reception of visitors from partner schools, joint authoring, and joint research. By direct contacts with people from different cultures, students may gain cultural awareness and accumulate their sociolinguistic knowledge. Van Lier (1996) provides a sequential development of language learning to move from being exposed to and being aware of the target language through being engaged in and autonomously participating in social activities, using the target language, and finally arriving at the level of proficiency in which language learners can actually master the language and use it in a creative way in an authentic environment. I would argue that, for a language learner to reach the final stage *proficiency*, it is, at least in part, the language teachers' responsibility to provide learners with a sociolinguistically rich learning environment, such as cross-cultural exchanges, to enrich students' learning experience.

A quick overview of reports on cross-cultural exchanges shows that most of the researchers report only from their own side and their own perspectives. The partners' side and their perspectives are always ignored. This one-side reporting phenomenon does not reflect a need in a sociolinguistic pedagogy and needs to be improved in an era moving towards globalization to equally appreciate and respect people from different cultures and to focus more on social or cross-cultural interactions. It can more meaningful and more comprehensive if researchers can collaboratively report of both sides of a cross-cultural exchange project. On the other hand, as Eckert (2018) discusses the third wave in sociolinguistics in her book, the future of sociolinguistics is actually involving a very wide range of elements, including style, ideology, gender, age, personae and identity. It is especially true in an era moving towards globalization when cross-cultural communications and population mobility are greatly enhanced by modern technologies and convenient transportations.

HEIGHTENED AWARENESS AND TOLERANCE OF LANGUAGE VARIETIES AND CULTURAL DIFFERENCES

As the development of the idea of *World Englishes*, People have a heightened awareness of language varieties. It is especially complicated when it comes to "the distinction among nation, state, and official language" (Davies & Dubinsky, 2018, p. 99). According to Davies and Dubinsky, a nation is

> a population with a shared identity based on culture, ethnicity, history, religion, language, or some other characteristic….A state…is a political entity, in which a government has sovereignty over a particular territory….An official language is a state language that is mandated by law or is written into the constitution of a state. (p. 99-102)

Based on this distinction, there is no wonder that people in Taiwan and people in the southern part of Fujian Provence, China speak the same dialect *Southern Min*.

In the case of English, even though English is used mostly for international communication, different accents and different expressions for the same idea can be seen everywhere, even on English proficiency tests, such as TOEIC, which involves speakers with different English accents in the listening comprehension test. There is no longer a so-called "standard English" (Fromkin, Rodman, & Hyams, 2014). Jindapitak and Teo (2013) argue that, in second language teaching approaches, we should not still stick to American or British English and insist on a native-like accent. Davies and Dubinsky (2018) argue that even African American English (AAE) are spoken differently by different speakers in different areas and situations for different purposes. EFL learners should be aware of English varieties in pronunciation, lexis, and other areas of grammar. Teachers should expose their students to different English speaking accents and environments. In cross-cultural exchange settings, it is especially important that students learn and be able to tolerate and even appreciate different language varieties.

In addition to language varieties, there are also language changes. As Fromkin et al. (2014) point out all "living languages change with time" (p. 337). There are sound, phonological, morphological, syntactic, and lexical changes. New words or expressions are also created all the time. Slangs or idioms can be created because of a currently occurring incident. Only people who have a good knowledge of the incident can associate new expressions with a current event. In cross-cultural exchanges, participants may learn firsthand the currently invented words or expressions in the target culture.

Awareness and tolerance of language varieties and changes should also be reflected in testing of languages. As Seargeant (2012) states "practical interventions in the wake of research into World Englishes are also being suggested for the revision of language assessment procedures" (p. 105). He argues that tests of English should be contextualized to include local norms and situations. On the one hand, it may reflect how the local varieties are developed and what are specific to the local culture. On the other hand, it is a good opportunity to raise the status of local varieties. From a sociolinguistic perspective, being able to communicate internationally in an era of high migration and mobility is one of the competencies required to develop as a global citizen, and to be able to communicate with people from different cultures appropriately requires a heightened awareness of language varieties.

Although raising cultural awareness and tolerating cultural differences has been a part of popular rhetoric and public discourse in a globalizing era, the issues of racism, or racial discrimination, still exist in different parts of the globe. As Caballero (2014) describes the reality of mixing races in Britain, even though mixed-race families have a long history in Britain, it has been a public debate. Theoretically, Britain presents itself as a multicultural and multiracial nation and mix-race families are living happily in the nation. In reality, as described by Caballero, mix-race families are always associated with low social class, lifestyles, and residential location and are traditionally perceived as "a simplistic, monolithic picture of sexually promiscuous" (p. 224). Caballero argues that most of the research studies done on mix-race families were generally outsider-led. He is worried that those outsider-led research findings may not be true voices and representative of those mix-race families and their children. He urges research studies to work into the actuality behind those mix-race families and into real people living complex and their everyday lives, and research studies on the topic should be moved away from outsider-led ones to include "factors of class, gender, ethnicity, geography, sexuality, [and] age" (p. 235). Caballero's study reveals an important message: cultural awareness may turn out to be political rhetoric in an era moving towards racial inequality existing in the globe.

Viewing from historical, geographical, and political perspectives, we understand that language varieties and, hence, discriminations are created by many different traumas and conflicts occurred between or among different ethnic groups or countries. One of the most significant goals of globalization is to prevent the global community from repeating all the historical mistakes. It is hoped that cross-cultural encounters can really bridge the gap between people speaking different languages or language varieties and from different cultures, and most importantly, people can have a tolerant and positive attitude towards people of different cultures.

COLLABORATION BETWEEN EDUCATIONAL INSTITUTIONS AND COMMERCIAL ORGANIZATIONS

Foskett (2010) states that "higher education (HE) is an international business operating in a global market" (p. 33). He describes the pressure faced by higher education leaders in the competitive global market. He acknowledges the contributions higher education has made to global economy, especially with the emergence of the "knowledge economy. Taylor (2010) also states that globalization "has rapidly established higher education as a commodity within international trade" (p. 85). Hodges, Watchravesringkan, Yurchism, Hegland, Karpova, Marcketti, and Yan (2015) cite Hynes and Richardson's words and claim that it is important to link "the university entrepreneurship course to examples within the real world....[E]ntrepreneurship education must focus on areas related to industry and to economic growth" (p. 316). Agarwal (2008) states that higher education is a big business opportunity, and he estimates that student enrollment will reach more than 300 million in 2025. All the claims mentioned here point to a tendency in a globalizing era in higher education that higher education will go hand in hand with commercial sectors and that the ultimate goal of education is the well-being of human beings. As many examples of cross-border collaboration mentioned throughout the book, education and commerce are closely related in modern society. In many cases mentioned in the book, financial difficulties are always the main factor that cause the failure of cross-border collaborations and many educational objectives aim at providing students with necessary skills to practice in their future business careers.

Cottom (2017) describes a phenomenon in higher education in the United States, the expansion of for-profit colleges, which she terms "lower ed." These colleges have emerged to respond to the needs of low socio-economic minority groups who are struggling to get a college degree in the hope of getting a better job in their future career. This phenomenon emerged as a result of inequality in education in the United States, and it is not really what we want to see in any place of the world. Collaborations between educational institutions and commercial organizations in private sectors do have potentials in bridging the gap in career opportunities between advantaged and disadvantaged groups of people as educators are working hard in minimizing the digital divides and as increasing collaborations between educational institutions and commercial organizations largely provide students with equal opportunities to access job training and options.

Kinser and Levy (2006) also describe U.S. tendencies of higher education, that is, the emergence of for-profit higher education. Although there are different ways to define and to regulate for-profit institutions, they explain that "many countries allow for-profit institutions for 'training' but not 'for education'" (p. 110). Kinser and Levy further classify for-profit institutions into four types: corporate universities, corporate-owned universities, non-degree granting institutions, and degree-granting institutions. Among them, corporate universities mainly aim at training employees of their own business and to build "their human resource capacity to sustain long-term profit" (p.113), while corporate-owned universities are universities "owned by corporations that seek to make profits from providing educational services" (p. 113). They aggressively open their branch campuses in other regions or other countries. As for non-degree granting institutions and degree-granting institutions, as their names suggest, the differences between the two types of institutions lie in whether they grant academic degrees or not. Non-degree granting institutions do not award degrees to their participants; rather, they provide short-term entry level training, while degree-granting institutions award mostly non-university level degrees. However, there are chances for participants to have substantial advanced education and to get a university or college degree.

Toma (2011), on the other hand, describes American higher education in rather straightforward and plain words as saying it has "increasingly become a commodity, its environment marked by intense competition and rhetoric associated with markets and efficiency" (p. 1). The fact shows that universities are applying whatever strategies they can to recruit students, to advance their ranking, and diversify their financial resources. Under this circumstance, universities have concentrated their attention on individual gains rather than on societal good, and states "are increasingly expressing their expectations that institutions demonstrate quality and contribute to local, state, and national economic development" (p. 2). As a result, universities are paying more attention to areas such as information technology, diversity, and international affairs. In this regard, different forms of cross-cultural exchanges, such as cross-border collaborations, distance education, cross-cultural videoconferencing or computer-mediated communications, and exchange of students or faculty, are encouraged, and programs less directly connected with the commercial sphere are diminished.

In the domain of cross-cultural exchanges, there are many cases showing that collaborations between educational institutions and commercial organizations may have its advantages and added values in promotion higher education if well organized and coordinated. As described in Chapter 7 of the book, in the case of the Gulf Region, for example, Dubai and Qatar, their Dubai International Academic City and Education City turned out to be successful international branch campuses particularly because they had financial support from either entrepreneurial investors or the Royal family. In contrast, the Japanese case is considered a failure, and their international campuses could hardly survive after a short period of operating. Among the reason for the failure are management and financial issues.

Another example illustrated in the same chapter is the cases of internationally collaborated campuses in Malaysia. Coincidentally, the two cases of collaboration in Malaysia are representative of success and failure. The successful one is the MUSCM campus and the unsuccessful one is the RMIT campus. According to Lane (2011), transaction costs and financial issues contributed a lot either to the success or failure of the cross-border collaborations. Viewing from the financial perspective, one might be worried about the quality of higher education. It is surely true that quality is very important in education. However, without sound finance, quality education may not be able to achievable.

In Southeast Asia, Welch (2011) describes the case of Malaysia. In order to survive the competitiveness in the international market, the Malaysian government had strategic policies to corporatize public sector higher education institutions. On the other hand, in the era of economic crisis, the Malaysian government also promoted franchise agreements between public and private higher education institutions and overseas partnerships such as the cases mentioned earlier. Under this circumstance, as described by Welch, Malaysia's higher education was seen as having "an increasing commercial rationale for internationalization" (p. 82).

In the case of India, Agarwal (2008) describes that a considerable number of foreign providers from various countries sought collaboration with Indian higher education institutions. Unfortunately, studies show that many of "these foreign providers were not recognized or accredited in their own countries, and…Indian partners were not affiliated with any Indian University" (p. 91). Generally, many programs offered by foreign providers in India are commercially motivated and can hardly maintain academic standards.

From the discussion above, we may conclude that collaborations between education and commerce may be inevitable in an era moving towards globalization. As Agarwal (2008) states, "In recent years, economic considerations have become the weightiest impetus for academic mobility" (p. 93). However, commercialization of higher education may at the same time cause many issues that need to be dealt with, such as quality of education, regulations to monitor cross-border collaborations and the impacts they may have on local education. Speaking of quality assurance, educators need to be reminded that commercialization and quality assurance are not mutually exclusive. On the contrary, they are complementary to each other. On the one hand, financial support from private sectors may help higher education institutions recruit sufficient and well-qualified faculty and equip advanced instructional facilities. On the other hand, quality education may contribute to economic development, especially in an era of a knowledge economy.

In addition to instruction in the education arena, academic research is also a great concern of some scholars. Heller, Pietikäinen, and Pujolar (2018) are concerned about the dissemination of research work outside the academic world, which they term *knowledge mobilization*. They argue that generally academic publications are mostly read by academics and thus only benefit the academic field. They urge to publish research results in other relevant domains. Academic researchers need to know that their research findings may be of concern of various interested groups, such as "any kind of professional group, government agency, private business, association, NGO, [and] political constituency" (p. 148). Heller et al. argue that, from a sociolinguistic perspective, the traditional conception that scientists are authorities and what they say are truths is no longer valid. They urge collaborations or co-designing research between or among different domains and organizations. They point out that "knowledge mobilization and outreach is basically conceived as a dialogue in which the voice and interests of non-academic participants must be allowed to be put on the table" (p. 149).

REGIONAL INTEGRATION IN HIGHER EDUCATION

In an era moving towards globalization, international collaboration can enhance competitiveness of each partner in the so-called knowledge economy and more effectively help them work together towards global issues and promote mobility in different areas of higher education. In international collaboration, there is a tendency towards regional integration. That is, countries in the same region may work together to more effectively achieve their mutual goals. Barrett (2017) describes the case of the European Higher Education Area (EHEA) partnered by the European Commission. They view higher education as "both recipients and agents of change in the political economy context" (p. 58) and aim at increasing social cohesion nationally and regionally and increasing social, academic cohesion nationally and regionally and increasing social, academic, and professional mobility. As Barrett describes, one of the important examples of regional integration in higher education is Erasmus International Student Exchange established by the European Commission, aiming at promoting the mobility of students for semester or year abroad study. In addition to Erasmus, there are also other "regional programs for higher education, life-long learning, vocational training, and ongoing student exchanges in Europe" (p. 60).

As mentioned earlier in the book, there is a tendency towards regional collaboration or integration. As described by Barrett (2017), the

> Bologna Process's policy reforms in Europe have been simulated by other regions of the world. Across regions, the degree of integration in higher education varies, from discursive organization as in Latin America to broader extents of cooperation in Asia. (p. 226)

In Europe, under the Bologna Process, member states worked together towards the goal of "Europe of Knowledge," aiming at socio-cultural and economic development as the main purposes of education. Examples of collaboration among European member states include "the degree structure, quality assurance, and academic recognition" (p. 229). For member states of the Bologna Process, on the one hand, they converged with higher education policy reform. On the other hand, they had sufficient freedom to adjust their policy reform to address their national situation and needs.

Barrett (2017) attributes the regional integration in Europe to three main factors: "competitive economic pressures through globalization, domestic policies through intergovernmentalism, and sociological and ideational processes stemming from the EU and European institutions through Europeanization" (p. 61). According to Barrett (2017), "Europeanization is the overall regional influence of Europe acting on national and institutional levels....intergovernmentalism is led by the states to make policy at European level" (p. 62). The dynamics of Europeanization and intergovernmentalism both expand national cooperation in higher education in Europe and economic interdependence to the advantage of member states, not to mention some unexpected benefits resulting from national cooperation. Under this circumstance, institutions actually play their roles at different levels: "the supranational level of the EU, the national level of the state, and the sub-national level of the higher education institution" (p. 65).

In addition to Europeanization and intergovernmentalism, and regional mobility, regional integration in Europe in higher education include international mobility. For example, higher education institutions are encouraged to provide "opportunities for students and researchers to study and to work beyond their home country," (p. 67) and student mobility is even used to measure institutions' success in their competitiveness and compatibility in the knowledge economy market. The rationale underlying international mobility is that "the international recognition of academic credits and degrees are expected to enhance educational quality, student learning outcomes, and economic development" (p. 67). As Barrett (2017) states, "Higher education mobility programs from the EHEA and Erasmus have been stimulated by other regions of the world, and outcomes thus far provide lessons for understanding, success, and challenges" (p. 69).

In addition to Europe, another example showing a tendency of regional collaboration is intercultural education in post-communist countries described by Bleszynska (2011). She states that post-communist countries share similar historical backgrounds, face similar issues in the post-communist era, and require collaboration to research on issues of mutual concerns. Bleszynska illustrated that the mutual concerns include "the problematics of indigenous minorities, cultural borderlands, reconstruction of multicultural traditions of the past, and establishing friendly and peaceful intergroup relations" (p. 78). Therefore, these countries collaboratively develop their intercultural programs of research centers in "regions where certain groups or social phenomena occur" (p. 78). For example, in Poland, the research group in Warsaw University focuses it research "on postmodern multicultural societies, immigrants, urban enclaves, intercultural competences, education and socialization in multicultural societies, as well as the role of education in the social integration of refugees and immigrates" (p. 78). Other examples, such as University of Bialystok working on Polish-Belarusian borderland affairs, Silesian University in Cieszyn researching on the problematic of ethnic socialization in the Polish-Czech contact area, and many other research centers in post-communist countries, show that almost all of the post-communist countries require immediate attention to similar issues after their political transformation, such as "globalization, migration, emancipating cultural minorities, combating racism, ethnic prejudice and xenophobia" (p. 76). Working together and combining "intercultural education with Global Education, Civic Education, Education on Human Rights and Education for Peace" (p. 76) are viewed as equally important and beneficial to post-communist countries.

In the case of Latin America, the "political will to make regional higher education cooperation a policy priority is needed to elevate the issue and to develop more structures of cooperation" (Barrett, 2017, p. 227), and the regional integration in Latin America has emerged. For example, the Union of South American Nations (UNASUR) was formed in 2008 and the Community of Latin America and Caribbean States (CELAC) was formed in 2010 (Barrett, 2017). Other regional Unions such as the Interuniversity Center for Development (CINDA) is based in Santiago, Chile and is connecting Ibero-American countries, which have historic ties to Portugal and Spain, …[to share] best practices" (p. 227). Member nations focus on "quality assurance and accreditation in higher education" (p. 227).

In the case of Asia, representatives "from the Association of Southeast Asian Nations (ASEAN) were present as observers and participants in the Bologna Policy Forum at the EHEA Ministerial Conferences in Bucharest in 2012 and in Yerevan in 2015" (p. 229). After the conferences, ASEAN started to initiate regional higher education collaboration.

Some of the ASEAN members of University Network are also members of the Asia-Pacific Quality Network (APQN), which "is a network that promotes regional and cross-border collaboration aimed at building capacity and strengthening quality assurance in higher education" (Sarvi, 2011, p. 252).

DIGITAL INEQUALITY EMERGED AS OPPOSED TO SOCIAL INEQUALITY

Social inequality, such as racism and sexism, has been widely discussed in a considerable amount of literature. In the digital and globalizing world, however, there are different types of inequality that deserve our attention. While people are praising and enjoying the advancement and convenience of modern technologies, they overlook the divides existing in the so-called information age. Wang (2015) describes the first, second, and third digital divide. The first digital divide is *access*. For those in poor countries, regions, or families, people cannot afford to own computer facilities or access to the Internet. In other words, they are deprived of their chances to enjoy learning and to get the most advanced knowledge through modern technologies. The second digital divide is *use*. For some people, although having access to modern technologies is not a problem for them, they have problems making use of these modern technologies. For example, people with less technical skills and people who do not read English may be prevented from using modern technologies. Age and gender differences are also sources of digital divide. The so-called digital natives are seen much more skillful in operating technical devices than digital immigrants are because they were born in a digital world and are used to modern technologies. On the other hand, in terms of gender, traditionally, males tend to be better than females in managing technical devices. Wang further described the third digital divide *learning*. Even though *access* and *use* are not problems for some people, how to make use of technical devices to learn lead to differences among or between technology users. E-learning or m-learning have become popular terms in the educational field. It is true that we can use our mobile devices anytime and anywhere to learn. However, how do you learn and what do you learn in the process of using technical devices? Surely we have to define *learning* in a broader sense, not confined to academic learning. Smart users of technical devices or luckier students of smart teachers can make the most use of technical devices to learn, be it academic learning, language learning, social learning, or cultural learning.

Ragnedda and Ruiu (2018) associate digital divide with social capital. Those who have better access to the digital world and who are better benefitted from the use of digital devices, just like those who own more powerful social capital in society, can make use of their digital capital to gain a lot of benefits, say job hunting, information gathering, and development of social networks. As pointed out by Hockly and Dudeney (2017), the "digital divide is unlikely to disappear by 2020, as it rests not on lack of access to technology online but corresponds to wider socioeconomic factors" (p. 244). In discussing higher education in Southeast Asia, Welch (2011) states that the quality of education "is closely intertwined with questions of social justice and democracy…[w]hen good-quality education is limited to a small elite, …not merely does quality go out the window, but the overall quality of the education system is substantially weakened" (p. 120). The same holds true when we view cross-cultural exchanges from this perspective. Those who are financially less advantaged may be deprived of their opportunities to participate in any cross-cultural activities, be it communicating online or taking a fieldtrip to another country. Furthermore, cross-cultural exchanges can be impossible because of different levels of technological development and incompatibility of technical specifications. Digital technicians, like sociologists in society, need to deal with the inequality in the digital world.

From the discussions in the entire chapter, we may conclude that whatever challenges people in the global world may face in the course moving towards globalization and what practitioners of cross-cultural exchanges can do to respond to these challenges are actually dependent on how we human beings are committed to developing a peaceful and harmonious globe. After all, globalization is not the goal we intend to achieve, but rather a peaceful and harmonious global community.

REFERENCES

Abungu, A. & Law, M. (2015). Surviving in a global environment: New skills for library development. In B. L. Eden (Ed.), *Partnerships and new roles in the 21st-century academic library: collaborating, embedding, and cross-training for the future* (pp. 159-170). Lanham, Maryland, USA: Rowman & Littlefield.

Agarwal, P. (2008). India in the context of international student circulation: Status and prospect. In H. D.Wit, P. Agarwal, M. E. Said, M. T. Sehoole, & M. Sirozi (Eds.), *The dynamic of international student circulation in a global context* (pp. 83-112). Rotterdam, The Netherlands : Sense.

Al-Barwani, T., Ameen, H., & Chapman, D. W. (2011). Cross-border collaboration for quality assurance in Oman: Contested terrain. In R. Sakamoto & D. W. Chapman (Eds.), *Cross-border partnerships in higher education: strategies and issues* (pp. 133-150). New York, USA: Routledge.

Allmen, M. R. (2011). The intercultural perspective and its development through cooperation with the Council of Europe. In C. A. Grant & A. Portera (Eds.), *Intercultural and multicultural education: Enhancing global interconnectedness* (pp. 33-48). New York, USA: Routledge.

Amirali, S. & Bakken, J. P. (2015). Trends and challenges of recruiting and retaining international graduate students: An internal perspective. In R. V. Nata (Ed.). *Progress in education. Volume 36* (pp. 147-155). New York, USA : Nova.

Ananta, A. & Arifin, E. N. (Eds.). (2004). *International migration in Southeast Asia*. Singapore: Institution of Southeast Asian Studies.

Arndt, R. T. & Rubin, D. L. (Eds) (1993). *The Fulbright difference, 1948-1992*. New Jersey, USA: Transaction.

Ates, O. (2012). Impact of case study method on an ESP business course. *International Journal of Business and Social Science, 3*(6), 135-140.

Attewell, P. (2001). The first and second digital divides. *Sociology of Education, 74*(3), 252-259.

Austin, A. E. & Foxcroft, C. (2011). Fostering organizational change and individual learning through 'ground-up' inter-institutional cross-border collaboration. In R. Sakamoto & D. W. Chapman (Eds.), *Cross-border partnerships in higher education: Strategies and issues* (pp. 115-132). New York: Routledge.

Bahry, S., Darkhor, P., & Luo, J. (2009). Educational diversity in China: Responding to globalizing and localizing forces. In G. A. Wiggan & C. B. Hutchison (Eds.), *Global issues in education: Pedagogy, policy, practice, and the minority experience* (pp. 103-129). Lanham, Maryland, US: Rowman & Littlefield.

Bano, S. (2018). From brain drain to reverse brain drain: Implications for South Asia and the United States of America. In K. Bista (Ed.). *International student mobility and opportunities for growth in the global marketplace* (pp. 64-79). Hershey, PA, USA: IGI Global.

Barrett, B. (2017). *Globalization and change in higher education: The political economy of policy reform in Europe.* Cham, Switzerland: Palgrave Macmillan.

Barnett B., & Jacobson, S. L. (2010). Higher education partnerships for studying and improving leadership preparation and development around the world. In F. Maringe & N. Foskett (Eds.), *Globalization and internationalization in higher education: Theoretical, strategic and management perspectives* (pp. 255-276). London, UK: Continuum.

Bazeley P. (2003) Computerize data analysis for mixed methods research. In A. Tashakkori & C. Teddlie (Eds). *Handbook of mixed methods in social & Behavioral Sciences* (pp. 385-422). Thousand Oaks, CA, USA: Sage.

Beauchamp, M. (2011). Face to Faith: Teaching global citizen. *Phi Delta Kappan, 93* (4), 24-27.

Ben-Zakan, A. (2010). *Cross-cultural scientific exchanges in the Eastern Mediterranean, 1560-1660.* Baltimore, USA: Johns Hopkins UP.

Bergmann, J. & Sams, A. (2012). *Flip your classroom: Reach every student in every class every day.* Eugen, Oregon, USA: International Society for Technology in Education.

Bernard, H. R. & Ryan, G. W. (2010). *Analyzing qualitative data: Systematic approaches.* Los Angeles, USA : Sage.

Bevis, T. B. & Lucas, C. J. (2007). *International students in American colleges and universities: A history.* New York, USA: Palgrave Macmillan.

Bleszynska, K. M. (2011). Intercultural education in post-communist countries. In C. A. Grant & A. Portera (Eds.). *Intercultural and multicultural education: Enhancing global interconnectedness* (pp. 69-82). New York, USA: Routledge.

Boeije, H. (2010). *Analysis in qualitative research.* Los Angeles, USA: Sage.

Brack, B. L. (1993). The missing linkage: The process of integrating orientation and reentry. In R. M. Paige (Ed.), *Education for the intercultural experience* (2nd ed.). (pp. 241-279), Main, USA: Intercultural Press.

Brislin, R. W. (1993). A cultural-general assimilator: Preparation for various types of sojourns. In R. M. Paige (Ed.). *Education for the intercultural experience* (2nd Ed.). (pp. 281-299), Main, USA: Intercultural Press.

Brooks, R. & Waters, J. (2011). *Student mobilities, migration and the internationalization of higher education.* London, UK: Palgrave Macmillan.

Brown, H. D. (2000). *Principles of language learning and teaching* (4th ed.). New York, USA: Pearson.

Brown, L. & Aktas, G. (2012). Turkish university students' hopes and fears about travel to the West. *Journal of Research in International Education, 11*(1), 3-18.

Brown, R. M. & Tignor, S. E. (2016). Preparing culturally competent teachers through faculty-led study abroad. In J. A. Rhodes & T. M. Milby (Eds.), *Advancing teacher education and curriculum development through study abroad* (pp. 57-73). Hershey, PA, USA: IGI Global.

Brunvand, S. (2016). Facilitating student interaction and collaboration in a MOOC environment. In R. Mendoza-Gonzalez (Ed.), *User-centered design strategies for Massive Open Online Courses (MOOCs)* (pp. 1-14). Hershey, PA, USA: IGI Global.

Bücker, J., Bouw, R., & Beuckelaer, A. (2018). Dealing with cross-cultural issues in culturally diverse classrooms: The case of Dutch business schools. In K. Bista (Ed.). *International student mobility and opportunities for growth in the global marketplace* (pp. 117-133). Hershey, PA, USA: IGI Global.

Caballero, C. (2014). Mixing race in Britam: The influence of academic publics. In Y. Taylor (ed.), *The entrepreneurial university: Engaging publics, intersecting impacts* (pp. 223-241). London, UK: palgrave Macmillian.

Callison, D. (1998). Authentic assessment. *School Library Media Activities Monthly, 14*(5), n.p.

Carbaugh, E. M. & Doubet, K. J. (2016). *The differentiated flipped classroom: A practical guide to digital learning.* California, USA: Corwin.

Carson, L. (2018). Teaching internationally for internationalization. In B. E. Bizzell, R. C. Kahila, & P. A. Talbot (Eds.), *Cases on global competencies for education diplomacy in international settings* (pp. 95-118). Hershey, PA, USA: IGI Global.

Casquero, O., Benito, M., Romo, J., & Ovelar, R. (2016). Participation and interaction in learning environments: A whole-network analysis. In K. Terry & A. Cheney (Eds.), *Utilizing virtual and personal learning environment for optimal learning* (pp. 111-131). Hershey, PA, USA: IGI Global.

Center for Innovative Teaching and Learning. *Authentic assessment.* Retrieved from Indiana University Bloomington Website http://citl.indiana.edu/teaching-resources/assessing-student-learning/authentic-assessment.

Chang, J. S. (2006). A transcultural wisdom bank in the classroom: Making cultural diversity a key resource in teaching and learning. *Journal of studies in International Education, 10*, 369-377.

Chang, S. & Gomes, C. (2017). International student identity and the digital environment. In B. K. Mikk & I. E. Steglitz (Eds.), *Learning across cultures : Locally and globally* (3rd ed.). (pp. 39-62). Washington, DC, USA: NAFSA: Association of International Education.

Chapman, D. W. & Sakamoto, R. (2011). The future of cross-border partnerships in higher education. In R. Sakamoto & D. W. Chapman (Eds.). *Cross-border partnership in higher education: Strategies and issues* (pp. 265-270). New York, USA: Routledge.

Cheng, C. M. (August 30, 2017) Interview by Ai-Ling Wang.

Cheung, K. S. (2007). A comparison of WebCT, Blackboard, and Moodle for the teaching and learning of continuing education courses. In P. Tsang, R. Kwan & R. Fox (Eds.), *Enhancing learning through technology* (pp. 219-228), Singapore: World Scientific

Cho, H. (2018). The pitfalls and promises of electronic portfolio assessment with secondary English language learners. In J. Perreu, K. Kelch, J-S Byun, S. Cervanted, & S. Safavi (Eds.), *Applications of CALL theory in ESL and ESL environments* (pp. 111-130). Hershey, PA, USA: IGI Global.

Chuah, C .K. P. (2007). Experience redesign: A conceptual framework for moving teaching and learning into flexible E-learning environment. In P. Tsang, R. Kwan, & R. Fox (Eds.), *Enhancing learning through technology* (pp. 37-50). Singapore: World Scientific.

Chun Shin Limited. (2012). *Global HRM & TOEIC*. Taipei, Taiwan: Author.

Chye, K. H., Gervais, G., & Kiu, Y. S. (2007). Using technology in education: The application of data mining. In P. Tsang, R. Kwan & R. Fox (Eds.), *Enhancing learning through technology* (pp. 185-198). Singapore: World Scientific.

Clifford, V. (2011). Moving from multicultural to intercultural education in Australian higher education. In C. A. Grant & A. Portera (Eds.), *Intercultural and multicultural education: enhancing global interconnectedness* (pp. 315-322). New York, USA: Routledge.

Clifford, V., Henderson, J., & Montgomery, C. (2013). Internationalising the curriculum for all students: The role of staff dialogue. In J. Ryan (Ed.), *Cross-cultural teachig and learning for home and international students: Internationalisation of pedagogy and curriculum in higher education* (pp. 251-264). London, UK: Routledge.

Collins, C. S. (2001). Cross-border collaboration in the service of human capacity development. In R. Sakamoto & D. W. Chapman (Eds.), *Cross-border partnerships in higher education: Strategies and issues* (pp. 228-247). New York, USA: Routledge.

Colwell, J., Nielsen, D., Bradley, B. A. & Spearman, M. (2016). Preservice teacher reflections about short-term summer study abroad experiences in Italy. In J. A. Rhodes & T. M. Milby (Eds.), *Advancing teacher education and curriculum development through study abroad programs* (pp. 91-111). Hershey, PA, USA: IGI Global.

Corbin, J & Strauss, A. (2008). *Basics of qualitative research: Techniques and procedures for developing grounded theory* (3rd ed.). Los Angeles, USA: Sage.

Cottom, T. M. (2017). *Lower ed: The troubling rise of for-profit-colleges in the new economy.* New York, USA: The New Press.

Crawford, A. & Witko, K. (2018). Developing cultural competencies in the conflict zone: Two teachers with one mission. In B. E. Bizzell, R. C. Kahila, & P. A. Talbot (Eds.), *Cases on global competencies for educational diplomacy in international settings* (pp. 77-94). Hershey, PA, USA: IGI Global.

Cronje, J. (2011). Using Hofstede's cultural dimensions to interpret cross-cultural blended teaching and learning. *Computer & Education, 56*(3), 596-603.

Croom, P. W. (2011). Motivation and aspirations for international branch campuses. In R. Sakamoto & D. W. Chapman (Eds.), *Cross-border partnerships in higher education: Strategies and issues* (pp. 45-66). New York, USA : Routledge.

Cruzado-Guerrero, J. & Martinez-Alba, G. (2016). Meaningful language and cultural experiences for future teachers in Puerto Rico. In J. A. Rodes & T.M. Milby (Eds.), *Advancing teacher education and curriculum development through study abroad programs* (pp. 160-176). Hershey, PA, USA: IGI Global.

Crystal, D. (2003). *English as a global language* (2nd ed.). Cambridge, UK: Cambridge UP.

Cuenat, M. E. (2018). PluriMobil: Pragmatic enhancement of intercultural learning before, during, and after study abroad. In J. Jackson & S. Oguro (Eds.), *Intercultural interventions in study abroad* (pp. 175-189). New York, USA: Routledge.

Currier, C., Lucas, J., & Arnault, D. S. (2009). Study abroad and nursing: From cultural to global competence. In R. Lewin (Ed.), *The handbook of practice and research in study abroad: Higher education and the quest for global citizenship* (pp. 133-150). New York, USA: Routledge.

Daniels, J. (2013). Developing capability: International students in doctoral writing groups. In J. Ryan (Ed.), *Cross-cultural teaching and learning for home and international students: Internationalisation of pedagogy and curriculum in higher education* (pp. 41-52). London, UK: Routledge.

Davies, W. D. & Dubinsky, S. (2018). *Language conflict and language rights: Ethnolinguistic perspectives on human conflict.* Cambridge, U.K.: Cambridge UP.

Dennis, M. J. (2018). *International student mobility and the new world disorder: Practical recommendations for international enrollment managers, deans and recruiters.* Naples, Flordia, USA: Old Post Books.

De Wit, H., Agarwal, P., Said, M. E., Sehoole, M. T., & Sirozi, M. (Eds.) (2008). *The dynamics of international student circulation in a global context.* Rotterdam, The Netherlands: Sense.

De Wit, H. & Beelen, J. (2013). Socrates in the low countries : Designing, implementing and facilitating internationalisation of the curriculum at the Amsterdam University of Applied Sciences (HvA). In J. Ryan (Ed.), *Cross-cultural teaching and learning for home and international students: Internationalisation of pedagogy and curriculum in higher education* (pp. 156-167). New York: Routledge.

De Wit, H. & Rumbley, L. E. (2008). The role of Anerican higher education in international student circulation. In H. de Wit, P. Agarwal, M. E. Said, M. T. Sehoole, & M. Sirozi (Eds.), *The dynamics of international student circulation in a global context* (pp. 199-231). Rotterdam, The Netherlands: Sense.

Dealtry, R. (2017). *The future of corporate universities: How your company can benefit from value and performance-driven organisational development.* Bingley, UK: Emerald.

DeLong, M., Geum, K., Gage, K., McKinney, E., Medvedev, K., & Park, J. (2011). Cultural exchange: Evaluating an alternative model in higher education. *Journal of Studies in International Education, 15*(1), 41-56.

Denise, L. (1999). Collaboration vs. C-Three (cooperation, coordination, and communication). *Innovating, 7,* (n.p.).

Devlin, S. & Peacock, N. (2009). Overcoming linguistic and cultural barriers to integration: An investigation of two models. In T. Coverdale-Jones & P. Rastall (Eds.), *Internationalising the university: The Chinese context* (pp. 165-184). London, UK: Palgrave Macmillan.

Diehl, W. C. (2013). M-learning as a subfield of open and distance education. In Z. L. Berge & L. Y. Muilenburg (Eds.), *Handbook of mobile learning* (pp. 15-23). New York, USA: Routledge.

Doring, N., Lahmar, K., Bouabdallah, M., Bouafia, M., Bauzid, D., & Gobsch, G. (2010). German-Algerian university exchange from the perspective of students and teachers: Results of an intercultural survey. *Journal of Studies in International Education, 14*(3), 240-258.

Doyle, S., Gendall, P., Meyer, L. H., Hoek, J., Tait, C., McKenzie, L., & Loorparg, A. (2010). An investigation of factors associated with student participation in study abroad. *Journal of Studies in International Education, 14*(5), 471-490.

Eckert, P. (2018). *Meaning and linguistic variation: The third wave in sociolinguistics.* Cambridge, UK: Cambridge UP.

Ellenwood, A. E. & Snyders, F. J. A. (2010). Virtual journey coupled with face-to-face exchange: Enhancing the cultural sensitivity and competence of graduate students. *Intercultural Education, 21*(6), 549-566.

Esteban, A. S., Ramos, J. S. & Seco, A. A. (2011). A method for adapting learning objects to students' preferences. In S. B. Eom & J. B. Arbaugh (Eds.), *Student satisfaction and learning outcomes: An introduction to empirical research* (pp. 316-338). Hershey, PA, USA: Information Science Reference.

Fabregas-Juneiro, M. G., Fabre, R. L., & Rosete, R. T. (2012). Developing successful international faculty led program. *US-China Education Review, B4,* 375-382.

Fielding, T. (2016). *Asian Migrations: Social and Geographical mobilities in Southeast, East and Northeast Asia.* New York, USA: Routledge.

Fong, P. & Postiglione, G. (2011). Making cross-border partnerships work: The case of China's Hong Kong systen. In R. Sakamoto & D. W. Chapman (Eds.) *Cross-border partnerships in higher education: Strategies and issues* (pp. 169-190). New York, USA: Routledge.

Foskett, N. (2010) Global markets, national challenges, local strategies: The strategic challenge of internationalization. In F. Maringe & N. Foskett (Eds), *Globalization and internationalization in higher education: Theoretical, strategic and management perspectives* (pp. 35-50). London, UK: Continuum.

Freeman, D., Katz, A., Gomez, P. G., & Burns, A. (2015). English for teaching: Rethinking teacher proficiency in the classroom. *ELT Journal, 69*(2), 129-139.

Fromkin, V., Rodman, R., & Hyams, N. (2014). *An introduction to language* (10th ed.), Florence, USA: Cengage Learning.

Garrison, D. R. & Anderson, T. (2003). *E-learning in the 21st century.* London, U.K.: RoutledgeFalmer.

Gebhard, J. G. (2017). *Teaching English as a foreign or second language: A self-development and methology guide,* 3rd edition. Ann Arbor, Michigan, USA: University of Michign Press.

George, P. G. (1995). *College teaching abroad: A handbook of strategies for successful cross-cultural exchanges.* Massachusetts, USA: Allyn and Bacon.

Gerstein, R. B. (2000). Video conferencing in the classroom: Special projects toward cultural understanding. In D. L. Johnson, C. D. Maddux, & L. Liu (Eds.), *Integration of technology into the classroom: Cases studies* (pp. 177-186). New York, USA: Haworth.

Granville, S., Janks, H., Mphahlele, M., Reed, Y., Watson, P., Joseph, M., & Ramani, E. (1998). English with or without g(u)ilt: A position paper on language in education policy for South Africa. *Language and Education, 12*(4), 254-272.

Gray, J. & Morton, T. (2018). *Social interaction and English language teacher identity.* Edinburgh, UK: Edinburgh UP.

Green, S. L. & Edwards-Underwood, K. (2015). Understanding and redefining multicultural education. In R. V. Nata (Ed.), *Progress in education, Volum 36* (pp. 121-134). New York: Nova.

Groos, L. S. & Goh, M. (2017). Mindful reflection in intercultural learning. In B. K. Mikk & I. E. Steglitz (Eds.), *Learning across cultures: Locally and globally* (3rd ed.). (pp. 167-190). Washington, D. C., USA: NAFSA, Association of International Educators.

Gulati, R., Wohlgezogen, F. & Zhelyazkov, P. (2012). The two facets of collaboration: Cooperation and Coordination in strategic alliances. *Academy of Management Annuals 6,* 531-583.

Haraway, D. J. (2000). A cyborg manifesto: Science, technology, and socialist—feminism in the late twentieh century. In N. Badmington (Ed.), *Posthumanism* (pp. 69-84). Houndmills, Basingstoke, Hampshire: Palgrave.

Hargittai, E. (2002). Second-level digital divide: Differences in people's online skills, *First Monday, 7*(4) April. Retrived from URL: http://firstmonday.org/issues/issue 7_4/hargittai/index.html.

Harkness, J. (2003). Questionnaire translation. In Harkness, J. A., Van de Vijver, F, J, R., & Mohler, P. Ph (Eds.), *Cross-cultural survey methods* (pp. 35-56). New Jersey, USA: John Wiley & Sons.

Harris, J. (2012). World Englishes and English as a lingua franca: Application in the English classroom in Japan. *Forum of Higher Education Research, 2*, 25-34.

Harrison, N. & Peacock, N. (2010). Interactions in the international classroom: The UK perspective. In E. Jones (Ed.), *Internationalisation and the student voice: Higher education perspectives* (pp. 125-142). New York, USA: Routledge.

Hartman, E., Kiely, R., Boettcher, C., & Friedrichs, J. (2018). *Community-based global learning: The theory and practice of ethical engagement at home and abroad.* Sterling, Virginia, USA: Stylus.

Harvey, T. A. (2017). Design and pedagogy for transformative intercultural learning. In B. K. Mikk & I. E. Steglitz (Eds.), *Learning across cultures: Locally and globally* (3rd ed.). (pp. 109-138). Washington, DC., USA: NAFSA, Association of International Educators.

Heller, M., Pietikäinen, S., & Pujolar, J. (Eds.). (2018). *Critical sociolinguistic research methods: Studying language issues that matter.* New York, USA: Routledge.

Hepple, E. (2018). Designing and implementing pre-sojourn intercultural workshops in an Australian university. In J. Jackson & S. Oguro (Eds.), *Intercultural interventions in study abroad.* (pp. 18-36). New York, USA: Routledge.

Herrington, J., Reeves, T. C., & Oliver, R. (2010). *A guide to authentic e-learning.* New York, USA: Routledge.

Higson, H. E. & Liu, K. (2013). Business lessons without business: Can arts-based training enhance cultural competence? In J. Ryan (Ed.), *Cross-cultural teaching and learning for home and international students* (pp. 110-124). London, UK: Routledge.

Hildenbrand, B. (2007). Mediating structure and interaction in grounded theory. In A. Bryant & K. Charmaz (Eds.), *The Sage handbook of grounded theory* (pp. 539-564). Los Angeles, USA: Sage.

Ho, K. (2012). Out of America: Exploring collaborative mural teaching in Bulgaria. *Teaching Artists Journal, 10*(2) 77-87.

Hockly, N. & Dudency, G. (2017). Digital learning in 2020. In M. Carrie, R. M. Damerow, & K. M. Bailey (Eds.), *Digital language learning and teaching: Research, theory, and practice* (pp. 235-245). New York, USA: Routledge.

Hodges, N., Watchravesringkan, K., Yurchism, J., Hegland, J., Karpova, E., Marcketti, S., & Yan, R-N. (2015). Assessing curriculum designed to foster students entrepreneuruial knowledge and small business skills from a global perspective. *Family and Consumer Sciences Research, 43* (4), 313-327.

Holton, J. A. (2007). The coding process and its challenges. In A. Bryant & K. Charmaz (Eds.), *The Sage handbook of grounded theory* (pp. 265-289). London, U.K.: Sage.

Hoult, S. (2018). Aspiring to postcolonial engagement with the other: Deepening intercultural learning through reflection on a South India sojourn. In J. Jackson & S. Oguro (Eds.), *Intercultural interventions in study abroad* (pp. 71-87). London, UK: Routledge.

Hurn, B. J. & Tomalin, B. (2013). *Cross-cultural communication: Theory and practice.* London, UK: Palgrave Macmillan.

Hyde, M. (2012). *The international student's guide to UK education: Unlocking university life and culture.* New York, USA: Routledge.

Hyde, M. & Hyde, A. (2014), *Going to university abroad: A guide to studying outside the UK.* New York, USA: Routledge.

Icbay, M. A., & Kocayoruk, E. (2011). Being an exchange student in Turkey: Adaptation to a new culture. *International Journal of Progressive Education, 7*(3), 27-39.

Institute of International Education. (n.d.). *The Fulbright program and IIE.* Retrieved from Institute of International Education Website: http://www.iie.org/Fulbright.

International Education and Resource Network (2016). *iEARN project book 2016-2017,* Author.

Iredale, R., Hawksley, C. & Castles, S. (Eds.). (2003). *Migration in the Asia Pacific: Population, settlement and citizenship issues.* U.K.: Edward Elgar.

Jackson, J. (2018). Optimizing intercultural learning and engagement abroad through online mentoring. In J. Jackson & S. Oguro (Eds.). *Intercultural interventions in stud abroad* (p. 119-136). London, UK: Routledge.

Jana, R. (1999). *How to get the most out of online learning.* Retrieved from: http://www.cnn.com/TECH/computing/9909/15/learn.online.idg/index.html.

Jane, E. (2018). Genered cyberhate : A new digital divide? In M. Ragnedda & G. W. Muschert (Eds.), *Theorizing digital divides* (pp. 186-198). London, UK: Routledge.

Jenkins, J. (2003). *World Englishes : A resourece book for students.* Cheltenham, UK: Routledge.

Jenkins, J. (2007). *English as a Lingua Franca: Attitude and Identity.* Oxford, UK : Oxford UP.

Jindapitak, N. & Teo, A. (2013). The emergence of world Englishes : Implications for English language teaching. *Asian journal of social sciences and humanities, 2*(2), 190-199.

Johansson, F. (2006). *The Medici Effect: What elephants and epidemics can teach us about innovation.* Boston, Massachusetts, US: Harvard Business School Press.

John, M. J. S. (1996). Business is booming: Business English in the 1990s. *English for Specific Purposes, 15*(1), 3-18.

Jones, E. (2010). 'Don't worry about the worries': Transforming lives through international volunteering. In E. Jones (Ed.), *Internationalisation and the student voice: Higher education perspectives* (pp. 83-97). New York: Routledge.

Jordan, M. K. A. C. (2018). *Cultural exchange programs: The case of Fulbright program in Taiwan* (unpublished master's thesis). Tamkang University, New Taipei City, Taiwan.

Kachru, Y. & Nelson, C. L. (Eds.). (2006). *World Englishes in Asian contests.* Hong Kong: Hong Kong University press.

Kartoshkina, Y. (2017). Neuroscience behind intercultural learning. In B. K. Mikk & I. E. Steglitz (Eds.), *Learning across cultures: Locally and globally* (3rd ed.). (pp. 87-107). Washington, DC., USA: NAFSA, Association of international educators.

Keengwe, J., Onchwari, G. & Oigara, J. (Eds.). (2014), *Promoting active learning through the flipped classroom model.* Hershey, PA, USA: IGI Global.

Kelly, P. P. (2018). Reflections on a troubled experience in Malawi. In B. E. Bizzell, R. C. Kahila, & P. A. Talbot (Eds.), *Cases on global competencies for educational diplomacy in international settings* (pp. 141-153). Hershey, PA, USA: IGI Global.

Kerr, P. (2015). Adaptive learning. *ELT Journal, 70*(1), 88-93.

Keskin, Y. (2014). Turkey's difficulty choice: European Union or Shanghai Cooperation Organization. *Tamkang Journal of International Affairs, 17* (3), 81-130.

Khan, B. H. (Ed.) (2016). *Revolutionizing modern education through meaningful e-learning implementation.* Hershey, PA, USA: IGI Global.

Kinser, K. & Levy, D. (2006). For-profit higher education: U.S. tendencies, international echoes. In J. J. F. Forest & P. G. Altbach (Eds.), *International handbook of higher education: Part One: Global themes and contemporary challenges* (pp. 105-119). Dordrecht, The Netherlands: Springer.

Kirk, D. (2009). Diversity, global practive, local needs: An international comparative study of preservice teachers' perceptions of initial teacher training in the United States, England, and United Arab Emirates. In G. A. Wiggan & C. B. Hutchison (Eds.), *Global issues in education: Pedagogy, policy, practice, and the monorty experience* (pp. 59-80). Plymoth, UK: Rowman & Littlefield Education.

Knight, J. (2011). Higher education crossing borders: A framework and overview of new developments and issues. In R. Sakamoto & D. W. Chapman (Eds.), *Cross-border partnerships in higher education: Strategies and issues* (pp. 16-41). New York, USA: Routledge.

Koh, K. H. (2017) *Authentic assessment*. Retrieved from: Oxford Research Encyclopedia of Education Website http://education.oxfordre.com.

Kolb, C. (2009). International studies and foreign languages: A critical American priority. In R. Lewin (Ed.), *The handbook of practice and research in study abroad: Higher education and the quest for global citizenship* (pp. 3-20). New York, USA: Routledge.

Kurt, Ő. E. & Simsek, E, I (2016). Evaluation of mobile learning with the eight-dimensional e-learning framework. In B. H. Khan (Ed.), *Revolutionizing modern education through meaningful e-learning implementation* (pp. 80-108). Hershey, PA, USA: IGI Global.

Kurt, S. (2017). *ADDIE model: Instructional design.* Retrieved from Educational Technology Website: educationaltechnology.net/the-addie-model-instructional-design/.

Lam, B-H. (2005). *Authentic learning.* Retrieved from The Hong Kong Institute of Education Website: https://www.eduhk.hk/aclass/Theories/AuthenticLearning_28June.pdf.

Lane, J. E. (2011). Joint ventures in cross-border in higher education: International branch campuses in Malaysia. In R. Sakamoto & D. W. Chapman (Eds.). *Cross-border partnerships in higher education* (pp. 67-90). New York, U.S.A: Routledge.

Lea, M., Oshea, T., Fun, P., & Spears, R. (1992). 'Flaming' in computer-mediated communication: Observation, explanations and implications. In M. Lea (Ed.), *Contexts of computer-mediated communication* (pp. 89-112). London, UK: Harvester-Wheatsh.

Leask, B. (2010). 'Beside me is an empty chair': The student experience of internationalization. In E. Jones (Ed.), *Internationalisation and the student voice* (pp. 3-17). New York, USA: Routledge.

Lee, W. Y. C. (1995). Authenticity revisited: text authenticity and learner authenticity. *ELT Journal, 49*(4), 323-328.

Little, D., Ushioda, E., Appel, M. C., Moran, J., O'Rourke, B., & Schwienhorst, K. (1999). *Evaluating tandem language learning by e-mail: Report on a bilateral project*. CLCS Occassional Paper No. 55.

Liu, M. & Lin T. B. (2011). The development of multicultural education in Taiwan: Overview and reflection. In C. A. Grant & A. Portera (Eds.), *Intercultural and multicultural education: Enhancing global interconnectedness* (pp. 157-176). New York, USA: Routledge.

Lombardi, M. M. (2007). Authentic learning for the 21st Century: An overview. *EDUCAUSE Learning Initiative*, (Edited by Diana G. Oblinger) 1-12.

Lorente, B. P., Piper, N., Shen, H. H., Yeoh, B. S. A. (Eds.). (2005). *Asian Migrations: Sojourning, displacement, home coming & other travels.* Singapore: National University of Singapore.

Lucas, J. M. & Blair, S. G. (2017). Learning outcoms and assessment. In B. K. Mikk & I. E. Steglitz (Eds.), *Learning across cultures: Locally and globally* (3rd ed.). (pp. 191-213). Washington. D.C., USA: NAFSA, Association of International educators.

MacNaughton, G., & Hughes, P. (2007). Teaching respect for cultural diversity in Australian early childhood programs: A challenge for professional learning. *Journal of Early Childhood Research, 5*(2), 189-204.

Mady, C. (2011). The results of short-term bilingual exchanges keep on ticking: Long-term impacts of brief bilingual exchanges. *Foreign Language Annals, 44*(4), 712-724.

Magnier-Watanabe, R., Benton, C., Herrig, H., & Aba, O. (2011). Blended learning in MBA education: A cross-cultural experiment. *Open Learning, 26*(3), 253-263.

Maharjan, G. & Sakamoto, R. (2011). Collaboration for instructional technology systems in agriculture. In R. Sakamoto & W. Chapman (Eds.), *Cross-border partnerships in higher education: Strategies and issues* (pp. 191-206). New York, USA: Routledge.

Malone, J. C. (1991). *Theories of learning: A historical approach.* Belmont, California, USA: Wadsworth.

Mann, C. & Stewart, F. (2000). *Internet communication and qualitative research: A handbook for researching online.* London, UK: Sage.

Maringe, F. (2010). The meaning of globalization and internationalization in HE: In F. Maringe and N. Foskett (Eds.), *Globalization and internationalization in higher education: Theoretical, strategic and management perspectives* (pp. 17-34). London, UK: continuum.

Maringe, F. & Foskett, N. (2010). Introduction: Globalization and universities, In F. Maringe & N. Foskett (Eds.), *Globalization and internationalization in higher education* (pp. 1-13). London, UK: Continuum.

Martin, F., Paker, M. A., & Ndoye, A. (2011). Measuring success in a synchronous' virtual classroom. In S. B. Eom & J. B. Arbough (Eds.), *Student satisfaction and learning outcomes in e-learning: An introduction to empirical research* (pp. 249-266). Hershey, PA, USA: IGI Global.

Martinez, M. D., Ranjeet, B., & Marx, H. A. (2009). Creating study abroad opportunities for first-generation college students. In R. Lewin (Ed.), *The handbook of practice and research in study abroad: Higher education and the quest for global citizenship* (pp. 527-542). New York, USA: Routledge.

Martinez-Alba, G. & Cruzado-Guerrero, J. (2016). Language teaching strategies: Five countries compared through study abroad. In J. A. Rhodes & T. M. Milby (Eds.), *Advancing teacher education and curriculum development through study abroad programs* (pp. 198-213). Hershey, PA, USA: IGI Global.

McArthur, T. (2003). *Oxford guide to world English*. Oxford, UK: Oxford UP.

McCaffery, J. A. (1993). Independent effectiveness and unitended outcomes of cross-cultural orientation and training. In R. M. Paige (Ed.), *Education for the intercultural experience* (2nd ed.) (pp. 219-240). Maine, USA: Intercultural Press.

McGrath-Champ, S., Zou, M., & Taylor, L. (2013). Exploring new frontiers in an internationalized classroom: Team-based learning and reflective journals as innovative learning strategies. In J. Ryan (Ed.), *Cross-cultural teaching and learning for home and international students: Internationalisation of pedagogy and curriculum in higher education* (pp. 27-40). New York, USA: Routledge.

McNaught, C. & Curtis, A. (2009). Using policy initatives to support both learning enhancement and language enhancement at a Hong Kong University. In T. Coverdale-Jones & P. Rastall (Eds.), *Internationalising the University: The Chinese context* (pp. 85-104). Hampshire, UK: Palgrave Macmillan.

Mede, E. & Dikilitas, K. (2015). Teaching and learning sociolinguistic competence: Teachers' cricital perceptions. *Participatory Education Research, 2*(3), 14-31.

Mehra, B., & Bishop, A. P. (2007). Cross-cultural perspectives of international doctoral students: Two-way learning in library and information science education. *International Journal of Progressive Education, 3*(1), 1-33.

Mendeloff. D., & Shaw, C. (2009). Connecting students internationally to explore postconflict peacebuilding: An American-Canadian Collaboration. *Journal of Political Science Education, 5*, 27-54.

Mertova, P. (2013). Internationalisation and quality in higher education: Perspectives of English, Australian and Czech senior academics. In J. Ryan (Ed.), *Cross-cutural teaching and learning for home and international students* (pp. 69-81). London, UK: Routledge.

Mfum-Mensah, O. (2009). Teaching and learning in a developing world context: Understanding the curriculum development for marginalized communities in Northern Ghana. In G. A. Wiggan & C. B. Hutchison (Eds.), *Global issues in Education: Pedagogy, policy, practice, and the minority experience* (pp. 131-150). Lanham, MD, USA: Rowman & Littlefield Education.

Mikitani, H. (2012). *Englishnization. Kodansha Ltd.* Taipei, Taiwan: Busingss Weekly.

Mikk, B. K. & Bjarnadottir, T. (2017). Intercultural facilitation. In B. K. Mikk & I. E. Steglitz (Eds.), *Learning across cultures: Locally and globally* (3rd ed.). (p. 139-165). Washington, D.C., USA: NAFSA, Association of international educators.

Mitakidou, S. (2011). Cross-cultural education in Greece: History and prospects. In C. A. Grant & A. Portera (Eds.), *Intercultural and multicultural education: Enhancing global interconnectedness* (pp. 83-97). New York, USA: Routledge.

Mohler, P. P. & Uher, R. (2003). Documenting comparative surveys for secondary analysis. In J. A. Harkness, F. J. R, Van de Vijver, & P. Ph. Mohler (Eds.), *Cross-cultural survey methods* (pp. 311-327). New Jersey, USA: John Wiley & Sons.

Molenda, M., & Boling, E. (2008). Creating. In A. Januszewski & M. Molenda (Eds.), *Educational Technology: A definition with commentary* (p. 81). New York: Lawrence Erlbaum Associates.

Montgomery, C. (2013). A future curriculum for future graduates? Rethinking a higher education curriculum for globalised world. In J. Ryan (Ed.), *Cross-cultural teaching and learning for home and international students: Internationalisation of pedagogy and curriculum in higher education* (p. 171-181). London, UK: Routledge.

Mousavi, S. A. (2002). *An encyclopedic dictionary of language testing* (3rd ed.). Taipei, Taiwan: Tung Hua.

Mueller, J. (2014). *Authentic assessment toolbox* Retrived from North Central College, IL, USA. Website: http://jfmueller.faculty.noctrl.edu/toolbox/whatisit.htm.

Murray, D. E. (2000). Protean communication: The language of computer-mediated communication. *TESOL Quarterly, 34*(3), 397-421.

Nathan, E. P. (2013). Global e-learning: A strategy for managing e-learning development project across cultures. In M. Hamada (Ed.), *E-learning: New technology, applications, and future trends* (pp. 257-274). New York, USA: Nova.

Natriello, G. (2006). *Bridging the second digital divide: What can sociologists of education contribute?* Retrieved from Teachers College, Columbia University, EdLab Website: http://edlab.tc.columbia.edu/files/EdLab_Bridging.pdf.

New York University (n.d.). Retrieved from New York University Website https://www.nyu.edu/students/communities-and-groups/international- student.html.

Ngo, M. (2014). Canadian youth volunteering abroad: Rethinking issues of power and privilege. *Current Issues in Comparative Education, 16*(1), 49-61.

Nieto, C., & Booth, M.Z. (2010). Cultural competence: Its influence on the teaching and learning of international students. *Journal of Studies in International Education, 14*(4), 406-425.

Nomora, K., Natori, Y., & Abe, O. (2011). Region-wide education for sustainable development networks of universities in the Asia-Pacific. In R. Sakamoto & D. W. Chapman (Eds.), *Cross-border partnerships in higher education: Strategies and issues* (pp. 209-227). New York, USA: Routledge.

O'Brien, L. & Richardson, J. (2015). Supporting research through partnership. In B. L. Eden (Ed.), *Partnerships and new roles in the 21st-century academic library: Collaborating embedding and cross-training for the future* (pp. 191-211). Lanham, MD, USA: Rowman & Littlefield.

Ochs, K. (2011). *Revisiting the implementation of the Commonwealth Teacher Recruitment Protocol: Furthering implementation and addressing critical steps in the recruitment process.* Papers of the sixth Commonwealth Research Symposium on Teacher Mobility, Recruitment and Migration, Addid Ababa, Ethiopia, 8-9 June, 2011. Edited by Johathan Penson and Akemi Yonemura (p. 24-32). London, UK: UNESCO and Commonwealth Secretariat.

Olcott, Jr. D. (2009). Global connections-local impacts: Trends and developments for internationalism and cross-border higher education. In T. Coverdale-Jones & P. Rastall (Eds.), *Internationalising the university: The Chinese context* (pp. 72-84). London, UK: Palgrave Macmillan.

Olesova, L. & Richardson, J. (2017). The effectiveness of feedback in asynchronous online courses for nonnative speakers of English. In M. Carrier, R. M. Damerow, & K. M. Bailey (Eds.), *Digital language learning and teaching : Research, theory, and practice* (pp. 79-92). New York, USA: Routledge.

Olsen, R. E, W-B & Kagan, S. (1992). About cooperative learning. In C. Kessler (Ed.), *Cooperative language learning: A teacher's resource book* (pp. 1-30). New Jersey, USA: Prentice Hall Regents.

Omolewa, M. (2011). *Toward a global response to teacher preparation, recruitment and migration.* Papers of the sixth Commonwealth Research Symposium on Teacher Mobility, Recruitment and Migration, Addid Ababa, Ethiopia, 8-9 June, 2011. Edited by Johathan Penson and Akemi Yonemura (p. 15-23). London, UK: UNESCO and Commonwealth Secretariat.

O'Neal, D. D., Ringler, M., & Rodriguez, D. (2008). Teachers' perceptions of their preparation for teaching linguistically and culturally diverse learners in rural eastern North Carolina. *The Rural Educator, Fall,* 5-13.

Ortloff, D. H. & McCarty, L. P. (2009). Educating for a multicultural Germany in the global era. In G. A. Wiggan & C. B. Hutchison (Eds.), *Global issues in education: Pedagogy, policy, practice, and the monorty experience* (pp. 81-101). Plymouth, UK: Rowman & Littlefield Education.

Ozcelik, H., & Paprika, Z-Z. (2010). Developing emotional awareness in cross-cultural communication: A video-conferencing approach, *Journal of Management Educationl, 34*(5) 671-669.

Paige, R. M. (1993). Trainer competencies for international and intercultural programs. In R. M. Paige (Ed.), *Education for the intercultural experience* (pp. 169-199). Maine, USA: Intercultural Press.

Pang, P. (2009). Strategy for the development of a global city: Study abroad in Singapore. In R. Lewin (Ed.), *The handbook of practice and research in study abroad: Higher education and the quest for global citizenship* (pp. 230-246). New York: Routledge.

Peachey, N. (2017). Synchronous online teaching. In M. Carrier, R. M. Damerow, & K. M. Bailey (Eds.). *Digital language learning and teaching: Research, theory, and practice* (pp.143-155). New York, USA: Routledge.

Pettey, G. R., Bracken, C. C., & Pask, E. B. (Eds.). (2017). *Communication research methodology: A strategic approach to applied research*. New York, USA: Routledge.

Phillipson, R. (2009). *Linguistic imperialism continued*. New York, USA: Routledge.

Portera, A. (2011). Intercultural and multicultural education: Epistemological and semantic aspects. In C. A. Grant & A. Portera (Eds). *Intercultural and multicultural education: Enhancing global interconnectedness* (pp. 12-30). New York, USA: Routledge.

Prensky, M. (2001). Digital natives, digital immigrant. *On the Horizon, 9*(5), 1-13.

Punteney, K. (2017), Social psychology in intercultural contexts. In B. K. Mikk, & I. E. Steglitz (Eds.), *Learning across cultures: Locally and Globally* (3rd ed.). (pp. 63-86). Washington, D. C., USA: NAFSA, Association of International Educators.

Ragnedda, M. & Ruiu, M. L. (2018). Social capital and the three levels of digital divide. In M. Ragnedda & G. W. Muschert (Eds.), *Theorizing digital divides* (p. 21-34). New York, USA: Routledge.

Rahman, M. M. & Ullah, A. A. (Eds.). (2012). *Asian migration policy: South, Southeast and East Asia*. New York, USA: Nova Publishers.

Reid, S. & Spencer-Oatey, H. (2013). Towards the global citizen: Utilising a competency framwork to promote intercultural knowledge and skills in higher education students. In J. Ryan (Ed.). *Cross-cultural teaching and learning for home and international students* (pp. 125-140). London, UK: Routledge.

Research eu Results Magazine (2015, April). *Dipping into the cultural barriers to 'social' media*. Luxembourg: Author.

Ritter, Z. S. (2016). Globalization of racism: Chinese, Japanese, and Korean international students' racial stereotypes and experiences with cross-racial interactions. In K. Bista & C. Foster (Eds.), *Exploring the social and academic experiences of international students in higher education institutions* (pp. 132-155). Hershey, PA, USA: IGI Global.

Robertson, R. (1995). Glocalization: Time-space and homogeneity-heterogenity. In M. Featherstone, S. Lash & R. Robertson (Eds.), *Global modernities* (pp. 25-44). London, UK: Sage.

Robinson, M. (2011). Think global, go local. *Teaching Music 19* (1), 48-50.

Robson, S., Leat, D., Wall, K., & Lofthouse, R. (2013). Feedback or feed forward? Supporting Master's students through effective assessment to enhance future learning. In J. Ryan (Ed.), *Cross-cultural teaching and learning for home and international students: Internationalisation of pedagogy and curriculum in higher education*. London, UK: Routledge.

Roudometof, V. (2016). *Glocalization: A critical introduction.* New York, USA: Routledge.

Ruberg, L. F., Moore, D. M., & Taylor, C. D. (1996). Student participation, interaction, and regulation in a computer-mediated communication environment: A qualitative study, *Journal of Educational Computing Research, 14*(3), 243-268.

Ruecker, T. (2011). The potential of dual-language cross-cultural peer review. *ELT Journal, 65*(4), 398-407.

Russell, M. & Vallade, L. (2010). Guided reflective journalling: Assessing the international study and volunteering experience. In E. Jones (Ed.), *Internationalisation and the student voice* (pp. 98-109). New York, USA: Routledge.

Sahin, Y. (2011). The importance of the foreign language learning contributing to world peace. *US-China Education Review, 8*(5), 580-588.

Said, M. E. (2008). International student circulation in Egypt. In H. d. Wit, P. Agarwal, M. E. Said, M. T. Sehoole, & M. Sirozi (Eds.), *The dynamic of international student circulation in a global context* (pp. 47-82). Rotterdam, The Netherlands: Sense.

Sakamoto, R. & Chapman, D. W. (Eds.). (2011). *Cross-border partnerships in higher education: Strategies and issues.* New York, USA: Routledge.

Samuels, H. (2013). 20th-century humanism and 21st-century technology: A match made in cyberspace. *English Teaching Forum, 51* (3), 2-9.

Sarvi, J. (2011). Cross-border collaboration for inculive and sustainable higher education: Searching for priorities. In R. Sakamoto & D. W. Chapman (Eds.), *Cross-border partnerships in higher education: Strategies and issues* (pp. 248-262). New York, USA: Routledge.

Sato, T. & Hodge, S. R. (2016). Asian international graduate students' academic and social experiences in American higher education institutions. In K. Bista & C. Foster (Eds.), *Exploring the social and academic experiences of international students in higher education institutions* (pp. 1-20). Hershey, PA, USA: IGI Global.

Sayers, D. (1991). Cross-cultural exchanges between students from the same culture: A portrait of an emerging relationship mediated by technology. *The Canadian Modern Languages Review, 47*(4), 678-696.

Schattle, H. (2009). Global citizenship in theory and practice. In R. Lewin (Ed.), *The handbook of practice and research in study abroad: Higher education and the quest for global citizenship* (pp. 3-20). New York, USA: Routledge.

Schenker, T. (2012). Intercultural competence and cultural learning through telecollaboration. *CALICO Journal, 29*(3), 449-470.

Schmitz, J. R. (2006). On the notions 'native'/'nonnative': A dangerous dichotomy for world Englishes? *Rask, 23*, 3-26.

Schwarz, N. (2003). Cultural-sensitive context effects: A challenge for cross-cultural surveys. In J. A. Harkness, F. J. R. Van de Vijver & P. Ph. Mohler (Eds.), *Cross-cultural survey methods* (pp. 93-100). New Jersey, USA: John Wiley & Sons.

Seargeant, P. (2012). *Exploring world Englishes: Language in a global context.* London, UK: Routledge.

Sekaran, U. (2003). *Research methods for business: A skill building approach* (4th ed.). New York, USA: John Wiley & Sons.

Sheley, N. S., & Zitzer-Comfort, C. Expand and contract: E-learning shapes the world in Cyprus and in California. *Studies in American Indian Literatures, 23*(2), 71-90.

Shiveley, J. M. & Van Fossen, P. J. (2001). *Using Internet primary sources to teach critical thinking skills in government, economics, and contemporary world issues.* West Point, Connecticut, USA: Greenwood Press.

Shivnan, J. & Hill, M. N. (2011). Global nursing: Sustaining multinational collaboration over time. In R. Sakamoto & D. W. Chapman (Eds.), *Cross-border partnership in higher education: Strategies and issues* (pp. 153-168). New York, USA: Routledge.

Shomoossi, N. & Ketabi (2007). A critical look at the concept of authenticity. *Electronic Journal of Foreign Language Teaching. 4* (1), 149-155.

Slethaug, G. & Vinther, J. (2013). The Challenges of multilingualism for international students in Denmark. In R. Janette (Ed.), *Cross-cultural teaching for home and international students: Internationalisation of pedagogy and curriculum in higher education* (pp. 82-94). London, UK: Routledge.

Smith, T. K. (2018). Developing competencies for global engagement: American fourth graders to Taiwan. In B. E. Bizzell, R. C. Kahila, and P. A. Talbot (Eds.), *Cases on global competencies for educational diplomacy in international settings* (pp. 1-19). Hershey, PA, USA: IGI Global.

Smolcic, E. & Martin, D. (2018). Structured reflection and immersion in Ecuador: Expandimg teachers' intercultural and linguistic competencies. In J. Jackson & S. Oguro (Eds.), *Intercultural intervention in study abroad* (pp. 190-205). New York, USA: Routledge.

Spencer-Oatey, H., & Franklin, P. (2009). *Intercultural interaction: A multidisciplinary approach to intercultural communication.* Hampshire, UK: Palgrave Macmillan.

Spiegel, A. (2018). Difference, spatiality, and sociability in the everyday life of expatriate managers. In A. Spiegel, U. Mense-Petermann, & B. Bredenkötter (Eds.), *Expatriate managers: The paradoxes of living and working abroad* (pp. 85-104). New York, USA: Routledge.

Stern, P. N. (2007). On solid ground: Essential properties for growing grounded theory. In A. Bryant & K. Charmaz (Eds.), *The sage handbook of grounded theory* (pp. 114-126). London, UK: Sage.

Stowe, J. E. (1990). *English language instruction in the schools in transition: The case of Taiwan in the 1980s* (Unpublished Doctoral Disseratation). Columbia University Teachers College, New York, USA.

Tabot, A., Oyibo, K., & Hamada, M. (2013). E-learning evolution: Past, present, and future. In M. Hamada (Ed.). *E-learning: New technology, applications and future trends* (pp. 1-32). New York, US: Nova.

Tang, Y. S. (2018), *The influence of Taiwan's higher education towards a Southeast Asian ethnic Chinese Community: A case study of Malaysian students* (unpublished master's thesis). Tamkang University, New Taipei City, Taiwan.

Tarling, N. (2004). *International students in New Zealand: The making of policy since 1950.* Auckland, New Zealand: The University of Auckland.

Taylor, J. (2010). The response of governments and universities to globalization and internationalization in higher education. In F. Maringe & N. Foskett (Eds.), *Globalization and internationalization in higher education: Theoretical, strategic and management perspectives* (pp. 83-96). London, UK: Continuum.

Toma, J. D. (2011) *Managing the intrepreneurial university*. New York, USA: Rutledge.

Tournès, L. (2018). New actors of the post-cold war world (Europe, China and India): Toward a genuine globalization scholarship program. In L. Tournès & G. Scott-Smith (Eds.), *Global exchanges scholarships and transnational circulations in the modern world*. New York, USA: Berghahn.

Tournès, L. & Scott-Smith, G. (Eds.). (2018). *Global exchanges: Scholarships and transnational circulations in the modern world*. New York, USA: Berghahn.

Training Industry (2013). Retrieved from Training Industry Website: *ADDIE Model* www.trainingindustry.com/wiki/content-development/addie_model.

Trotman, A. & Wiggan, G. (2009). Inclusive education in the global context: The impact on the government and teachers in a developing country—Trinidad and Tobago. In G. A. Wiggan & C. B. Huttchison (Eds.), *Global issues in education: Pedagogy, policy, practice and the minority experience* (pp. 297-309). Lanham, MD, US: Rowman & Littlefield.

Tsai, R. C. H., & Redmer, G. (Eds.). (2014). *Language, culture, and Information technology*. Taipei, Taiwan: Bookman.

Tsou, W. (2015). From globalization to glocalization: Rethinking English language teaching in response to the ELF phenomenon, *English as a global language education, 1*(1), 47-63.

Tu, C. H. & McIsaac, M. (2002). The relationship of social presence and interaction in online classes. *The American Journal of Distance Education, 16*(3), 131-150.

Turner, Y. (2013). Pathologies of silence? Refleting on international learner identities amidst the classroom chatter. In J. Ryan (Ed.), *Cross-cultural teaching and learning for home and international students: Internationalisation of pedagogy and curriculum in higher education* (pp. 227-240). London, UK: Routledge.

Turner, Y. & Robson, S. (2009). Conceptions of internationalisation and the implications for academic engagement and institutional action: A preliminary case study. In T.

Coverdale-Jones & P. Rastall (Eds.). *Internationalising the university: The Chinese context* (pp. 13-32). London, UK: Palgrave Macmillan.

Twenty, D. (1999). *Opinion: Distance learning is no substitute for real-world education.* Retrived from: heep://www.cnn.com/TECH/computing/9905/21/distlearn.idg/index.html.

van Deth, J. W. (2003). Using published survey data. In J. A. Harkness, F. J. R., Van de Vijver, & P. Ph. Mohler (Eds.), *Cross-cultural survey methods* (pp. 291-309). New Jersey, USA: John Wiley & Sons.

van Lier, L. (1996). *Interaction in the language curriculum: Awareness, autonomy & authenticity.* New York, USA: Longman.

Vigilance, C. (2011). Migration and development: Key issues for consideration for the Commonwealth. Papers of the sixth Commonwealth Research Symposium on Teacher Mobility, Recruitment and Migration, Addid Ababa, Ethiopia, 8-9 June, 2011. Edited by Johathan Penson and Akemi Yonemura (p. 5-14). London, UK: UNESCO and Commonwealth Secretariat.

Vincent-Lancrin, S. (2011). Cross-border higher education and the internationalization of academic research. In R. Sakamoto & D. W. Chapman (Eds.), *Cross-border partnerships in higher education* (pp/ 93-114). New York, USA: Routledge.

Vinther, J. (2011). Enhancing motivation with cultural narratives in computer-mediated communication. *Computer Assisted Language Learning, 24*(4), 337-352.

Wainwright, P., Ram, P., Teodorescu, D., & Tottenham, D. (2009). Going global in the sciences: A case study at Emory University, In R. Lewin (Ed.), *The handbook of practice and research in study abroad* (pp. 381-398). New York, USA: Routledge.

Wals, A. E. J., & Sriskandarajah, N. (2010) Mediated cross-cultural learning through exchange in higher agricultural education. *Journal of Agricultural Education and Extension,.16* (1), 5-22.

Walsh, L. & Kahn, P. (2010). *Collaborative working in higher education: The social academy.* New York, USA: Routledge.

Wang, A. L. (1997). *Bridging the cultural gap through computer-mediated cross-cultural communications: A Case Study of Chinese College Students in Taiwan* (Unpublished Doctoral Dissertation). New York University, New York, USA.

Wang, A. L. (2008). *Raising college students' real voice through online dialogue journal writing.* Taipei, Taiwan: Crane.

Wang, A. L. (2013). Engaging students in language learning via successful cross-cultural videoconferencing. In M. Hamada (Ed.), *E-learning: New technology, applications and future trands* (pp. 241-256). New York, USA: Nova Science.

Wang, A. L. (2014). Key to developing cross-cultural collaboration: Three cases of collaborative projects. In S. Rutherford (Ed.), *Collaborative learning: Theory, strategies and educational benefits* (pp. 15-34). New York, USA: Nova Science.

Wang, A. L. (2015). From E-learning to M-learning: The emergence of a third digital divide—learning. In R. V. Nata (Ed.), *Progress in education Volume 36* (pp. 107-120). New York, USA: Nova Science.

Wang, A. L. (2018). Issues of cross-cultural communication in a globalizing era. In D. Tafazoil, M. E. Gomez Parra, & C. A. Huertas-Abril (Eds.), *Cross-cultural perspectives on technology-enhanced language learning* (pp. 100-116). Hershy, PA, USA: IGI Global.

Wang, D. (2016). From English-only to multilingualism: English in the language policy of the Uited States. *International Journal of English Language Teaching, 3*(1), 2016, 32-41.

Weber-Bosley, G. (2010). Beyond immersion: Global engagement and transformation through internation via student reflection in long-term study abroad. In E. Jones (Ed.), *Internationalisation and the student voice* (pp. 55-67). New York, USA: Routledge.

Welch, A. (2011). *Higher education in Southeast Asia: Blurring borders, changing balance.* London, UK: Routledge.

White, C. (2003). *Language learning in distance education.* Cambridge, UK: Cambridge UP.

Wible, D. (2005), *Language learning and language technology: Toward foundations for interdisciplinary collaboration.* Taipei, Taiwan: Crane.

Wicaksono, R. (2013). Raising students' awareness of the construction of communicative (in)competence in international classrooms. In J. Ryan (Ed.), *Cross-cultural teaching and learning for home and international students: Internationalisation of pedagogy and curriculum in higher education* (pp. 241-250). London, UK: Routledge.

Wiggan, G. (2009). Paying the price, globalization in education: Economics, policies, school practices and student outcomes. In G. A. Wiggan & C. B. Hutchison (Eds.), *Global issues in education: Pedagogy, policy, practice, and the minority experience* (pp. 21-34). Lanham, Maryland, USA: Rowman & Littlefield.

Wiggins, G. (1990). The case for authentic assessment. *Practical Assessment, Research & Evaluation, 2*(2), n.p. Available online: http://paraonline.net/getvn.asp?=2&n=2.

Wikipedia (n.d.). Fulbright program. Retrieved from Wikipendia Website: http://en.wikipedia.org/wiki/Fulbright_Program.

Wikipedia (n.d.). George Leslie Mackay. Retrieved from Wikipedia Website: https://en.wikipedia.org/wiki/George_Leslie_Mackay.

Wilkinson, J. S. & Wang, A. L. (2007). Crossing borders: How cross-cultural video-conferencing can satisfy course goals in dissimilar subjects. In P. Tsang, R. Kwan, & R. Fox (Eds.), *Enhancing learning through technology* (pp. 109-123). Singapore: World Scientific.

Williams, G. M. & Case, R. E. (2016). When in Rome: Socializing international teaching assistants into the US higher education norms. In K. Bista & Faster (Eds.), *Exploring the social and academic experiences of international students in higher education institutions* (pp. 156-174). Hershey, PA, USA: IGI Global.

Williams, Q. (2017). *Remix multilingualism: Hip hop, ethnography and performing marginalized voices.* London, UK: Bloomsbury.

Winer, M. B. & Ray, K. (1994). *Collaboration Handbook: Creating, sustaining and enjoy the journey.* Saint Paul, MN, USA: Amhert H. Wilder Foundation.

Winks, R. W. (1993). Afterwards. In R. T. Arndt & D. L. Rubin (Eds.), *The Fulbright difference, 1948-1992* (pp. 470-475). New Jersey, USA: Transaction.

Wu, W. V., & Marek, M. (2010). Making English a "habit": Increasing confidence, motivation, and ability of EFL students through cross-cultural computer-assisted interaction. *Turkish Online Journal of Educational Technology, 9* (4), 101-112.

Yogman, J., & Kaylani, C. T. (1996). ESP program design for mixed level students. *English for Specific Purposes*, *15*(4). 311-324.

Young, C. A. & Moran, C. M. (Eds.). *Applying the flipped classroom model to English language arts education.* Hershy, PA, USA: IGI Global.

Yu, X.., Isensee, E., & Kappler, B. (2016). Using data wisely to improve international student satisfaction: Insides gained from international student barometer. In K. Bista & C. Foster (Eds.). *Exploring the social and academic experiences of international students in higher education institutions* (p. 212-232). Hershey, PA, USA: IGI Global.

ABOUT THE AUTHOR

Ai-Ling Wang, PhD
Associate Professor, Tamkang University,
New Taipei City, Taiwan

Dr. Ai-Ling Wang is Associate Professor of the English Department at Tamkang University, New Taipei City, Taiwan. She got her M.A. in Bilingual Education from Texas A & I University, Texas, U.S.A. and Ph.D in Bilingual Education from New York University, New York, U.S.A. Her research interests and courses offered include cross-cultural exchanges and communications, bilingual education, second language acquisition, teaching English to speakers of other languages, computer-mediated language learning, e-learning and m-learning, cross-cultural videoconferencing, teaching methodologies, discourse analysis, linguistics, English for specific purposes, World Englishes and English varieties, globalization and internationalization, and dialogue journal writing.

Dr. Wang had many experiences of cross-cultural collaboration with educators from different countries, including Japan, Hong Kong, France, and the United States. She welcomes international collaborations with educators from all over the world to enrich students' global view and to enhance their intercultural competencies

INDEX

A

abuse, 72, 203
academic learning, 134, 219, 278, 309
academic performance, 25, 69, 71, 88, 99
access, 3, 8, 10, 29, 32, 33, 48, 58, 62, 63, 74, 116, 118, 124, 132, 141, 152, 192, 194, 195, 198, 199, 203, 211, 215, 217, 219, 220, 261, 290, 291, 304, 309
accessibility, 216
accommodation, 122, 300
accreditation, 122, 124, 162, 220, 262, 308
action research, 264
adjustment, 78, 80, 100, 153, 177, 283, 300
administrative support, 111, 149, 211
administrators, vii, x, xi, 6, 7, 9, 17, 26, 27, 102, 135, 137, 139, 148, 242, 282, 283, 296
advancement, 3, 38, 57, 98, 120, 144, 154, 196, 212, 218, 219, 241, 246, 276, 298, 300, 309
African Americans, 138
African-American English, 198
age, 3, 60, 63, 120, 144, 148, 199, 202, 203, 210, 211, 215, 230, 245, 275, 291, 298, 301, 303, 309
agencies, 91, 160, 161, 162, 220, 223, 276
aging population, 144
aging society, 221
agriculture, 52, 104, 254, 322
altitude sickness, 137
American culture, 105, 188
anxiety, 25, 87, 158, 189, 199
appointments, 149, 166, 168
Asia, 3, 5, 12, 17, 18, 19, 22, 35, 96, 97, 108, 111, 122, 124, 130, 141, 156, 161, 162, 240, 261, 262, 297, 305, 307, 308, 310, 311, 319, 324, 331
Asia-Pacific Quality Network (APQN), 309
assertiveness, 75
Assessing Learning across Cultures, 276
assessment, x, 21, 46, 71, 81, 146, 170, 174, 175, 176, 192, 201, 248, 254, 257, 269, 270, 271, 272, 273, 274, 275, 276, 277, 279, 280, 281, 282, 283, 285, 286, 299, 302, 313, 314, 321, 322, 324, 326, 331
assessment procedures, 302
Association of Southeast Asian Nations (ASEAN), 111, 308
asymmetry, 124
asynchronous communication, 65, 94, 204, 290
attitudes, 1, 3, 9, 21, 23, 24, 25, 32, 52, 63, 75, 76, 85, 89, 117, 128, 135, 149, 162, 163, 167, 168, 189, 207, 209, 232, 234, 281, 293, 296
Australia, 2, 15, 17, 21, 24, 28, 36, 58, 70, 85, 110, 112, 121, 124, 127, 130, 138, 142, 143, 152, 153, 185, 259, 296
authentication, 174
authenticity, 169, 170, 171, 174, 175, 186, 272, 321, 328, 330
authority, 6, 150, 154, 181, 183, 202, 207, 282, 293
autonomy, 178, 216, 217, 227, 292, 330

B

background information, x, 19, 190
barriers, 132, 148, 153, 155, 167, 188, 254, 316, 326
basic education, 264
behaviors, 16, 76, 82, 89, 146, 150, 174, 202, 232, 300
benefits, vii, 3, 29, 54, 61, 64, 66, 93, 99, 117, 118, 121, 131, 136, 154, 164, 169, 179, 182, 183, 193,

195, 219, 252, 257, 267, 268, 283, 287, 307, 309, 330
bias, 58, 68, 276
bilateral, 92, 119, 321
bilateral relationship, 119
bilingual education policy, 31
bilingualism, 31, 294
blended communication, 185, 210, 211, 241
blends, 106
brain, 14, 81, 137, 139, 143, 144, 145, 159, 161, 174, 220, 312
brain drain, 14, 144, 145, 220, 312
brain train, 220
Brain-Circulation, 143
brainstorming, 204
business management, 39, 48, 52, 66, 229, 236, 240, 246
business partners, 100
buyers, 34

C

campaigns, 112, 141
candidates, 251, 275
capacity building, 110
career development, 123
case study, 131, 311, 328, 329, 330
categorization, 167
Caucasians, 121
changing environment, 248
chat rooms, 214
children, 5, 19, 20, 22, 32, 34, 58, 140, 159, 235, 296, 300, 302
Chinese government, 10, 107
circulation, 97, 110, 121, 124, 125, 144, 145, 148, 311, 315, 316, 327
citizens, 2, 8, 13, 22, 31, 71, 117, 252, 260, 262, 283
citizenship, 8, 118, 136, 143, 315, 319, 321, 322, 325, 327
civic life, 236
civil servants, 240
class size, 19, 67, 156, 254, 286
classes, 20, 66, 158, 171, 187, 214, 239, 250, 329
classroom, 7, 8, 9, 14, 24, 25, 28, 29, 36, 38, 58, 66, 73, 74, 75, 82, 83, 84, 86, 105, 110, 115, 116, 123, 134, 135, 139, 145, 146, 147, 148, 149, 150, 151, 152, 154, 156, 159, 164, 170, 172, 174, 175, 183, 186, 187, 198, 199, 204, 207, 213, 215, 217, 218, 241, 245, 270, 273, 281, 285, 291, 293, 294, 296, 297, 312, 313, 317, 318, 320, 322, 323, 329, 332
classroom culture, 152, 156, 285
classroom management, 66, 152
classroom teacher, 105, 147, 218
coaches, 28
coding, 42, 44, 45, 46, 47, 48, 59, 60, 279, 319
coercion, 141
cognition, 69
cognitive development, 217
cognitive skills, 212
cognitive tool, 216
Cold War, 2, 14, 108, 141
collaboration, vii, viii, ix, xi, 4, 8, 9, 22, 36, 42, 55, 67, 77, 91, 92, 96, 97, 99, 100, 101, 102, 103, 104, 111, 128, 131, 158, 166, 172, 179, 180, 182, 188, 211, 212, 215, 218, 219, 221, 224, 234, 238, 240, 242, 243, 244, 245, 248, 249, 252, 253, 254, 255, 256, 258, 259, 260, 262, 264, 265, 266, 267, 283, 286, 297, 298, 299, 303, 305, 306, 307, 308, 311, 312, 313, 314, 318, 327, 328, 330, 331, 333
collateral, 58
collectivism, 74, 82
college campuses, 138
college students, 118, 132, 147, 155, 187, 211, 219, 234, 238, 239, 241, 322, 330
colleges, 15, 18, 91, 106, 108, 112, 114, 128, 129, 137, 155, 246, 251, 255, 262, 294, 304, 312, 315
commodity, 13, 92, 101, 220, 303, 304
communication, ix, 25, 26, 33, 35, 36, 37, 38, 39, 54, 57, 63, 65, 66, 67, 68, 76, 83, 91, 92, 93, 95, 96, 127, 135, 140, 146, 151, 152, 154, 163, 177, 185, 189, 190, 191, 192, 193, 195, 196, 198, 199, 200, 201, 203, 204, 205, 206, 207, 208, 209, 210, 211, 212, 213, 214, 216, 218, 229, 230, 231, 233, 234, 240, 241, 245, 255, 282, 292, 294, 295, 299, 300, 321, 322, 330
communication competence, 140, 230, 234
communication skills, 63, 83, 135, 207, 229, 231, 233, 240
communication technologies, ix, 33, 35, 37, 38, 39, 57, 65, 91, 196, 212, 213, 216, 218, 255
communicative competence, 207, 208, 229, 230, 231, 233, 234
communities, 6, 9, 28, 77, 136, 147, 148, 167, 170, 196, 209, 215, 236, 292, 295, 323, 324
community, x, xi, 2, 6, 17, 28, 33, 34, 39, 53, 71, 76, 77, 86, 94, 96, 98, 110, 111, 113, 116, 124, 129,

134, 136, 137, 141, 142, 148, 149, 154, 165, 166, 172, 177, 184, 195, 196, 197, 199, 200, 201, 202, 204, 219, 230, 243, 248, 251, 259, 263, 278, 292, 294, 295,296, 297, 303, 310
Community of Latin America and Caribbean States (CELAC), 308
competition, 5, 70, 94, 121, 137, 141, 142, 183, 212, 252, 266, 271, 294, 304
competitiveness, 18, 70, 92, 97, 144, 155, 165, 212, 220, 249, 255, 284, 305, 306, 307
computer, viii, ix, 29, 36, 37, 38, 39, 43, 48, 62, 65, 66, 67, 74, 88, 94, 95, 103, 154, 185, 191, 192, 193, 194, 196, 198, 199, 203, 205, 211, 213, 214, 215, 218, 248, 254, 274, 275, 293, 298, 305, 309, 321, 324, 326, 330, 332, 333
computer adaptive approach, 275
computer conferencing, 215
computer networks, 43, 103, 191, 196
computer-mediated communication, viii, 29, 39, 66, 94, 95, 154, 185, 191, 198, 199, 214, 218, 298, 305, 321, 324, 326, 330
Computer-Mediated Communication (CMC), 191
conference, 4, 58, 60, 103, 205, 206, 209, 274
conflict, 35, 82, 94, 136, 150, 159, 277, 292, 315
conflict resolution, 277
Confucius Institutes, 104, 107
consensus, ix, 4, 23, 39, 55, 61, 67, 94, 99, 100, 119, 169, 181, 197, 205, 209, 267, 298
construction, 49, 138, 176, 331
content analysis, 41, 42, 55, 59, 60, 279
conversations, 116, 158, 200
cooperation, vii, viii, ix, 13, 15, 62, 77, 97, 100, 107, 162, 179, 180, 181, 182, 183, 188, 203, 235, 238, 243, 260, 271, 307, 308, 311, 316
cooperative learning, 156, 181, 182, 271, 299, 325
coordination, 100, 180, 182, 227, 238, 316
Coordination, 100, 179, 181, 182, 318
cost, 62, 113, 126, 132, 143, 191, 193, 219, 275, 283
Council of Europe, 20, 235, 311
course content, 201
creativity, 60, 66, 74, 85, 157, 158, 164, 176, 200, 212, 237, 273, 277, 290
critical thinking, 5, 60, 66, 74, 89, 146, 150, 158, 164, 176, 207, 212, 236, 272, 273, 290, 298, 328
Cross-Border Collaboration, 255, 256, 259, 261
cross-cultural education, 23, 131
cross-cultural exchange project, vii, viii, ix, x, 37, 38, 39, 42, 45, 48, 50, 51, 52, 53, 55, 56, 58, 60, 62, 63, 66, 72, 78, 89, 92, 108, 157, 172, 179, 181, 186, 201, 210, 224, 225, 230, 236, 237, 240, 241, 246, 269, 270, 272, 273, 274, 282, 283, 284, 285, 286, 287, 301
cues, 76, 191, 196, 200, 201, 202, 203, 204
cultural awareness, viii, 46, 70, 73, 74, 75, 83, 84, 85, 131, 142, 146, 149, 171, 178, 182, 183, 197, 205, 210, 211, 218, 225, 231, 232, 234, 294, 300, 302
cultural beliefs, 232
cultural differences, 24, 26, 75, 79, 80, 82, 83, 85, 130, 139, 147, 149, 150, 151, 152, 164, 167, 183, 187, 190, 197, 206, 207, 208, 219, 225, 240, 245, 247, 250, 253, 276, 277, 293, 299, 302
cultural heritage, 12, 26, 77
cultural identities, 85, 106
cultural learning, 26, 36, 39, 47, 52, 69, 87, 131, 134, 154, 164, 165, 177, 181, 184, 186, 206, 218, 224, 225, 228, 229, 234, 235, 236, 237, 239, 274, 276, 282, 292, 309, 327, 330
cultural norms, 83, 156, 216, 268, 270
cultural practices, 105
cultural stereotypes, 190
cultural values, 81, 84
cure, 137
curricula, 8, 15, 16, 21, 28, 142, 280, 284
curriculum, 11, 14, 16, 18, 21, 27, 28, 31, 32, 81, 84, 85, 91, 133, 156, 171, 174, 176, 183, 192, 193, 245, 256, 257, 263, 289, 299, 313, 314, 315, 316, 319, 322, 323, 324, 326, 328, 329, 330, 331
curriculum development, 263, 313, 315, 322, 323
cyberspace, 178, 234, 258, 327
Czech Republic, 15, 238, 239

D

data analysis, 41, 43, 46, 50, 51, 54, 312
data collection, 41, 43, 45, 46, 47, 57, 58, 61
data gathering, 48, 49
database, 57, 58, 60, 61, 131
decision makers, 194, 247
decision-making process, 99
deduction, 42, 44, 54
deductive reasoning, 42, 75
deficiencies, 48, 163
democracy, 21, 260, 310
depth, 61, 63, 127, 185, 296
designers, viii, 180, 241, 270

developed countries, 3, 5, 18, 117, 119, 124, 160, 196, 259
developing countries, 119, 136, 160, 216, 255
development banks, 255
dialogues, 187, 240
dichotomy, 138, 162, 229, 230, 272, 327
digital communication, 39
digital divide, 13, 63, 69, 194, 195, 199, 202, 304, 309, 311, 318, 319, 324, 326, 330
digital technologies, 36, 191, 195, 298
diplomacy, 33, 77, 106, 107, 141, 236, 238, 313, 315, 320, 328
direct observation, 276
discrimination, 2, 8, 11, 26, 72, 89, 139, 162, 189, 296, 302
discs, 38
discussion groups, 270
diseases, 198
displacement, 322
distance education, viii, 65, 91, 146, 185, 212, 213, 214, 215, 216, 217, 218, 219, 220, 273, 305, 316, 331
distance learning, 14, 210, 211, 214, 217, 218, 219
distribution, 6, 99, 183, 213, 220, 242, 255
diversity, 9, 20, 24, 27, 68, 133, 138, 184, 196, 198, 203, 235, 260, 296, 304, 312, 313, 322
dominance, 29, 32, 70, 94, 197, 198, 199, 230

E

earnings, 121
ecology, 10
economic change, 21
economic cooperation, 107
economic development, 97, 109, 157, 243, 304, 306, 307
economic growth, 141, 303
economic status, 5, 11, 63, 72, 148, 194
economic systems, 130
educational background, 138, 291
educational exchanges, 105
educational institutions, 19, 24, 192, 224, 253, 264, 265, 304, 305
educational materials, 60, 215
educational objective, 303
educational practices, 145, 282
educational settings, 30, 33, 257

educational system, 5, 6, 7, 8, 10, 135, 145, 205, 242, 253
educators, vii, x, 7, 21, 23, 26, 28, 31, 85, 103, 165, 169, 192, 195, 203, 215, 217, 223, 248, 253, 273, 275, 290, 291, 304, 306, 320, 322, 323, 333
egocentrism, 235
elders, 75
e-learning, 36, 38, 68, 75, 76, 77, 177, 193, 195, 200, 201, 210, 217, 238, 273, 284, 291, 318, 320, 321, 322, 324, 333
e-mail, 36, 37, 39, 62, 65, 103, 178, 191, 192, 203, 211, 213, 214, 215, 226, 227, 228, 234, 242, 245, 292, 321
emergency, 89
emergency response, 89
empathy, 39, 118, 134, 135, 231, 233, 277, 278
empirical studies, 43, 56, 63, 82, 223, 234, 236
employability, 15, 118, 262, 284
employment, 3, 89, 110, 112, 113, 121, 141, 145, 270
employment opportunities, 110, 113, 121, 145
encouragement, 69, 76, 153, 176, 181, 200, 261
enrollment, 9, 24, 89, 111, 112, 113, 118, 121, 137, 155, 212, 263, 315
entrepreneurs, 195, 240, 257
environment, 10, 12, 17, 21, 24, 39, 66, 68, 69, 72, 73, 80, 81, 82, 83, 114, 115, 116, 117, 118, 122, 128, 131, 134, 139, 147, 148, 155, 156, 158, 159, 165, 167, 168, 169, 170, 171, 172, 177, 182, 184, 188, 198, 199, 201, 202, 204, 207, 210, 212, 214, 218, 226, 232, 242, 243, 248, 251, 263, 290, 293, 295, 299, 301, 304, 311, 313, 314, 326
environments, 67, 82, 217, 290, 302, 314
equality, viii, 21, 22, 27, 70, 94, 120, 175
equipment, ix, 105, 161, 172, 210
Erasmus scholarship programs, 107
erosion, 10
essay question, 272, 273
ethical issues, 68, 69, 78, 201
ethnic groups, 2, 10, 20, 22, 76, 138, 139, 303
ethnicity, 5, 63, 122, 147, 182, 202, 230, 301, 303
Europe, 5, 19, 20, 34, 97, 107, 115, 122, 130, 143, 197, 235, 307, 308, 312, 329
European Commission, 306
European Union, 2, 70, 96, 97, 110, 127, 197, 239, 260, 320
evidence, 55, 59, 112, 132, 136, 157, 228, 233, 271, 273, 279, 280
evil, 196

evolution, viii, 21, 38, 258, 328
examinations, 164
exchange students, vii, 58, 70, 72, 86, 102, 126, 127, 128, 185, 190
expatriate manager, 166, 167, 168, 232, 233, 328
expertise, 19, 85, 93, 111, 157, 180, 182, 188, 202, 240, 244, 250, 266, 285
exposure, 73, 130, 150, 153, 184, 186, 197, 232, 238, 240, 298, 299

F

face-to-face, viii, 36, 61, 63, 65, 76, 103, 110, 172, 178, 185, 186, 190, 198, 200, 203, 209, 210, 211, 212, 213, 217, 229, 242, 254, 261, 281, 290, 292, 298, 316
facial expression, 60, 218
facilitators, 83, 85, 86, 203, 291, 292
factories, 10, 187
faculty development, 91, 179, 256, 265
faculty mobility, 17, 19, 109
families, 9, 43, 118, 132, 133, 162, 166, 245, 296, 302, 309
family history, 7
farming techniques, 11
feedback, x, xi, 12, 54, 81, 134, 135, 151, 153, 172, 193, 200, 214, 215, 226, 227, 229, 266, 269, 270, 275, 278, 280, 281, 282, 283, 287, 325
feelings, 15, 80, 163, 176, 178, 200
financial, 2, 15, 18, 19, 70, 88, 89, 93, 99, 100, 101, 104, 106, 113, 118, 122, 124, 132, 135, 142, 143, 169, 185, 201, 224, 236, 246, 247, 250, 252, 254, 255, 257, 259, 263, 265, 266, 275, 303, 304, 305, 306
financial institutions, 224
financial resources, 15, 143, 304
financial support, 15, 19, 70, 88, 101, 104, 106, 118, 169, 185, 236, 252, 259, 263, 266, 275, 305, 306
fine arts, 39, 241
first generation, 132, 213
flexibility, 31, 192, 214, 231, 233, 275
flipped classroom, 86, 291, 293, 313, 320, 332
focus groups, 25, 281, 286
force, 3, 15, 61, 83, 101, 121, 165, 173, 292, 299
foreign language, 29, 30, 35, 115, 116, 134, 147, 158, 163, 175, 179, 197, 205, 211, 226, 227, 228, 229, 231, 232, 240, 294, 295, 298, 321, 327
formal education, 166, 269

formation, 2, 148, 205, 260
foundations, 85, 331
framing, 238, 289
France, 2, 18, 70, 76, 103, 104, 105, 112, 124, 135, 141, 210, 240, 248, 333
freedom, 195, 196, 218, 265, 287, 292, 307
friendship, 76, 117, 200, 282, 287, 292
Fulbright Program, 105, 106
funding, 15, 18, 92, 101, 142, 245, 265
funds, 14, 124, 144, 259, 263

G

gender differences, 309
General Agreement on Trade in Services, 109
geography, 1, 83, 162, 303
German-Algerian exchange program, 189
gestures, 82, 218
global communications, 171
global competition, 5, 121, 142, 294
global economy, 5, 257, 303
global education, 1
global issues, 2, 4, 9, 10, 11, 25, 28, 39, 104, 117, 142, 159, 211, 235, 244, 245, 255, 258, 261, 276, 297, 306
Global Networking Intercultural Capabilities (GNIC)., 85
globalization, vii, ix, 1, 2, 3, 4, 5, 6, 7, 8, 9, 10, 11, 12, 13, 14, 17, 19, 20, 22, 23, 26, 30, 33, 38, 39, 71, 74, 81, 94, 110, 112, 117, 122, 124, 128, 130, 139, 142, 145, 150, 157, 159, 164, 170, 224, 230, 241, 255, 258, 261, 270, 276, 284, 289, 290, 299, 301, 303, 305, 306, 307, 308, 310, 322, 329, 331, 333
glocalization,, 11, 12
governments, 4, 106, 123, 125, 224, 252, 253, 260, 294, 329
grading, 38, 74, 120, 149, 164, 165, 180, 271
graduate program, 24, 130
graduate students, 24, 104, 134, 200, 213, 281, 311, 316, 327
grants, 104, 105, 106, 108, 119
Greece, 2, 23, 34, 323
Grounded Theory Method (GTM), 42, 44
group processes, 278
group work, 155, 181, 183, 271, 274

growth, 19, 25, 87, 91, 105, 117, 125, 129, 140, 141, 144, 189, 262, 267, 271, 277, 279, 280, 290, 312, 313

H

harassment, 137, 203
harmonization, 70
harmony, 96, 244
health, 7, 89, 113, 137, 140, 142, 235, 241, 242, 258
health care, 7, 140, 142, 242
health condition, 137
hegemony, 2, 3, 32, 196, 230
higher education, vii, viii, 5, 7, 13, 14, 15, 16, 17, 18, 19, 21, 27, 70, 91, 96, 97, 98, 101, 107, 108, 109, 111, 112, 113, 118, 121, 123, 124, 125, 126, 128, 134, 141, 142, 143, 144, 157, 161, 162, 166, 207, 212, 220, 223, 224, 245, 246, 247, 248, 252, 253, 254, 255, 256, 259, 261, 262, 264, 265, 267, 284, 294, 303, 304, 305, 306, 307, 308, 310, 311, 312, 313, 314, 315, 316, 317, 320, 321, 322, 323, 324, 325, 326, 327, 328, 329, 330, 331, 332
history, 6, 14, 17, 23, 30, 31, 32, 33, 35, 37, 43, 57, 59, 60, 81, 83, 93, 100, 104, 107, 116, 119, 120, 122, 135, 143, 215, 225, 230, 236, 237, 242, 297, 301, 302, 312
home culture, 84, 139, 155, 165
homework, 73, 92, 93, 137, 155, 214, 253
homogeneity, 2, 23, 326
host, vii, 2, 19, 26, 36, 56, 69, 74, 76, 78, 82, 83, 84, 86, 102, 113, 114, 115, 116, 117, 123, 124, 126, 128, 129, 134, 135, 136, 137, 139, 142, 144, 145, 148, 149, 152, 154, 156, 157, 158, 165, 166, 167, 185, 187, 189, 233, 244, 246, 249, 251, 252, 270, 271, 279
hot spots, 92
housing, 117, 125
human, 2, 3, 10, 12, 14, 20, 22, 23, 29, 33, 35, 36, 37, 38, 40, 48, 74, 109, 111, 138, 144, 156, 212, 215, 220, 235, 246, 253, 255, 260, 265, 275, 293, 298, 303, 304, 310, 314, 315
human capital, 144, 220
human interactions, 36, 38, 293
human right, 2, 10, 20, 22, 23, 29, 235, 260
humanistic perspective, 178

I

ideal, 56, 167, 238, 253, 295
identity, 8, 20, 72, 78, 81, 88, 129, 133, 138, 140, 147, 148, 162, 163, 197, 202, 301, 314, 317
ideology, 13, 26, 36, 69, 133, 152, 163, 196, 203, 238, 268, 301
idiosyncratic, 279
iEARN, 261, 297, 319
image, 77, 95, 138, 139, 248, 254
immersion, 54, 122, 130, 133, 140, 142, 167, 295, 328, 331
immigrants, 20, 21, 23, 24, 121, 144, 170, 235, 294, 308, 309
immigration, 36, 113, 121, 126, 141, 221, 270
imperialism, 3, 27, 197, 325
improvements, x, 43, 63, 64, 114, 123, 188, 283, 285, 287
income, 5, 19, 118, 132, 194, 255
incompatibility, 100, 210, 219, 252, 310
independence, 14, 32, 111, 123, 217
India, 2, 12, 30, 96, 97, 104, 108, 112, 118, 123, 124, 125, 129, 144, 161, 196, 197, 230, 236, 245, 248, 256, 305, 311, 319, 329
individuals, 38, 49, 62, 75, 77, 85, 136, 138, 144, 149, 186, 194, 204, 220, 224, 235, 252, 259, 276, 283
Indonesia, 14, 18, 97, 116, 161, 162
induction, 42, 54
industrialized countries, 20, 235
industry, 7, 189, 221, 256, 303
ineffectiveness, 6, 9
inequality, 2, 5, 6, 8, 11, 18, 72, 118, 122, 124, 175, 194, 195, 303, 304, 309, 310
information sharing, 38, 261
information technology, 144, 172, 258, 304
infrastructure, 14, 83, 101, 195, 201, 249
ingredients, 39, 98, 266
institutions, x, 4, 8, 11, 12, 14, 18, 27, 70, 88, 91, 92, 97, 99, 100, 107, 108, 111, 113, 118, 120, 121, 123, 124, 125, 141, 143, 154, 157, 161, 162, 179, 185, 187, 193, 201, 216, 220, 224, 234, 236, 240, 243, 246, 247, 248, 252, 253, 255, 259, 260, 261, 262, 263, 264, 267, 294, 304, 305, 306, 307, 326, 327, 331, 332
instructional materials, viii, ix, 9, 10, 115, 134, 163, 171, 176, 207, 213, 216, 217, 257, 267, 283, 293

integration, 20, 21, 64, 68, 148, 150, 154, 290, 306, 307, 316
intellectual property, 246, 254, 265
intercultural competence, 16, 39, 48, 63, 64, 81, 83, 84, 87, 122, 124, 149, 168, 207, 224, 230, 232, 234, 236, 241, 270, 276, 277, 279, 280, 284, 308
Intercultural Interaction Competence (ICIC), 230
intercultural learning, 25, 26, 75, 78, 81, 86, 96, 138, 148, 183, 184, 185, 235, 272, 277, 278, 279, 315, 317, 318, 319, 320
intercultural training program, 78, 80, 82, 85, 86, 89, 184
interdependence, 100, 218, 235, 271, 307
Interdisciplinary Learning, 244
international branch campus, 102, 157, 246, 247, 305, 315
international communication, 29, 152, 294, 301
International Monetary Fund, 263
International Organizations, 263
international relations, 66, 102, 107
international standards, 162, 220, 262
international student identity, 147, 148
international trade, 31, 145, 220, 239, 303
international volunteering, viii, 65, 69, 80, 135, 136, 172, 250, 271, 320
internationalism, 325
internationalization, ix, 1, 13, 14, 15, 16, 17, 19, 24, 25, 27, 28, 29, 33, 98, 102, 110, 121, 124, 125, 126, 127, 150, 154, 164, 170, 238, 251, 272, 284, 305, 312, 313, 317, 321, 322, 329, 330, 333
internship, 129, 220
interpersonal communication, 140
interpersonal interactions, 75
Interuniversity Center for Development (CINDA), 308
intervention, 89, 153, 185, 264, 270, 278, 279, 328
investment, 101, 125, 145, 161, 201, 223, 248, 250
isolation, 15, 76, 117, 147, 153, 200, 214, 215, 219

J

Jewish English, 198
job position, 153
Jordan, 106, 141, 320
journalism, 12, 39, 54, 66, 67, 179, 205, 248

K

kidnapping, 137
knowledge acquisition, 170, 219, 272
knowledge economy, 5, 92, 96, 109, 110, 143, 220, 248, 255, 258, 303, 306, 307

L

labor market, 255
lack of confidence, 207
language barrier, 26, 72, 106, 167, 190
language development, 224
language proficiency, ix, 29, 30, 54, 66, 68, 70, 71, 72, 73, 88, 92, 93, 115, 116, 147, 151, 154, 163, 205, 206, 208, 211, 225, 226, 230, 232, 275, 281, 294, 295
language skills, 68, 71, 72, 73, 74, 115, 118, 131, 154, 158, 163, 171, 207, 220, 234, 294
language varieties, 94, 152, 163, 207, 208, 209, 216, 219, 229, 230, 270, 276, 299, 301, 302, 303
languages, 3, 5, 9, 10, 13, 29, 31, 32, 63, 68, 69, 71, 92, 93, 94, 99, 152, 158, 163, 172, 184, 191, 192, 194, 196, 197, 198, 206, 209, 216, 219, 225, 227, 233, 245, 250, 251, 254, 290, 294, 295, 302, 303, 333
lead, 17, 18, 20, 46, 50, 51, 53, 62, 70, 77, 88, 97, 98, 99, 138, 149, 180, 181, 186, 197, 201, 202, 229, 241, 250, 255, 256, 285, 290, 297, 299, 300, 309
Learning about Business Management, 240
Learning about Design, 241
Learning about Diplomacy, 238
Learning about Educational Leadership and Administration, 242
Learning about Literature and History, 237
Learning about Music, 236
Learning about Nursing, 241
Learning about Political Science, 238
Learning about Public Policy, 243
Learning about Religious Harmony, 244
learning activity, 171, 290
learning environment, 21, 24, 38, 68, 76, 77, 112, 113, 149, 152, 156, 158, 169, 171, 172, 175, 176, 177, 178, 181, 184, 191, 195, 200, 201, 204, 210, 212, 215, 216, 217, 218, 219, 226, 228, 229, 272, 273, 290, 291, 292, 293, 297, 301, 313, 314

learning outcomes, 16, 77, 175, 176, 177, 195, 201, 216, 241, 270, 271, 276, 278, 280, 290, 307, 316, 322
learning process, 88, 93, 129, 164, 172, 176, 195, 214, 257, 291, 292
learning styles, 81, 92, 149, 151, 156, 293
Learning to be Engaged in Global Issues, 245
Learning to Do Research Cross-Culturally, 244
life experiences, 45
life sciences, 31, 245
lifelong learning, 30, 176
lingua franca, 15, 29, 71, 93, 115, 152, 196, 197, 198, 206, 211, 295, 318
linguistics, 174, 231, 232, 299, 333
literacy, 62, 219, 263, 280
literature survey, 41, 55, 56, 58
living conditions, 83, 128

M

magazines, 12, 45, 113, 170
majority, 16, 18, 22, 128, 144, 163, 262, 286, 299
Malaysia, 97, 112, 124, 143, 248, 249, 305, 321
management, 11, 38, 49, 58, 66, 71, 74, 91, 97, 101, 149, 185, 192, 201, 215, 233, 240, 249, 252, 259, 264, 295, 300, 305, 312, 317, 322, 329
marketplace, 18, 172, 312, 313
Maryland, 102, 311, 312, 331
mass, 38, 42, 113, 120, 138, 140, 197, 207
Massive Open Online Course (MOOC), 204
materials, viii, 28, 30, 38, 69, 73, 84, 86, 125, 134, 135, 146, 156, 162, 163, 169, 170, 171, 172, 174, 175, 176, 177, 186, 212, 213, 214, 216, 217, 237, 246, 257, 265, 272, 275, 282, 283, 292, 297
matter, 6, 67, 71, 164, 171, 184, 198, 199, 275, 318
meaningful tasks, 273
media, 2, 38, 57, 69, 113, 138, 148, 189, 280, 326
medical science, 12, 131, 248
medicine, 34, 104
Mediterranean, 34, 96, 312
melting, 98, 133, 182
messages, 13, 17, 48, 79, 80, 104, 150, 186, 191, 199, 200, 213, 214, 217, 225, 226, 228, 268, 300
methodology, 28, 42, 43, 44, 55, 325
migrants, 22, 36, 144, 147, 235, 297
migration, 8, 23, 36, 110, 145, 148, 160, 161, 297, 302, 308, 311, 313, 325, 326
miniature, 150

minorities, 5, 9, 24, 94, 133, 235, 308
minority groups, 10, 20, 23, 63, 94, 118, 122, 149, 235, 304
minority students, 5, 10, 23, 36, 71, 122
miscommunication, 198
mission, 30, 248, 315
misunderstanding, 174, 229
mixing, 155, 302
mobile device, 291, 309
models, 20, 93, 99, 104, 111, 118, 127, 148, 153, 193, 213, 214, 215, 258, 316
modern society, viii, 17, 39, 230, 232, 290, 296, 303
mother tongue, 10, 22, 29, 31, 33, 119, 194, 196, 197, 198, 202, 251, 295
motivation, 18, 114, 115, 116, 147, 172, 178, 216, 233, 330, 332
multicultural education, 10, 21, 22, 297, 311, 312, 314, 317, 321, 323, 326
multiculturalism, 2, 8, 9, 21, 22, 78, 136, 296
multilingualism, 294, 328, 331
multimedia, 38, 83, 215, 218
multinational companies, 12
multinational corporations, 2, 166
Muslim, 72, 76, 189, 244
mutual respect, 98, 127, 223, 300
mutuality, 98, 99

N

narratives, 178, 330
national culture, 79
national interests, 104
national policy, 265
National University of Singapore (NUS), 129, 244
nationalism, 138
nationality, 19, 79, 147, 151, 230
native-speaker prejudice, 226, 295
natural disaster, 35, 137
natural science, 31
negative attitudes, 186
negotiation, viii, 75, 94, 100, 151, 210, 227, 292, 295
networking, 257, 261, 264, 277
neural network, 82, 139
neutral, 189, 196, 198
New Zealand, 36, 70, 118, 119, 120, 121, 122, 124, 142, 242, 328
non-educational organizations,, 224, 253
non-instructional purposes, 224, 253, 256

O

objective reality, 49
online learning, 39, 67, 204, 212, 319
openness, 139, 167, 199, 231, 233, 234
opportunities, xi, 18, 82, 84, 87, 92, 100, 104, 106, 112, 113, 114, 117, 118, 122, 125, 126, 131, 136, 142, 144, 145, 149, 152, 153, 172, 179, 180, 182, 188, 190, 196, 199, 201, 205, 212, 213, 217, 232, 243, 244, 246, 248, 252, 254, 256, 265, 270, 279, 292, 296, 304, 307, 310, 312, 313, 322
oral presentations, 52
Organization for Economic Cooperation and Development, 223
organize, viii, 50, 51, 53, 59, 66, 67, 72, 81, 88, 102, 118, 126, 151, 173, 177, 191, 211, 214, 224, 225, 229, 236, 237, 239, 251, 289, 294
overseas sojourn, 85

P

Pacific, 75, 87, 122, 128, 239, 240, 261, 262, 309, 319, 324
parents, 5, 6, 9, 88, 114, 132, 173, 195, 219, 245, 263
participants, vii, viii, ix, x, 7, 25, 26, 27, 37, 39, 42, 43, 46, 47, 50, 51, 52, 53, 54, 56, 61, 62, 63, 65, 67, 68, 71, 72, 73, 74, 76, 78, 79, 81, 86, 94, 95, 100, 103, 118, 127, 130, 132, 133, 134, 137, 140, 152, 153, 169, 174, 175, 178, 179, 180, 181, 185, 186, 189, 190, 191, 192, 196, 197, 198, 199, 200, 202, 203, 205, 206, 207, 208, 210, 212, 214, 216, 219, 231, 236, 240, 242, 243, 256, 257, 260, 266, 278, 279, 281, 282, 284, 286, 287, 292, 295, 296, 297, 298, 300, 302, 304, 306, 308
partners., 13, 37, 42, 78, 92, 93, 96, 99, 100, 102, 108, 183, 186, 190, 200, 205, 206, 208, 223, 224, 226, 228, 253, 259, 266, 267, 271, 274, 294, 297, 300
pedagogy, 21, 28, 85, 134, 136, 146, 184, 216, 217, 301, 314, 315, 316, 318, 323, 324, 326, 328, 329, 331
peer assessment, 282
personal autonomy, 233
personal computers, 36
personal development, 16, 88
personal learning, 68, 73, 313
personal relationship, 75, 223
personality, 60, 76, 114, 116, 138, 139, 147, 175, 186, 191, 200, 231, 232, 257
Philippines, 30, 97, 112, 143, 197, 230, 267
phonology, 208
physical environment, 175
physical properties, 252
platform, 37, 192
playing, 50, 83, 283
PluriMobil, 84, 85, 315
policy, 6, 11, 16, 18, 22, 23, 29, 31, 32, 33, 105, 108, 121, 124, 195, 253, 274, 284, 294, 295, 296, 307, 308, 312, 317, 320, 323, 325, 326, 328, 329, 331
policy makers, 6, 11, 18, 23, 108, 121, 124, 195
policy reform, 307, 312
politeness, 77, 201, 202, 300
political instability, 253, 266
politics, viii, xi, 1, 4, 13, 31, 33, 36, 83, 92, 98, 104, 109, 141, 143, 203, 214
population, 7, 17, 21, 23, 24, 35, 110, 112, 119, 122, 123, 127, 138, 139, 146, 149, 150, 179, 188, 197, 212, 220, 242, 244, 247, 251, 255, 276, 284, 296, 297, 301
portfolio, 250, 280, 285, 314
portfolio assessment, 280, 314
power relations, 12, 98, 149, 198, 201, 209, 226, 266, 268
preparation, 8, 73, 83, 87, 129, 133, 140, 160, 259, 260, 296, 312, 325
preservice teachers, 7, 122, 187, 188, 320
pre-service teachers, 133
prestige, 29, 92, 98, 120, 196, 247, 252, 262, 265
prevention, 137
primary school, 8, 173
principles, viii, xi, 17, 32, 44, 75, 80, 92, 104, 135, 159, 176, 227, 248, 253, 279
private education, 250
private sector, 12, 108, 161, 239, 252, 295, 304, 306
problem solving, 11, 176, 204, 298
problem-solving, 74, 176, 199, 217, 274, 277
professional development, 129, 154, 160, 223, 272
professionals, 4, 32, 105, 142, 144, 173, 256
profit, 143, 249, 252, 304, 315, 320
promote innovation, 111
pronunciation, 94, 198, 302
protection, 20, 160, 265
psychological health, 140
public policy, 243
public schools, 296
public sector, 127, 305

Q

qualifications, 161, 162, 220
qualitative research, 43, 44, 48, 53, 62, 312, 315, 322
quality assurance, 21, 31, 91, 162, 220, 246, 262, 265, 306, 307, 308, 309, 311
quality of life, 75, 152, 241
quantitative research, 59, 257
questionnaire, 62, 63, 185, 189, 257, 271, 283

R

race, 122, 132, 138, 194, 202, 230, 302, 313
racism, 26, 136, 137, 138, 139, 149, 302, 308, 309, 326
reading, 54, 66, 78, 158, 173, 186, 199, 213, 233, 276, 279
reality, vii, 9, 25, 96, 110, 165, 179, 202, 246, 258, 299, 302
reasoning, 49, 75, 277
reciprocity, 111, 119, 154, 227, 235
recognition, 127, 162, 220, 236, 237, 247, 248, 264, 307
recommendations, iv, ix, x, 32, 33, 99, 285, 286, 315
recruiting, ix, 14, 15, 16, 65, 69, 70, 71, 112, 118, 119, 120, 124, 137, 141, 144, 149, 155, 157, 164, 188, 226, 245, 246, 252, 284, 311
redistribution, 121
reflective practice, 7, 277, 278
reflexivity, 279
regional collaboration, 97, 111, 307, 308
regional integration, 306, 307, 308
regionalization, 97
regions of the world, 94, 96, 98, 104, 141, 307, 308
regulations, 20, 21, 69, 88, 89, 112, 139, 203, 204, 253, 265, 306
reinforcement, 215
relevance, 27, 61, 172, 174, 258, 300
reliability, 60, 62, 64
religion, viii, 1, 4, 8, 20, 33, 36, 39, 53, 72, 96, 97, 98, 110, 148, 202, 203, 245, 301
religious beliefs, 69, 151
reputation, 34, 77, 112, 113, 137, 165, 190, 252
requirement, 62, 150, 250
requirements, 21, 70, 72, 73, 101, 113, 119, 122, 125, 150, 184, 187
researchers, 4, 5, 10, 13, 19, 22, 26, 27, 41, 42, 44, 47, 48, 49, 50, 53, 55, 56, 57, 58, 60, 61, 62, 63, 64, 72, 73, 81, 86, 91, 92, 96, 103, 107, 108, 127, 130, 136, 142, 166, 174, 182, 188, 190, 191, 197, 200, 202, 203, 204, 210, 211, 213, 229, 233, 238, 240, 244, 245, 248, 254, 258, 271, 277, 280, 281, 282, 285, 286, 301, 306, 307
resilience, 231, 233
resource allocation, viii
resources, 6, 29, 32, 81, 84, 98, 99, 112, 113, 119, 148, 151, 152, 156, 162, 163, 191, 195, 196, 210, 215, 217, 246, 248, 261, 262, 264, 266, 295, 313
response, 5, 10, 12, 18, 49, 76, 84, 89, 97, 103, 177, 180, 199, 200, 226, 246, 273, 275, 296, 325, 329
revenue, 17, 110, 121, 247, 248, 265
rewards, 18, 161, 263, 267
rhetoric, 18, 302, 304
rights, iv, 9, 10, 20, 32, 88, 175, 198, 235, 246, 315
rules, 20, 27, 54, 72, 98, 112, 139, 163, 175, 196, 202, 207, 208, 232, 253, 265, 300

S

safety, 88, 137, 245
scholarship, 104, 107, 108, 112, 125, 132, 242, 329
school, x, 5, 6, 7, 8, 9, 10, 19, 23, 28, 29, 32, 34, 35, 36, 37, 67, 69, 70, 87, 88, 92, 94, 95, 99, 100, 102, 103, 113, 115, 116, 118, 119, 120, 123, 125, 129, 132, 133, 135, 137, 139, 140, 145, 146, 150, 156, 159, 161, 166, 171, 173, 176, 183, 185, 187, 192, 206, 207, 210, 213, 229, 232, 235, 241, 242, 244, 245, 246, 252, 260, 261, 263, 264, 271, 274, 282, 284, 289, 296, 300, 313, 328, 331
school activities, 271
science, 1, 5, 48, 77, 98, 106, 108, 127, 130, 131, 132, 143, 154, 172, 221, 236, 238, 245, 248, 255, 261, 265, 323
science majors, 131, 132, 238
scientific knowledge, 34, 35, 131
second language, 28, 30, 178, 197, 225, 230, 234, 299, 302, 317, 333
secondary education, 112
secondary schools, 106, 119
security, 17, 133, 137, 190, 193, 275, 297
segregation, 6, 23, 140, 167
self-awareness, 148, 183, 231
semi-structured interviews, 25
sensitivity, 54, 117, 136, 184, 211, 233, 234, 271, 316
service provider, 168

sex, 137
sexism, 309
Shanghai Cooperation Organization, 260, 320
shock, 26, 76, 80, 87, 88, 122, 129, 137, 139, 140
short-distance cultural exchanges, 296
showing, 56, 76, 106, 112, 132, 159, 179, 194, 200, 204, 228, 232, 248, 254, 300, 305, 308
Singapore, 18, 30, 97, 129, 185, 197, 230, 234, 243, 244, 258, 294, 311, 314, 322, 325, 331
small businesses, 214, 257
social activities, 48, 57, 64, 113, 166, 177, 187, 293, 301
social behavior, 47, 48
social capital, 117, 195, 309
social context, 12, 175, 199, 200, 232, 274
social environment, 116, 186
social interactions, 163, 176, 299
social justice, 22, 81, 132, 160, 297, 310
social learning, 207, 309
social network, 35, 68, 95, 195, 204, 300, 310
social norms, 149, 165, 196, 202, 203, 204
social presence, 68, 76, 77, 199, 200, 201, 329
social sciences, 106, 121, 130, 131, 261, 281, 320
social services, 243
social status, 20, 116, 198, 202
society, xi, 5, 6, 9, 10, 11, 12, 13, 15, 18, 22, 23, 29, 31, 32, 33, 74, 77, 104, 105, 137, 138, 141, 150, 154, 165, 168, 194, 196, 198, 233, 234, 236, 258, 272, 294, 295, 297, 309
socioeconomic status, 242
sociolinguistic competence, 208, 232, 299, 323
solution, 258
South America, 239, 308
South Asia, 12, 105, 111, 144, 312
Southeast Asia, 3, 22, 96, 97, 108, 156, 161, 162, 297, 305, 310, 311, 328, 331
species, 131
specific knowledge, 130, 219
specifications, 310
speech, 196, 205, 300
Statistical analysis, 64
statistics, 63
stereotype, 137, 138, 149, 182
stereotypes, 79, 83, 84, 136, 138, 149, 234, 266, 326
stigma, 163
strategic planning, 155
stress, 46, 48, 79, 123, 159, 161, 163, 231, 241
structure, 7, 8, 35, 94, 98, 123, 156, 172, 177, 180, 181, 195, 202, 207, 293, 307, 318

structuring, 278
student enrollment, 113, 120, 121, 155, 284, 303
student teacher, 7, 133, 134
study abroad programs, 14, 58, 111, 114, 122, 124, 126, 130, 132, 143, 187, 212, 271, 315, 322
styles, 24, 86, 128, 146, 156, 182, 199, 200, 208, 209, 233, 251, 264
subjectivity, 61
sub-Saharan Africa, 97
summer program, 130
sustainability, 21, 27, 101, 243, 261, 266, 267, 283, 284, 287
sustainable development, 261, 262, 324
Switzerland, 135, 312
sympathy, 122
synergistic effect, 129

T

Taiwanese students, 37, 179, 181, 205, 206, 211, 228, 245
tandem type communication, 206
target, 53, 72, 93, 114, 115, 131, 144, 147, 152, 163, 165, 170, 171, 174, 178, 214, 224, 225, 226, 227, 229, 232, 246, 248, 255, 295, 298, 300, 302
Task Authenticity, 173
teacher mobility, viii, 4, 126, 145, 155, 157, 160, 161, 220
Teacher mobility, 145
teacher training, 7, 96, 133, 146, 150, 160, 161, 235, 320
teacher-student relationship, 146
teaching strategies, 21, 135, 147, 151, 152, 158, 243, 322
teams, 130, 240, 285
technical support, x, 67, 95
techniques, 57, 60, 80, 155, 254, 275
technological advancement, 77
technologies, vii, 2, 3, 12, 33, 35, 36, 37, 38, 39, 40, 48, 62, 114, 141, 154, 156, 158, 186, 191, 195, 196, 202, 210, 212, 215, 216, 217, 218, 219, 224, 232, 237, 238, 241, 246, 254, 276, 280, 289, 290, 291, 293, 294, 298, 300, 301, 309
teleconferencing, 36
television stations, 187
territory, 85, 94, 188, 301
test scores, 176
testing, 44, 91, 174, 270, 272, 275, 302, 324

textbook, 66, 150, 215, 227, 298
think critically, 291
thoughts, 61, 80, 214, 277
threats, 114, 141, 194
Tibet, 244
time lags, 95
time periods, 35, 57
TOEFL, 115, 126
tourism, 7, 77
trade, 77, 109, 220
Traditional Assessment, 270
trainees, 74, 75, 79, 80, 81, 82, 83, 84, 87
training, viii, ix, 7, 12, 20, 25, 36, 38, 53, 65, 69, 71, 72, 73, 74, 75, 77, 78, 79, 80, 81, 82, 83, 84, 85, 86, 87, 88, 89, 97, 108, 125, 126, 130, 134, 136, 140, 149, 160, 161, 173, 184, 211, 217, 219, 229, 233, 239, 245, 257, 271, 296, 298, 304, 311, 318, 323, 324
training programs, viii, 36, 72, 74, 75, 78, 79, 80, 82, 83, 85, 86, 88, 97, 184, 271
transformation, 15, 25, 140, 290, 308, 331
translation, 34, 45, 58, 62, 63, 163, 318
transportation, 3, 25, 97, 101, 141, 207, 224, 232, 241, 246, 255, 292, 298, 300
Trinidad & Tobago (T&T), 6
tuition, 18, 70, 88, 112, 113, 119, 122, 124, 142
Turkey, 2, 58, 127, 128, 189, 260, 299, 319, 320

U

UNESCO, 160, 161, 162, 223, 324, 325, 330
Union of South American Nations (UNASUR), 308
United Arab Emirates (UAE), 6
United Kingdom, 7, 70, 112, 118, 122, 124, 132, 141, 142, 143, 144
United States, vii, 2, 4, 5, 6, 7, 11, 17, 59, 66, 70, 100, 105, 106, 112, 118, 120, 121, 122, 124, 127, 128, 134, 135, 141, 142, 144, 148, 158, 159, 179, 185, 197, 198, 245, 247, 248, 251, 254, 256, 259, 260, 294, 296, 304, 312, 320, 333
universities, 7, 15, 17, 18, 24, 32, 34, 91, 92, 96, 100, 102, 106, 107, 111, 112, 113, 114, 115, 119, 120, 121, 125, 126, 129, 137, 143, 157, 189, 190, 212, 219, 223, 233, 241, 242, 246, 247, 250, 251, 254, 255, 256, 259, 261, 264, 282, 286, 294, 304, 312, 316, 322, 324, 329
university education, 255

unstructured interviews, 72

V

validation, 91, 174, 262
variables, 56, 59, 60, 286
variations, 45, 52, 262
varieties, 9, 94, 152, 163, 198, 207, 208, 209, 216, 219, 229, 230, 270, 276, 299, 301, 302, 303, 333
variety of domains, 4
videos, 45, 78, 84, 146, 158, 171, 196, 237, 257, 291, 293
virtual communities, 195, 219, 270
visa system, 121
vision, 174, 248, 260, 267
visions, 248
vocabulary, 12, 158, 163, 198, 232
vocational education, 264
vocational education and training, 264
vocational training, 8, 307

W

wages, 161
Washington, 234, 258, 314, 317, 318, 320, 322, 323, 326
water shortages, 10
web, 154, 192, 254, 275, 292
websites, 37, 39, 68, 69, 158
well-being, 2, 3, 109, 144, 159, 243, 253, 284, 303
Western countries, 26, 98, 108, 128, 247
Western Europe, 20, 36, 235
workers, 7, 20, 121, 143, 144, 221, 235, 275
working conditions, 143, 157
workplace, 114, 165, 173, 176, 257, 273
World Bank, 223, 255, 263, 264
World Wide Web, 38, 215

X

xenophobia, 308

Y

yellow fever, 137
young people, 19, 136, 245

Related Nova Publications

A Virtual Higher Education Campus in a Global World: The Role of the Academic Campus in an Era of Technological Progress

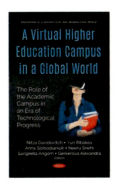

Editors: Nitza Davidovitch, Yuri Ribakov, PhD, Anna Slobodianiuk, Neeru Snehi, Sangeeta Angom, and Alexandra Gerkerova

Series: Education in a Competitive and Globalizing World

Book Description: This book focuses on the challenges of academic teaching in an era of technological advances. The challenges of pedagogy and technology are an important topic in the debates of academic scholars on the instructor's role in an era of technological progress.

Hardcover ISBN: 978-1-53615-784-0
Retail Price: $230

Problems in Higher Education: Closures, Sexual Violence and Rising Costs

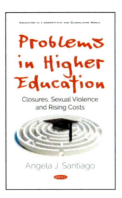

Editor: Angela J. Santiago

Series: Education in a Competitive and Globalizing World

Book Description: Chapter 1 provides an explanation of the options a postsecondary student may pursue in the event the IHE he or she attends closes, any financial relief that may be available to such students, and other practical implications for students following a school's closure.

Hardcover ISBN: 978-1-53615-591-4
Retail Price: $195

To see a complete list of Nova publications, please visit our website at www.novapublishers.com

Related Nova Publications

HIGHER EDUCATION: BACKGROUND, TAX BENEFITS AND COLLEGE CREDITS

EDITOR: Isaac Mario

SERIES: Education in a Competitive and Globalizing World

BOOK DESCRIPTION: The Higher Education Act of 1965 authorizes numerous federal aid programs that provide support to both individuals pursuing a postsecondary education and institutions of higher education (IHEs). Chapter 1 provides a brief overview of the major provisions of the HEA.

HARDCOVER ISBN: 978-1-53616-028-4
RETAIL PRICE: $195

TEACHING PRACTICES: IMPLEMENTATION, CHALLENGES AND OUTCOMES

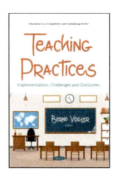

EDITOR: Bernd Vogler

SERIES: Education in a Competitive and Globalizing World

BOOK DESCRIPTION: The opening chapter of *Teaching Practices: Implementation, Challenges and Outcomes* specifically addresses the challenges we have faced during more than ten years of research into different topics regarding teaching practices, from subjects such as the relationship between the planning of practices and their application in specific classroom contexts to others linked to task management in the direct teaching of content.

SOFTCOVER ISBN: 978-1-53615-900-4
RETAIL PRICE: $82

To see a complete list of Nova publications, please visit our website at www.novapublishers.com